The *Titanic*
on Film

The *Titanic* on Film

Myth versus Truth

LINDA MARIA KOLDAU

McFarland & Company, Inc., Publishers
Jefferson, North Carolina, and London

LIBRARY OF CONGRESS CATALOGUING-IN-PUBLICATION DATA

Koldau, Linda Maria.
    The Titanic on film : myth versus truth / Linda Maria Koldau.
    p.   cm.
    Includes bibliographical references and index.

    ISBN 978-0-7864-6311-4
    softcover : acid free paper ∞

    1. Titanic (Steamship) — In motion pictures. I. Title.
PN1995.9.T56K65 2012
791.43'621634 — dc23   2012008980

BRITISH LIBRARY CATALOGUING DATA ARE AVAILABLE

© 2012 Linda Maria Koldau. All rights reserved

No part of this book may be reproduced or transmitted in any form or by any means, electronic or mechanical, including photocopying or recording, or by any information storage and retrieval system, without permission in writing from the publisher.

On the cover: *Titanic*, 1997 (Twentieth Century Fox/Photofest)

Manufactured in the United States of America

McFarland & Company, Inc., Publishers
   Box 611, Jefferson, North Carolina 28640
   www.mcfarlandpub.com

To Magnus, Vanessa,
and Anna

Table of Contents

Preface	1
Introduction: The Archetype of Maritime Disaster	9

Part I. History, Myth and Film

1. The Historical Event	21
2. The *Titanic* Myth	29
The Parameters and Their Codification in Film	29
The Historical Development	38
3. *Titanic* in Film	46
Titanic *in Film from 1912 to the Present Time*	48
EARLY FILMS AND NEWSREELS, 1912–13	49
THE 1929 *ATLANTIC* AND SELZNICK'S FOUNDERED *TITANIC* PROJECT	55
THE SIX MAJOR *TITANIC* PRODUCTIONS	59
TITANIC EPISODES AND FANTASIES	66
The Dying Queen: Documentaries of the Wreck	70
The Perfect Script	77
THE BASIC INGREDIENTS	77
MAKING IT ORIGINAL: SUBPLOTS AND STRUCTURAL MODELS	81
FRAMING DEVICES	85

Part II. Major *Titanic* Films

4. The Nazi *Titanic* (1943): Unfit for Propaganda	95
Greed as Main Theme: The Plot and the Protagonists	97
Propaganda Failed	105
Epilogue	110
5. *Titanic* (1953): Myth Turned into Melodrama	111
First Class with a Gender Conflict	113
Religion and Redemption	117
The Subplots and Their Relation to the Main Plot	119

Table of Contents

6. *A Night to Remember* (1958): The "Real Story" — 129
   - The Main Plot: The Ship as Star — 129
   - Social Microcosm: Class as Main Theme — 134
   - The Ideal of British Middle-Class Virtue — 136
   - Gender and Religion — 141
   - The "Titanic *Code*": Authenticity and Nostalgia — 143

7. *S.O.S. Titanic* (1979): Great in Detail, Weak in Plot — 148
   - The Frame Structure and Its Significance for Characterization — 148
   - Strictly Historical: The Representation of the Various Social Spheres — 153
   - Problems of Plot—Nevertheless an Impressive Film — 160

8. *Titanic* (1996): Poor Plots with an Impressive Disaster — 167
   - Structure and Plots — 169
   - Striving for Authenticity: Historical Motifs — 174
   - The Climax — 177

9. James Cameron's *Titanic* (1997) — 182
   - The Main Categories of the Titanic *Myth and Their Treatment in Cameron's* Titanic — 184
   - Postmodernist Features in Cameron's Titanic — 195
   - The Recipe for Success — 206

10. The *Titanic* Code: Recurrent Motifs in *Titanic* Films — 223
    - Recurrent Motifs: History, Myth, and Fiction — 224
    - Music to Drown By: Music in the Titanic *Myth* — 234
      - THE FINAL SONG — 236
      - MUSIC AND CLASS — 241
      - THE FILM MUSIC — 244
      - THE SOUNDS OF DEATH — 256

Conclusion: Making Titanic *Immortal* — 259

Chapter Notes — 265

Bibliography — 287

Index — 293

Preface

For many people today, "Titanic" is synonymous with James Cameron's tremendously successful film of 1997. For them, the media event, not the disaster, has become the core of "Titanic." Cameron, however, only built on the rich ground prepared for him both in cultural history and in film history. The main story of his film is not new, many of the people are not new, most of the details are not new, even some of the dialogue is not new: He simply followed the *Titanic* code.

The examination of the *Titanic* myth and the various major feature films on the *Titanic* disaster shows how in the course of the 20th century a clearly defined pattern in the cinematic representation of the disaster developed. I have chosen to call this pattern the "*Titanic* code." The *Titanic* code is a narrative combination of scenes, motifs and details from the *Titanic* story based on the main storyline of the ocean liner *Titanic*'s voyage, collision and sinking in April 1912, and integrating numerous legends from the *Titanic* myth. The *Titanic* code is a pattern that returns again and again in *Titanic* literature and film. From the very start, the audio-visual film medium strongly contributed to shaping this code.

The historical *Titanic* story, the cultural historical *Titanic* myth, and film have developed in close interaction since 1912. In their symbiosis, central themes in Western storytelling have been negotiated, each time in relation to the specific historical, political and social context in which the *Titanic* tale was retold:

> [E]ach generation has rewritten the myth of the *Titanic* to fit its own prejudices and preoccupations, and ideas of gender, class and nation have been inscribed in each recycling of the story. The cinema has played a major role in the evolving myth of the *Titanic*.[1]

Titanic offers a unique example how one single event in Western history can be turned into a myth — a myth that not only integrates the most urgent social and political issues of its time, but also anchors them in the collective consciousness of an entire century by negotiating them repeatedly in the most popular medium of the 20th and 21st centuries. As Steven Biel showed in his analysis of the *Titanic* myth in American culture, *Titanic* has functioned as a kind of "social drama" in which conflicts were played out and "American culture thought out loud about itself."[2] Typically for a modern myth, this drama has primarily been unfolded in the popular media, most strikingly, in the form of the feature film.

Film with its overwhelming force of visibility has decisively contributed to determine the exact pattern of the historical story: What is shown on screen is "true"—whether it is legend or not. With *A Night to Remember* (1958), based on Walter Lord's documentary novel of 1955, the *Titanic* code definitely became fixed. Nobody asked about the fallacies of oral history, on which Lord's novel to a great part is built, nobody asked about the legends that Lord presented as "truth"—and even the fictional dialogue from Lord's novel would be inserted as an "authentic" part of the historical *Titanic* story in new film productions. Film thus entrenched many legends surrounding the *Titanic* disaster.

With regard to the cinematic retellings, though, the delicate question of truth is not relevant. Film calls for drama, even in the documentary genres (they, too, eventually serve entertainment and thus ask for a more or less dramatic mode of presentation). The *Titanic* story has the tremendous advantage that the historical event in itself offers the perfect drama, with a structure and many details corresponding to classical tragedy. The true event was turned into legend while the ship still was sinking. Truth and legend became so entangled that they inseparably merged and thus formed the *Titanic* myth.

In fact, the pitfalls of history versus legend open up everywhere in the *Titanic* complex. *Titanic* enthusiasts will probably detect a number of mistakes regarding the historical summary of the *Titanic* disaster in Chapter 1—or whatever they take for "mistakes." This is in fact part of the game: What is history, what is legend? What is true, what is fiction? It is not the aim of this study to offer a "definite" version of the *Titanic* story, and certainly not to answer the questions that have not been solved in the past one hundred years. *Titanic* indeed is the perfect case to show the essential problem of historical research—and to demonstrate the enormous liberty that the "true history" of the *Titanic* offers to screenwriters and directors. You have got a ship the size of a little city, with some 2,200 people on board, about 700 of whom survived the disaster. That is, you get 700 different versions of the story. Or even more, with people changing their minds and adopting details they found in the newspapers or heard from other survivors. The process of myth-making started right after the collision, and some of the most important legends became already fixed as survivors talked their traumatic experiences through on the *Carpathia*. Thus, important questions were "answered" before experts even had discussed them.

Likewise, the protocols from the 1912 inquiries give the perfect example of the complexity and chameleon-like character of "historical truth." They comprise more than two thousand pages, covering all conceivable aspects, from the construction of the *Titanic* via the circumstances before departure up to all the details of the sinking and the night in the lifeboats. They leave just as many open questions as they offer answers. Right from the start it was a hopeless venture to aim at a plausible, linear reconstruction of the events. No witness could know what actually had happened in other quarters of the ship, on other decks, even on the other side of the deck they had been on. Passengers were unaware of seamanship and nautical routine, inexperienced crew members lacked important knowledge, rising panic impaired perception, and finally there was the darkness and the chaos of the sinking — objective observation, sound judgment, and unambiguous facts could hardly be expected. In the inquiries, the technique of interrogation as well as cross examination contributed to the overall confusion: A single witness would be asked questions by several persons, and about a broad spectrum of aspects. Quite often in an individual interrogation, important points are not followed up, but attention is abruptly directed to other aspects in the middle of one argumentation line. There are statements about one specific aspect at very different points in the protocols — statements by various people, made on various days. This patchwork does not lead to conclusive answers at all.

Finally, there is the question of interests. Both the parent trust International Mercantile Marine and the subsidiary White Star Line — as well as the Marconi Wireless Telegraph Company — had no wish for defects in navigation and the conduct of their employees to be found. In turn, no employee acting as witness desired to lose their job or have their career impaired. Numerous testimonies therefore are additionally influenced by personal and economic interests.

On such premises, it is hopeless to seek an "historical truth." The historian has to rely on approved methods: source studies, broad and deep-reaching contextualization, common sense. Among the studies on the *Titanic* that build on analyses of the protocols, Diane E. Bristow's voluminous *Titanic: Sinking the Myths* (1995) displays these qualities to the greatest degree. Her analysis has been led by the profundity of the historian, the unquenchable curiosity of an enthusiastic scholar, and the common sense of a professional in the public transport service. The book is by no means flawless, yet it offers many convincing theses regarding the most controversial questions. Another good source is the Encyclopedia Titanica website, which not only contains detailed biographies of the passengers and crew, but a wealth of sources (such as the transcription of newspaper articles from 1912 up to today), the discussion of countless details regarding the *Titanic* disaster, and a great number of well-researched, specialized studies.

Yet finding the "historical truth" by no means is the purpose of this book. On the contrary: It is exactly the general myth and the numerous legends surrounding the *Titanic* disaster that are of primary importance for an analysis of how the *Titanic* story has been translated into film. Film as narrative medium strongly builds on spectacular legends and on the central human and social questions that constitute the myth. In narrative film, the (essentially problematic) concept of "authentic history" always must be put into inverted commas — authenticity in the depiction of an historical event certainly is desired, but only as long as it does not impair the conclusiveness of drama. In the case of *Titanic* films, the relation between "history" and fiction in fact is the vital point. As mentioned above, history and fiction are extremely close to each other in this special case, since the historical *Titanic* story in itself was turned into fiction as soon as the ship had sunk and thus offered the perfect matrix for a dramatic script right from the start. *Titanic* film versions have greatly profited from this symbiosis of history and fiction. While the basic, well-known storyline guaranteed the audience the gratifying effect of recognition, the many open questions and the enormous number of unknown individual fates offered ever new opportunities to create enthralling film drama.

In the context of the ensuing examination, it would yield no useful insights to discuss the question if one film is more "authentic" than another, just as a goof hunt in the individual films would make little sense, unless it is a matter of intentionally inserted anachronisms that serve to emphasize features going beyond the historicist presentation of a 1912 event and thus give insight in the film's cultural historical context. The interest is, instead, directed towards the *Titanic* code: Which role does the historical story play in the drama, how are the central themes of the myth treated, which are recurring stock motifs and how do they interact with the plot? In the most convincing *Titanic* films, the cinematic translation of the *Titanic* myth is almost identical with the *Titanic* code, using the stock motifs of the historical story as metaphors for class distinction and social tension, for the concept of humanity and mankind's place in the universe, for man's possibilities and limitations. Thus, it is the general aim of this study on representations of the *Titanic* in film to examine this unique, symbiotic interrelation of history and fiction that turned one of the great disasters of the 20th century into the perfect subject matter for the century's most popular medium. As a result, it will become clear how the unique combination of a singular disaster at a very specific point in Atlantic history has led to a multitude of 20th century film renderings that live up perfectly to the central demands of cinematic art.

The relationship between history and film has been increasingly discussed in recent scholarship, especially with regard to various forms of docudrama in feature film and television.[3] In the case of the *Titanic*, the negotiation of this complex relation not only takes place within the respective film and its specific translation of the *Titanic* story and myth. It already starts with the very choice of media context and genre: feature film, docudrama, TV mini-series and TV documentary as well as the various film genres that can be combined with the disaster story (romance, melodrama, action and adventure, to name only a few) all have their own sets of aesthetics and contingencies which in turn influence the relation to "authenticity" in the presentation of the historical event. While in a classic Hollywood epic, the disaster primarily plays an instrumental role, offering a tragic foil for the fictional plot, docudrama aims at an historical reconstruction, concentrating on the *Titanic* and her story and using the historical characters as additional "human interest" only. Accordingly, the 1953 Hollywood melodrama *Titanic* and the 1958 British docudrama *A Night to Remember* follow essentially different aesthetics, while Cameron's *Titanic* takes yet another choice by inseparably entangling the story of the ship with the story of the fictional heroine. In the light of the *Titanic* myth with its elementary fusion of history and legend, all these approaches are equally legitimate: The *Titanic* myth not only offers a perfect dramatic script, but also — despite its irreversibly fixed order of events — an incredible freedom for cinematic translation. If the basic pattern of outset-collision-sinking is heeded, all that pleases is permitted.

Thus, the *Titanic* myth, translated into varying cinematic guises, has grown almost unchecked. John Wilson Foster defines this process of gradual transformation through reproduction as the development of a commodified *Titanic* "mythology":

> Over the decades the event has become a culture in the figuratively biological sense. It has reproduced itself until we seem to understand how history becomes legend and thence (through the large imprecise gestures of its lessons) in the end mythology, a case-study in the making of deep culture, human memory at its most significant. Or, more disturbingly, until we seem to understand how nowadays the reality of death and disaster can in the other direction be distorted in representation so often, and represented so variously, that it ceases to be reality and is merely a set of images (trite or frantically fresh) to be exhibited, bought and sold....[4]

It is this process of "the making of deep culture, human memory at its most significant," that makes the development of the *Titanic* myth through representation in film so important. The commodification of the myth can most clearly be seen in the myth's postmodern phase, which is not only codified in James Cameron's 1997 blockbuster and the innumerable tie-in products connected with this film, but also represented by other post–1997 *Titanic* productions (many of them using set-pieces from Cameron's *Titanic* for parody), by *Titanic* tourism, and by the memorabilia market, which by now is drowning in kitsch.

The *Titanic* story, partly true, partly myth, has been retold again and again. Just by itself, the story offers something for everyone:

> To social historians, it is a microcosm of the early 1900s. To nautical enthusiasts it is the ultimate shipwreck. To students of human nature it is an endlessly fascinating laboratory. For lovers of nostalgia it has the allure of yesterday. For daydreamers it has all those might-have-beens.[5]

Translated into film, the "story for everyone" can be adapted to almost any genre and form — although the 2001 animated musical film, which implies that the disaster was not that tragic after all, indeed does challenge the limits of taste (just as the two porno productions do). Since May 1912, the *Titanic* has appeared in more than a hundred films — narrative and documentary, large-scale retellings of the disaster or fictional dramas that include the *Titanic* story just as a single episode, docudrama, documentary or real-life TV shows. In the art of film, the *Titanic* indeed appears as a passe-partout.

It is the cinematic retellings of the disaster story as such that are most interesting from a cultural historical perspective. In this book, they will be referred to by the term "*Titanic* film," in contrast to those films that insert the *Titanic* story only as a single episode, but do not set it in focus. In building on the *Titanic* story and the *Titanic* myth, *Titanic* films most clearly expose great themes of storytelling, namely issues of gender, class, nation, race, religion, and human hubris. In the analysis of the six major *Titanic* productions, covering the period from 1943 to 1997, it will be shown how these constitutive elements of the *Titanic* myth are negotiated, how they respond to the social and political concerns of their varying context, and how they interact with the increasing demand for an "authentic" representation of the *Titanic* disaster.

The approach of this study is cultural historical, treating feature films as documents — or, in the terminology of postmodernist analysis, "texts" — that give evidence of their historical, social, political, and cultural context. It is my interest to disclose the essential symbiosis of history, myth, and film, for which the *Titanic* disaster offers such a unique example. This symbiosis is in fact at work wherever outstanding historical events are translated into art, especially into the popular cinematic art of the 20th and 21st centuries.

For several reasons, the *Titanic* offers the perfect example for this symbiosis and therefore the perfect case for analysis: First, due to several excellent cultural historical studies on the *Titanic* complex, the mechanisms how the myth came into being right in the hours of the sinking and how it then was solidified in public discourse and various forms of art have been laid bare in singular detail, offering a clear matrix for analysis.[6] Secondly, more than most other major disasters, the *Titanic* disaster crystallizes the issues of gender, class, nation, race, religion and hubris into one single, enthralling story, which in its historical unfolding displays a perfect dramatic pacing. Thirdly, the *Titanic* has been linked with the film medium right from the start and throughout the entire 20th century. Fourthly, each of the major *Titanic* films not only offers a significant example for the translation of the *Titanic* code into film, but equally reflects decisive concerns of its own historical, social, and political context. Finally — and this reason should not be underestimated — the *Titanic* is an issue of lasting general interest, now just as it was in the past decades. Why has this interest persisted, even fifteen years after Cameron's "last word" on it? How does film, whether motion picture or documentary, contribute to this ongoing interest?

My approach is cultural historical. This means that cultural theories and theories of film are explicitly or implicitly integrated where adequate, but they are by no means the starting point and red thread of the analysis: It is the historical document and its relation to its context that is the focus of the scholarly interest. Indeed, cultural historical analysis opens up the diversity and richness of cultural expression, while its interdisciplinary and comparative approach helps to identify patterns and recognize long-term structures in mentality and aesthetic thought. It is these patterns and structures that can be discovered in the symbiosis of the historical *Titanic* story, the *Titanic* myth and their representation in film, yielding telling insights why this specific disaster has been of such great relevance to so many people worldwide throughout.

The book falls into two parts. The first part offers the cultural historical fundament with chapters on the historical event, on the development of the *Titanic* myth and on the translation of this myth into film throughout the 20th century. The historical surveys are supplemented with systematical chapters that display the elements of the myth and the structural reasons why the *Titanic* story offers "the perfect script" according to the art of classic script writing. The second part focuses on the analysis of the six major *Titanic* films, covering the 1943 German National Socialist production, the 1953 Hollywood film, the 1958 British docudrama *A Night to Remember*, the 1979 television production *S.O.S. Titanic*, the 1996 mini-series *Titanic* and the 1997 James

Cameron blockbuster. The final chapter summarizes the dominant motifs that on the whole constitute the *Titanic* code, a fixed pattern with ample possibility of variation. Special attention is eventually paid to an aspect that, at least in film analysis, often is forgotten: the music, which in film constitutes a decisive element for emotional design and impact.

Since the focus lies on the *Titanic* story and not on film history, the actors' names are only given where they are important for the analysis.[7] They can be looked up on the Internet Movie Database. Since the detailed data for every film are easily accessible in this online database, there is no filmography at the end of the book.

Two remarks on style and nautical usage should be added. In maritime transport, it is incorrect to say "on the ship"; one always travels or works as crew member "in" a ship.[8] Nevertheless, in common, non-professional language, "on" is ubiquitous. In *Titanic* literature, "on" is almost exclusively used, with authorities like Lawrence Beesley (1912) and Walter Lord (1955) setting the pattern. Since this book is about the popular reception of the *Titanic* story and the *Titanic* myth through film, this common usage has been chosen. References to the ship, in turn, often adopt traditional nautical custom in common usage: As usual in professional nautical language until today, the ship is referred to as "she." In the *Titanic* myth, this coincides with the notable personification of the "maiden ship" as a female being.[9] The more neutral term "ship," in contrast, is in common usage mainly referred to with the neutral "it." Again, this common usage, reflecting the popular perception of the *Titanic* and her story, has been adopted in this book. The cinematic basis of sources for this book are films featuring the *Titanic* disaster in the period 1912–2011. Since the manuscript was completed and sent to the publisher in August 2011, it has not been possible to integrate the many documentary and fictional productions that have been broadcast in the days around the 100th anniversary on 14/15 April, 2012.

I am deeply grateful to the librarians of the Statsbibliotek at Aarhus and at the library of my own institute, who have given me access to *Titanic* books and sources from all over the world. Without their excellent service, this source-intensive study would not have been possible. I am equally grateful to the many researchers and *Titanic* enthusiasts, who generously share their research on Internet forums such as the Encyclopedia Titanica, and who have dedicated much of their leisure time to transcribe historical sources such as the protocols from the *Titanic* inquiries, making them generally accessible on the Internet. This work, unpaid and mostly unrewarded in academic context, is of inestimable help in the scholarly research on the cultural history of the *Titanic*.

Introduction
The Archetype of Maritime Disaster

"The Entire World Aghast at Most Stupendous of Marine Disasters" was the tagline of an advertisement published by a New York film company in 1912.[1] The advertisers were frank: Their animated film, *Titanic Wreck*, was based on the public's insatiable desire for sensation, and thus it was a question of selling the *Titanic* incident as "the most stupendous" of all maritime disasters in order to attract spectators and get the highest profit out of the ocean liner's sinking.

This little ad represents a process of media exploitation that set a new standard in the early days of film. While the *Titanic* still was sinking, news about the disaster was sent over the Atlantic via wireless telegraphy; this news immediately was spread in multiple forms. The *Titanic* and her hapless passengers became one of the great media events in the early 20th century. Simultaneously, the disaster was turned into one of the most viable 20th-century myths, concentrating cultural history, social development, the progress of technology, and national self-awareness into a single event. In the course of the following decades, public interest in the *Titanic* ebbed and flowed, being intermittently incited anew by media events such as the large-scale success of various *Titanic* films, the publication of Walter Lord's documentary novel *A Night to Remember* (1955), the discovery of the wreck in 1985 and James Cameron's movie of 1997.

As authors on the myth of the *Titanic* frequently stress, it must be asked why it was this single ship among the hundreds that have sunk in the past 200 years, why it was this specific group of around 1,500 passengers among the tens of thousands dying in maritime disasters that have called for such an overriding attention worldwide. There have been other maritime disasters since the sinking of the *Titanic*, and with much greater loss of life. The German ship *Wilhelm Gustloff*, which sank on January 30, 1945, in the Baltic Sea with more than 9,000 refugees on board, is frequently cited as the greatest maritime disaster in history. In peace time, one of the worst disasters ever registered was the collision of the Philippine ferry *Doña Paz* with the oil tanker *Vector* on December 20, 1987, with a loss of over 4,300 lives. Numerous other incidents involved the deaths of tens of thousands altogether — and yet the names of the vessels and the people who drowned, were burnt, crushed to death, who suffocated or froze to death are forgotten; none of these disasters ever received attention that could be compared to the craze about the *Titanic* both at the time of the event and in later decades.

Why the *Titanic*? The answers generally evolve from what has become a crucial part of the *Titanic* myth: The sinking of the *Titanic* has been turned into a metaphor for the end of the 19th-century world order with its fixed class-based society and its optimistic belief in the limitless possibilities of modern technology. Along with the two World Wars and the end of the Cold War in the 1990s, the *Titanic* disaster has been regarded as one of the great watersheds in the 20th century — and, lately, as a typological forerunner of the 9/11 attack on the World Trade Center, whose destruction again marked the end of an old world order, of the illusionary certainty of a fixed, Western system of values. The constellation of a single, disastrous event and a clearly discernable change of the established world order bestowed mythical qualities on the incidents, qualities that became enhanced in the course of decades.

The central medium to disseminate and establish the myth of the *Titanic* has doubtlessly been film. It is one of the many coincidences linked with the sinking of the *Titanic* that film right at the time of this disaster was developing into the dominant form of mass entertainment and news dissemination. From the very beginning, film has been the perfect medium to transform the incident into a myth. The emphasis in the representation of the *Titanic* disaster quickly shifted from news coverage to storytelling and entertainment. Thus the myth was molded: With its focus on dramatization, narrativity, and emotional impact, film decisively contributed to engraining the story of the *Titanic* into the public consciousness of an entire century. The real incident, with the ship as its main persona, constituted the skeleton to the various film scripts. Individual storylines, giving a personality to selected passengers and transforming their registered names and origins into enthralling human drama, served as flesh on these bones. In each new version, fictional film gave a distinguishable face, a palpable form to the archetypal vignettes that would recur again and again in *Titanic* narratives, such as the brave officers and their captain, Bruce Ismay, Thomas Andrews, the "unsinkable Molly Brown," the Astor and the

Straus couples.[2] To these historical motifs each film added its own storylines and agendas with fictitious characters, be it romance, family drama, social criticism or political propaganda.

An event of mythical quality thus meets with a medium that is perfect to enhance and convey this very quality to a mass audience. *Titanic* has been qualified as the "archetypal shipwreck"[3]; there is little doubt that film has vitally contributed to raise this single maritime disaster above so many other tragic incidents at sea.

There are, however, more facets to the "archetypal" quality of the 1912 disaster which are taken up in film. Two distinguishable traits of epic quality have been adopted and enhanced in almost every fictional rendition of the *Titanic*'s fate, be it in literature, film, music or the arts.

First, the incident is tightly linked to classical tragedy. Thomas Hardy's famous poem on the *Titanic* disaster, "The Convergence of the Twain" (published in 1915), entirely builds on a tragic, cosmic destiny ("the Immanent Will") that preordains two forces, one constructed by humans, the other created by nature, to "converge." The sinking of the *Titanic* has thus been elevated to cosmic preordination; human emotion — negligible from this universal perspective — is not a subject in this poem.

The sequence of the historical events equally resembles classical tragedy. Several authors have emphasized the perfect pacing of the *Titanic* story, opening with splendor and confidence, which is confirmed and extended in the first, celebratory part of the voyage, until the unexpected event of the collision triggers a slow, gradually accelerating process of awakening and rising anxiety, ending in spectacular tragedy. The popular reception and translation of the event in the media would then add a calm, dignified finale to the disaster, encapsulated in the hymn "Nearer, My God, to Thee." The *Titanic* story offers everything: hubris, dramatic irony, nemesis, catharsis — it is a tragedy that must be narrated. Or, even better, put on screen.

Numerous film versions take up these traits of classical tragedy, of preordination and inevitable doom, be it as part of the overall structure — Jean Negulesco's 1953 *Titanic* film starts with a gigantic iceberg calving in the Arctic; it then takes more than one film hour with episodes on the *Titanic* until "the twain" finally meet, be it in the construction and motivic enrichment of individual scenes. The litany of "ifs," frequently recited in *Titanic* literature and implicitly taken up in every single *Titanic* film, is part of the transformation of the disaster into timeless tragedy: If Captain Smith had heeded the ice warnings, if the last warning had been taken up to him, if the ship had turned just a few seconds earlier or later, if the wireless operator of the *Californian* had listened yet a little longer to the nightly traffic, if the distress rockets had been recognized as a call for help, and so on. Every film with its careful depiction of these endless "ifs" builds up new hope for an alternative ending — and then relentlessly destroys it. Tragedy, the preordained "convergence of the twain" is inevitable.

Yet it is not only the splendid ship, whose virginal state (*maiden* voyage) turns it into a most tragic victim: Tragedy is inscribed in the personal destiny of every passenger and every crew member. The Edwardian law of gentlemanly behavior, for which the *Titanic* has become an icon — "women and children first" — inevitably enforced the ripping apart of couples and families. None of the *Titanic* films misses out on this perfect potential for human tragedy. In fact, this aspect is the disaster story's greatest strength in cinematic terms: Since every single *Titanic* film invariably involves one or more love plots (the dominant ones fictitious, a few others historical), the tragedy of the disaster is most palpably translated into human terms through the forced separation of the main characters. It is the love plot and its tragic twist that enables the audience to "let the *Titanic* story in" (to use a phrase coined by director James Cameron).

Finally, an additional facet in the aligning of the *Titanic* disaster to the principles of classical tragedy are the astoundingly detailed premonitions of the event years before the actual disaster took place.[4] Thus, the reference to Morgan Robertson's novella of 1898 about the collision of a gigantic ocean liner called *Titan* with an iceberg serves as an uncanny prologue to the tragedy that Walter Lord unfolds in his documentary novel *A Night to Remember*.[5] Another oft-quoted fictional precursor of the actual disaster is Gerhard Hauptmann's novel *Atlantis*, which was published one month before the sinking of the *Titanic*.[6] Read in their cultural historical context, these novels simply reflect the period's unease with the imperialist spirit of the time, with the imperturbable confidence in technical progress that allegedly foreshadowed mankind's absolute control of the natural forces, and with an ever-increasing gap between the wealthy and the poor. Luxury ocean liners like the *Olympic* and the *Titanic* offered the perfect incarnation of this *Zeitgeist*— and the fate of the *Titanic*, ship of superlatives, eventually yielded the ultimate evidence that the premonitions of preachers and writers like Robertson and Hauptmann were justified. Mankind in its hubris was doomed.

Secondly, there is another old myth at work that has fascinated mankind over thousands of years: the relation between man and sea and, closely linked to it, the gruesome fascination of shipwreck. While two famous literary examples, Herman Melville's *Moby Dick* (1851) and Ernest Hemingway's *The Old Man and the Sea* (1952), primarily focus on the struggle between man and a creature of the sea, literary reflections on man's relation to the sea itself reach back to antiquity. Both in Greek mythology and in the Bible, the sea is used as a metaphor for man's essential inner struggles. Man's life is seen as a voyage (*The Odyssey*, *The Argonauts*, imagery in the Old and New Testaments), where human community and solidarity, common faith as well as moral and social codes serve as a safe vessel. Beyond this metaphorical use, boats and ships have been used in world literature as a motif for man's domestication of the natural force of the sea, be it for the purpose of sea trade or maritime warfare. Accordingly, Roland Barthes in his *Mythologies* (1957) identifies the ship as a token for man's absolute, unlimited control:

> Most ships in legend or fiction are, from this point of view, like the *Nautilus*, the theme of a cherished seclusion, for it is enough to present the ship as the habitat of man, for man immediately to organize there the enjoyment of a round, smooth universe, of which, in addition, a whole nautical morality makes him at once god, the master and the owner (*sole master on board*, etc.). In this mythology of seafaring, there is only one means to exorcise the possessive nature of the man on a ship; it is to eliminate the man and to leave the ship on its own.[7]

Barthes offers a solution to break the hubris of man's god-like control which, however, has more rarely been chosen by authors and artists throughout centuries: The ship makes itself independent of man. The ancient legend of the ghost ship, oft revived in Western narrative tradition, is among the most prominent examples for this maritime variant of a human construct (or machine) developing a life and will of its own.[8] In contrast, the standard device in maritime literature to break man's dominance is to eliminate the ship, that is, man's creation, *together* with man, to let them both go down: *Titanic*.

Sea vessels therefore represent man's superiority and mankind's fulfillment of the biblical imperative to "rule over the fish of the sea and the birds of the air and over every living creature that moves on the ground" (Genesis 1:28). Yet they equally stand for man's vulnerability and eventual downfall due to the old cardinal sin of *superbia* (hubris). The *Titanic* disaster presents the perfect example for this duality, a modern fulfillment of ancient warnings. From the very start of its documentation and reflection in the media, in literature, and in film, the incident has been interpreted along this line. At the same time, the disaster has struck a fundamental chord in collective, image-oriented perception: The iconic image of the gigantic ocean liner being helplessly sucked down into the maritime abyss has incited the public's imagination from the very start.

Titanic news, *Titanic* literature and *Titanic* films have strongly relied on the general hunger for sensation and thrilling disaster. The sheer size of the *Titanic*, her superlatives of being not only the biggest but also the most

The iconic *Titanic*: a dying giant (Filson Young, *Titanic*, London: G. Richard, 1912).

luxurious ocean liner ever built, and above all the *Titanic*'s famous epithet of being "practically unsinkable" made the ship the perfect subject for a maritime disaster scenario. The concatenation of unfortunate events, distilled in the litany of "ifs," and the peculiar sinking process itself, leaving time for the tragic awakening, painful farewells, and gradually rising panic, added to making this incident *the* maritime disaster of all times. The time factor, the terribly high loss of lives and the overall context of peace time and confidence in technical prowess were vital instances to make the *Titanic* unforgettable: Disaster scenarios ask for sudden catastrophe on the foil of a peaceful setting, for a merciless race against time, and, to heighten tragedy, for a considerable loss of life.

The mechanism of a disaster plot that turned the *Titanic* into the epitome of maritime catastrophe can be highlighted by the comparison with the sinking of the *Andrea Doria* on July 25 and 26, 1956. Although equally considered one of the biggest, fastest and safest ocean liners of her time, the Italian passenger ship received remarkably scarce attention in the aftermath of its sinking; until today, not a single *Andrea Doria* movie has been produced, although the event does offer a considerable array of elements for a disaster plot. The ship simply took too much time to sink (almost eleven hours), and there were enough ships around to assist in good time after the disaster, so that almost all passengers and crew members were saved, including the captain, Piero Calamai. Gender, class, nation and race, religion and hubris — the elements that proved vital both in the *Titanic* story and in the ensuing myth — did not play a notable role in this scenario. Nor would the sinking of the *Andrea Doria* come to be regarded as an omen of impending world war; it had little chance of reaching a status of *Titanic* degree. And who would want to highlight the fate of the poor but zealous passengers with their life-affirming music, when the 1912 Third Class emigrants have been replaced by the tourists of the 1950s? Even the aesthetic aspect failed on the *Andrea Doria*: An ocean liner rearing up among icebergs under a starry sky in the moment of its death is quite another sight than the pathetic gradual capsizing of a lame giant in full daylight. There was no way the *Andrea Doria* could ever reach a comparable presence in film and media.

Given the singular combination of cultural historical as well as artistically enticing factors in the case of the *Titanic* disaster, it is not surprising that the *Titanic* has been a subject for film productions over and over again. In his *Titanic* bibliography, D. Brian Anderson lists nineteen fictional films as well as fifty-two documentaries and TV shows on the *Titanic* from 1912 up to 2005.[9] Both the publication of Walter Lord's novel in 1955 — the first systematic account of the disaster, based on interviews with over sixty survivors — and the discovery of the wreck in 1985 have encouraged new film projects leading up to James Cameron's movie, whose format and unbeaten success have set a temporary end to further feature film renditions of the subject (excepting parodies referring to Cameron's film).

Although the subject of the *Titanic* is unique and forces filmmakers to

A dismal sight: the capsizing of the *Andrea Doria* on July 20, 1956 (Mariners' Museum, Newport News, Virginia).

adhere to a strictly circumscribed storyline, a vital aspect of *Titanic* films must be seen as part of a broader tradition. Just as the actual event itself received overwhelming attention and emotional reaction due to its being part of the age-old tradition of literary tragedy and maritime lore, the audiovisual rendering of the *Titanic* disaster can draw on the narrative, aesthetic, visual and auditory traditions of several film genres. Melodrama with its focus on human interest (love stories, family conflicts, social drama) is enriched by vital elements of the romance, the disaster, and the action genre. Cameron's film, in turn, despite its many postmodernist features, strongly evokes the tradition of the Hollywood epic, while European *Titanic* films represent various schools of filmmaking, culminating in the restrained British documentary style of *A Night to Remember*. TV productions again have to follow their own aesthetic principles, with the epic disaster subject of the "archetypal shipwreck" provoking hybrid forms that combine the artistic constraints of the TV drama with the pretense of the large-scale motion picture. The *Titanic* complex thus is absorbed into a broader cinematic context, which adds artistic freedom, individual profile and emotional poignancy to the storyline of the well-known subject.

Hence, a highly fruitful interaction between the historical *Titanic* complex — constituted by the symbiotic relationship between history and myth — and its cinematic translations throughout the 20th century can be observed. The various *Titanic* films that have been produced since 1912 exploit the wealth of motifs and social agendas that the 1912 disaster had to offer; over the decades they reflect the experience of a century that has decisively been characterized by technical invention with both its benefits and its shady sides as well as by social and political conflict and its escalation in disaster.[10] The *Titanic* tragedy, being depicted from the perspective of varying cinematic traditions and various national backgrounds, has become an icon for the experience of this century with its numerous calamities on a hitherto unknown scale. It is this symbolic quality that makes the sinking of the ocean liner more than "just" an accident — and it is for this reason that this archetypal shipwreck again and again has fascinated audiences worldwide in its various cinematic renditions.

Part I
History, Myth and Film

1

The Historical Event

The *Titanic* story is known to all; even toddlers get it in the form of mini-books with "basic knowledge for the youngest." The *Titanic* was the biggest ship in her time and the pride of her company, the British White Star Line. She was the second of the three luxury ships of the "Olympic Class," which had been designed to cross the Atlantic in a regular weekly service. On April 10, 1912, the *Titanic* started on her maiden voyage from Southampton, scheduled to arrive in New York on April 17. On April 14, at 11:40 P.M., she collided with an iceberg off the Newfoundland coast and sank within two hours and forty minutes. About 1,500 people lost their lives, while little more than 700 were saved in lifeboats.

Many books have been written on the *Titanic* and her ill-fated voyage, and countless theories have been developed on what exactly happened that night and why this splendid ship, equipped with the highest safety standards, sank with such a great loss of life. Numerous details have never been clarified; only a few of the open questions could be answered when the *Titanic*'s wreck was discovered at a depth of almost 13,000 feet on September 1, 1985. To this day, *Titanic* fascinates a worldwide audience, and *Titanic* enthusiasts meticulously research and retell the individual passengers' lives, every thinkable detail of the voyage, and the immortal "life" of the *Titanic* after her sinking.

Cultural historians distinguish between the "historical" and the "mythical" *Titanic*.[1] The historical ship disappeared from the surface on April 15, 1912, at 2:20 A.M. The mythical ship emerged at exactly the same moment and has since absorbed the imagination of millions. This distinction can, of course, not be absolutely drawn; the factual *Titanic* still played an important role both in the inquiries following the disaster and, much later, as a wreck in the story of the rediscovery. But it is indeed the mythical *Titanic*, the greatest, most beautiful ship of the world, the "ship of dreams," that has since dominated the general notion of "the *Titanic*."

In this chapter, the outline of the historical events is given, including a balanced presentation of the contested details of the *Titanic*'s collision and sinking.[2] It is not the aim to give a definite answer to the unresolved questions; instead, the possibilities for various interpretations are presented.

The background to the *Titanic* story is the transatlantic traffic in the early 20th century. The strong competition between the various passenger lines led to a fast development of ships regarding size, speed, and luxurious design. The White Star Line, originally an independent British company, had been incorporated into John Pierpont Morgan's mega-trust "International Mercantile Marine" (IMM) in 1901. Morgan sought to monopolize the transatlantic traffic, combining it with his network of North American railway lines. White Star was only one of several British shipping companies that were bought out by Morgan. Its president, J. Bruce Ismay, retained his position with White Star, but additionally became general manager of the IMM. This meant for the *Titanic* and her sister ships that they were registered as British ships in Liverpool, but in fact were owned by an American trust controlling the White Star Line's capital. Until today, the *Titanic* is regarded as a "British" ship, but also strongly linked to the United States due both to the general ownership of the IMM and the prominent American passengers who perished in the sinking.

The fiercest competitor in the transatlantic traffic was the Cunard Line. Its liners RMS *Lusitania* and RMS *Mauretania*, which both embarked on their maiden voyage in 1907, with a tonnage of almost 32,000 GRT, were the largest passenger ships of their time and held the Blue Riband for the fastest crossing of the Atlantic in 22 years. In 1907, Ismay and Lord William Pirrie, chairman of the Belfast shipyard Harland & Wolff, designed a new class of ships that should outdo Cunard in two vital aspects: size and luxury. The Olympic Class ships were not designed to beat the Cunard liners in speed, but they were larger by fifty percent and offered a hitherto unknown luxury. Thus, they should attract the two important categories of customers: the thousands of emigrants (who due to the hard competition between the various lines had the opportunity to choose a passage on a ship giving them more room and convenience) and, in contrast, the very rich traveling regularly between the United States and Europe. These business priorities were later transformed into an important part of the *Titanic* myth, namely the persistent focus on First Class and Third Class and their contrasts in *Titanic* narratives and films.

On June 14, 1911, the first ship of the new class, the RMS *Olympic*, started on her maiden voyage. She was the great attraction to the general public: of unprecedented size, of unprecedented luxury, displaying unimaginable splendor in her First Class localities. The *Titanic* was just the second ship.³ Although slightly larger with regard to gross tonnage (but not in her outward dimensions with a length of 882 feet and a height of 175 feet), she was not the object of worldwide interest — until she sank. The *Titanic* left Southampton on April 10, 1912, after some delay of the maiden voyage due to a coal miner strike that paralyzed part of the transatlantic traffic in that spring. Coal from other ships was transferred to the *Titanic*, and a number of Third Class passengers who had booked passage on other ships were glad to hear that White Star Line had changed their tickets to the luxurious new liner without any extra charge. After stops at Cherbourg, where a number of the richest passengers boarded, and Queenstown (Cobh), where Irish emigrants entered their Third Class quarters, the *Titanic* steered out onto the open Atlantic. The first days of the voyage were uneventful. On Saturday, April 13, a fire that had smoldered in one of the coal bunkers since departure was finally extinguished. At the same time, the wireless operators received ice warnings from ships crossing the region outside the Newfoundland coast. Ice in this region was nothing new to Captain E.J. Smith and his officers. It was a regular danger, and every experienced officer knew how to cope with it. In fact, there had been numerous ice warnings published for exactly this region since late March, so that the officers of the *Titanic* knew that they were entering the ice zone in the evening of April 14. This was equally indicated by the weather. A sudden fall in temperature, the sudden drop of the wind, that had hitherto blown strongly from north-northwest, and the calm, oily water (which is in fact the very first stadium of ocean water turning into ice, called "frazil ice" in glaciology) — all these signs indicated that they were entering the lee side of the ice field which they had been warned of. Yet this fact was later denied in the official inquiries; it would have caused tremendous damage to the White Star Line. Nevertheless, Second Officer Lightoller's later testimony regarding the final change of guards confirms that the officers knew that they had reached the ice. The much-discussed question of which of the wireless warnings the officers had received and which had not found its way up to the bridge therefore is largely irrelevant. In *Titanic* films, however, it is a favorite moment of dramatic irony when wireless operator Jack Phillips spikes the message from the British passenger ship *Mesaba* with its succinct coordinates of ice instead of sending it up to the captain.

At 11:40 P.M., lookout Frederick Fleet became aware of something large looming darkly before the ship in the moonless night. First Officer William Murdoch, who held watch on the weather side of the outer bridge, must have seen the berg moments earlier than Fleet, since the ship already began to turn when Fleet rang alarm to the bridge. In *Titanic* films, in contrast, the dramatic moment of the first sighting generally is given to the lookouts in their crow's nest far above the deck. This in no way corresponds to the professional procedures on a ship: It is the watch officers on the bridge who are responsible for the safety of a ship. From their lower position they are able to see any object in front of the ship earlier than the lookouts far above the deck. They have the necessary experience to identify objects and to react. The lookouts only are an additional safety measure. It is quite clear that First Officer Murdoch saw the iceberg before the lookouts on April 14, 1912.

Murdoch gave order for a port-around maneuver, the correct way to react with an object right in front of the bow. The command "hard astarboard" brought the bow to port; after the object had passed the ship by about a third of her length, the counter-command "hard aport" brought the stern away from the berg.[4] It was a maneuver right out of the textbook — and it was not Murdoch's fault that it did not prevent the collision. The iceberg had simply been too close.[5]

The slight "heaving," "huge crash of glass," or "long-drawn, sickening crunch" at collision (a few statements of survivors, whose memories, however, probably were influenced by the disaster that followed) in fact gave evidence of an irregular damage along the starboard side of the hull. The "300-feet gash" is one of most popular common legends about the *Titanic* disaster — and the dramatic moment of the iceberg tearing into the hull again provides a favorite visual detail in *Titanic* films. Yet ultrasound examinations of the wreck have shown that the ship was by no means "ripped open like a tin can." Instead, a few of the hull's steel plates were pushed in at irregular intervals, so that the rivet heads holding them together popped away. Obviously, the ship bumped and grazed against the berg several times. Six seams opened up, relatively short fissures only — but distributed over a length of about 300 feet. This meant that the *Titanic* was doomed to sink. Enormous quantities of water entered six compartments. Until today, no ship can resist such a damage.

It is not quite clear how aware the officers, the crew and the passengers were of the ship's doom and the short span of time they had. There is no clear evidence for ship architect Thomas Andrews informing Captain Smith and the officers about a time limit of one hour or a little more. This conversation is a legend started by the novel-like description in Walter Lord's *A Night to Remember* (1955): Lord connects his patchwork of countless testimonies by means of fictitious little scenes and dialogues. Andrews's diagnosis resulting in the "mathematical certainty that the *Titanic* will sink" is such a fictitious scene; there is no evidence that this diagnosis was given on the bridge. The words are by Walter Lord.[6] In *Titanic* films, however, they are inevitably quoted in an allegedly "authentic" scene in order to heighten the urgency and prepare the audience for the drama to come.

In the inquiries, some of the surviving officers and crew claimed that they were not aware of the urgency of their situation. Did the captain and the senior officers really know that the ship had less than three hours to live? Captain Smith's peculiar measures to summon help seem to indicate that he either did not know or did not want to believe that the *Titanic* was bound to sink.[7] First, the distress signal sent by the wireless operators was by no means the international standard SOS, which had been ratified by all seafaring nations in 1908. Operator Jack Phillips instead sent CQD, the distress signal of the Marconi Company, thus signaling that the *Titanic* was in dire need of help — but that the captain desired help by British ships, which, in contrast to ships from most other nations, were equipped with Marconi telegraphs. Assistant operator Harold Bride, who survived the disaster, stated that they had not taken the situation seriously and only later began to send SOS. Equally, the distress rockets which were fired from the bow at 12:45 A.M. were white and thus did not signal distress in accordance with the International Rules of the Road. Only rockets with colors would have signaled to ships of any company and any nation that the *Titanic* was in dire straits (this rule is valid in seafaring until today). At the inquiries after the disaster, there was some discussion of this specific point, yet it was never clarified. There is indeed reason to believe that several open questions were covered up, serving the interests both of the White Star Line and the Marconi Company.

In fact, there were a number of ships quite close to the *Titanic*. To a non–British ship, the combination of the CQD signal and the white rockets would have signaled "We are in need of help, but wish this from a British ship only." This does make sense, since the salvage fee for a ship was (and is) tremendous. If the ship comes from the same company, there is no salvage fee to pay, and if it comes from the same nation, there is still some possibility of negotiation. Thus, it is logical that a British captain with his ship in distress would try to signal a British ship first, preferably of his own company — unless in dire straits. Were Captain Smith, his officers and the wireless operators indeed unaware of the short time span the *Titanic* actually had? This would not be surprising; after all, countless other ships, frailer than the *Titanic*, had suffered severe damage from collisions, yet could hold themselves afloat for many hours or even for days. There is reason to surmise that Smith — with the president of the White Star Line being on board — hoped to avoid salvage fees and thus fatally misjudged the situation.

It is unclear if wireless operator Phillips in fact rejected a possible offer of help from a German ship, the *Frankfurt*.[8] He and Harold Bride concentrated on the *Carpathia*, a British liner that was 58 sea miles away and came to rescue with full speed (and they also communicated with the *Titanic*'s sister ship *Olympic*, asking the captain to have his lifeboats ready, despite the hopeless distance between the two ships). One of the most contested aspects in the *Titanic* story is the position of another ship, the *Californian*. At the 1912 inquiries, attention quickly focused on this ship, a smaller passenger liner that lay stopped in ice close to the *Titanic*. In fact, the *Californian*'s wireless operator Cyril Evans had warned the *Titanic* of field ice just before the collision, but was rudely cut off by overworked Jack Phillips. Later, the watch officers of the *Californian* did see the rockets — but their captain Stanley Lord, informed that they were white and not in color, correctly did not interpret them as distress signals. In the inquiries, the *Californian* and her captain were welcome as scapegoats; suspicion of failure to render assistance soon focused entirely on them. Walter Lord's book *A Night to Remember* and *Titanic* films since 1958 eventually have cemented the public opinion that the *Californian* could have saved the *Titanic*'s passengers (which in no way is true). Screenwriters throughout the 20th century gratefully took up this motif, since it yields another opportunity for poignant dramatic irony.

At 12:25 A.M., evacuation into lifeboats started. Since the *Titanic*'s crew was in no way prepared and there were no general rules for such an emergency, many lifeboats left the ship only partly filled. The officers followed the principle "women and children first," which had been established in the Western world with the sinking of the British troop ship *Birkenhead* in 1852 (in this case, the officers made sure that the soldiers' families on board were put into lifeboats). The interpretation of this principle, however, was crucially different on the port and the starboard sides of the *Titanic*'s Boat Deck: First Officer Murdoch on port allowed husbands to be evacuated together with their wives and also let single men enter the lifeboats when there were no women left on deck. Second Officer Lightoller interpreted the principle as "women and children *only*," categorically denying access to men and even to male teenagers. Thus, lifeboats with many empty spaces (which could well have been filled with passengers) were lowered.

The Third Class passengers had the worst chances, not because of a set policy to evacuate First and Second Class first, but since they were far down in the ship, there was no standard procedure, and communication was made difficult by many emigrants not understanding English. In some cases, the way of Third Class passengers up onto the Boat Deck was additionally blocked by gates. These gates were locked due to American Immigration Law and not because of ill will — but it was an inexcusable negligence that the crew forgot to unlock them in the course of the evacuation. In one case, a gate was broken down by desperate Irishmen, who fought to let at least the women get through to the Boat Deck. Again, these incidents provided popular motifs for film, showing how the underprivileged have to fight in order to at least get a chance.

By 2:05 A.M., all the lifeboats had left the ship; the officers were fighting to cut loose the last two collapsible boats from the roof of their quarters on the Boat Deck. At 2:10, Jack Phillips sent his last signal, at 2:17, the bow definitely went under water, at 2:18 the lights went out and the ship, rising high up into the air, broke in two. At 2:20 A.M., the *Titanic* went down.

Hundreds of people fought and died in the icy water; a few lucky ones reached Lifeboat 4 and the two collapsibles that had been swept off the ship. Collapsible B in fact floated upside down, offering a precarious raft to some thirty men balancing on its keel for hours. At 3:30 A.M., the *Carpathia* arrived on the scene; at 8:30 A.M. the last survivors were taken on board. The *Carpathia* changed its direction and steamed for New York, where it arrived in the evening of April 18.

One important reason why the sinking of the *Titanic* became more prominent than any other ship disaster: the passengers who were on board. Among the 2,200 passengers and crew, there were some of the richest and most prominent men of their time: the American millionaires John Jacob Astor, Benjamin Guggenheim, Henry Sleeper Harper, George Widener, Isidor Straus, John Thayer, Charles Melville Hays, Arthur Ryerson. Most of them were with their wives, some even with children. Except for Henry Sleeper Harper, all of them died in the sinking. Isidor Straus went down together with his wife Ida, who — famously — refused to be separated from him. It was the doom of these rich and prominent ones that shocked and fascinated the world.

Another prominent passenger was J. Bruce Ismay, president of the White Star Line. He traveled on a complimentary ticket in one of the two luxury suites with its own promenade. After the collision, Ismay — rather clumsily — tried to assist with the evacuation of the passengers and eventually entered Collapsible C, since there were free places and no more passengers close by. This was later regarded as an unforgivable act of cowardice, which eventually prompted Ismay to resign from his post and completely withdraw from social life. In the official inquiries it was of greatest importance to him to insist that he had been "only a passenger" and thus had no responsibility for the navigation of the ship. Rumors said, however, that he pressed Smith to break a speed record for the Atlantic crossing. While it is out of question that the *Titanic* was supposed to break the record for the Blue Riband, it is plausible that Ismay wished the newly built ship with its strong engines to beat her "older sister" *Olympic* on the Atlantic crossing. There is some evidence that he acted in his role as president of the White Star Line on the *Titanic* rather than as an ordinary passenger.

A special figure in the *Titanic* history and myth is the Denver millionairess Margaret Tobin Brown, notoriously represented as Molly Brown in later *Titanic* legend. She traveled together with the Astor couple and distinguished herself by her brave, energetic behavior both in Lifeboat 6 and on the *Carpathia*, where she immediately organized a relief fund for the needy Third Class survivors. The character of this extraordinary woman was gratefully taken up in almost every single *Titanic* script,[9] yet the fictitious Molly Brown offers a predominantly distorted image of Margaret Brown's real personality, instrumentalizing her to provide the perfect contrast to the stiff establishment within First Class.

In New York and London, the United States Senate inquiry and the British Wreck Commissioner's inquiry tried to uncover the reasons for the collision and the sinking of the *Titanic*. Over several months, they examined aspects of her construction, nautical routines, questions of wireless communication and distress signals, the number and manning of lifeboats and many more details. Captain E.J. Smith, Chief Officer Henry Wilde, First Officer William Murdoch, ship architect Thomas Andrews and wireless operator Jack Phillips having died in the sinking, key persons were missing, who could otherwise have been able to throw light on many of the unanswered questions. But even if they had been able to bear witness, it is unlikely that the inquiries would ever have led to a convincing line of events and argumentation. The examination technique, the high number of witnesses, the necessarily fragmented knowledge of an individual witness and — above all — the clear interests on part of the White Star Line, the International Mercantile Marine, and the Marconi Company, made sure that a reliable result never could be achieved.

There is indeed well-founded suspicion, especially with regard to the British inquiry, that a few delicate questions pointing to the White Star Line's responsibility were covered up. In the end, the committees came to no clear result regarding liability. The survivors claimed an overall compensation of $16,800,000. White Star Line refused, referring to the inquiries' open result. In 1916, the court eventually decided that altogether $663,000 had to be paid to the claimants. Many of the families who had lost a father, a son or a brother and thus their main providers only survived due to the international Titanic Relief Fund.

2

The *Titanic* Myth

The "mythical *Titanic*" emerged at the moment of the sinking, with the historical details being woven into a tale of heroism, tragic death, and religious redemption. Wireless technology turned the *Titanic* disaster into a media event even before the ship had gone: With Jack Phillips's distress signals, news of the *Titanic*'s dire straits spread over the Atlantic while she still was sinking. The sheer dimension of the event — the biggest and most luxurious ship in the world sinking on her maiden voyage, with the cream of American society on board — immediately turned it into something far beyond normal news. *Titanic* became a myth.

The Parameters and Their Codification in Film

According to social anthropological theory, myths encode abstract values and beliefs in a concrete form, which — in modern time — is disseminated through representations of popular culture.[1] Regardless of artistic quality, popular culture with its straightforward transmission of values can turn certain objects, persons or historical events into myths, transforming them into "a sophisticated social representation; a complex relationship between history, reality, culture, imagination and identity."[2] And it was indeed popular culture — film, magazines, illustrations, amateur poetry — rather than intellectual debate that turned *Titanic* into a modern myth right in 1912.

There are deep-lying structural reasons why the ship disaster of April 14, 1912, became a myth that has endured throughout the 20th and well into the 21st century. Cultural historians Tim Bergfelder and Sarah Street have identified the unique potential of this disaster that turned it into a key event in the 20th century:

> *Titanic* has inspired a great wealth of representations across different art forms and media, and across a multitude of different national and cultural contexts.

The tragedy has been appropriated to articulate and justify a wide spectrum of ideological positions on issues such as class, gender, national identity, capitalism and media manipulation, political propaganda, and collective mourning and remembrance. The history of the *Titanic* is thus a prism which facilitates an almost infinite range of different stories to be narrativised.[3]

As cultural analyses of the *Titanic* myth point out, several prime issues of contemporary debate were crystallized in the *Titanic* story: the gender issue of "women and children first" (including notions of appropriate chivalrous behavior on part of the men); the class issue exemplified in the structure of *Titanic*, which resembled a microcosm of Edwardian society and had serious consequences for the Third Class passengers' chances to survive; the nation issue in the contrasts between British crew and American passengers just as between the "Anglo-Saxon race" and allegedly panicking "Latins"; and religious issues epitomized by the chorale "Nearer, My God, to Thee" and the notion of human hubris.[4] In addition, *Titanic* figured prominently in contemporary criticism of the increasing dominance of ruthless capitalism (often targeted in religious and moral sermons on the "lesson of the *Titanic*") and the manipulative potential of the media.

In the debates after the disaster, the buzzword "Titanic" generally served to confirm and sustain a strongly conservative view on Protestant Anglo-Saxon society. In times of social upheaval on both sides of the Atlantic, *Titanic* seemed to be the perfect answer to any attempt at change and reform.[5] Although various interpretations of the incident can be distinguished, it was a single "master narrative" that immediately dominated the general perception of the *Titanic* disaster, presenting itself as "common sense" and thus treating the truths of the *Titanic* as "self-evident."[6] This conventional narrative of the disaster confirmed the orthodox notion of gender roles, of "gentlemanly" behavior and "true manliness," it affirmed the "natural order" of class distinction (with the chivalrous conduct of the millionaires confirming the "innate nobility" of the upper class), it strengthened the traditional conviction of the superiority of the "Anglo-Saxon race." (Protestant) Christian religion finally was used to turn *Titanic* into a tale of redemption, with the hymn "Nearer, My God, to Thee" conducting the victims to Heaven and comforting those who were left behind. As a whole, the conventional narrative of the *Titanic* appeared as a "parable of the natural goodness of class, racial, ethnic and gender hierarchies,"[7] serving to perpetuate the traditional social order.

In this respect, the *Titanic* myth offers the perfect subject matter for any Hollywood film. With its clear categories of gender, class, nation and religion, the dominating *Titanic* narrative reflects core issues in Western society — and constitutive motifs in film production. Classic Hollywood drama notoriously confirms and codifies conservative values. The *Titanic* story and its myth offer the perfect subject to reaffirm these values and the perfect vehicle to spin strong tales of love that inevitably result in tragedy — but also in redemption.

The gender motif is the strongest in *Titanic* films, not only because screenwriters tend to build the main plot around a love story, but also because the (almost) inescapable separation of the sexes in the hours of evacuation offers perfect material for melodrama and tragedy. *Titanic* films mostly reconfirm the traditional gender roles: crying and destitute women are put into lifeboats, their husbands stay back in manly demeanor. Surviving men, in turn, need a justification: They are young heroes who fall into the lifeboat while helping the officers (and get injured in this accident, so that they cannot protest against their salvation), they are explicitly ordered by the authority of an officer as helpers or professionals into the boats, or they get swept overboard and survive through a physical and thus manly ordeal.[8] While the women meekly sit in the lifeboats and cry. And most films make use of the Straus couple, thus confirming the sanctity of marriage. The famous episode is either added as a poignant detail in the frenzy of evacuation, or it is adapted to fit into the main love story — Rose jumping out of the lifeboat to stay with her beloved Jack (with Rose's "Remember: You jump — I jump" being a rather crude variation on Ida Straus's biblical oath "Where you go, I go"[9]).

Class is an important means of contrast in *Titanic* films. Early films almost exclusively focus on the rich First Class passengers, reflecting the general disregard for the poor emigrants in the *Titanic* debate of 1912.[10] Highlighting the notables of contemporary American society, these films perpetuate the myth of first-cabin heroism, that is, the millionaires' chivalrous behavior in the face of death, thus re-affirming orthodox class distinctions. Third Class passengers are occasionally used for some ethnic contrast in the early films; not before the 1958 production *A Night to Remember* do they figure as personalities in their own right. Typically, they are often called "steerage passengers" in *Titanic* literature and film, which additionally deprives them of their individuality: The White Star Line made a specific point of calling this class "Third Class" and not "steerage," indicating the higher standards of accommodation. The term "steerage" would have represented the large, open dormitory-style accommodation typical for emigrant quarters. Such an accommodation did not exist on the *Titanic*; instead, Third Class passengers slept in cabins with several bunks. Nevertheless, the term "steerage" prevailed in common use, contributing to the usual characterization of this class as "the common people" with little individuality.[11]

It took a long time until Third Class was deemed worthy of a subplot of its own in *Titanic* films. The films up to *A Night to Remember* use Third Class passengers as exotic interludes that may have an instrumental function within the main, First Class–oriented plot, but not a true plot of their own. *A Night to Remember* grants at least a little bit of individuality to a group of Irish emigrants, yet they are still treated as "types" rather than as individuals. The *Titanic* films of 1979, 1996, and 1997 eventually give Third Class representatives a plot of their own, following a notion of "political correctness" in the late 20th century — but they equally subject these passengers to the film business's predilection for stereotypes of innocent folksy life.

Since 1943, *Titanic* films present the inevitable dance scene in the Third Class common room, referring back to the historical "party" with dance, which was held there on Saturday, April 13. Filmmakers generally use this scene for a display of earthy joy of life — and, of course, for spinning new love interests. These innocent, affirmative and zealous emigrants are turned into victims at a later stage: During the evacuation, Third Class adds dramatic scenes of underprivileged, helpless people being locked in a deadly trap, while productions from 1958 onwards gratefully take up the historical dramatic episode of vigorous Irishmen breaking down a gate. Nevertheless, these productions do by no means concede equality to Third Class. "Steerage" is reduced to folksiness and stereotypes verging on caricature. The main plot of the various films still dwells on the First Class, using the *Titanic*'s potential for a display of splendid settings and beautiful costumes. Even James Cameron's Jack Dawson is by no means a real Third Class hero, but a bohemian who continually crosses the borders and can easily adapt to any class.

Second Class passengers in turn are notoriously ignored, both in the *Titanic* myth and in *Titanic* films.[12] They are inconspicuous and belong to the somewhat boring middle class, not fit for drama and high sentiment. The only Second Class passenger who achieved some degree of fame is the college teacher Lawrence Beesley, whose 1912 book *The Loss of the SS. Titanic: Its Story and Lessons* offers an excellent and detailed report of the sinking. Beesley later served as adviser in the production of the 1958 film *A Night to Remember*. According to a popular anecdote, he attempted to stay on the ship as the sinking was filmed, but director Roy Baker would not allow this, since it would have been a union violation endangering the entire production.[13] Thus Beesley, who had been quite regularly saved in a lifeboat in 1912, for a second time in his life missed the "chance" to go down with the *Titanic*. The 1979 film *S.O.S. Titanic* eventually took up his character, presenting him as a somewhat profiled personage with a subplot of his own.[14] Typically, even this production turns him into the personification of the boring ordinariness of Second Class; this class simply did not offer good material for the *Titanic* myth in film.

The crew had class distinctions of its own. The top are the officers on the bridge, the middle are the seamen of lower rank as well as the vast body of stewards, waiters, cabin and kitchen personnel and whatever else was needed on this vast hotel ship. The "underlings," in turn, have to toil among the burning furnaces of the *Titanic*'s underworld. It is no coincidence that Harold Bride's story of the fight in the wireless office just minutes before the sinking involves a smeary stoker, who sneaks into the cabin and steals the life vest from poor Phillips, the young white-collar hero, who is frantically sacrificing the last moments of his life to summon help.[15] There is good reason to doubt this story[16]; nevertheless, it again offers a perfect dramatic contrast in the *Titanic*'s tale of self-sacrifice and heroism. Accordingly, many films include this scene. The officers, in turn, are generally depicted as reliable professionals who faithfully fulfill their duty (again, with certain exceptions in the anti–British 1943 film). Projecting the outcome back onto their actions and character, however, film directors often present them as somewhat weak and helpless: After all, they cannot stop the *Titanic* from sinking.[17]

The third category that plays a vital role in the public perception and discussion of the *Titanic* disaster is nation, often in combination with race. There are several aspects of nation and race that were highlighted in the 1912 *Titanic* debate and then were transferred into the cinematic codification of the myth. First of all, *Titanic* serves to promote the conservative conviction that the "Anglo-Saxon race" in many ways is superior to any other race and nationality. Many films focus on stereotypical British values, codified in the legendary final admonition of Captain Smith, "Be British!"[18] Indeed, Englishman Captain E.J. Smith himself, who bore the ultimate responsibility for the *Titanic*'s collision with an iceberg at full speed, was regarded as beyond any reproach. Although the inquiries in fact criticized the fact that the *Titanic* had been driven through an ice field with excessive speed, it was concluded that Captain Smith had simply acted according to custom.[19] In public opinion, he was fully exonerated from the blemish of responsibility for the disaster: After all, he had fulfilled the seaman's code of honor and gone down with the ship. Tellingly, various legends about his behavior in the sinking seek to impose a heroic aura on him; the most popular is the story that Captain Smith, swimming in the water, had saved a child, put it into a lifeboat and then, upon hearing that First Officer Murdoch had not survived (how should the survivors in the boat know?), refused to be saved himself.[20] The major *Titanic* films, though, do not adopt such legends, apart from Smith's (allegedly) stoic death on the bridge.

Another British favorite is ship architect Thomas Andrews, who was invariably depicted by crew and passengers alike as gentle, kind-hearted, dutiful, committed, and selfless. Tellingly, not a single film makes a notable issue of his being Northern Irish rather than English — the "Irish" stereotype only pertains to the poor Third Class emigrants.[21] Andrews, the renowned architect of the *Titanic* and nephew of the shipyard owner Lord Pirrie, is a member of the upper class and thus represented as essentially "British." Just as Captain Smith, he was specially ennobled by having gone down with the ship. His final pose in the First Class Smoking Room before the painting *Plymouth Harbor*, with his lifebelt nonchalantly discarded, offers a perfect image of British composure and stoicism.[22] Just like Smith and Andrews, the group of British senior officers, especially surviving hero Charles Herbert Lightoller, incarnate British virtues: sense of humor, sense of duty, stoicism, tolerance, and a certain individualism that, however, is moderated by the common duty and the common fate. The common fate also turns the heroic American First Class passengers into "honorary Brits"— or, as Archibald Gracie exulted in his 1913 book *The Truth About the* Titanic, into paragons of the more broadly defined "Anglo-Saxon race."[23] Gracie offers a welcome expedient to the problem of national difference and competition in the North Atlantic traffic: *Titanic*, the British ship owned by an American trust, unites the British and the U.S.-American passengers into the noble "Anglo-Saxon race." His eulogy on Anglo-Saxon virtues blatantly confirms the social reality of racial inequality in the United States: "Americans" are simply equated with white people of Anglo-Saxon descent. The rest of the "melting pot" is blinded out. Characteristically for the United States, however, it is wealth and social standing that crucially contribute to the racial ennoblement into "Americans": The true racial identity of Ida and Isidor Straus is hardly ever pointed out (the Jew Isidor Straus, by the way, was of German descent). In general discourse, they were, just like millionaire Benjamin Guggenheim with his noble final gesture, depicted as exemplary representatives of "the Anglo-Saxon race."[24]

In 1912, preachers and writers saw the *Titanic* as crucible for "true racial character." According to Filson Young's philosophical musings, the Anglo-Saxon race after "long years of peace and increase in material comfort ... had deteriorated in courage and morale."[25] *Titanic* offered the opportunity to prove that the "genetic" strength of character and inner nobility could not, after all, be eliminated by transient slackness due to comfort and tranquility: A true disaster, such as the *Titanic*, would call forth and openly display the finest traits of the Anglo-Saxon race.

The most outstanding ethnic group on the *Titanic* besides the British and American were the Irish. More than 120 passengers on the *Titanic* were Irish; about two-thirds of them died in the sinking.[26] They almost exclusively were emigrants, hoping to start a better life in the United States. Thus, Irish men, women, and children constituted the largest contingent of one single nationality in Third Class. In combination with romantic notions of "Irishness," this has led to a specifically "Irish note" in *Titanic* films from 1958 onwards. In *A Night to Remember*, Irish passengers for the first time play a conspicuous role. With a certain focus on a group of poor Irish emigrants and a shy love story between a young Irishman and a Polish girl, the film presents the stereotype of the poor but life-affirming Third Class passengers; for the first time it is Irish music and dance that become the symbol of this stereotype. In Cameron's *Titanic*, Irishness then becomes commodified, with a film score giving a universal "Irish feel" to the film. Even though main character Jack Dawson is not Irish at all, he is closely linked to the emigrants' culture, which symbolizes freedom, zeal for life, and closeness to a natural, healthy way of living.[27] In contrast, the historically extremely detailed and accurate film *S.O.S. Titanic* displays "Irishness" on the *Titanic* in a much more differentiated way. In the rich kaleidoscope of historical details and incidents, the Irish Third Class passengers are by no means the only instance of "Irish zeal for life" on the *Titanic*. For the first time, both their transfer on the tender (with passenger Eugene Daly playing lively Irish airs — another authentic detail) and the Irish traders are featured; they used the stop of the *Titanic* at Queenstown to sell souvenirs to the rich passengers. Yet more importantly, Irishness is also found in the other spheres of the ship: The common link to their beloved Ireland is the starting point in a delicate relationship that develops between Northern Irish ship architect Thomas Andrews and the Irish stewardess Mary Sloan. Accordingly, in *S.O.S. Titanic* Irishness is not exclusively connected with a poor and simple life, yet it more generally represents an extraordinary sensibility and humanity regardless of class and standing. The representation of Irishness on the *Titanic* thus is both realistic and treated metaphorically in this film.

The issue of race becomes more virulent with regard to the behavior of the passengers during the evacuation. While emigrants from Scandinavia and Germany were regarded as the poor relatives of "the Anglo-Saxon race" so to say, the notion of the strange, unknown and therefore menacing Other was projected onto the emigrants from Southern Europe, Middle East, and Asia. In the 1912 discussion of the disaster, they are depicted as inordinate, cowardly, wild and brutish. If there was a panic during the evacuation, it was the "Italians" or — after the Italian ambassador in the U.S. had protested — the "immigrants belonging to the Latin races" who were the delinquents.[28] It is remarkable, though, that the racial vilifications originally came from one and the same person: It was Fifth Officer Harold Lowe — the only crew member who was so noble as to turn back with Lifeboat 14 and pull a few of the victims out of the water — who discredited both the Italian (or "Latin") emigrants and the Chinese passenger whom they saved after the sinking (calling him a "Jap" and a "little blighter"). Was it a personal racist attitude that immediately was taken up and implemented as a general racist feature in the *Titanic* myth? It is clear that Lowe's disparaging words reflect a general attitude towards Southern European and Asian people in 1912,[29] yet it is conspicuous that the most outspoken racist statements came from the same person.

Nation and race emerge again and again as vital issues in *Titanic* films up to 1997. Not surprisingly, the 1943 propaganda film makes the most of racial stereotypes, conveniently drowning those who were not desired in national socialist racial ideology. Later films are more cautious in this respect — yet in the Cameron film, it is still Jack Dawson's Italian friend Fabrizio who is in the first row of those trying to enter a lifeboat as the situation turns desperate. (Tellingly, the stereotype has changed: While in 1912, Italians were denounced as emotional, effeminate, and wild, in 1997 the Italian stereotype Fabrizio represents Mediterranean charm and zest for life. The 1950s cliché of "bella Italia" has left its traces even in the *Titanic* myth.) Generally, the predominantly Anglo-American film productions follow the discourse on nation and race as it was established right after the disaster, focusing on the British crew and the American passengers as paragons of reliability and manly virtue.

Religion plays an important role in the overall design of the *Titanic* narrative. In public discourse, the *Titanic* disaster story quickly became a tale of redemption — the triumph of prevailing Anglo-Saxon Protestant values even in the face of disaster and death. Typically, in such a transformation a few elements were elevated and exaggerated, while less agreeable historical aspects were completely blotted out, such as the question of the navigational causes of the disaster, the defective equipment, the lack of coordination in the evacuation, and the general social inequality on the ship. Popular *Titanic* narratives chose only those aspects that fitted into the desired image of the disaster — and this image served to make sense of an event that surpassed human understanding. Historical elements were selected and combined into a narrative that transformed tragedy into triumph.[30]

It was, of course, the religion of the "superior race" that was instrumental in this transformation. The disaster, with its elements of divine intervention, human tragedy and eventual resignation into God's will, downright called for religion as connecting link. The Protestant hymn "Nearer, My God, to Thee"— which had been used by several Anglo-Saxon Protestant denominations since the middle of the 19th century — became the paradigm for a distinctly Anglo-Saxon religiosity in the *Titanic* myth, exhorting the Christian believers to resign into God's benevolent will.[31] Tellingly, it is Protestant and not Roman Catholic religion that has become part of the *Titanic* myth: Catholicism is only occasionally used as a religious *couleur locale*, focusing on the historical character of Father Thomas Byles, who reportedly helped Third Class passengers up to the deck and into boats, heard confessions and prayed with those who remained on the deck. The Catholic priest was stylized into a hero after the model of the biblical "Good Shepherd" and is frequently depicted in *Titanic* films.[32] Yet this is only a little vignette; the vast majority of texts that used the *Titanic* disaster in religious exhortations comes from a Protestant context and ignores Catholic aspects of faith on board the *Titanic*.[33]

The religious dimension of the *Titanic* myth is not restricted to the New Testament aspects of comfort and resignation into God's benevolent will. The disaster equally had Old Testament dimensions: God's punishment for human hubris, the Deluge and Noah's Ark. According to biblical description, the measures of Noah's Ark were quite close to those of the *Titanic*—yet while Noah purposefully declined to participate in the sinful excesses of his time and therefore was allowed to save a microcosm of living creatures for a better world to be re-established after the Deluge, mankind in the early 20th century consciously surrendered to the excessive luxury of the *Titanic*.[34] And therefore the ship with its social microcosm on board was doomed to sink.

The image of divine retribution, however, also has non–Christian roots in antiquity, referring to the gods' acts of punishment for human hubris. In 1912, it was the alleged claim of "unsinkability" that became the leitmotif in the discourse on hubris and God's just punishment.[35] *Titanic* films gladly use this motif: "The ship is unsinkable," "*Titanic* herself is a lifeboat"— dramatic irony, highlighting the passengers' overconfidence and silly pride that soon will be turned into deadly dismay. Indeed, the proud claim of the *Titanic* being "unsinkable" was the talk of the town in 1912 — but only *after* the *Titanic* had sunk. The presumptuous claim conveniently emerged after the opposite had happened. In the official promotional descriptions of the new Olympic class ships, the unusually high degree of safety is stressed, displaying the hull with its sixteen watertight compartments that are separated by fifteen watertight bulkheads.[36] The word "unsinkable" is used several times in the White Star Line's brochure and in shipbuilders' magazines — but always with the cautionary modification "practically." Neither the White Star Line nor the shipbuilders Harland & Wolff ever claimed that the *Titanic* was unsinkable. However, an official of the White Star Line, possibly Phillip A.S. Franklin, vice president of the International Mercantile Marine, was imprudent enough to launch an official statement on April 15, 1912, at 9 A.M.: "There is no danger that *Titanic* will sink. The boat is unsinkable and nothing but inconvenience will be suffered by the passengers."[37] At this time, the *Titanic* had of course already foundered. It still took some twelve hours of misguided and incorrect news, but then it was certain: The *Titanic* had gone down.[38] For the press and the public, Franklin's word confirmed the incredible hubris of a company, a hubris that — according to the nascent myth — "had led" to disaster. A little detail, the occasional word of the *Titanic* being "practically unsinkable," had been turned into the actual *reason* for her sinking.[39] And thus, the historical event is turned into myth, on equal footing with Greek tragedy, a story of hubris and nemesis, of pride and fall, in one line with Daedalus and Prometheus, who transgressed the boundaries of the permissible to man. (Prometheus, of course, was neither man nor god, but — a *titan*.) In the case of *Titanic*, this blasphemy was not committed by single individuals but, according to preachers and moralists in 1912, by the entire Western society. Or by mankind as such. And therefore the *Titanic* had to sink, even before her maiden voyage was consummated.

The myth has its morale. In the end, tragedy is turned into triumph, and thus the disaster is given a meaning. Myths serve to create order in an arbitrary world. The interests of certain social groups are elevated to general truths; senselessness thus begins to make sense, in the interest of the society that creates the myth. The various elements of the *Titanic* myth, extracted from the historical event, served to stabilize and sacralize the values of conservative Western society: marriage as a holy institution, the noble behavior of the upper class men, the feminine meekness of their women, the natural superiority of the Anglo-Saxon race. The triumph of the *Titanic* is a triumph of these values, and as such it was anchored in Western collective memory. And therefore, almost all *Titanic* films somehow lead to a happy end — although the ship inevitably sinks.

Gender, class, nation, race, and religion (including human hubris) are elements anchored in the historical event, but they became at once isolated, magnified and instrumentalized in the discourse on the disaster, which started on April 15, 1912. In his analysis of the *Titanic* myth, Steven Biel shows how the process of making sense of the disaster by telling and retelling the conventional narrative itself was a serious attempt to reassert authority.[40] Thus, the myth with its specifically highlighted elements offers the perfect subject matter for the popular film medium, which in its mainstream form of the narrative motion picture serves to stabilize conservative values in (Western) society.

The Historical Development

The myth of the *Titanic* displays a clearly discernible development throughout the 20th century. Basically, there are three periods that can be distinguished: 1912–1955, with a strong start in the years 1912–1914; 1955–1985, framed by the publication of Walter Lord's *A Night to Remember* in 1955 and the discovery of the wreck in 1985; and then from 1985 to the present time, with a specific highlight in 1997, when James Cameron's film made *Titanic* a major topic worldwide.

In the two years between the event and the outbreak of the First World War, *Titanic* initially figured as a media event and then was broadly used as a metaphor for human hubris in articles, essays and books. The disaster's strongest impact, however, came through popular culture, where the issue acted as a draw in various forms of literature, arts, music, and film. Right after the disaster, multiple forms of popular commemoration were used, from postcards to commemorative handkerchiefs, with motifs and discourses that anchored the various basic elements of the myth in public perception.[41] Not all approved of the dominant narrative: George Bernard Shaw for instance openly criticized the clichés used in public discourse. (He was in turn acidly "corrected" by his friend Arthur Conan Doyle, who would not accept any blemish on the *Titanic* tale.) Joseph Conrad—an experienced sailor himself—attacked the amateurish investigation of the disaster as well as the British Board of Trade's regulations. Counter-narratives satirized the prevailing stereotypes in the *Titanic* story; tellingly, they came from those quarters that did not enjoy the privileges of the Anglo-Saxon upper class.[42] Generally, however, the conservative master narrative of the *Titanic* was accepted and used as moralistic tale until the outbreak of the First World War directed attention to more urgent matters.

Except for Ernest Raymond's theater play *The Berg* and the 1929 film *Atlantic* based on this play, there was no general interest in the *Titanic* during the 1920s. In the 1930s there were a few notable "revivals": in literature, the epic poem *The Titanic* of the Canadian poet E.J. Pratt (1935) as well as the two German novels by Robert Prechtl (*Titanensturz: Roman eines Zeitalters*, 1937[43]) and Josef Pelz von Felinau (*Titanic—Tragödie eines Ozeanriesen*, 1939[44]). The 1943 German propaganda film *Titanic* would use motifs from both novels. In the American film industry, there actually was some well-publicized stir around *Titanic* in the 1930s, with producer David O. Selznick trying to tempt director Alfred Hitchcock into making a big *Titanic* movie.

The most enduring "*Titanic* event" in the 1930s, though, was the invention of "Molly Brown."[45] It was only after her death in 1932 that the courageous Denver millionairess Margaret Tobin Brown became a fixed element in the *Titanic* myth. In the years of the Depression, she was turned into a token for America's prevailing triumph: The "rags-to-riches tough gal" from the American West who had been a minor legend in Colorado became a national asset, another prominent personage in the cabinet of the American myth. Margaret Tobin was born in 1867 into a family of Irish emigrants in Hannibal, Missouri. After a rather thrifty childhood, she moved to Leadville, Colorado, where she married the miner John Joseph Brown, whose parents had immigrated from Ireland. In the 1890s, John, who had by then become superintendent of all Ibex mining properties, developed a method to win gold from the Little Johnny Mine. Due to shares and John's leading position, the Brown family became tremendously rich and moved to the finest quarter of Denver in 1894. In Leadville, Margaret Brown had already been involved in the women's right movement; in Denver, she became one of the leading personalities advocating education, human rights and suffrage. Due to her social and political commitment, she was known in the leading American circles, who appreciated both her personality and her social activities. Thus, she was a good friend of the Astor couple, with whom she traveled back from an Egypt tour to America on the *Titanic*.

During the evacuation and in Lifeboat 6, Margaret distinguished herself by her courageous behavior. Even more important, though, was her extraordinary social engagement on the *Carpathia*: Once saved, she immediately started to assist the Third Class survivors (resisting the First Class doctor of the *Carpathia*, who tried to keep her away from the lower classes), and only a few hours after having been taken onto the *Carpathia*, she had already founded the Survivors' Committee and organized an aid fund for destitute emigrants who had lost the little they had possessed. By the time the *Carpathia* arrived in New York on April 18, this fund had collected $10,000 (about $220,000 in present time value[46]). At the dock, Margaret did not leave the *Carpathia* with the other passengers, but stayed aboard with those of the survivors who had nobody to welcome and help them, and saw them off the ship the next day. By contacting embassies and reminding the White Star Line of its obligations, she made sure that her poorer fellow survivors were taken care of.[47] This individual relief operation was organized from her suite in the Ritz-Carlton hotel, where Margaret stayed on for several days together with her brother and her New York friend Genevieve Spinner, assisting foreign-born survivors before she finally traveled home to Denver. Scandalized by the fact that she as a woman was not allowed to testify in the American *Titanic* inquiry, Margaret Brown eventually wrote her own account that was printed in various international newspapers.

The legend of "Molly Brown" started in 1933, with local journalist Gene Fowler publishing a strongly embellished "story" of Brown under the title *Timberline*. A few years later, Fowler's folk tale was taken up by sensationalist writer Carolyn Bancroft, whose fully fictionalized account *The Unsinkable*

Mrs. Brown was first published in a romance magazine in 1936, then came out separately as a little book, which was subsequently taken up in several radio broadcasts in the 1940s.[48] On this basis, the Broadway musical *The Unsinkable Molly Brown* was written in 1960 (renaming Margaret "Molly"); it was turned into a motion picture by MGM in 1964, starring Debbie Reynolds. The musical film definitely entrenched in public perception the popular — and faulty — image of the uncouth newly rich millionairess with a demonstrative lack of good manners and education, but a golden heart. Typically for a legend, it is not the person of Margaret Tobin Brown that is the theme of the "Molly Brown" narrative, but rather American resiliency and triumph.

The Molly Brown myth serves the promotion of a symbol of the triumphant American nation; it also represents the domestication of a woman who distinguished herself by her courageous, self-reliant and extraordinarily responsible and helpful conduct in the *Titanic* disaster. Brown was indeed a highly exceptional woman, interested and strongly involved in contemporary questions of social equality, education, politics, and women's rights. As such, she was a woman outside the norm.[49] The legend turned her into a stereotypical protagonist in the myth of the American West: strong, independent, liberated from the fetters of culture, thus personifying the American dream of a classless society with equal chances for all. At the same time, though, the legend domesticates the "unfeminine" demeanor of the real Brown, declaring it the exceptional conduct of an almost mythical figure — and thus, of no menace to the traditional allocation of gender roles in 1912 and in the decades to come.

Titanic films transport the legend rather than a truthful representation of the real Margaret Brown. She is one of the few historical characters who can be used for comic relief, but she also offers instances of unusual (because female) heroism. Her allegedly brash and down-to-earth behavior in First Class gives relief to the — stereotypically — stiff atmosphere in the finer circles of the rich; in some films, these scenes amount to parody. Her assistance in the evacuation — encouraging hesitant ladies to enter the lifeboats — equally provides a humorous moment, as she herself is put into a lifeboat against her will. The scenes in Lifeboat 6, however, are serious, emphasizing her courage and assertiveness.[50] Yet there are hardly references to Brown's social commitment on the *Carpathia* and in the aftermath of the disaster.[51] In general, she is depicted as a cliché of a headstrong woman, and thus as an exception to the rule. "Molly Brown," an American heroine, indeed was made "unsinkable," but it is not the real Margaret Brown who is the subject of this myth.

As the Second World War broke out, the subject of the *Titanic* again was superseded by other, more atrocious disasters. The great "event" that catapulted *Titanic* back into worldwide consciousness and thus opened up a new phase in the history of the *Titanic* myth was the publication of Walter Lord's documentary novel *A Night to Remember* in 1955. For the first time, a narrative version of the *Titanic* disaster came out that was based on as many first-hand testimonies as possible. For the first time, an account was published that entirely focused on the crucial two and a half hours between the collision and the sinking, trying to untangle as many of the unanswered questions as possible. Lord offers a kaleidoscope of perspectives, ranging from the officers via the passengers down to the few surviving stokers. Born in Baltimore in 1917, Lord had "tasted blood" during an Atlantic crossing on the *Olympic* in 1926. The experience of traveling on the *Titanic*'s sister ship prompted him to collect everything about the *Titanic*—but, more importantly, to search for and contact as many survivors as possible. *A Night to Remember* is a collage of the memories and testimonies of more than sixty survivors, a modernist, highly visual narrative that retells the disaster minute by minute.[52] The multiple perspectives are molded into a coherent mosaic, taking the reader from the upper decks down into the ship's bowels to let them experience the drama so to say in real time, as an omnipresent observer. Contrary to other novels, it is not Astor, nor Smith, nor Ismay, who are the focus of the narrative: main protagonist and tragic hero is the *Titanic*, the ship itself. *A Night to Remember* is exciting reading, due to its fast pace and the multiplicity of perspectives: the drama unfolds moment for moment, in multiple views, a complex network of observations and memories. For the first time since 1912, the *Titanic* appears to be within grasp again, the real ship, the real experience, quite contrary to the overdone melodrama or philosophical musings of the *Titanic* novels hitherto published. However, oral history was not yet a scholarly discipline in 1955: The pitfalls of the complex interferences of personal memory with outward influences were not yet discussed as decisive factors in private testimonies of an historical event. Thus, the countless survivors' statements in Lord's novel have been taken as "truth," turning *A Night to Remember* into the "Bible" for *Titanic* research. In fact, the novel with its uncritical presentation of "authentic memories" and its countless fictional dialogues serving as "glue," has decisively contributed to establishing many of the legends as "authentic." Once again, history and legend became inseparably entangled in the *Titanic* complex. With the appearance of Lord's novel, the myth can no longer be distinguished from the historical event.

Lord's "analytical" approach intrigued a worldwide audience. However, his analytical stance is forcefully countered by the broad curtain of nostalgia drawn over the disaster, which overwhelmingly won the sympathy of the readers. With Lord's novel, a new view on the *Titanic* disaster was established: "Never again will the world be as it was" is the mantra that echoes throughout the book. It has, ever since the sweeping success of Lord's novel, shaped the perception of the *Titanic*. With *A Night to Remember*, nostalgia has become the hallmark of the *Titanic* myth. In Lord's view, the *Titanic* set an end to an era in which everything somehow had been easier and better: Everybody knew where they belonged (preferably in First Class!), men still were gallant, women meek, crews were considerate, couples were loyal, families stuck together, business managers took a personal and sincere interest in the well-being of their customers. There still was faith in the fundamentally good — the good in technology, in progress, in man. All this was lost, in a single night, due to a single iceberg. "Never again would they be quite so sure of themselves" — this is Lord's essential statement about mankind after the *Titanic* ordeal.[53] Wistful nostalgia is coupled with an almost modernist narrative stance: Time is running, all too fast, rushing towards doom — at the same time, an entire era of man's history is passing within these two and a half hours.

The *Titanic* myth is given a new dimension. Lord does mention the injustice of the class system, hubris and the unconditional admiration of richness and power, but all this is folded up in a nostalgic image of a golden era that allegedly existed in serene innocence until April 14, 1912. Reality in the U.S. and Europe in the spring of 1912 was quite different — but this is ignored in Lord's *A Night to Remember*. The myth became wrapped up in nostalgia. The need for such a "wrapping" must be seen in the historical context of Lord's publication: after two world wars and Hiroshima, under the constant menace of the Cold War, the *Titanic* offered the dream of "the old days," in which — despite a few little blemishes — everything still was manageable and never really devastating.[54] Compared to air attacks and atomic bombs, the *Titanic* disaster was downright human. It gave its victims time: time to say goodbye, time to prepare themselves for a "good death," to die "as gentlemen" and in acceptance of God's divine will. Modern technology is less merciful; the *Titanic* disaster still had a human face.

Finally, Lord's novel also started a new tradition in *Titanic* lore: "What if...?" With *A Night to Remember*, the many speculations on alternatives and contingencies — which, of course, had been voiced much earlier — became an indispensable part of the *Titanic* narrative. Lord himself later called the "ifs" an element of Greek tragedy: mankind's revolt against merciless doom, human speculation on what would have happened if... If Captain Smith had reduced speed, if lookout Fleet (or, as it was, First Officer Murdoch) had seen the iceberg moments earlier, if there had been sufficient lifeboats (which, incidentally, would not have helped more passengers to survive[55]), if the *Californian* had reacted to the rockets. The series of "ifs" is endless. It is contrasted by the brutal fact that the *Titanic*, in a chain of unfortunate events, collided with an iceberg at a certain place and a certain point of time in a way that inevitably led to her sinking. *Titanic* authors preferably translate this into a doom of universal dimensions:

> A slight shift of time — several minutes more, or several minutes less — would have changed the ship's position and put her ahead of or behind the precise spot where the berg was struck. But once the flow of time began, there could be no modification. The inevitable was already set in motion. *Titanic* had but one destination: the disaster which was her doom.[56]

Lord's documentary novel had an impact like no other *Titanic* book. It unleashed a new wave of *Titanic* interest, which continuously increased over the following decades. In 1956, the one-hour television drama *A Night to Remember*, based entirely on Lord's book, was broadcast as an episode in the NBC series *Kraft Television Theatre*; the teleplay by George Roy Hill and John Whedon was included among the 1956 prize plays of the Writers Guild of America.[57] Yet it was the British film *A Night to Remember* (1958), combining literal quotations from Lord's scene-by-scene depiction of the disaster with a few plausible fictional additions, that turned into a major success and made the title *A Night to Remember* known worldwide.

Lord's book itself has been regarded as "the *Titanic* Bible" by *Titanic* enthusiasts, who began to multiply and in the early 1960s established themselves as an organization. In 1963, Edward Kamuda from Indian Orchard, Massachusetts, founded the Titanic Historical Society (originally called "*Titanic* Enthusiasts of America") with the aim to preserve the memory of the *Titanic*. Originally a very little circle consisting of six active (i.e., paying) members and some forty-five honorary members (mostly aged survivors), the society began to grow. From the late '60s onwards, the annual conventions attracted more and more people, and its cooperation with the media got the little society increasing public attention. A decisive step to make the *Titanic* Historical Society famous worldwide was the establishment of a contact between leading members and American oceanographers. The society's emphatic support eventually contributed to a sensation that turned out to be the next milestone in the development of the *Titanic* myth: the discovery of the wreck.

That event, on September 1, 1985, became a worldwide media circus, which neither the *Titanic* enthusiasts nor oceanographer Robert Ballard had foreseen. Public interest in the *Titanic*, which never really had died away, virtually exploded. The myth entered a new phase — and Ballard's career soared. With him, the media, camera teams, writers and artists profited from the new

2. The Titanic Myth 45

Titanic hype. As in 1912, the media and the myth formed a profitable symbiosis: Ballard's scientific principle that modern oceanography should rely on images and not on sonar screening, was in perfect harmony with the public's desire for pictures.[58] The audience wanted to *see* the *Titanic*, to become immediately involved in the dives to the wreck. Thus, numerous "life documentations" were made in the years after the discovery, taking the audience to the wreck in real-life broadcasts. Once again, the name *Titanic* became connected with the triumph of modern technology, but this time, high-tech was instrumental in "redeeming" the lost maiden ship.[59] The *Titanic*, which according to the myth had sunk in 1912 "due" to human hubris, was resurrected, now in nostalgic, quaint, and deeply moving guise.

The discovery of the wreck launched a flood of publications and documentary films, and soon a heated debate on the salvage of "artifacts" from the wreck broke out. Both scientists and scholars from the humanities began to focus on the ship, analyzing data from the wreck or the cultural historical phenomenon of the *Titanic* myth respectively. In 1995, the IMAX film *Titanica* with its giant pictures of the wreck enchanted a global audience, and in 1997, James Cameron summed up the *Titanic* myth in his mega-movie, combining nostalgia with high-tech, a young woman's emancipation with Hollywood romantics, the splendid, vigorous ship with the dignified wreck, crowning the film with an apotheosis of the immortal *Titanic* as a paradisiac vision. It was a movie spectacle, magnified by a global media spectacle that turned *Titanic* into *the* event of popular culture at the end of the '90s.[60]

With the Cameron film, *Titanic* had indeed become an asset in popular culture: Wrapping paper with the portraits of the film's cast sold just as well as replica of fictional Rose DeWitt Bukater's evening gowns and jewelry. The members of the *Titanic* societies, which by now had spread in several countries worldwide, were not amused: Their elite hobby had been turned into a mass phenomenon; *Titanic* memory had been debased to *Titanic* kitsch.[61] Collecting, a serious branch in the *Titanic* societies, became problematic: It was no longer the refined hunt for the original or the limited facsimile—the market became flooded with replicas of artifacts and film props, *Titanic* rulers, stationery and pens. Or *Titanic* ice cube trays (with *Titanic* sinking vertically in your gin and tonic glass), an inflatable mini–*Titanic* for the bath tub (including the iceberg) and, of course, recipes for *Titanic* cakes.

Has the myth reached its final stage? With Cameron's film, *Titanic* reached the climax of popularity, yet at the same time it has sunk into an abyss of popular kitsch. Postmodern society has created its postmodern *Titanic*, it is a question of the general cultural development how the unforgettable ship will fare in the decades to come.

3

Titanic in Film

Titanic is simply *made* for fiction. The historical event offers the perfect structure, the myth supplies the perfect main themes — and the 2,200 passengers and crew, whose biographies have been investigated on a singular scale in the history of disasters, offer a multitude of individual plots that can be worked out within the *Titanic* framework. Together, they form a constellation that with the 1958 film version of Walter Lord's documentary novel *A Night to Remember* would be crystallized into the "*Titanic* code": a combination of the historical story and its dramaturgically perfect pacing with the basic elements of the *Titanic* myth, with a certain number of individual scenes regarded as "authentic," and with the historical personages. This code, fixed in its outline and basic ingredients, is then supplemented with fictional characters and plots. In the earlier films, these fictional plots are the focus, while the sinking is used as background only. With the fixation of the code in the 1958 film *A Night to Remember*, though, it is the *Titanic* code itself that forms the very basis of *Titanic* film scripts; fictional plots can only unfold in close interaction with this code. Since the *Titanic* code is dramatically so strong that it can constitute a perfectly functioning feature film in itself, with almost no fictional addition, the *Titanic* disaster and its mythologization indeed were just made for film.

The historical story of the *Titanic* displays a truly classic narrative rhythm[1]: the splendid outset with the brilliant new ship and correspondingly high expectations, serene life on board throughout the first days of the voyage, then the collision as a sudden, unexpected impulse which, however, ironically is registered by a few only. Then the drama of the two and a half hours until the sinking: the gradual awakening, starting with curiosity, gradually changing into inquietude, concern, anxiety and finally turning into desperation. The end, however, offers a finale of symphonic dimensions, followed by tranquility and a dignified acceptance of fate. This perfect design is supported by classic elements of Greek tragedy — hubris, dramatic irony, nemesis, catharsis — and vitalized by numerous opportunities for the dramatic juxtaposition of opposites. It is no surprise that *Titanic* was taken up by countless writers, screenwriters and film producers immediately after the disaster had taken place: The story just had to be told.

The myth of the *Titanic* is universal by highlighting universal human issues — and thus, *Titanic* films again and again articulate themes of class, nation, ethnicity, gender, and religion, with the *Titanic* being a sort of "index" around which the individual (often fictional) plots are constructed. The *Titanic* itself constitutes the fundament to these plots, "a cautionary tale, even a fable."[2] Without this fundament, the fictional tales of love and jealousy would be banal. The sinking, however, invests them with a dimension of universal suffering and aspiration. Each script for a *Titanic* film must come to terms with this myth; each screenwriter must seek a convincing link between the fictional plot and its universal fundament.

The passengers and crew, finally, are the material to play with. There are some stock characters and motifs that form the "*Titanic* grid": The historical voyage is the stage, the historical characters like Captain Smith, Bruce Ismay, Thomas Andrews and a number of passengers, both notorious and nameless, are the players. In their historical authenticity, the passengers and crew offer the basic pairing of opposites that Steven Biel has identified as an important pattern of the *Titanic* myth.[3] These opposites are linked to the categories of main themes of gender, class, and nation, serving to highlight their popular stereotypes: noble First Class American vs. panicking Third Class foreigner, dutiful wireless operator vs. smeary and thievish stoker; Anglo-Saxon vs. foreign; prominent individuals vs. the nameless mass; hysterical females vs. unsinkable Molly Brown. These contrasting elements also help to profile the various strands in multiple-plotting. In fact, *Titanic* is the very object made for multiple plots. As a microcosm and a layered structure, the ship offers seven possible spheres:

1. First Class
2. Second Class
3. Third Class
4. Officers' sphere: bridge, chart room, officers' quarters, wireless office[4]
5. Crew's quarters
6. Engine rooms
7. First Class passengers' servants

Most films focus on the contrast between First Class and Third Class, integrating professional spaces such as the bridge, the wireless office, and the engine rooms. These features form the basic spatial and social structure for *Titanic* tales. Only the meticulously researched productions of 1958 and 1979 involve Second Class strands, and the 1979 *S.O.S. Titanic* alone includes a few minor scenes in the crew's quarters. The individual servants of the First Class passengers remain anonymous — except for the maid of the Allison family, Alice Cleaver, an historical character whose fate on the *Titanic* is fictionalized in the 1996 film.

Few filmmakers, however, content themselves with the historical cast. Generally, the *Titanic* and her historical protagonists form only the background for some larger human drama. Although some historical characters may shine through in fictional characters, such as author William Thomas Stead in the fictional writer and philosopher John Rool (the 1929 film *Atlantic*) or Father Thomas Byles in the priest George Healey (the 1953 film *Titanic*), the main plot of most *Titanic* films is purely fictional, liberating the screenwriter from the demands of historical correctness. Instead, the laws of filmmaking are to be obeyed: great romance or melodrama, wrought into the storyline of a well-known disaster.

Yet even the historical *Titanic* story itself asks for a certain degree of fictionalization. The *Titanic* complex builds on a broad gamut of unanswered questions that have led to unending speculation. Film can finally give the definite answers, can finally *show* "how it really was." We finally get the missing links: What happened in the moment of the collision? Who is to blame? What were the machinations behind the disaster? Capitalism, blind faith in technology, English arrogance, American greed? And what exactly happened on the ship, in the course of the voyage, during the final two hours? How did the disaster change the lives of the survivors and the victims' families?

Titanic films give answers, again and again. They construct history. Sworn to "authenticity," they pick up aspects of the legend and imprint it into collective memory as "reality" and "truth," decisively supported by the power of the image, the music, and the emotions. *Titanic* has everything to offer: heroism, melodrama, love, despair, pleasure and pain, failure and triumph, memory and eternal guilt. The luxury of "those above" and the poor but honest life of "those below." A ship of clichés, just made for film.

Titanic *in Film from 1912 to the Present Time*

Titanic had sunk at exactly the right point of time — at least from the perspective of film history, as it was. In 1912, film still was a young and fresh medium which had just begun to conquer the world.[5] In 1895, the first performances of silent films had spellbound audiences in Berlin and Paris. In the beginning, film was used to represent little scenes from daily life or humorous anecdotes. Within a few years, though, film turned into the dominant narrative medium in Western society. Shortly after 1900, the first short feature films were made, and in 1910, the first film producers settled in Hollywood. The master works of early film history — *The Great Train Robbery, Cabiria, Birth of a Nation* — were all made in the years around 1912. *Titanic* was the perfect subject for the medium. Early silent film with its expressive gestures and stark contrasts concentrated on events of global significance (seen from a Western perspective), on disasters and human tragedy. *Titanic* was such an event — at least it was perceived as such in the Western world and the media helped to magnify the incident into a tragedy of universal dimensions.

Early Films and Newsreels, 1912–13

Filmmakers immediately grasped the potential of the story. One of the *Titanic* survivors was the singer, dancer, model and actress Dorothy Gibson, who had already starred in a number of silent films in 1911 made by the American branch of the French Eclair Motion Picture Company.[6] On the *Titanic*, the 22-year-old traveled First Class together with her mother; both women were saved in Lifeboat 7. Eclair at once decided to exploit both the incident and the fact that one of their actresses had been involved: Within two weeks, a motion picture was made starring Dorothy Gibson. It was released exactly one month after the disaster, on May 14, 1912. The story is that of the *Titanic* disaster, wrapped in a fictional plot about a young woman who survives the disaster and, due to the traumatic experience, is almost dissuaded from marrying her sea-faring fiancé. Of course, a happy end is provided, "Miss Dorothy" gets her husband and he, despite *Titanic* risks, remains in the Navy, loyal to his duty to flag and country. The media made a lot out of Gibson re-enacting "the real experience" and even wearing the clothes she had worn in the night of April 14. The actress worked on the script herself, embellishing it with details taken from the *Titanic* myth, which had rapidly spread in newspaper reports and — largely fictionalized — publications on the disaster: a more or less helpless crew, panic among the Third Class passengers, men being shot.[7] As the first dramatic film reconstruction of the disaster, *Saved from the Titanic* immediately became a success and quickly crossed the Atlantic, with enthusiastic reception in various European countries. Today, the ten-minute motion picture is lost, having been destroyed in a fire at Eclair Studios in 1914 — a severe loss for research on the *Titanic* myth.

Saved from the Titanic was only the prelude to an entire tradition of motion pictures that take up the disaster and present it in ever new constellations of human interaction, political and moral messages, and changing film aesthetics. In the second half of the 20th century, this playful and pragmatic handling of the event gave way to an ever more obsessive aspiration at "authenticity," combined with an ever more passionate mystification of the disaster.

In the beginning there were the newsreels. As soon as the *Titanic* had sunk, theater managers became obsessed with showing the "real" story of the *Titanic*. There was great potential for profit here:

> [T]he sinking took place at the dawn of the newsreel age, when the public was becoming accustomed to seeing a selection of filmed news at their local picture palaces, in newsreels including Pathé Gazette, the Animated Weekly and Topical Budget. So somehow, to satisfy expectations if nothing else, the *Titanic* story had to be covered on film, and finding or shooting appropriate news images became of urgent importance to these companies. They tackled this task with speed and energy.[8]

The problem was that the ship only became famous after it had disappeared. Thus, authentic *Titanic* footage was unavailable. There existed a considerable number of newsreels and short films presenting the *Olympic* (the flagship of the White Star Line, the first ship of the new Olympic class), which had been the great sensation and the star. After April 15, however, the worldwide audience was no longer interested in seeing the *Olympic*: It was the *Titanic* that entirely absorbed public interest. And this public audience had, as Stephen Bottomore points out, by now become accustomed to watching the latest news in the theaters — on film, displaying the real pictures and the real people. Demand was overwhelming worldwide, but authentic footage of the *Titanic* was scarce goods. Only the laying of the keel on March 31, 1909, had been filmed, the transport of the giant anchor, the launch on May 31, 1911, the *Titanic*'s departure from Belfast to Southampton, and a few moments that had been filmed on 10 April 1912, just before the *Titanic* set out on her maiden voyage.[9] There was nothing about the splendid interior, nothing that could show the audience that the *Titanic* indeed had been "the ship of dreams."

There are several twists of fate with regard to the *Titanic* and documentary footage. A notable Second Class passenger on the *Titanic* was cinematographer William Harbeck, who had a high reputation for his film documentaries (among others, a documentation of the aftermath of the 1905 San Francisco earthquake).[10] In his luggage, he had five up-to-date film cameras and some 110,000 feet of film, that is, over a hundred reels which he brought from Europe and intended to present in American theaters. Besides, Harbeck was not idle while traveling on the *Titanic*: According to a note of the *Moving Picture News*, Harbeck was "under a $10,000 contract with the White Star line to take moving pictures of the giant vessel on her maiden trip to America."[11]

He was supposed to leave the *Titanic* in a tug before entry into New York harbor, so that he could film the *Titanic*'s arrival at the White Star dock. It must therefore be assumed that a considerable amount of original *Titanic* footage went down to the bottom of the Atlantic on April 15, 1912.

Another twist of fate is the story of Charles Urban, known as one of the first major figures of early cinema.[12] An expert on documentary and news film, he proposed a documentation about the construction of the Olympic class ships to Harland & Wolff as early as September 1907. The shipbuilding company was delighted by the offer for cost-free publicity and gladly accepted. Originally, Urban intended to film the construction of both ships, which lay side by side in the two giant berths specifically constructed for this purpose by Harland & Wolff. For some reason, Urban ended up filming the *Olympic* only, from 1909 to 1911. The six-minute film *S.S. Olympic* was released in British theaters in the fall of 1911 and became a major success both in England and other European countries.[13] The *Titanic*, however, was ignored — and this was the worst blow for Urban, as it turned out in April 1912: He had simply chosen the "wrong" ship. A similar film on the *Titanic* would have been the coup of his life.

Most filmmakers resorted to montage: a cut-together of anything "authentic" to be had, the original film scenes from the keel-laying to the departure, additional still pictures and short films. In standard short films, Captain Smith and icebergs open the stage, an exposition, so to speak, of the "protagonists."[14] Then, in brutal contrast, the departure of the search ships from Halifax, their return with hundreds of bodies, scenes of desperate relatives in front of the New York White Star Office, the arrival of the *Carpathia*, pictures of the survivors, and finally the heroic presentation of the *Carpathia*'s crew and of Guglielmo Marconi, whose wireless technology was praised for having saved hundreds of lives. And the "in between," on which public interest entirely was focused? Merciful darkness veiled the disaster, interrupted by an intertitle with the distress signal "C.Q.D." that was "flashed on in vivid reality."[15] None had filmed the sinking (or if they did, the camera had gone down with the filmmaker), so the episode which the audience was most interested in was not available. Since there also was some discussion about the decency of showing the disaster in the media, the one-minute silence in complete darkness — no doubt a somewhat frightening experience for the audience — was a fine compromise. The flashing of the "C.Q.D." then both imparted a sense of urgency and cemented the belief that the wireless operators had used the correct signal to call for help.

Still, the amount of authentic footage was meager. Soon, some additional material was included, showing "Captain Smith on the Bridge" or "on his ship"—but it was not specified that this ship was the *Olympic*. After all, the *Olympic* had been Captain Smith's ship up to the *Titanic*'s maiden voyage. In fact, some controversy developed on this issue: The audience had a right to "authenticity."[16] However, there generally was a thin line between fact and fiction in the days of early cinema. Newsreels and dramatic films were aesthetically close to each other, "documentaries" exploited the dramatic and dramatizing possibilities of the medium, while motion pictures were extremely short and shared the aesthetics of the newsreels, with abrupt changes of short scenes and sequences. Authentic or not: The 1912 audience generally was content with the newsreels—as long as it could believe that it saw the *Titanic*.

Dramatized versions of the disaster could therefore easily integrate footage from documentaries or imitate the aesthetics of the newsreels. Typically, the German film *In Nacht und Eis* ("In Night and Ice"), that was announced for May 1912 but eventually premiered on August 17, 1912, in Berlin, starts almost like a newsreel, providing the following fictionalized plot with a high degree of authenticity.[17] The acting, in turn, often tends to the melodramatic: Captain Smith's extended outbreak of despair as he (!) spots the iceberg from the bridge indeed verges on parody, at least if seen from today's perspective. In fact, the mixing of "reality" with melodrama, which is so pervasive in this film, was to become a specialty of director Mime Misu, who made his first significant appearance with *In Nacht und Eis*.[18] The meticulous representation of the *Titanic*'s boiler rooms and the obvious fascination with an inferno of water, steam, fire, and smoke resulted in positive reviews, praising the realism of this "educational picture." Interestingly, there is a strong emphasis on the wireless operator and his efforts to the last minute to summon help. In this respect, the film is indeed "realistic," since it effectively reflects the joint effort of the White Star Line and the Marconi Company to turn the Marconi operators into heroes and stylize the disaster into a stroke of fate, against which man (and the White Star Line) simply was powerless. Mime Misu took up a popular motif in the *Titanic* debate; it turned out to be the best promotion Marconi and the White Star Line could have hoped for. Another legend perpetualized in this film is the alleged death of Captain Smith, who was said to have saved a child while swimming in the water and to have put it into a lifeboat, but then declined any help with the words "I will go down with the ship." And, as the intertitles tell us, the band does indeed play "Nearer, My God, to Thee"—again a cinematic consolidation of a popular myth right from the start.

Apart from these legendary elements, Misu offered ample insight into life on board before the collision. This provided the international audience with what they had hoped for and dearly missed in the newsreels: the luxury and splendor of the *Titanic*. This element of cinematic props and staging was to become indispensable in later *Titanic* films, strongly influencing plots and perspectives on the disaster.

In *Nacht und Eis*, released with the title *Shipwrecked in Icebergs* in the U.S., enjoyed considerable success in several countries. After being almost entirely forgotten, this first full-length *Titanic* motion picture was rediscovered in the wake of Cameron's *Titanic* in early 1998; it is now available in the slightly shortened length of 35 minutes on YouTube (with German intertitles).

Denmark, a little seafaring nation, released two silent films heavily building on aspects of the *Titanic* disaster. On October 3, 1912, *Et drama paa havet* ("A Drama at Sea") opened in Copenhagen; in the U.S. the short film was shown from January 1913 onwards under the title *The Great Ocean Disaster, or The Fire at Sea*.[19] The romantic plot focuses on a ship catching fire at sea. Thus, the most notable *Titanic* feature, the iceberg, is eliminated. Yet in contrast to *In Nacht und Eis*, the film makes an issue of the fatal shortage of lifeboats, which was a highly discussed subject after the sinking of the *Titanic*. *Et drama paa havet* shows passengers fighting for places in the lifeboats, thus turning another *Titanic* legend into film drama.

In December 1913, Nordisk Film released *Atlantis*, directed by the notable Danish film director and producer August Blom.[20] The film — one of the longest silent films to date worldwide — is based on Gerhart Hauptmann's homonymous novel, which was published a month before the sinking of the *Titanic* and, featuring an episode of a sinking ocean liner, was regarded as a prophetic vision.[21] Due to the ship disaster in Hauptmann's novel, which is a crucial event in the unfolding of the main plot, film director Blom could draw on the massive public attention engendered by the *Titanic* disaster. Hauptmann tells the story of the physician Dr. Friedrich von Kammacher, who tries to escape the bleak reality of his wife's insanity as well as his own professional failure by traveling in Europe and to the U.S. Both the novel and the film focus on Kammacher's complicated relationship with the dancer Ingigerd Hahlstroem, whom he follows on a voyage to the U.S. The film depiction of the passenger ship S.S. *Roland* contains episodes that will come to be regarded typical in the later *Titanic* film tradition: scenes in First Class (both on the deck and in the interior rooms), on the bridge, in the boiler rooms, and in steerage. (In this case, the term "steerage" is correct, with large common rooms where the poor emigrants stay and sleep during the voyage.) A tongue-in-cheek effect is the great commotion in First Class as their relatively small ship meets a major ocean liner: In the middle of dinner, all passengers rush out on deck to wave — *Titanic* passing by? The ship has only three funnels, yet otherwise, it quite resembles the *Titanic* in this 1913 film. Since the plot of *Atlantis* unfolds in the late 19th century, that is, at a time when liners of such a dimension did not yet exist, this little detail doubtlessly constitutes a *Titanic* connection. The scene is followed by a single, lonely Dr. Kammacher standing on the starboard side of the deck, looking at a beautiful large sailing ship close by, calm and dignified, in gentle motion: The time of the great sailors is past.

The disaster, however, is not quite "Titanic." As the S.S. *Roland* hits a wreck lying deeply in the water, it is clear from the start that the situation is fatal. The wireless operator sends "SOS." This is another anachronism in the light of a late 19th-century plot: Wireless telegraphy was not installed on ships until the early 20th century, and the international distress signal SOS was agreed upon by the seafaring nations only in 1908. An "authentic" *Titanic* plot would in any case have used the Marconi Company's CQD. Yet it is not only the distress signal that is somewhat "un–*Titanic*" in this shipwreck episode: In contrast to the historical *Titanic* disaster, panic breaks out quickly, passengers fight wildly, and there certainly is no word of "women and children first." Boats get crowded before they are swung out, and people die in flooding cabins and in the boiler room. Surprisingly, though, the sinking takes many hours: While the collision happens at 3:20 A.M., the ship goes down in open morning light. In the end, only one boat with a handful of passengers remains on the surface; of course, Kammacher and Ingigerd (whom he saved from her cabin) are among the survivors. The traumatic event eventually moves Ingigerd to accept Kammacher's love, yet in New York, her constant flirting and indifference to Kammacher finally drives him away. In the end, the surgeon meets another woman and marries her after his wife has died.

Titanic— or rather: the sinking of the S.S. *Roland*— is but an episode in this film, yet it plays an important role as rite of passage from Europe to the U.S., turning out to be the catalyst in the relationship between Kammacher and Ingigerd. Unlike the earlier silent films featuring the *Titanic* disaster, it involves a great number of extras in order to make the event appear authentic: filming the sinking scenes on the Norwegian liner *C.F. Tietgen*, Blom let 500 passengers plus officers and crew fight in the bay of Køge (Denmark) to create a realistic impression of the sinking. Accordingly, the film was praised as "the last word in film realism" and the scene of the shipwreck as "one of the most remarkable and realistic ever produced in films."[22] The *Titanic* alias S.S. *Roland* is not much more than a prop in the Danish film adaptation of the Hauptmann novel. Nevertheless, it added decisively to the general attractiveness of the film. In Norway, however, the film was banned, since it was considered inappropriate to turn the recent tragedy into commercial entertainment: Filming a ship disaster in 1912–13 could only be associated with the *Titanic*.

In Blom's *Atlantis*, the story of the ship disaster figures as an episode within a larger plot. From 1913 onwards, motion pictures featuring the *Titanic*, whether directly or with a veiled name, can be divided into two categories: Films that use the famous disaster just as an episode and films that entirely focus on the voyage and its disastrous outcome. It is the latter that kept the myth of the great disaster going and transformed it in the course of the 20th century.

The 1929 *Atlantic* and Selznick's Foundered *Titanic* Project

After the beginning of the First World War, cinematic interest in the *Titanic* dwindled. It took fifteen years for the ship to resurge on screen.[23] In 1929, shortly after the introduction of sound in film, came *Atlantic*, a production by British International Pictures at Elstree. German director Ewald André Dupont made it with three different casts in three languages: German, English, and French.[24] In Germany, *Atlantic* was the first sound film to be released.

The motion picture puts the popular English theater play *The Berg* (1929) by Ernest Raymond on screen; it shares the philosophical stance of the play. Thus, the story of the disaster is turned into a somewhat static drama taking place in the First Class Smoking Room and covering the final few hours of the doomed ship's life: a chamber play, in which the different world views and attitudes of the two main characters, the stoical atheist author John Rool and an Anglican Priest called "Padre," clash. Their intellectual interplay is accompanied by the bland little melodramas of the minor characters and unfolds on the foil of the ship's catastrophe. Like Raymond's play, Dupont's film appears to be more allegory than drama, although great pains were taken to add cinematic dimensions: *Atlantic* was praised and admired for the impressive design of the ship's interiors. Besides the Smoking Room, which constitutes the center of the film, individual scenes are filmed in the engine room, on the bridge, in the chart room, in the wireless office, on the Grand Staircase, in a First Class suite, and on deck.[25]

Atlantic is the first full-length motion picture on the fate of the *Titanic*, covering the final three hours of the ship. However, everything was done *not* to name *Titanic*—not least, since the White Star Line tried to interfere several times in order to prevent the production of a feature film that would arouse undesired memories and thus cause damage to the company's image once again.[26] In Raymond's play, the name "Titanic" is just as much avoided as any direct references to the famous White Star ship. The film, in contrast, more explicitly alludes to *Titanic*, although the name of the doomed ship is "Atlantic" and none of the historical characters appears by name.[27] Nevertheless, correspondences with historical persons such as the author William T. Stead, the priest Father Thomas Byles, John Jacob Astor and his wife, the Straus couple, and Captain E.J. Smith are obvious. Apart from this, the film script includes a number of succinct allusions to the disaster, such as the famous remarks on the weather and the unusual smoothness of the sea, which according to the 1912 inquiries had been voiced on the bridge just prior to the collision.[28] In the eventual film, these allusions to the *Titanic* are cut — was this consideration for the White Star Line's concerns or a simple (and necessary) reduction of an overloaded script? In any case, the veiling strategies were well-meant, but useless. The international audience did, of course, know exactly what was being played: a luxurious ocean liner, an iceberg, remarks about an "unsinkable" ship, too few lifeboats, and in the end the strains of "Nearer, My God, to Thee"—the name "Titanic" indeed was superfluous.[29]

Yet the correspondences in detail are less significant than the overall attitude: *Atlantic* appears as a resurrection of the *Titanic* myth in full vigor. The attitude displayed in the film is just as conservative as the myth of 1912: courage and self-sacrifice, traditional gender roles, a generally accepted social hierarchy,[30] in the end, the humble acceptance of God's will and a quiet triumph of Christian religiosity — all this is being presented in rather longwinded dialogues and pregnant pauses.[31] The aspect of nation is underlined in the film script, which contains Captain Smith's legendary final admonition "Be British!" In the film, the scene is conspicuously absent; the proud "Be British!" was probably deemed inadequate for a trilingual film with a non-British (or even latently anti–British) audience in mind.[32] Still, almost all characters are British (whether played by English, German or French actors), and there is at least one scene in which the "superiority of the Anglo-Saxon race" is blatantly demonstrated: As the lifeboats are loaded, two lowly men fight their way through the crowd and force their way into a lifeboat. As they refuse to leave the boat, they are shot by an officer and their bodies are thrown into the sea. They are black.[33]

Taking up and endorsing vital aspects of the *Titanic* myth right at a time that was characterized by fears of revolution and social disorder, by the overturning of established ideas of femininity, and by a record divorce rate, *Atlantic* appears as a self-reliant affirmation of traditional values, ennobled by the tragedy of the sinking.[34] After the long silence surrounding the *Titanic* disaster, *Atlantic* proved the unsinkable potential of the event, both in terms of film drama and moral message. The international audience was enthusiastic: *Atlantic* turned out to be one of the most successful European films of the period.

Eventually, Hollywood directed its attention towards the "greatest ship disaster of all times." In 1936, producer David O. Selznick (head of Selznick International Pictures) saw a chance that an old dream of his could come true: to make a magnificent motion picture out of the *Titanic* disaster.[35] The trigger for his initiative was news about the aged liner S.S. *Leviathan* being sold for scrap. Selznick intended to go all out and sink a real ship. However, the appropriate prop was not sufficient to realize the dream.

Back in 1912, Second Officer Lightoller stated at the British Inquiry with regard to the special conditions of the disastrous night: "Everything was against us."[36] Looking back at Selznick's effort to realize the great *Titanic* motion picture, one could equally state that everything was against him. Selznick did not get the S.S. *Leviathan*. He got the director — no one less than Alfred Hitchcock — but it turned out that Hitchcock never made the film. Selznick's dream got entangled in all kinds of problems: legal, diplomatic, competitive, artistic. The main problem maybe was Selznick's own indecisiveness and fear of lawsuits. The picture never was made.

Generally, the idea was fine. *Titanic* was, as ever, a great issue of general interest (as the 1929 film had shown) and offered the perfect ingredients for a spectacular feature film. Selznick counted on the potential the subject had for an international audience, especially including the film market of the British Empire. The first setback concerned the rights to the title and the script: Film producer Howard Hughes owned a script for a *Titanic* film written by Wilson Mizner and Carl Harbraugh. In late 1937, Selznick protested as Hughes registered the title. Selznick's own plans for a *Titanic* film then led to threats of a lawsuit, raised by Hughes' lawyer Neil McCarthy. Although there actually was no legal ground for that, Selznick was not happy about the prospects of a suit. Further legal worries arose when *Variety* announced on June 1, 1938, that Selznick would be rushing *Titanic* into production for a late summer release. The response was overwhelming: Selznick International Pictures was deluged by offers of advice and material from survivors and other people. For Selznick, this was too much of a good thing: "My enthusiasm is tempered with a great worry that we are going to wind up with all kinds of lawsuits, especially from people who may have some deluded notion that they may have submitted material or ideas to us for which they should be paid."[37] A young lawyer was hired to work out guidelines for the production; he issued an extensive legal guide for writers on the *Titanic* project, explaining matters of infringement, libel, and right of privacy, and how to avoid potential pitfalls. Selznick International Pictures clearly was nervous.

Meanwhile, Selznick had negotiated with Hitchcock, who had gladly accepted the offer to direct the film. As it was, the English director quite obviously was not keen on the subject itself, but regarded the project as a passport to the enticing American film industry. Various anecdotes circulate in Hitchcock biographies regarding his misgivings about a *Titanic* film; although they are probably legends, they give evidence of Hitchcock's reservations about the project.[38] After all, the end was known — how should he build up suspense culminating in an unexpected turn? It eventually turned out that Hitchcock's American career started with *Rebecca* (1940); at least, Selznick would achieve an Academy Award with this film. Yet Selznick himself remained unsettled about his choice of director for the *Titanic* picture. Long after Hitchcock had been publicly announced as the director of *Titanic*, Selznick continued having second thoughts and considering other choices. And it was just as difficult for him to decide about a screenwriter and an adequate script.

Meanwhile, a new and serious problem arose in England: White Star (which in 1933 had merged with the Cunard Line), the British Board of Trade, and the Merchant Marine began to stir. The White Star officials remembered the 1929 fiasco with the film *Atlantic* quite well. This time, it was easier to convince the British Censor Board that a *Titanic* film would do serious damage to the British shipping industry; after all, it was a foreign and not an English company that intended to produce a film about the disaster. The American Ambassador Joseph Kennedy became involved; the *Titanic* film began to turn into a diplomatic case. Hitchcock, still in England, was asked to represent Selznick International Pictures, convincing the British authorities that the film was supposed to become "a glorification of the bravery and efficiency of British seamen."[39] Despite Hitchcock's efforts at an official meeting on September 2, 1938, the managers of the shipping body and Cunard White Star Ltd. were not convinced. The project was seen as a menace to British reputation; objections were voiced in political and mercantile circles on both sides of the Atlantic.

And still another obstacle emerged. Selznick International Pictures received news about a European *Titanic* film project, allegedly by the French company Milo Film. It was not clear if there was anything to the rumor, yet it was still regarded as another stumbling block for Selznick's project. While waiting for definite information from Europe, Selznick had a treatment written by British novelist Richard Blaker. Since Selznick insisted on including the elderly actress Maude Adams as star, the screenwriter's freedom was seriously impaired. His script might still have been turned into a tolerable Hitchcock film — yet Selznick did not like it.

Selznick's *Titanic* met obstacles in every respect. By the end of 1938, the project had all but died. It was scarcely mentioned at the studio, while all efforts were concentrated on the production of *Gone with the Wind* (1939) and *Rebecca*. In March 1939, news that another producer had taken over the French *Titanic* project gave a new impetus, but even then, Hitchcock's efforts towards an original script did not lead to anything. Selznick continued being indecisive, and when the war broke out in September, he saw his potential European market for a *Titanic* film lost. By 1940 the project had died. Selznick still clung to the remains of his dream, proposing in a 1950 memo to produce the film — but his "magnificent picture" never was made. Hollywood's first *Titanic* project had sunk before the pre-production phase was consummated.

Nevertheless, the subject proved unsinkable. Just a few years after Selznick's drowned project, national socialist Germany released a *Titanic* motion picture that definitely was not a glorification of British seamanship and efficiency. While *Atlantic* still had focused on intellectual debate, the 1943 *Titanic* set the line — great melodrama on a ship, an interplay of contrasting stereotypes on the foil of a grandiose tragedy.

The Six Major *Titanic* Productions

The six large-scale *Titanic* films from the period 1943 to 1997 will be discussed in detail in Part II of this book, but their varying focuses and their relation to the *Titanic* myth will be briefly summarized here.

The German 1943 *Titanic*, directed by Herbert Selpin, is a piece of propaganda, trying to exploit the elements of nation and race for political ends. John Jacob Astor — transformed into a British "lord" — and Englishman Bruce Ismay are the villains who risk the ship and the passengers' lives because of their unlimited greed. In order to disparage the British enemy (with whom Germany had been at war since September 1939), the *Titanic* crew was supplemented with an efficient German First Officer, who turns out to be the only responsible and upright officer on ship. Racial undertones are found in Third Class, with the raucous representatives of undesirable races eventually being drowned. Gender, in turn, is not highlighted; in fact, the villains' love interests do certainly not correspond to the standard image of the destitute female passenger. Nevertheless, officer Petersen's German love interest, First Class passenger Sigrid Olinsky (they do only get together after the sinking — flirtation on the ship would have been against the rule and ruined Petersen's professional reputation!), gradually is converted from an "anomalously" independent woman into a socially minded helper and finally finds her appropriate female place in a lifeboat. It is clear that she will eventually turn into a fine housewife and give birth to Petersen's children. Religion plays no role in this film: National socialist ideology was not interested in supporting an attitude that resigns into God's will.

The first great Hollywood *Titanic* film, in turn, is devoid of political issues. Instead, the 1953 *Titanic* (director: Jean Negulesco) focuses entirely on melodrama — and thereby on the imparting of social values. As in the German 1943 production, the ship primarily serves as foil and means for a moralistic cause. Again, the focus is on the upper class (with a few stereotypical shots in Third Class), but this time it is a family drama that unfolds during the last hours of the *Titanic*. Using the finest stars of the time, Hollywood tells the story of an estranged couple, which in the face of disaster finds back to their old love and the true virtues of American family life. The father and the twelve-year-old son are sacrificed for the sake of this insight, but this is part of the game. Since the film confirms a conservative set of values, the gender issue plays a vital role: Julia Sturges is by no means a meek woman; she takes responsibility for her children in order to save them from the obsolete and stifling European upper class culture. Yet in the course of the tragic event, she is transformed from her somewhat unbecoming independence and inner strength to the characteristic wife, who in tears obeys her husband's gentlemanly request to enter a lifeboat. Class itself is no issue; the Hollywood *Titanic* is an upper class drama which does not question the "natural" boundaries between the life of the rich and the tragedy of the poor. In the end, all are united, singing "Nearer, My God, to Thee" as the ship goes down. As in the *Titanic* myth, Anglo-Saxon religion gives its blessing to the chivalrous heroism of the upper class.

Besides the "appropriate" gender roles in an American family, nation plays a major role in this *Titanic* tale. Hollywood's *Titanic*, produced in the early phase of the Cold War, champions sound American values, which are profiled against derelict European ways. The context of the early 1950s is clear: While Old Europe has definitely been destroyed in the Second World War and the coming end of the British Empire begins to show, hope gleams at the Western horizon. The true American spirit, simple, independent, liberal and full of vitality, is the message of this film. In order to bring it home to everybody, the ship has to sink.

The 1958 British production *A Night to Remember* (director: Roy Baker) appears almost as a counter-production to the Hollywood tale. In fact, it is to a great part a one-to-one translation of Walter Lord's 1955 bestseller into film. Instead of melodrama and romance, *A Night to Remember* offers the bare facts, told as a tale of decent heroism and self-sacrificing sense of duty. Although it was the aim of the producer William MacQuitty to avoid any sort of mythification, central aspects of the *Titanic* myth again are taken up and confirmed. In documentary aesthetics, the black-and-white film propagates values regarded as "essentially British." An emphatic plea for "true

Britishness" seems to echo throughout the film, depicting crew and passengers alike as amiable, reliable, and committed. There are no villains; even J. Bruce Ismay — despite his stepping into a lifeboat — is represented as a broken and pitiable man, harassed by the disaster he helplessly has to witness. There is no word of pressing the *Titanic* into a speed record: It is doom, not human error, that causes the *Titanic* to sink.

In contrast to the earlier *Titanic* motion pictures, class is a central issue in the film, exposed at the very beginning and pursued in the various subplots of First, Second and Third Class passengers. Yet it is regarded as given, a "natural" aspect of British society and by no means a problematic issue. The heroes, however, come from the middle class. Thus, the dominant upper class focus of the *Titanic* myth has been decisively shifted. Although the film follows Lord's book by showing as many facets and perspectives as possible, it clearly concentrates on Second Officer Lightoller as paragon of duty and reliability. Again, it is the historical context that explains the specific emphasis in this *Titanic* film: With the middle class having become the new fundament of a postwar British society in the 1950s, it is the middle-class officer who becomes the true hero of the British *Titanic* tale. Together with supporting protagonists, Lightoller exemplifies British national character in its purest ideal.

The aesthetics of the 1958 *Titanic* film are novel: documentary and sober, relying on as many "facts" as possible, trying to tell "the real story" on the basis of historical evidence. From now on, no *Titanic* film could afford taking liberty with the historical facts. *A Night to Remember*, still regarded as "best *Titanic* film ever" by many *Titanic* enthusiasts, became the benchmark for any *Titanic* production to come. This film set the *Titanic* code, in its most pristine form.

Indeed, "authenticity" turned into a veritable fetish for filmmakers following the famous English production. The matrix of the *Titanic* code was perfect: the historical event, increasingly researched since the publication of *A Night to Remember*, offered the best fundament a filmmaker could wish for — a tremendous disaster in perfect timing, a clearly defined setting in a constricted space, which, however, in itself constituted a microcosm of society, and a broad spectrum of protagonists with their individual stories to choose from. The skeleton is given, it can be fleshed out again and again, picking from the broad cast of historical *Titanic* characters.

In 1979, a serious attempt was made at translating the "real story" with the historically known characters into an "authentic" drama. Take the facts, twist them ever so slightly, and you get all you need. The best "material" was the historical characters who are known by name, but not with a detailed biography that would confine poetic license: Why should Martin Gallagher, an Irish bachelor in Third Class, not be matched with a love interest — for example the nameless "Irish beauty" mentioned in Lawrence Beesley's 1912 report? What about the warm-hearted descriptions of Thomas Andrews by members of the crew? Could this not be turned into a little bit of decent flirtation? And Lawrence Beesley himself, best-known of all Second Class passengers — he deserves indeed to be put into the spotlight of a film camera. Since he appears just a little bit too pedantic in his book, some embellishment is required: In the film, he is equally equipped with a love interest. Even this lady is authentic: The screenwriter chose the anonymous American teacher that Beesley himself mentioned in his book.

When the mini-series *S.O.S. Titanic* was broadcast on television in 1979 (director: William Hale), Lawrence Beesley had been dead for twelve years. Luckily, one feels tempted to say — it is not very probable that the *Titanic* survivor would have appreciated his representation as a somewhat prudish, pedantic lover. A more detailed analysis of the television drama does, however, show that the mini-series actually has turned out quite well. It continues what had started with *A Night to Remember*: a narrative of the *Titanic* story, true to detail, as authentic as possible. *S.O.S. Titanic* is a mosaic made of multiple survivors' impressions, of statements, episodes and anecdotes that turn history into drama and thus into a functioning film. Even though the fictitious love plots and dramatizations may not be the best in film history (after all, it was just a television production with a low budget), the film is indeed worth watching. But make sure to take the original version, as broadcast on YouTube: As will be shown in Chapter 7, the reduced DVD version distorts the script and turns the series into cheap melodrama. The original version, in contrast, has its merits: an unprecedented wealth of historical detail transformed into a poignant representation of the *Titanic* story.

After the wreck's discovery and the major media hype in 1985, the way was open for action film director and technophile James Cameron. In many ways, Cameron's motion picture, made between 1995 and 1997, appears to be the ultimate *Titanic* story. It offers the perfect blending of masterly Hollywood handicraft and romantic kitsch; the international success of the film proved the validity of the formula. Cameron makes use of everything that the historical *Titanic* story as well as his predecessors in the film business had to offer. And he adds the wreck, taking the story right into present time (in the film, 1996). His success formula is the inextricable link between the audience's contemporary time and the *Titanic*'s past, personified in the character of Rose, who is introduced as a 101-year-old lady and then takes the audience back to her memories of the voyage on *Titanic*, where she, a seventeen-year-old First

3. Titanic *in Film*

Class beauty, fell in love with an independent drifter and artist. The film thus is turned into a coming-of-age tale of a demonstratively modern female character, attractive to a large audience worldwide.

Again, the *Titanic* is both the foil and the indispensable means to effect the change from a spoiled and socially fettered First Class girl to an independent, life-affirming young woman. Third Class passenger Jack Dawson is, of course, instrumental in this change, yet it is the *Titanic* that offers the platform for their coming together, their love, and Rose's transformation through love and tragedy. Gender plays a vital role, but its meaning in the *Titanic* myth has been reversed: Cameron's *Titanic* is not a story of "women and children first," but a romanticized tale of female emancipation. It is not by coincidence that Rose jumps out of the lifeboat back onto the *Titanic*: not to stay and die with her beloved, like Ida Straus did, but to fight together with him to survive. The final moments of the film, scrolling back on Rose's life after the *Titanic* disaster by showing the photos of her career, prove that she has fulfilled the promise she gave to her lover as he was dying in the icy Atlantic: never to give up, "no matter what happens." The *Titanic* disaster, in combination with Rose's love for Jack, has decisively changed her life and given her a new direction. She leaves the *Carpathia* under a new name and with the American future open to her.

Cameron's *Titanic* also takes up the issue of nation. Despite its demonstrative equalizing between Third and First Class and between the various nationalities in Third Class, the characters offer but the usual stereotypes— lively and life-affirming Third Class, coming from all kinds of nations, and suffocatingly stiff First Class, represented almost exclusively by Americans. But being American has two sides in Cameron's film. On the one hand, there are the rich, stiff and arrogant American First Class passengers. They indulge in fake aristocratic behavior—a "denatured" rip-off of an obsolete European caste. This is Americanness as it should *not* be, according to Cameron's *Titanic* doctrine. In contrast to these rich First Class passengers, Jack and his alumna Rose offer an American alternative: free, independent, adventurous — making "every day count." Characters like them make the American dream come true. The British, in contrast, are reduced to the officers and kind Mr. Andrews; they appear as rather colorless: The issue of nation focuses on the wrong and the right way of being American, suggesting that some melting pot injection of lively nationalities in Third Class could be quite healthy for true Americanness. Irishness, in turn, is largely recommended (especially through music) as a way of leading an independent, healthy life. This is, of course, a cliché and has nothing to do with the reality of the Irish emigrants on board the *Titanic*, who do not even figure prominently in Cameron's film.

With regard to class, the same stereotypes are propounded. First Class is predominantly bad and corrupt, Third Class is good and innocent. Cameron uses all available incidents to display his "political correctness" in depicting the Third Class passengers: lively dance and joy, loving parents and their children (no paternal or motherly love is demonstrated in First Class), vigorous youths who fight against upper class cruelty by breaking down a locked gate as the ship sinks. As to Second Class, Cameron relinquishes the historical correctness displayed in the 1958 and 1979 films: Second Class has again completely disappeared. The boring middle class simply is not adequate for a Hollywood epic.

Race plays a minor role in the Cameron film, yet it is latently present in the presentation of the Third Class passengers. Interestingly, Cameron revises some of the historical stereotypes of race — just to adopt the modern ones. As already mentioned, Jack's best friend Fabrizio is one of those unruly Italians, who were regarded with open contempt in 1912. In the 1997 film, the emigrant is turned to the modern stereotype of the young Italian: charming, vital, open-hearted, quick to laughter, quick to honest indignation. Both the unruly "Latins" and the life-affirming Italian youth are stereotypes; the latter is in line with Cameron's demonstration of a politically correct attitude.

Religion is given homage in a few shots. First, the Sunday service scene, then the inevitable "Nearer, My God, to Thee," played by the band as their final piece just before the sinking. As the crowd moves to the rising stern, historical passenger Father Byles prays with the doomed. Yet Christian religion is not really respected in Cameron's modern *Titanic* tale. Instead, it has become substituted by a sort of secular religion: Romantic love has become the alternative for religion. Eternity is granted not through faith in God, but through everlasting love — notoriously codified by Celine Dion's "My Heart Will Go On." It is love that links old Rose to her ageless beloved Jack, and this love forms a link between the "ship of dreams" and the dignified wreck. In the end, the wreck is redeemed through love. *Titanic* promises eternity, in everlasting beauty.

Cameron takes all he can get, and he combines it with his own predilections for deep-sea technology. As Hollywood epic on a grand scale, the film is a masterwork. But it was not necessarily loved by those who love *Titanic*.

In odd vicinity to the Cameron hit, a homonymous television miniseries was produced: the American Zoetrope *Titanic*, broadcast a year earlier than Cameron's film (in November 1996). It is unclear if the production of this series was prompted by the buzz around the Cameron project or if it was just a coincidence. After all, a new motion picture had been overdue since the discovery of the wreck in 1985, making use both of the insights into some facts of the sinking and of modern technology in film production. It is of course hardly possible to compare the television production with Cameron's film. Yet if the mini-series is regarded in its own right — taking the low budget and narrow time-frame for production into account — it is in fact remarkable how much director Robert Lieberman made out of the potential the *Titanic* story has to offer.

Like the 1979 production, the mini-series focuses on the entire voyage of the *Titanic*. Yet it even takes the survivors to New York — the first time that the representation of the *Titanic* story is taken that far in film, excepting the early silent film *Saved from the Titanic* as well as the German 1943 movie that ends with a British court scene for propaganda purposes. Although the three romantic plots of the 1996 mini-series are equally contrived as in the 1979 production (at least, the love stories are all-fictional and therefore free from the awkward fetters of history), the movie does convince — especially because it focuses more and more on the disaster of the ship and thus on the actual human suffering.

Gender is not a specific subject in this film, excepting stereotype conflicts such as an illegitimate romantic love affair throwing a respectable woman out of balance and a poor innocent girl being raped by a villain. The three dominant plots do in any case not focus on gender issues but on ordinary love stories and their troubles. Classes are set off by individual plots, but their representatives remain, in contrast to Cameron's cross-class love story, neatly separated. There is neither class mixing nor any open critique of the class system, except the barricades for adventurer Jamie, who would like to explore First Class but is blocked by the gates. Just as with gender, there is no effort to throw the social system into relief and to question its mechanisms. Nation is at the most used as folkloristic color: innocent Aase from Denmark (who, despite her modest background, obviously has no problem communicating in English), a spectrum of English characters (from the pure and deeply religious Jack family via the good-hearted thief Jamie to the cartoonish villain Doonan), and some cosmopolitan Americans. Generally, however, national or racial differences play no role whatsoever. Religion, finally, is highlighted in a few rather unusual ways. It plays a certain role in the Third Class plot, since fictional Aase has joined an equally fictional family of English proselytes who seek a new life in the U.S.[40] The most striking "religious" instance is the design of the sinking episode, which is introduced by the Jack family praying the Lord's Prayer in the face of death and then turns into a quite impressive larger-than-life sequence, alluding to universal flood disasters. "Nearer, My God, to Thee," in contrast, is hardly heard, although it is played by the band.

Altogether, the various aspects of the myth, which are so apt for film drama, are not thrown into relief in this *Titanic* version. This may be one reason why the mini-series, despite some good acting and a relatively well-done setting, never received much attention. Beside Cameron's movie, it simply drowned.

Titanic Episodes and Fantasies

Beyond the six major *Titanic* feature films in the period 1943 to 1997, there are quite a number of films that made use of the *Titanic* without actually constructing their plots around the famous disaster. Just as in the Danish *Atlantis* of 1913, the disaster has been used as a catalyst whenever convenient in numerous films and television episodes: to get rid of a protagonist in an elegant way, to start or to save a love relationship, to reunite an estranged couple. Or simply to add a special twinge of tragedy, as in the Oscar-winning family saga *Cavalcade* (1933, director: Frank Lloyd), where the promising son Edward dies together with his young wife Edith on their splendid honeymoon trip on the *Titanic*. A more unusual plot is presented in *Whom the Gods Destroy* (1934), where the famous motif of a man escaping the sinking ship dressed in women's clothing kicks off an intricate psychological family drama. Titanic as a tragic disaster thus has become a popular motif for numerous films and television-series in the course of the 20th century.[41] After Cameron's mega-success, though, the tip has been turned towards its parodic potential.

A few years after *Cavalcade*, *History Is Made at Night* (1937, director: Frank Borzage) featured a melodramatic *Titanic*-like episode, putting the heroine — incidentally the ship-owner's wife — on a large ocean liner on its maiden voyage; it collides with an iceberg and sinks with 3,000 people on board. The episode is the final climax of this romantic melodrama, helpfully leading to the suicide of the heroine's villainous husband (whom she has tried to divorce throughout the entire film) and opening the way for her to become happy with her honest lover. By the way, the villain is called Bruce Vail (rather than Bruce Ismay), he owns the ship and tries to beat it into an Atlantic speed record on its maiden voyage, resulting in the collision.[42] And, of course, the passengers sing "Nearer, My God, to Thee" as they face death on the sinking liner. Yet as fate has it, the crucial bulkhead unexpectedly does hold, the ship does not sink, and the captain announces that help is on its way. All are saved and live happily ever after. The romance offers the "alternative ending" that the audience keeps hoping for in vain in the major *Titanic* movies.

From the 1950s onwards, it was especially television that made use of *Titanic* for minor episodes. London Weekend Television's series *Upstairs, Downstairs* (1971–75), featuring the life of the wealthy Bellamy family in the period from 1903 to 1933, had to solve the problem of actress Rachel Gurney having decided to leave as the third season was about to go into production.

Titanic offered just the right incident to give Lady Marjorie Bellamy a suitably dramatic exit. As it was, fictional Lady Marjorie was turned into another Ida Straus, rejecting a seat in a lifeboat, yet making sure that her maid would be saved.

Television also exploited the *Titanic*'s potential for the paranormal, featuring premonitions of the disaster. A rather amusing stance was taken in NBC's *Night Gallery*, which in its 1970 episode "The Lone Survivor" made use of the popular motif of a man escaping from the *Titanic* in women's clothes. Combining this motif with ancient myths of eternal punishment, the series turns this unmanly survivor into a maritime Ahasver who crosses the ocean in a lifeboat only to be picked up again and again by ships that are doomed to sink. Thus, he is taken on board by the *Lusitania*, which was torpedoed and sunk in 1915. As he again survives in a lifeboat, the liner *Andrea Doria*, which sank after a collision in 1956, shows up at the horizon to pick him up.

The most famous *Titanic* episode in a television series doubtlessly was the opening episode in Irwin Allen's science fiction series *The Time Tunnel* (Twentieth Century Fox Television, 1966–67). The series builds on a time machine that enables scientists to move freely between present, past, and future. In order to demonstrate the project's validity to the government, scientist Dr. Anthony Newman tests the Time Tunnel and promptly ends up on the *Titanic*. His warnings are thrown to the winds; Captain E.J. Smith does not even heed a newspaper report on the sinking presented to him by scientist Dr. Douglas Phillips, who has entered the Time Tunnel to save his friend. In the sinking, the Tunnel operations staff succeed in taking the two scientists out of the 1912 time zone — but due to problems with the unproved technology, they cannot bring them back. Newman and Phillips are trapped in time and swung from one period to another: The *Titanic* experience sets the start for an entire series that amusingly plays with major historical events.[43]

Indeed, *Titanic* proved to be a popular asset in time-travel series and fantasy films, making, amongst others, a prominent appearance in the 1981 fantasy film *Time Bandits* (1981) and in NBC's series *Voyagers* (1983). The disaster's potential for comedy — due to transformations of some of its aspects into stock-in-trade motifs — and for the supernatural were exploited in various films in the 1980s; its parodic potential would be tapped after the megasuccess of Cameron's *Titanic*.[44] Thus, the famous wreck has been turned in the great white sharks' lair in the animated comedy film *Shark Tale* (2004): Shark boss Don Lino has chosen the *Titanic* reading room as his personal headquarters, with the notorious drawing of Rose DeWitt Bukater hanging on the wall. Much more famous than this cheap drawing is, of course, the pose of Rose and Jack at the *Titanic*'s bow. It has become a worldwide standard for parody in cartoon and film and is even taken up in car advertisements.

One of the worst parodies — especially because it was not meant as a parody at all — is the 2001 Italian animated film *Titanic: The Legend Goes On* (*Titanic, mille e una storia*, or: *Titanic: La leggenda continua*, director: Camillo Teti), a failed Disney imitation that excels in bad taste.[45] Due to the many allusions to and rip-offs from Cameron's *Titanic*, the film can partly be seen as a parody, yet in fact it is meant as a musical fairy tale using the *Titanic* story and involving all kinds of talking, singing and rapping animals. The only interesting feature may be the reversal of class and gender in the main love story: This time, the heroine comes from Third Class and falls in love with a First Class youngster. Notably, almost all the "good" characters in the broad spectrum of protagonists survive and eventually get happily married, implying to a children audience that the *Titanic* disaster was not really a tragedy after all.

A more serious role is given to the *Titanic* disaster in *No Greater Love*, a 1996 television romance based on Danielle Steel's novel of the same name. The disaster becomes the starting point for the entire plot, doing away with the parents of four siblings and thus putting a heavy burden on a woman who is actually too young to shoulder it. After the opening disaster episode, the film focuses on the Winfield children (who enjoy the privileges of the upper Boston circles) and tells the story of Edwina, who as the eldest takes responsibility for her brothers and sister and sacrifices her own chances for youthful life and love.

The opening sequence on the *Titanic* gives an amusing *déjà vu* experience: All the scenes on the *Titanic*, in the lifeboats and at the boarding of the *Carpathia* that do not involve the main actors are taken from the 1979 film *S.O.S. Titanic*.[46] The effect is somewhat curious, a constant alternation between a serious representation of the *Titanic* disaster and a kitschy romance that only uses the sinking as a melodramatic point of departure for an equally melodramatic (or, rather, non-dramatic) story to develop. There is one point of interest, though: In a way, the disaster of the *Titanic* is made up for in the course of the film. The ill-fated voyage is balanced by the main character Edwina going on an Atlantic trip again after twelve years. The ship does not sink — and spinsterly Edwina even falls in love on the voyage, many years after she lost her fiancé in the *Titanic* disaster and then sacrificed the flower of her youth to raise her orphaned siblings.

As so often, *Titanic* has been instrumentalized: The disaster only sets the stage, with a hint of the Straus story in family mother Kate Winfield's refusal to leave her husband on the *Titanic*. The famous ship disaster thus offers the medium to create an unusual constellation for a family drama to unfold. And it provides a highly dramatic episode to start with; the rest of the film is banal.

Finally, there are two films that use *Titanic* in a rather unusual way—and both are so cheap that they hardly deserve attention.

Titanic II, a 2010 DVD production directed by Shane Van Dyke (released in good time for the anniversary in 2012), tries to update the ship disaster by combining it with an ecological drama. In April 2012, entire parts of Greenland break down into the Atlantic and cause a mega-tsunami. Meanwhile, the luxury cruiser *Titanic II* has set out from New York, crossing the North Atlantic right at the time of the 100th anniversary of the *Titanic* disaster. Filled with a crowd of arrogant and superficial passengers, the cruise ship meets some serious problems because of the eco-disaster, incidentally right at the position where the *Titanic* sank. The supermodern equipment (including lifeboats for all) do not help the passengers to survive. The heroine finally is saved by her Coast Guard daddy. The blue-eyed super-hero—her ex-lover, at the same time the arrogant owner of the ship who is converted to true love and true values in the course of the disaster—sacrifices his life for her. The film does not really live up to a *Titanic* plot.

Raise the Titanic, directed by Jerry Jameson, at least is better known—after all, it was nominated for the first Golden Raspberry Award, Category Worst Picture, in 1981.[47] The big-budget film is a failed adaptation of Clive Cussler's 1976 adventure novel *Raise the Titanic!* It proved to be a box office bomb, grossing only $7 million (plus $16.8 million in video rentals), which led British producer Lew Grade to the legendary statement that it would have been cheaper to lower the Atlantic Ocean.[48]

After a successful career in television, Grade took up an idea that had haunted the *Titanic* community since 1912: to raise the ship from the bottom of the ocean. Shortly after the disaster, rumors about treasures in the sunken ship spread, and soon ideas were developed how the *Titanic* could be raised. (It should be noted that until the discovery of the wreck in 1985, the belief prevailed that the *Titanic* had sunk intact.) Understandably, none of these ideas came to anything. Clive Cussler integrated the idea into his adventure novel, in which a rare and tremendously precious mineral, "byzanium," turns out to have been transported on the *Titanic*. Since the American government needs it in defense against the Soviets, a costly expedition is started, ending with the retrieval of the *Titanic* from the bottom of the ocean. The mineral is eventually not found on board the ship, but discovered in a false grave in England. Thus, the efforts actually were in vain—but both in the book and in the film, the raising of the *Titanic* makes for a highly attractive effect.

In order to achieve as much realism as possible, Grade purchased the 9,237-ton liner *Athinai*, whose decrepit exterior after twelve years of quiet rusting offered just the right touch. For the actual raising sequence and the large-scale exterior shots, an extremely costly model was built, at the scale of one-sixteenth, thus 55 feet long.[49] The raising sequence is the climax of the film — and with its three-minute length the only instance of any interest to an audience lured by the name "Titanic." It indeed makes a fine effect as the ship breaks through the surface. Somehow, an old dream seems to come true, despite the dilapidated state of the wreck.

After a few problems with the Soviets, who stand by during the raising and even enter the wreck at some stage, the vessel is towed to and docked in New York. As it is discovered that the byzanium is not on board, the *Titanic* has played its role. *Raise the Titanic* thus offers an odd resurrection tale that leads to nothing and actually leaves a rather dreary impression of the "ship of dreams."

For *Titanic* lovers worldwide, the failure of this poor "*Titanic* film" must have been satisfying. A few years later they would get the chance to see the real wreck, which in due course was ennobled by the famous IMAX documentary *Titanica* in 1995.

The Dying Queen: Documentaries of the Wreck

Films focusing on the wreck of the *Titanic* cannot be counted as *Titanic* films. They document what is palpably left of the *Titanic* story, but they do not seek to narrate the story itself by means of cinematic drama. Nevertheless, they are inseparably linked to the *Titanic* and its story, offering another picture of the "ship of dreams": Having rested quietly in almost 2.5 miles depth, the famous ship now possesses the dignity of a fragile dying queen.

In her present form (which has deteriorated considerably since Robert Ballard's discovery of the wreck in 1985), the *Titanic* offers a poignant view. Images of tremendous destruction alternate with shots of lasting beauty; indeed, the elegant line of the intact bow has become another icon for the *Titanic*. The silence is part of the fascination, just like the fish and crabs that occasionally are illuminated and for a short moment disclose their secret life in symbiosis with the wreck of the *Titanic*. The documentaries use this fascination for expressiveness: Typically, they spice up their sober narrative style with emotional and dramatic elements in image and sound. Again, the *Titanic*, with her tragic history and her pitiable remnants, offers the perfect object for this technique.

3. Titanic *in Film*

In his book *The Discovery of the Titanic* (1987), oceanographer Robert Ballard describes how he fought for his project for over 15 years, until his dream of finding the wreck finally was fulfilled. It is, as Steven Biel has shown, not only a tale of scientific triumph, but very much also a tale of the 1980s, reflecting the "frontier spirit" of the Reagan era by offering a triumphant narrative "of a revitalized American masculinity and a resurgent nation" to the entire world.[50] In his self-presentation, Ballard combines the features of the *Titanic* enthusiast (characterized by nostalgia and a quasi-religious veneration for the *Titanic*) with the character traits of the frontier and military hero that played so important a role in Reaganism. While Reagan's Star Wars program sought a place in the frontier of space, maritime scientist Ballard — tellingly describing himself as a "submarine cowboy"— explored the frontiers of the oceanic depths. His quest led to tremendous success on a global scale.

Ballard's description of the decisive moment on the night of September 1, 1985, indeed is gripping. The reader can feel the excitement as the first pieces of debris and then, finally, an identifiable boiler are sighted — after weeks and weeks of enervating, vain search, just a few days before the expensive mission had to be ended.[51] In the description of his personal reaction as well as in the official press statement he gave after his triumphant return to the Woods Hole Oceanographic Institution, Ballard invokes the religious vein of *Titanic* veneration:

> The *Titanic* lies in 13,000 feet of water on a gently sloping alpine-like countryside overlooking a small canyon below. Its bow faces north and the ship sits upright on the bottom. There is no light at this great depth and little life can be found. It is a quiet and peaceful and fitting place for the remains of this greatest of sea tragedies to rest. May it forever remain that way and may God bless these found souls.[52]

This quasi-religious aura would not leave the wreck. It combines the nostalgia that had dominated the *Titanic* myth since the publication of Walter Lord's *A Night to Remember* with the moving pictures of the dying *Titanic*.

Contrary to the belief of many who had reckoned that the extreme pressure and low temperatures at the bottom of the ocean would preserve the ship, all organic parts of the wreck (and the bodies) have been eaten away over the decades, first by fish and crabs and then by molluscs that corroded the major part of the wooden interiors. Almost nothing is left of the fabulous Grand Staircase, nothing of the beautiful carvings and the precious paneling. The process of slow destruction continues even now: The metal parts are slowly being eaten away by iron-eating bacteria that first cover the *Titanic*'s elegant forms with bizarre "rusticles" (a word Ballard coined to describe the icicle-like rivers of rust running down most parts of the wreck) and then,

The eerily lit bow of the *Titanic* in *Ghosts of the Abyss* (Walt Disney Pictures et al.).

eventually, let the wreck dissolve. The process of degradation and eventual decay has been dramatically accelerated by the great number of visitors to the wreck and by submersibles landing on the ship. Scientists expect that the wreck will disappear in the course of the next few decades. Thus, the *Titanic* indeed is a "dying queen."

Since the discovery, the wreck has been examined in numerous ways, leading to important insights with regard to unanswered questions. First, the discovery has finally resolved the question of the final position: The wreck was found at 41°43' 55" N, 49°56' 45" W, which is 13 miles from the last position reading that was transmitted through the *Titanic*'s distress call. This led to a reassessment of the distance relations between the *Titanic* and the *Californian*—albeit with no conclusive result.[53] Second, it could now, after 73 years, finally be confirmed that the *Titanic* had broken in two as the ship plunged. The wreck lies in two parts on the bottom of the ocean, with 1,970 feet between the bow and the stern section and two large fields with debris surrounding the hull pieces. Until 1985, it was generally believed that the *Titanic* had gone down in one piece, reflecting the opinion of the majority of survivors (and the desire of the White Star Line to demonstrate that the hull had been strong and stable). Other survivors, however, stated that the hull broke apart just before the final plunge.[54] The discovery now confirmed that they had been right. Up to 1985, *Titanic* films let the ship sink in one piece (and the raised wreck in *Raise the Titanic* is decrepit, but intact). Now the discovery of the pathetic sections offered an additional scene of exciting drama in the middle of the sinking; James Cameron, lover of action, high-tech, and spectacular effects, would make the most of it. Ultrasound examinations also corrected the popular notion of the "300-foot gash" that was so impressively used in the 1953 film.[55] From now on, *Titanic* films would show the less dramatic but more plausible scenario of individual steel plates being pressed in; after all, this slighter but equally fatal damage was the precondition for the cinematically "perfect" pacing of the disaster, namely the slow process from gradual awakening to growing anxiety to open panic, as the bow gradually fills with water.

Finally, the exploration of the wreck site would still offer another dramatic scene (which, however, has not yet been exploited in narrative *Titanic* film): the sinking of the wreck to a depth of almost 13,000 feet, where the two sections crashed onto the bottom and dug themselves deeply into the ocean floor. A submarine drama, powerful and poignant. The bow section probably reached the bottom in hardly more than six minutes. Due to the large amount of water that had already entered the forward part of the *Titanic* while she still was afloat, the increasing pressure in the depths did not destroy that much of the bow section. The superstructures and the enormous funnels, though, were torn away, probably by the enormous strength of the slipstream as the wreck reached the ground. The stern section, in contrast, was utterly devastated in the sinking, with its decks imploding, the plating of the hull peeling outward, and the decks collapsing on top of each other "like a stack of pancakes."[56] For the next several hours, a silent shower of light and lightest debris would drift down — until utter stillness concluded the drama. No film has yet attempted to show this touching submarine spectacle; in narrative *Titanic* films, attention invariably remains directed to the human tragedy on the surface.

Yet it is the wreck as such and its poignant condition that quickly caught the attention of filmmakers. In fact, pictures and film were the very starting point of Ballard's long story of the spectacular discovery, which actually began in 1973. Just as the sinking of the *Titanic* in 1912 perfectly coincided with the rise of film as narrative medium, the discovery is linked to a decisive development in oceanography, highlighting visual imaging as central means of deep-sea exploration. As a young scientist at the Woods Hole Oceanographic

Institution, Ballard belonged to the group of marine geologists that emphatically advocated visual methods of exploring the deep seas, in contrast to the geophysicists, who would prefer sonar.[57] Since the necessary technology for deep-sea photography yet had to be developed, many years of the preparatory phase were taken up by the costly construction of unmanned submersibles equipped with video cameras. Thus, the discovery of the *Titanic*, effected by the use of deep-sea visual imaging technology, in fact was a triumph in a scientific controversy — and no other object than the *Titanic* could have asserted this triumph with such an overwhelming echo all over the world.

It was the *Titanic* that fascinated a world-wide audience, and this audience desired an immediate visual experience. Accordingly, Ballard was under pressure to provide "pictures," and when he succeeded in taking them (again, with an exciting background story of almost-failure and eventual triumph), he had to realize that international media would pirate them even before he had arrived on shore.[58] Very quickly, *Titanic* again became an object for film. Yet except for the opening sequence of Cameron's *Titanic*—celebrating the triumph of underwater high-tech — no motion picture has yet made use of the wreck in a fictional tale. Is this due to respect for the dead? After all, a controversy with regard to the salvage of objects (reverently called "artifacts") has been raging since the late 1980s, with the opposing party emphasizing that the *Titanic* is a grave site and salvage therefore grave robbery. However, filmmakers would hardly mind this moralistic controversy if they saw the chance to make a profit with a motion picture. It is rather a problem of possible scenarios for an adequate story. A fictional yet still somewhat realistic story focusing on the wreck would involve a large contingent of underwater scenes and, due to the rather hostile conditions at almost 2.5 miles depth, only very limited possibilities for human interaction. What about a submarine ghost story then, or a high-tech science fiction scenario? The script has yet to be written — and it is the question if a good film could come out of it.[59]

Instead, the wreck has been glorified in documentary film. Countless documentaries have been made, covering all possible aspects. Every expedition has been accompanied by camera teams; in many cases, the media representation was an important factor in the sponsoring scheme.[60] Thus, documentary is turned into "drama" as the audience is taken along on exciting visits down to the dying queen. The documentary genre in fact continues the success recipe of the discovery tale, combining the serious stance of technology and sober research with the excitement of exploring a strange underwater world.

Two documentary films on the wreck have had considerable success: the

1995 IMAX film *Titanica* and James Cameron's 2003 documentary *Ghosts of the Abyss*. *Titanica* compels through the beauty of its large-scale images. The aim was to make the wreck visible as never before; thus, the main problem was light. This was solved with rather radical means: Two mini-submarines carrying high-intensity lights (altogether 70,000 watts) brought light to the eternal darkness of the depths. The result was breathtaking: It was *Titanica* that turned the wreck into a new icon for the *Titanic* tale, with images of saddening beauty. The viewer is engulfed in the mysterious silence of the deep sea, fascinated by the magnificence of the wreck, spellbound by the colors and the image sharpness. Narrative elements and even a pinch of comedy — explorer Richard White squabbling with the Russian pilot of the submersible about a mysterious 1912 suitcase that White would love to take along and open — add excitement to the documentary presentation of the scientific mission. *Titanica* does, in fact, tell the *Titanic* tale, not as a fictional story, but rather with short historical retrospective scenes (using original footage, photos, and period music) that present the essential stations in the short life of the ship. The present-day scenes as the research vessel sets out are in turn combined with dramatic film music, signaling that serious science can be an adventure — especially if the object of exploration is the *Titanic*. With its elements of visual beauty, drama, and entertainment, all this mounted in the assuring seriousness of exact science, *Titanica* offers a new version of the *Titanic* tale, making the wreck both the starting point and focus. *Titanica* has become a classic in *Titanic* film: Instead of a gripping plot, it offers the fascination of science and confirms the famous beauty of the *Titanic*, even in her final stage.

Cameron's *Ghosts of the Abyss* never reached the cult status of *Titanica*. Nevertheless, it is a fascinating documentary that explores the wreck in (pardon the pun) unprecedented depth. For the first time, the stained glass windows of the First Class Smoking Room are seen again, revealing their undiminished intensity of color in the light of the diving robot. Their counterfeits can be seen in the White Swan Hotel in Alnwick (Northumberland), whose owners bought parts of the *Olympic*'s First Class interiors as *Titanic*'s sister ship was scrapped in the mid–1930s. Much of the beautiful carvings, paneling, stained glass windows, and ceilings preserved in the hotel's "Olympic Suite" reveal what would have been seen on the *Titanic*, turning the White Swan Hotel into an attraction for *Titanic* enthusiasts. Cameron's film art indeed brought some of the *Titanic*'s original beauty back to life: first with his meticulous reconstruction of the ship in his 1997 movie, giving the illusion that the *Titanic* indeed had been resurrected, then with the discovery of some of the still existent luxuries in the wreck that are highlighted in the documentary film. It seems utterly unnecessary that Cameron inserted short visions of the *Titanic*'s "ghosts" in this documentary, featuring glimpses of the 1912 people in various places of the wreck. The impact of the film would have been stronger without this embarrassing touch of nostalgic kitsch.

In many ways the discovery of the wreck has completed the *Titanic* tale. Finally, there is a grave site to visit, an underwater mausoleum to see, the dignified body of the ship to venerate. Documentaries invariably dwell on the poignancy of the wreck, translating into film what Ballard expressed after having concluded his second mission in 1986:

> The *Titanic* is truly gone for good, home-ported at last.... Although she is still awesome in her dimensions, she is no longer the graceful lady that sank five days into her maiden voyage in April 1912. Her beauty has faded; she is broken in two and age has withered her. Her massive steel plates have begun to melt into rivers of rust. Her once-proud bulkheads are squashed and buckled. Her ornate wooden elegance has been eaten away and almost obliterated by armies of wood-boring molluscs. Her innards are scattered unceremoniously across the muddy ocean floor.... The bottom of the ocean is a quiet place, a peaceful place, fitting for a memorial to all the things that sank when the *Titanic* went down. The wreck we found and photographed can stand as a monument to a mistake of arrogance, to a lost age, and to a kind of innocence we can't recover—and to the people, both guilty perpetrators and innocent victims, who figured in the drama. In future, when I think of the *Titanic*, I will see her bow sitting upright on the bottom, dignified despite the decay, and, finally, at rest.[61]

The tragedy of the *Titanic* is immortal, codified in the images of destruction and death. Yet it has turned into a poignant, nostalgic tragedy, where a bittersweet tone prevails. The wreck confirms the image of the *Titanic* that was formed by Walter Lord in 1955. (Tellingly, Lord wrote the preface to Ballard's book, underlining how the wreck reinforced this spirit of nostalgic remembrance.)

Yet the wreck is also a token for triumph. Ironically, it first and foremost asserts the triumph of technology — history is "fixed," the technological failure of 1912 has been redeemed by technological triumph in 1985.[62] Thus, the story of the *Titanic* eventually is given a happy end. It is this decisive aspect of the story of the wreck that Cameron would adopt and transform into narrative film in his *Titanic*, combining the emotional impact of a fictional tale with the poignancy of the dying "ship of dreams." Until now, nobody has followed Cameron's example and made the wreck the prop in a fictional film. Yet despite its resistance to an overall fictionalization, the wreck of the *Titanic* continually invites documentary filmmakers to let it interact with fictional elements, offering the missing link for a quasi-religious conclusion to the *Titanic* tale.

The Perfect Script

There is one central rule in screen writing: You begin with the ending.[63] The entire story and every detail in the script are determined by the final climax. As script adviser Raymond G. Frensham puts it:

> [I]n your screenplay, you are working towards one eventual goal — your final climactic scene in Act III (not necessarily your last scene). Every piece of description, every image, line of dialogue, detail of characterization, every obstacle met, every set-back, and every conflict resolved, should be pushing towards that final climax to achieve maximum emotional effect."[64]

In this sense, the *Titanic* disaster undoubtedly offers the perfect script: You are sure that you have got a big climax. And with some 1,500 people dying in the icy Atlantic, while many of the surviving women have been torn away from their doomed husbands, you can be sure this end *is* emotional. There is just one problem: Everybody in the audience knows the outcome from the start.

In fact, Cameron made a point of this when suggesting his idea to Twentieth Century Fox for the first time.[65] If one is not James Cameron (who had a good selling name in the movie world before *Titanic*), it may be quite risky to take up an event whose outcome is one of the best-known disasters in the 20th century. Nevertheless, the high number of *Titanic* films and the success that some of them achieved prove that the *Titanic* disaster is perfectly adaptable to film, even if everybody knows beforehand that the ship is going to sink.

The Basic Ingredients

There are a number of strong reasons why the various aspects of this disaster add up to the ideal fabric for a feature film:

1. story: the linear progress towards the inevitable catastrophe — which is regarded as "the greatest ship disaster in the world"
2. plot, structure and setting: the multi-layered social structure as setting for romantic and dramatic subplots, with historical characters to use as stable background figures and plenty of contrasting motifs
3. themes: the various elements of the *Titanic* myth as themes of fundamental human interest — gender, class, race, nation, religion, hubris (cf. Chapter 2)

The story of a film is the series of events as they happen in chronological order. Plot, in contrast, is the most interesting and dramatically effective way of telling the story.[66] This means that in many cases the linear storyline is broken up, often by a frame narrative, but also within the main narrative by way of interweaving subplots or using flashbacks and flash-forwards. It is the relation between the two, story and plot, that compensates for the *Titanic* script "problem" and actually turns it into an asset: The *Titanic* with its microcosm of Edwardian life offers the opportunity to arrange a number of subplots against the structure of a well-known, dramatically strong story.

The crucial question is, "Who is the protagonist?" A classic film script depends on a main character who is confronted with a problem somewhere close to the beginning and then spends the rest of the film solving it, undergoing a process of personal growth (often in combination with an inner or external journey). In the 1958 and 1979 *Titanic* films, the "main character" is the ship itself: It is the maiden voyage of the *Titanic* and her sinking that make up the storyline, with all other plots being subordinated. However, a ship in a realistic setting has no character to develop, and there is a very limited number of possible unexpected turns in the well-documented voyage of the *Titanic*. The result is a film with a predominantly documentary character. Both *A Night to Remember* and *S.O.S. Titanic* have been described as docudramas; the 1958 film was highly praised for this "sober" attitude to the tragic story. The producers of *S.O.S. Titanic*, in contrast, sought to offset the documentary quality by adding several fictional subplots that involve historical *Titanic* passengers, so that the story was turned into an ensemble piece with several main characters whose story is told on the background of the *Titanic* disaster.

The other solution is more congenial to classic film production: Choose a fictional person and tell their story within the splendid setting of a doomed luxury liner. The voyage is thus used as a time frame and a metaphor for the development of the character; the disaster is turned into a background, in the worst case reduced to staffage (as, for example, in the 1929 film *Atlantic*). Several of the major *Titanic* films use the technique of highlighting the personal development of a fictional character in combination with the *Titanic* tragedy:

- 1943: Sigrid Olinsky: coming of age (love before money)
- 1953: Richard Sturges: finding his identity as American and father of the family
- 1996: Isabella Paradine: coming of age (true love interest; value of her family)

  Jamie Pierce: coming of age (conversion from a thief to an honest man)
- 1997: Rose DeWitt Bukater: coming of age (emancipation and liberation)

Typically, *Titanic* films that focus on a human main character strongly involve the theme of love — in romantic, melodramatic or tragic guise. Thus, all of the characters named above are involved in love stories that further their personal development. Another strong motif is family ties, which offers opportunity for melodrama, again on the historical background that the loss of hundreds of husbands, fathers, brothers, and sons who were not granted a place in the half-empty lifeboats remained one of the most heartrending aspects of the *Titanic* disaster.

It is typical for *Titanic* stories, though, that they set up strong subplots or even rivaling main plots. In the 1996 mini-series, it is not necessarily Isabella Paradine's tragic love story that is the focus. The congenial, open-hearted thief Jamie Pierce could equally be regarded as the main character; he is "redeemed" in the course of the voyage due to his growing love for the pure maiden Aase. The development of the rich Baltic countess Sigrid Olinsky in the 1943 film, in contrast, is rivaled by the overall propaganda theme of the film: It is hardly the personal development of any passenger that plays the central role in this film, but the national socialist invective against the alleged avarice of British money nobility that, according to the film, had caused the sinking of the *Titanic*.

Nevertheless, the formula "personal fate + tragic setting" perfectly works in these films, not least because the specific background of the disaster offers ample opportunity for one of the strongest rhetoric devices in film. Due to the general knowledge about the outcome of the *Titanic*'s maiden voyage, dramatic irony dominates throughout large parts of the film. We know what the protagonists in the film do not suspect until the moment when the ship definitely is sinking. The great advantage of dramatic irony is that it creates wonderful moments of suspense: Spectators find themselves hoping that Frederick Fleet might still see the iceberg a little sooner or that Captain Lord on the *Californian* will get the idea after all and steer his ship towards the sinking liner. At the same time, dramatic irony supplies the audience with a sort of satisfaction, since they are a step ahead of the characters. This satisfaction, though, is balanced by the tragic character of the story: As it is clear that there is little chance that the film director will decide to let the *Titanic* go ahead to New York or at least remain on the surface until everybody is saved, the audience's knowledge about the near future adds a tinge of poignancy to all positive events happening on board up to the collision. And, of course, dramatic irony builds up further suspense around the fictional protagonists, since we do not know if they will be saved. Therefore the *Titanic* story's great "flaw," the audience's general awareness of its outcome, is in fact an asset rather than a problem for a screenwriter.

Story and plot design are supported by the strong shares that the story of the *Titanic* offers with regard to story archetype, film genre and general theme. In scriptwriting, eight archetypes of story are identified.[67] *Titanic* narratives use and combine at least three basic types:

- Orpheus: tragedy of a great loss
- Faust: inescapability of Fate
- Romeo and Juliet: boy meets (or loses) girl

Depending on where producers and screenwriters put the emphasis, additional aspects from other story types — e.g., "Tristan" with the triangle love relationship in the 1996 film — can be integrated. In any case, the *Titanic* story guarantees at least one of these strong narratives, so that the necessary "comfort zone," i.e., a certain degree of familiarity, is given. At the same time, the ship's multi-layered social structure and the sheer number of passengers — with individual fates and stories — offer countless variations on these archetypes, which in turn guarantee the necessary measure of novelty.

The combination of the general disaster narrative ("Orpheus" and, if combined with a moral lesson, "Faust") with an individualized plot and several subplots automatically leads to a combination of story archetypes. *Titanic* screenwriters have used the potential of such combinations, integrating mainly the most favorite type, "Romeo and Juliet," into the disaster. The profit of such a combination can be seen in negative comparison: The subplot of the Allison family and their nurse Alice Cleaver in the 1996 *Titanic* is not as effective as the romantic subplots, since it only adds the personal disaster of the Allison family to the general disaster of the ship. The result is a doubling and not an enhancement of the dramatic potential.

A corresponding effect of heightened drama is seen in the choice of genre. A disaster story, of course, asks for the visual and narrative traditions of the disaster film genre.[68] Any *Titanic* film has an impending or ongoing disaster at its core, and most *Titanic* films evince the typical narrative setup of the disaster film, namely multiple plotlines (often with a cast of several well-known actors) that, at least after the collision, focus on the struggle to survive the disaster. However, the historical fact of the *Titanic*'s sinking greatly limits the potential of a disaster film: The suspense effect of mainstream disaster films (will the hurricane hit? will the dam hold? when will disaster strike?) is not given, and there is almost nothing the protagonists actually can do to cope with the calamity. Therefore, the integration of subplots that lead to a mixing both of story archetypes and film genres so often dominates *Titanic* films.

In the mixing of genres, it is again romance and melodrama that dominate. Crime would be too far-fetched for the well-explored *Titanic* story: There definitely was not any major crime on the *Titanic*, and various conspiracy theories never really took hold.[69] Fortunately, no producer has had sufficiently bad taste so far to take up the many historical premonition stories and use them to turn the *Titanic* story into a large-scale thriller. The two cheap porno productions are not worth mentioning.[70] Under the roof of the blockbuster then, several genres can be combined at once: As seen in Cameron's *Titanic* film, romance, action-adventure, disaster, heritage, and historical epic can easily be fused into a sweeping Hollywood tale.

The question of theme is at the core of any *Titanic* film: What is the universal statement about the human condition the script makes? No subject would be more perfect than the *Titanic* disaster with its myth involving gender, class, nation, race, and religion. Producers and screenwriters have an entire spectrum to choose from, and again, several themes can be combined under the framework of the disaster. While Cameron chose to focus on gender and class, the 1943 propaganda film highlighted nation (and, less directly, race). And wherever the hymn "Nearer, My God, to Thee" is used, the theme of religion and morality shines through, most blatantly in the ending of the 1953 Hollywood melodrama. The *Titanic* became famous and immortal due to its myth, and this myth is constituted by themes that will prevail and be the subject of film productions at any time. Therefore, the *Titanic* has never gone out of date as a subject, from 1912 up to the present time.

The ample historical detail helps to flesh out these basic themes. The *Titanic* story offers everything a screenwriter would need to establish background and setting: the structure and mechanisms of British and American society in 1912, clear-cut contrasts in economy that serve to highlight the class differences both in society and on the ship, ethics, social rituals, conventions of conduct, and, of course, the wonderful opportunity for a luscious setting that the most luxurious ocean liner of its time affords. In a way, the *Titanic* story is foolproof as a setting and a theme—but this writer-friendly aspect is offset clearly by the tremendous difficulty of making the well-known story original and palatable once again.

Making It Original: Subplots and Structural Models

The standard producer question, "What is original about the story?" indeed is a difficult one. The basic story, the *Titanic*'s maiden voyage and its sinking, is so well-known that it definitely means a problem to a screenwriter. The solution lies within the story: As a microcosm of Edwardian life (including a considerable number of "non–Edwardian" passengers whose fate and stories yet await cinematic exploitation), the *Titanic* presents ample possibility for subplots — and, as demonstrated above, an excellent background for a main plot, if the screenwriter and producer choose to focus on a specific person rather than the ship itself. Generally, subplots are the perfect way to enhance a story, since they offer the opportunity to show parallel action, reveal backstory, subtext and different aspects of the main character, create suspense by delaying the development of the main story, and introduce other characters, thus generating variety and depth. The historically documented facts of the *Titanic* voyage and sinking supply a multitude of possible subplots — in fact, some 2,200 individual fates that can be used to construct subplots around a main plot. However, it is this multitude that again means a certain risk in *Titanic* stories: Some of the *Titanic* films lack coherence, since they combine too many strands, motivated by the desire to show the microcosm that the ship constituted. Classic feature films do ask for several subplots (one of which again can assume the status of "main subplot"), but the number should be limited, and the primary rule of writing "backwards," i.e., from an end that motivates every strand and detail of the story, must be strictly heeded. Thus subplots must have a clear and purposeful relationship to the main plot: "The joy of a well crafted script is that not only does it manage to carry so many stories simultaneously, it integrates them, along with the theme, with consummate ease — you don't notice it and can't see or feel the joins."[71]

If the main plot is the sinking, every event on the ship is of course linked to it. Yet, as seen above, a main plot with a ship as protagonist has its problems, so that the most successful *Titanic* films — except *A Night to Remember* — resorted to a fictitious story as main plot, focusing on a human protagonist. This again involves the problem of linking up the main plot with the subplots: Not in all cases did the combination of a person-oriented main plot with several subplots on the ship succeed.

There are other structural models quite adequate to the *Titanic* story: The great variety of spheres on the ship, not only the three passenger classes, but also the different strata within the crew (officers, stewards and stewardesses, engine rooms), is ideal for a multiple plot setting, that is, an ensemble piece with several main characters who each has a story to tell. In such a setting, the subplots are more or less of equal weight and need not be closely interlinked, though they are often built around a single thematic idea. It is interesting, for instance, how much *S.O.S. Titanic* focuses on problematic love relationships, while the 1943 film subjects all subplots to the theme of greed. The greatest problem in a multiple plot setting is the fact that every plot demands its own development and resolution, which engenders the danger of kaleidoscopic cuts that obscure or even prevent the development of the strands. The *Titanic* story, though, is not subject to this danger: The *Titanic* code, namely the fundament of the well-known disaster story and the occurrence of a few well-known personae and incidences, creates the strong framework of a single environment and the restriction of a short time span that unites even the most unrelated strands. Kaleidoscopic cuts, in turn, are amply used as a technique of visual acceleration both before the collision and as the slow process of the sinking reaches its final dramatic minutes. This technique is rarely bound to the individual plots, though, but rather used as a visual (and auditory) device to impart the density and increasing drama in the various spheres of the ship as disaster strikes.

A screenwriter could even go one step further by choosing the portmanteau structure, in which the individual strands run back to back. (In extreme cases, such a film even consists of several short films directed by different directors.) In the portmanteau film there is no dramatic interlinking of the various plots. In some films, these plots are, if at all, linked by a single, often unobtrusive tie, such as the same premise, the same location, or a brief event common to the various strands. In other films, the various protagonists' paths do actually cross, but there is no dramatic interaction leading to a real interweavement of the individual plots. At first sight, the *Titanic* story is unapt for the portmanteau structure; after all, the sinking of the vessel, on which the various plots unfold, is not really "unobtrusive." However, there is a link between this sort of film scenario and the *Titanic* that appears to be striking with regard to the early dramatizations of the ship disaster: One of the earliest portmanteau films that became paradigmatic for this structure is the 1932 MGM production *Grand Hotel*, which for the first time in American cinema featured an all-star cast and combined several plots under the framework of a hotel setting. Besides the strictly confined setting, the subplots are linked by several of the protagonists' lives reaching a point of crisis during their stay in the hotel, which in one case even leads to death. It is no coincidence that several of the early *Titanic* feature films apply the same format, concentrating entirely on events in First Class, which corresponds almost exactly to the *Grand Hotel* setting. Most of the silent films and the 1929, 1943 and 1953 *Titanic* motion pictures focus on interior settings (which kept the budgets down) and use the sea only for the dramatic collision and the sinking. Nevertheless, these First Class–focused films display one decisive difference to the *Grand Hotel* format: While the famous framing slogan in *Grand Hotel*, "People come and go. Nothing ever happens," is perfectly applicable to a hotel setting, there is a strict limit on the coming and going of passengers (= hotel guests) in the *Titanic* setting once the ship has set out. Both the time frame, the physical fact of being on a ship in the middle of an ocean, and the historical story of the *Titanic* put a limit on the format, providing at the same time a strong factor of suspense and linearity, which the looser structure of portmanteau films does not have.

Of course, there is no compulsion of linearity in *Titanic* films. Especially later films, such as the 1979 and the 1997 productions, work with framing devices, flashbacks and flash-forwards, so that the strictly linear storyline is broken up. As will be seen in the discussion of these films, this looser handling of structure serves to add dramatic momentum and to focus on an individual protagonist and his or her inner experience. Tellingly, in these films the sinking is not the end: The retrospective as typical technique in framing narratives automatically leads to the question about the protagonist's afterlife. In Cameron's film, this is in fact the central question in the coming-of-age story, while *S.O.S. Titanic* sticks more closely to the historical event and its immediate aftermath.

What about the end in a *Titanic* film then? The final act in the classic three act–structure (whose principles are at work even in more extended four- and five-act structures) must lead the story action to a strong climax, resolve its central problem and provide a satisfying ending.[72] "Satisfying" need not be "happy": A fundamental consideration in scriptwriting is to decide how the *audience* feels after leaving the theater. There are *Titanic* films that end tragically and leave the audience with feelings of sadness and maybe helpless anger, while other productions provide the feeling of a happy end, flavored with a wistful sadness:

- 1943: bitterness and anger
- 1953: tragedy with bittersweet catharsis
- 1958: tragedy with a comforting exposition of the insights and improvements it brought
- 1979: tragedy
- 1996: happy end despite the tragedy
- 1997: happy end despite the tragedy

More than in the other films, the ending of the 1943 *Titanic* must be regarded in its historical context: The tone of acid reproach at the end of this production is part of the national socialist propaganda against England. It is therefore that the historical fact of the inquiries with their indeterminate results has been included; for the sake of propaganda, the true scandal of the 1912 inquiries is turned into film. As part of the Nazi propaganda, though, the critique cannot be taken seriously. None of the other films, in turn, has taken up the inquiries.[73]

The other motion pictures make tragedy the dominant note in their endings. Almost invariably, though, tragedy is sweetened by comfort. The 1953 film constructs a redemption drama with the sinking as catharsis, while the 1996 and 1997 productions focus on character development of an individual protagonist who, despite terrible loss in the sinking, ends up being more mature and fit for life's challenges. All three films have in common that the story of some fictitious characters is bound up with the tragic fate of the *Titanic*. Since this story involves coming-of-age stories and personal development, the tragedy is alleviated by the feeling of having learned from disaster. Tragedy and catharsis have had their educational purpose. Thus, there resounds a certain feeling of happy end in these feature films, most strongly in the productions of 1996 and 1997.

Only the two films with the most documentary approach, that is, the 1958 and 1979 productions, focus simply on the sinking as the end, so that a feeling of tragedy prevails. This is only slightly alleviated in the 1958 *A Night to Remember* by ending with a summary of the "comfort" Walter Lord provides in his book, accompanied by an orchestral version of "Nearer, My God, to Thee":

> But this is not the end of the story—for their sacrifice was not in vain. Today there are lifeboats for all, unceasing radio vigil, and, in the North Atlantic, the International Ice Patrol guards the sea lanes making them safe for the peoples of the world.[74]

The 1979 production *S.O.S. Titanic*, in contrast, is the most radical in its documentary realism. It takes the audience to the verge of sanity, focusing on Bruce Ismay as a victim who is about to lose his mind as he is taken onto the *Carpathia*. The frame with the dreary scenes on the *Carpathia* and the icy seascape with ragged and harsh ice offers no alleviation. This is indeed tragedy.

Framing Devices

Having decided about how a specific *Titanic* script is to end, the decisive question is how the script begins and how this beginning is linked to the end. Steven Spielberg, famous for the mythical quality of his film stories, set utmost priority on this relation: "I'm very keen to get right the opening five minutes and closing five minutes of a film—they are crucial."[75] The beginning must set the story in motion, indicate the theme of the story, establish the protagonist (if not at once, very soon after the first scene)—always with a look to the end. Again, the *Titanic* story offers quite a spectrum of choices for the beginning of the famous story. A popular device is a sort of "documentary" prologue about the *Titanic*, using original footage of the launch and photos taken under production and at the outset of the voyage—or corresponding scenes in sepia brown coloring, simulating the "original" quality of the events shown (cf. the opening of the 1958, 1979, 1996, and 1997 productions). Such a prologue provides both nostalgia and dramatic irony, since it celebrates a triumph of technology which — as every spectator knows — will end in disaster.

Besides this "realistic" introduction, additional devices are used to link the beginning with the end. Framing devices are a favorite to construct a strong, overarching link in films with a classic plot design. *Titanic* films contain such frames in varying degree of conspicuity. The 1953 and 1958 productions with their linear narrative structure represent the minimum degree; the "frame" is constituted by the juxtaposition of the vital components, "glorious outset"—"disastrous end." In the 1953 Hollywood *Titanic*, a visual link is added by the ragged British ensign, which Captain Smith hoists at the Southampton departure as a sign for his adherence to British tradition and which is again seen fluttering in the wind immediately before the sinking, representing the demise of an outdated system of society. Yet more importantly, an "environmental frame" is set by the seascape with icebergs, which is set as a prologue with the dramatic calving of a berg (doubtlessly the one that will become the *Titanic*'s fate: a cinematic translation of Thomas Hardy's *The Convergence of the Twain*) and then ends with the historical scene of the lifeboats drifting among the icebergs in the morning after the sinking. In the 1958 film, the contrast between beginning and end is visually enhanced by the juxtaposition of the splendid launch and (fictional) christening scenes at the beginning with the image of pathetic flotsam in the end. Yet these juxtapositions do simply follow the bare skeleton of the historical *Titanic* story, so that they can hardly be regarded as a framing technique.

The other *Titanic* productions make ample use of the narrative and dramatic potential that framing devices offer to create a strong and convincing link between beginning and end. The 1943 anti–British propaganda film, starting with an extraordinary share holder meeting at the White Star Line, displays the cause that leads to the inevitable end. However, the moral structure of cause and punishment is broken up by an additional scene after the sinking, which presents the bitter fact that the guilty person actually is *not* punished; this end links up to the beginning, underlining the national socialist plea for fighting the inhuman reign of British greed. Another typical arching technique is used in the 1996 television mini-series, which starts (after the sepia brown picture sequence) with the ill forebodings of the nurse Alice Cleaver that eventually turn real in the sinking. The dead baby she visualizes floating on the water is finally "redeemed," since Alice saves little Trevor Allison; again, a touch of irony is added by the fact that (according to the film) Alice did not actually *save* the baby, but snatched him away from his mother and thus caused the rest of the Allison family to remain on board in order to search for Trevor, eventually perishing with the *Titanic*. The arch is closed: The two-part series started with Alice setting out (and having nightmares of a ship disaster and a drowned baby), and it ends with her arrival in New York, holding little Trevor in her arms. Nevertheless, this overall frame is weak, since the focus of the series does not lie on Alice Cleaver, but on the romantic account of Isabella Paradine and Jamie Pierce, who both survive the disaster and, matured through tragedy, arrive in New York to enter a new life.

The 1979 and 1997 productions apply more complicated framing structures. Both films use an actual frame narrative into which the main narrative, namely the *Titanic*'s voyage and sinking, combined with various love stories, is embedded. In both films, several devices in plot and imagery are used to construct a strong link between beginning and end, and in both films, it is not only the frame narrative that is connected, but also the beginning and the end of the embedded main narrative:

S.O.S. TITANIC (1979)

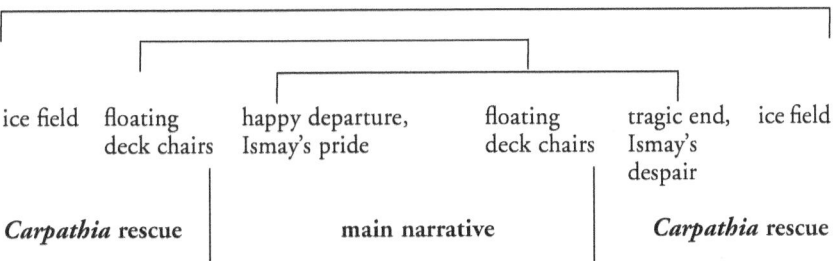

There are several framing devices at work in the original television version of *S.O.S. Titanic*.[76] On the visual (and acoustic) plane, the film starts with the uncanny zoom over an ice field in the North Atlantic, underlaid by sinister, dramatic music. The main narrative then is punctuated by short shots of the ice field and individual bergs, but it is only at the end that the camera lingers on the ice field again. Thus, an overarching theme of "Nature's power and indifference" is set. The narrative framework is constituted by the *Carpathia* rescue, into which the main narrative is inserted, starting as a flashback in Ismay's mind. The psychological process of remembering is triggered by deck chairs floating on the water; this will then be the final shot of the main narrative, leading back to the *Carpathia* frame. The main narrative, too, evinces an arch following the principle "from innocence to experience": It starts with happiness and ends in tragedy. Ismay's pride at the outset of the main narrative is met by his despair in the final *Carpathia* scene. The main narrative thus begins and ends with the tragic flotsam, while Ismay's state of mind builds a bridge between frame and main narrative.

The structure of Cameron's female narrative contains more layers as well as more substantial insertions. While the treasure hunt, which introduces old Rose as narrator, constitutes a clear frame with a lengthy sequence at the beginning and a shorter one at the end, the main narrative is additionally interspersed with short scenes on the research ship *Keldysh* at major turning points:

TITANIC (1997)

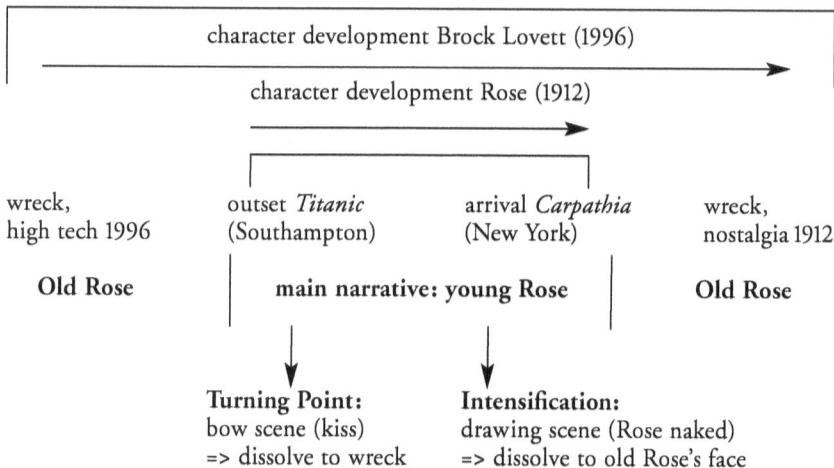

The frame is constituted by old Rose telling about how she experienced the voyage and the sinking of the *Titanic* and developed into a mature person through meeting Jack and falling in love with him. While the character of old Rose remains stable and unchanged in this frame setting, the frame nevertheless contains a minor coming-of-age story, namely that of treasure hunter Brock Lovett, who in the end pathetically declares: "Three years, I've thought of nothing except *Titanic*; but I never got it ... I never let it in." This person-oriented combination of symmetry (Rose) and development (Lovett) in the frame narrative is strengthened by a ship-oriented symmetry and development: The film starts with the wreck of the *Titanic* as it is exposed to the underwater explorers. They break the dignity of her grave by penetrating the maiden ship with a diving robot to wrest away the treasure allegedly resting in her bowels. In the end, the violation of the ship (and grave site) is made up for in two ways: physically by Rose throwing the blue diamond into the sea as a tribute to her lover, who had given her greater riches than any husband lavishing jewelry on her could have done, and metaphysically in Rose's final dream, where the wreck is transformed into the beautiful, immaculate "ship of dreams" that it was in April 1912. This restoration is nevertheless a development, since in Rose's dream all passenger classes and crew members are united at the Grand Staircase to celebrate her and Jack's love — a utopian dream using the ship as staffage.[77]

The main narrative, too, is spanned by an arch, starting with the *Titanic*'s outset at Southampton (with dock and pub scenes) and ending with the survivors' arrival in New York on the *Carpathia*. In fact, this arch is a film realization of one of the most poignant historical "summaries" of the tragedy, presented by Walter Lord in his book *A Night to Remember*:

> Even the Social Register was shaken [by the *Titanic* disaster]. In these days the ship that people traveled on was an important yardstick in measuring their standing, and the Register dutifully kept track. The tragedy posed an unexpected problem. To say that listed families crossed on the *Titanic* gave them their social due, but it wasn't true. To say they arrived on the plodding *Carpathia* was true, but socially misleading. How to handle this dilemma? In the case of those lost, the Register dodged the problem — after their names it simply noted the words, "died at sea, April 15, 1912." In the case of the living, the Register carefully ran the phrase, "Arrived *Titan-Carpath*, April 18, 1912." The hyphen represented history's greatest sea disaster.[78]

It is probable, though, that Cameron did not have the 1912 Social Register in mind when choosing to end the main narrative with the arrival in New York. This arrival, of course with the symbol of the Statue of Liberty (incorrectly situated), represents Rose's entry into a new, liberated life. Yet in order to realize this liberation, she does indeed take the step that the 1912 Social Register so carefully chose to deny: At Southampton, she conspicuously boarded the ship as a wealthy First Class lady, and in New York she arrives as a penniless Third Class passenger. Her character development offsets this voluntary loss of social status: The spoiled girl has turned into a determined young woman ready to fight for her life and liberty. The end of the frame narrative displaying Rose's collection of photographs (another arch: she carefully arranges them in her cabin when arriving on the *Keldysh* in the beginning of the film) proves that she has indeed turned Jack's advice into reality and "made every day count" throughout her life.

The insertion of scenes from the frame narrative (1996) into the main narrative serves to enhance the poignancy of the loss, to document how fresh the memory of her voyage on the *Titanic* still is to 101-year-old Rose, and to underline the continuity of spirit and feeling both in Rose and in the ship, to which her life has been inseparably linked. Technically, this is effected through a seamless visual dissolve: In the bow scene, the beautiful ship against the blazingly colorful sunset is transformed into the tragic wreck in the bluish darkness of the abyss; the same technique is used for cross-fading from young

Rose's eye to the eye of the old woman, illustrating that behind the body's changed exterior Rose's intensity and zeal for life have remained the same. It is, of course, no coincidence that these transformations from past to present time happen at the most intense points in the main narrative, which serve as turning points in the dramatic flow: The first instance is the famous scene at the bow, where Rose finally dares open herself to her incipient love for Jack and is rewarded with a unique moment of freedom — and their first kiss. This scene leads to a point of intensification, the drawing scene (with the second dissolve), and this in turn leads to the consummation of their love in the car. In terms of dramatic structure, the bow scene is the first decisive turning point in the development of the drama, a decision or choice on part of the protagonist, which engenders a crucial change in the story, catapulting it in a new direction.

While the first part of the frame narrative is clearly separated from the main narrative, contrasting the tragic wreck with the splendid ocean liner — the main narrative indeed begins with a blazing front view of the "ship of dreams," a stark contrast to the wreck that is shown in the first minutes of the film — and the old narrator with the beautiful young girl, the ending of the main narrative more gently leads back into the frame story by way of several overlaps. At first, there is a change into present time shortly before the end of the main narrative: Young Rose's determined call for help on the water, i.e., her decision to survive after Jack has died, switches over to old Rose recalling how many people perished in the sinking, while only one single lifeboat went back and altogether no more than six passengers were saved from the water. However, this change is not effected through a dissolve punctuating the main narrative; it rather serves as a preparation for the final transition back into present time. The remaining part of the main narrative are stupor-like scenes that cover the arrival of the *Carpathia* in a surreal morning seascape strewn with icebergs, a short scene on the *Carpathia* and Rose's lonely arrival at the feet of the Statue of Liberty. The final frame narrative in turn has a short flashback to Rose standing on the deck of the *Carpathia* as she discovers that she has the blue diamond in the pocket of the coat. This serves as a wordless explanation why old Rose has the diamond which Brock Lovett spent so many years trying to find.[79] However, the frequent changes between past and present in this final part of the film also imply that the initial contrast has turned into a continuum: Old Rose telling about the end of the *Titanic* is the same person as the determined young woman who had arisen from the disaster; it is only the beginning of the journey that is "far away in the distance," while the ship's end opens up to the continual thread of Rose's long and rich life.

3. Titanic *in Film*

Cameron's framing technique serves to link past with present, thus making the *Titanic* story once again palatable to a young, present-day audience (especially teenage girls, as audience analyses show). The seamless transition between the two time-levels of the frame and the main narrative in the two dissolve shots helps the modern audience to identify with Rose as a character of timeless youth, whether she is presented as a beautiful teenager on the *Titanic* or as a life-affirming 101-year-old on the present-time research ship. The frame makes clear that it is Rose who is the focus of this film: The *Titanic* story (taking up 85 percent of the film after all) set off a process in her character development that eventually led to a happy end, namely a rich and fulfilled life, as it is shown in the frame narrative.

The variety of endings and the manifold ways how beginning and end are linked in the major *Titanic* film productions display the persistently high dramatic potential in the well-known story. Although the end is so clear and unchangeable in a *Titanic* narrative, screenwriters and producers do in fact have a broad gamut of choices for the design of the story and its final climax. The *Titanic* code, that is, the historical *Titanic* story with its many details and the myth subsequently developed around the ship's maiden journey and sinking, provides ample material for stories based on the famous disaster. Both poetic license and the numerous possibilities of structure variation and dramatic technique make it possible to retell the story of *Titanic* again and again. The famous maritime disaster indeed offers the perfect basis for a film script.

Part II
Major Titanic *Films*

4

The Nazi *Titanic* (1943)
Unfit for Propaganda

An ocean liner run by a British company, filled with British businessmen and American millionaires on the one hand, modest and orderly people on the other, going down at night in the icy Atlantic, with most of the simple people losing their lives — can this be used for propaganda? Joseph Goebbels, minister of propaganda under Adolf Hitler, thought so. Cultural life in Nazi Germany was centralized and strictly controlled, and film was consistently used to strengthen and impart national socialist ideology.[1] Shortly after the outbreak of the war, Goebbels, as president of the *Reichskulturkammer* — an institution which he had founded to subject film, radio, theater, music, literature, publishing and the press to government control — launched a program of anti–British propaganda in order to kindle a stronger hatred for the enemy. Films like *My Life for Ireland* (1941) and *Attack on Baku* (1942) were made to denounce a tyrannical British Empire built on a decadent aristocracy and an exploitative plutocracy, oppressing other (of course, Aryan) peoples.[2] The *Titanic* story has so much to offer in terms of gender, class, nation, race, and religion — why not emphasize the nation aspect and show that the disaster solely was a result of British greed and ruthlessness?

The problem was that it did not really work out. The 1943 *Titanic* film failed as a propaganda film in many respects. Most conspicuously, it did not promote Nazi ideology to a German audience under the national socialist regime at all, since the film was not at all shown in Germany until 1950. There is evidence that a German release indeed was planned in 1943: Programs were printed for its German premiere.[3] However, for reasons not known, a German premiere did not take place. Eventually, the film was released in Prague and was run in most German-occupied territories as well as in several other European countries (Switzerland, Sweden, Finland, Greece, Spain,

Belgium), frequently breaking box office records.[4] Yet a German audience did not come to see the film under the NS regime. Although the film had been rated "staatspolitisch wertvoll" (of political merit) and "künstlerisch wertvoll" (of artistic merit) by the German Film Evaluation Office, it remained withheld from distribution in Germany, obviously upon personal intervention on the part of propaganda minister Goebbels.[5] Robert Peck discusses possible reasons for this seeming paradox: the deteriorating war situation (with the disastrous loss of German submarines in May 1943 having evoked a special sensitivity about sea disaster); Goebbels' possible dissatisfaction with the film's propaganda line; a general decline in the importance of the propaganda film in the period from 1941 to 1943; the danger of the *Titanic* being understood as a metaphor for the impending collapse of the Third Reich (which would subvert the intended propaganda and turn *Titanic* into a resistance film against the Nazi regime); or a deliberate subversion treating the *Titanic* as such a metaphor from the start, that is, a sort of intellectual sabotage of NS ideology on the part of director Herbert Selpin. The latter assumption is linked up with the fact that Selpin was arrested and (presumably) murdered by the Gestapo because of his derogatory remarks about the armed forces shortly before production was finished.[6] Yet as Peck shows, most of the named reasons can be ruled out, however plausible they may seem in retrospective. Although there is some likelihood that the film was withheld due to the Selpin affair, it will eventually remain a riddle why Goebbels did not allow the distribution of the propaganda piece he himself had ordered. The Germans had to wait until the 1950s until they were allowed to watch "their" version of the disaster.[7]

Whatever the reason for withholding distribution in national socialist Germany, it is clear that *Titanic*'s primary objective was propaganda — and that it did not reach the people who were first and foremost supposed to be influenced by it. However, the complicated distribution history is only an outward reason why Goebbels' anti–British version of the *Titanic* disaster did not succeed as an invective against England (after all, the film was shown in many other European countries, which could have got the message). The crucial reason lies in the theme itself. To put it simply, the *Titanic* story is not fit for propaganda. Of course, Goebbels and national socialist screenwriter Walter Zerlett-Olfenius did take up the nation aspect of the *Titanic* myth — but the *Titanic* story as such simply is not adequate to generally denounce the British and highlight German virtue. In the *Titanic* myth, nation is almost exclusively used to contrast stereotypes of British character and American values. In *Titanic* films, this is turned into a plea for American liberalism (most decidedly, the 1953 Hollywood film) or into a wistful memory of a world in which British virtue and chivalry still did count (*A Night to Remember*). The paradigm of nation in the *Titanic* myth thus is a British-American contrast: In film production until today, all other nations represented on the *Titanic* are reduced to stereotypes that add little touches of color — the oft-discussed hot-temperedness of the "immigrants belonging to the Latin Races" who had to be held at bay by pistol shots, the earthy steadiness of Scandinavian passengers, and, of course, Irish joy for life. The German passengers did not even qualify for such a role: As a stereotype, they are too close in mentality to British or Scandinavian passengers, so they do not stand out in terms of nation. And in First Class, there was not a single German passenger of sufficient interest to be turned into a leading character in a *Titanic* retelling.[8] Zerlett-Olfenius therefore had to invent — and he used a formula that resulted in poor (because it was entirely unconvincing) propaganda. Ironically, the German 1943 *Titanic* film can thus be used to analyze what a "propaganda failure" is — and why the *Titanic* story simply does not work for propaganda.

Greed as Main Theme: The Plot and the Protagonists

Walter Zerlett-Olfenius certainly was familiar with the *Titanic* myth as well as with the historical facts known at his time. Most conspicuously, though, he includes aspects of two best-selling German *Titanic* novels, Robert Prechtl's *Titanensturz* (1937) and Josef Pelz von Felinau's *Titanic — Tragödie eines Ozeanriesen* (1939). From Prechtl, the strong focus on John Jacob Astor is borrowed; yet the film script turns the character into a parody of what Prechtl presents. Prechtl's Astor is an intellectual, continually musing personage who in the end becomes morally cleansed through the disaster. The film script in contrast focuses exclusively on Astor's presentation as a White Star shareholder with the sole interest to increase his profit; there is no cleansing and no redemption. From Josef Pelz von Felinau came the idea of putting an external, non–British officer onto the *Titanic*, an experienced observer and the only clear-sighted character amongst the crew. While Captain Smith, as a sort of opponent to this First Officer, is characterized as irresponsible, indeed an incarnation of human hubris founded on modern technology, the fictional German officer Petersen is a paragon of virtue, making his responsibility and the passengers his highest priority.[9] For the Nazi film, Zerlett-Olfenius intensified the contrast between Petersen and the British in order to "prove" the superiority of the national socialist stereotype of the "upright German."

He also uses historically verifiable characters and incidents: White Star president J. Bruce Ismay, Captain E.J. Smith, the Astors as a couple, officer

Murdoch (here not serving as First Officer), wireless operators Jack Phillips and Harold Bride, the shortage of lifeboats, the lack of red distress rockets, the *Californian* (shortly hinted at in a conversation on the bridge), finally the British inquiry. Some famous aspects are turned to another use: The legend of Captain Smith saving a child is transferred to the fictitious German First Officer Petersen (who, in contrast to the legend about Smith, accepts being taken into the lifeboat), and the collision with the iceberg is turned into a didactic demonstration of what underwater ice can do to a ship, again delivered by infallible Petersen.

But that's about all there is to "historical fact" and generally known aspects of the myth in Zerlett-Olfenius's script. The interesting point about this script is how the facts are treated — and what parts of the *Titanic* myth are suppressed. It is not surprising that some of the famous historical aspects do not figure since they clash with national socialist ideology. Thus, the Straus couple and Benjamin Guggenheim, ideal emotional staffage used in all other *Titanic* films, are left out; it would have been inconvenient for the national socialist regime to demonstrate the virtues of loyalty and chivalry in the face of death using historical characters who were Jews. Molly Brown does not figure, either: A self-confident, entrepreneurial and politically active millionairess has no place among national socialist typologies of acceptable women — and her demonstration of civil courage would certainly not be desirable in the suppressive Nazi system. The indisputably positive British characters are equally left out: Neither Thomas Andrews nor Second Officer Lightoller appear. Even before the 1958 film *A Night to Remember*, Lightoller (the highest-ranking surviving officer) was regarded as a paragon of the dutiful officer. These characteristics are transferred to the German First Officer Petersen in the national socialist version of the *Titanic* tale.

The other historical characters are used as caricatures to fulfill the needs of propaganda. Ismay, whose British decadence is heightened by the title "Sir," is a sheer parody: the arch-villain responsible for the disaster. Captain Smith is but a puppet to the company's director, while the Astors — ennobled with the British titles "Lord" and "Lady"[10] — have been turned into an ice-cold, bickering couple whose "love" is measured in stocks and jewels. In order to make this cabinet of caricatures work, Zerlett-Olfenius filled the empty spaces with virtuous and orderly Germans. They represent a list of German archetypes within national socialist ideology:

1. First Officer Petersen: a paragon of male virtue and duty (his uniform adding a military touch and underlining his representation of law and order)

2. First Class passenger Prof. Bergmann: the stoical scholar who lives for his scientific world alone
3. Third Class passengers Jan and Anne: the perfect rural couple, personifying simple German life
4. Crew members Hedi and Franz: innocent and good-humored middle class, model of an acceptable love relationship[11]
5. Sigrid Olinsky: the "dangerous woman": dark and enigmatic (yet in the end tamed)[12]

These characters are stereotypes — and terribly boring in their impeccable virtue. Only the Baltic millionairess Sigrid Olinsky, played by German film star Sybille Schmitz, is allowed some character development throughout the film. But again, this development is stereotypical. In the first part of the film, she appears enigmatic and melancholic — without any reason and thus somewhat unsatisfying as starting point for a dramatic development. Later, it turns out that she must have had a love affair with First Officer Petersen on a voyage to Cairo. (This is not really a convincing story given Petersen's axiomatic adherence to the rules that demand a clear personal distance between crew and passengers.) Since Olinsky somehow jilted Petersen back in Cairo, she now behaves like an offended queen; he doubtlessly considers her a superficial bitch. In fact he does, but, as a paragon of courtesy, he would never say so. It is duty that eventually drives him to the utmost step: When the *Titanic* is in danger of running into an ice field at full speed (Petersen is, of course, the only one on board heeding this danger), he transgresses the iron rule that he must not enter a passenger's cabin and entreats Olinsky — who sits on the floor in her First Class stateroom in a decorative arrangement of her dress and lavish flowers, which would have been a rather unlikely sitting position for a German lady in 1912 — to use her influence with Ismay to make him reduce the speed of the ship. She melodramatically refuses — not telling him that the telegram in her hands has just informed her that she has lost all her fortune and thus also the possible influence she could have exerted over greedy Ismay. We do of course know the contents of the telegram and begin to feel sympathy for the poor former millionairess, who so effectively begins to brood and sigh after Petersen stormed out with the accusation, "I took you for a woman that only had the bad luck to be rich. For a woman that one could love if it were otherwise. I have been wrong. Excuse me."

Everything on this *Titanic* is a question of money, even for Petersen and Olinsky. Only when Olinsky tells him, in the middle of incipient turmoil, that she has lost all her money, does he allow his former love for her to rekindle. Immediately, haughty Olinsky turns soft — and then finally begins to show her good side. In line with Nazi preferences, she is transformed into a mixture of woman soldier and war-time nurse, helping to organize the passengers to enter the lifeboats. Yet it is Petersen, the man in charge, who gave her his overcoat and thus a uniform to play a soldier nurse for a little while. When he conveniently is taken into her lifeboat after the sinking, appearing as a hero out of the dark water with a child in his arms, she of course returns this sign of authority to him. The only interesting point in this pathetic romance is the moment where Petersen orders Olinsky herself into a lifeboat: "In my capacity as officer I *order* you to enter the lifeboat — never has an order been so hard for me like this one."[13] She desperately looks up to him while the boat is being lowered: did Cameron watch this film?

Using a handful of historical facts, Zerlett-Olfenius created a melodrama that uses the *Titanic* as luxurious staffage. But Olinsky's development, dramatized through her love for Petersen, is by no means the main plot. There is but one central protagonist in this *Titanic* tale: money. Goebbels wanted an anti–British propaganda film. Therefore, the screenwriter had to take up the sole motif that could be used against the British: the accusation of negligence of safety measures on the part of White Star for the sake of increased profit. Zerlett-Olfenius does everything to drive this message home. The film starts with two scenes at the White Star Line's London office: first a meeting of the main shareholders with Ismay, in which he announces that the escalating construction costs for the *Titanic* (no word of the other Olympic class ships!) have begun to ruin the White Star Line and that the share prices are falling dramatically. In the following scene, a meeting with the board of directors, Ismay announces a strategy to save the White Star Line. To the audience, his words are, of course, pure dramatic irony:

> Next week the *Titanic* will start her maiden voyage across the Atlantic. And you, gentlemen, will take part as my guests. On this voyage, you are in for a sensational surprise. A surprise that will make our shares rise in unprecedented measure. [*staring obsessively into the air*] Gentlemen, I'd rather not say more today. Please trust me. Just as we all trust in our *Titanic*, the proudest ship in the world [*the* Titanic, *splendidly lit on the sea, is shown to these words*], which soon will set sail to the honor of our White Star Line. To England's glory!

The invited directors will indeed be in for a sensational surprise — which none of them will survive. In the light of historical fact, Ismay's plan is complete nonsense: Both the speed record (the "surprise") and the intended stock manipulation connected with the record would have been impossible. It is clear that the *Titanic* never was built for a speed record and that the White Star Line never had the ambition to win the Blue Riband with her or any of the other three Olympic class ships.[14] Equally, there was no way of using the

4. The Nazi Titanic (1943)

***Titanic* (1943):** The lifeboat scene of a woman parted from her lover — long before Cameron's movie (UFA, actor: Sybille Schmitz).

Titanic for gambling on the stock exchange: By 1912, the British White Star Line was a subsidiary of the International Mercantile Marine owned by the American J.P. Morgan. There were no White Star shares publicly traded at the stock market. In Zerlett-Olfenius's script, though, the White Star Line appears as an independent enterprise fighting to reach solid ground again after the shares have been dramatically falling.

Thus, the script takes up one of the best-known, but also best-refuted myths about the *Titanic*, namely the alleged ambition for an Atlantic speed record, forcing Captain Smith to run the *Titanic* full speed against all nautical experience and caution. While in most *Titanic* films the speed motif is present, but not vital, the German propaganda version entirely focuses on this motif as a symbol for the heedless greed of Ismay and his like.

The stock manipulation plot is intensified by the rivalry between Ismay and Astor, which unfolds on the voyage: As the shares continue to fall despite the world-wide dissemination of the news of an expected new speed record, Ismay realizes that there is some other force at work marring his plans. Like Ismay himself, Astor intends to press the share price of the White Star Line further and further down in order to then make a killing and gain control over the company. Interestingly, his main interest is the ship itself, which for him represents power: "You see, the *Titanic* is not just a bunch of shares. She is a tangible asset. Tangible assets create power, and power is a means to whatever you want." The motif of power is inseparably linked to the motif of love:

> JOHN JACOB ASTOR: To each his own, Madeleine. For me, more power, for you, more jewelry.
> MADELEINE ASTOR: Jewelry is also an asset.
> JOHN JACOB ASTOR: But not always stable. Even gems are subject to fluctuation. And they can only be accurately judged when they are taken out of their mounting. Just like women.[16]

In the sphere of Ismay, Astor, and their like, love is a commodity, linked to luxury and shares. The relationship between Astor and Madeleine is characterized by cold calculation and distrust. Ismay, too, is given a (fictitious) companion, Gloria, whose only interest is to bind him (and his fortune) by marriage upon their arrival in New York. Both women are clearly subordinated to the men's financial interests. But it was not Goebbels's intention to arouse pity with British millionaire women: Madeleine and Gloria are ice-cold, calculating, and just as manipulative as their men. For Gloria, it is perfectly all right that Ismay begins to flirt with Sigrid Olinsky in order to gain control of the Baltic millionairess's (assumed) riches — as long as this does not present an obstacle to their imminent marriage. Yet as Petersen blandly informs them that the ship is sinking, she discloses her true character, which makes her a perfect match for Ismay:

> GLORIA: And what will become of us now?
> ISMAY: I don't know.
> GLORIA: You don't know. You don't know? [*goes and grabs her jewels*] And if something really happens? If we go down?
> ISMAY (*stricken*): Absurd... The game is over.
> GLORIA: Yes! The game is over! Up to now you have acted the big shot quite enough! But now, I am going to tell you something!
> ISMAY (*yells*): I told you to leave me alone!
> GLORIA: [*standing with her jewels in front of him*] I see, I should leave you alone. Before, I was good enough for you. You have been talking about marriage for years. You've taken away all my other chances. Now it's *I* who has the last chance, do you get it? *Me*, not you! Because I am a woman! Yes, a woman! And they say, women and children first!

Gloria's only interest is to grasp as many of her jewels as possible — her lover is discarded, since he is no longer of any use to her. But Gloria's arrogant indifference not only strikes Ismay: When the First Class women crowd on the Boat Deck, she haughtily demands precedence because of her position "as wife of president Ismay," and as soon as she sits in the lifeboat, she urges the officer to lower it down, regardless of the people who still could enter and thus be saved.[16]

Madeleine Astor is not much better: She plays both with the temptation of infidelity and with the feelings of poor Lord Douglas, arrogantly sending him away after she first has encouraged him. She prefers to remain in a cold but luxurious marriage after all. The audience is certainly not supposed to have sympathy for these women because the capitalist interests of their men destroy their chances for a happy marriage.

In this tale of greed leading to personal catastrophe, the *Titanic* disaster is made the touchstone for personal integrity: The news of the irrevocable sinking turns Ismay into a wailing coward, while Astor keeps his countenance, but of course intends to buy a place for himself in a lifeboat. Astor goes down with the ship (a punishment for his greed and coldness?), while Ismay does by no means sneak into security: It is First Officer Petersen, always in charge and always correct, who announces that he will personally guarantee a place in a lifeboat for Ismay, "so that you will be called to account by the Maritime Board of Inquiry!" But this does not happen in the end: The original version of the film ends with a scene in court, where the jury finally decides — despite Petersen's powerful testimony — that all blame is put on the deceased Captain Smith, while both Ismay and the Board of Management are acquitted. In this finale, Petersen assumes the grand "J'accuse" stature of an Émile Zola — and the film closes with the final title card, "The death of 1,500 people remained unatoned. An everlasting condemnation of England's lust for profit."

According to the wishes of propaganda minister Goebbels, Zerlett-Olfenius thus decided to make the greed of the White Star Line and the rich passengers the main plot of the *Titanic* film. This greed leads to the destruction of society, epitomized by the ship with its various social strata — a clear plea to continue fighting England with its decadent plutocracy. The greed motif is combined with a love motif showing two contrasting possibilities, the defeat and the triumph of love:

Plot level	*Theme*	*Contents*
Main plot	greed destroying society	stock manipulation => sinking of the *Titanic*
main subplot	love triumphing over money	relationship Olinsky-Petersen
subplot 2	money triumphing over love	relationship Ismay-Gloria
subplot 3	money triumphing over love	relationship J. J. Astor–Madeleine Astor

The subplots about the relationships of the rich and greedy are inseparably linked to the theme of the main plot: The destructive potential of greed starts in the immediate personal surroundings and ends with the ruin of society. The theme "money triumphing over love" is counterbalanced by the subplot that stands strongest against the main plot: the developing relationship between Petersen and Olinsky, which finally can unfold when she confesses that she has lost all her fortunes and thus has become "a woman that can be loved." The melodramatic scene in her cabin is the turning point in this relationship; from then on, things move uphill for Sigrid Olinsky, while the ship is going down.

There are further subplots, but they are no more than vignettes without a convincing dramatic development:

Subplot	Theme
Hedi and Franz	poor but happy, innocent love fulfilled
Jan and Anne	loyalty and simplicity prevail
Marcia (and the Levantine) vs. Henry and Bobby	cunning of the lower races vs. loyal friendship
Mendoz vs. Prof. Bergmann	"Latin" cunning and deceit vs. German virtue and stoicism

The subplots are stereotypes imbued with national socialist race ideology. None of them really develops, nor do they convincingly display the various spheres of the ship: Third Class does not constitute an alternative locale for dramatic development that would constitute a sustainable contrast to First Class, onto which the focus of the film is set. It must be said, though, that the 1943 *Titanic* for the first time in film uses the dramatic device of contrasting the refined First Class atmosphere (heightened by a fictitious ballroom) with the more earthy entertainment of the Third Class. Although the sensual dance of the gypsy Marcia — a somewhat curious musical mixture of a Spanish habañera and more Eastern influences, ending with a shy attempt at striptease — in ideological terms serves to display the depravity of the "lower races," the sheer length of this scene shows that the filmmakers also wanted to tickle the upright German audience's senses. It is not a coincidence that even prudish Anne in the end joins in the general clapping to the gypsy girl's dance.

The setting for this rather square-cut combination of main plot and subplots is the *Grand Hotel* format. The clear focus on First Class allowed for lavish sets that dwell on the luxuries of the famous ocean liner. Again, this focus displays a sort of double standard: While the film actually condemns the decadent First Class excess, the sets are opulent, doubtlessly to give the German audience something to enjoy in the midst of ongoing war. However, the objective is not a display of *maritime* grandeur: The Atlantic and the vast dimensions of the ocean liner are hardly ever seen. Instead, director Selpin

4. The Nazi Titanic (1943)

Titanic (1943): The splendid interiors of the 1943 *Titanic*, including a fictitious ballroom, both commented on excessive British luxury and provided a visual treat to a war-stricken audience (UFA).

set the focus on claustrophobic interiors; even the enormous ballroom is crowded by people and thus loses its large dimensions.[17] The setting reflects the capitalist protagonists' state of mind: They are fixed on money and their scheming, locked in by their greed, and thus eventually condemned to perish with the ship.

Propaganda Failed

The propaganda line of the film is clear: The motif of greed is used to discredit a capitalist British plutocracy, whose scheming causes both personal and universal disaster. Against this, the bravery, selflessness, and moral superiority of the Germans are highlighted: As Paul Malone shows in his analysis of *Titanic*, characters like Petersen "represent the German 'us,' standing alone against the forces of modernity, internationalism, capitalism, etc."[18] This "us" is underlined by minor characters like the "positive" couples Jan-Anne and Hedi-Franz, who stand for a simple but sincere *Volkscharacter* (character of the German people). An additional aspect of propaganda is the race issue, which is not strongly emphasized, but nevertheless visible on the ship: Negative character traits are relegated to the "lower races," such as the seductive gypsy girl Marcia, who tries to destroy the loyal friendship between Third Class passengers Bobby and Henry, the "Levantine" (a man of Eastern Mediterranean origin and thus probably Jewish), who slips a knife to Bobby when he fights his friend because of Marcia, and the Cuban thief Mendoz. The way how these "lower races" eventually are done away with almost seems humoristic:

> Later, as the ship is sinking, the Levantine instigates a riot. In the confusion, Henry leaves Marcia to rescue Bobby; as Marcia and the Levantine attempt to climb a rope ladder into a descending lifeboat, a desperate Mendoz attacks them. The two struggling men fall into the lifeboat, which plunges from its davits into the sea, neatly taking all three racial undesirables with it and demonstrating the fruit of non–Aryan underhandedness.[19]

This sort of racial didactics is a joke — and this exactly is the problem with it. Such a banal form of propaganda does not work. The negative sides of the rich and greedy as well as of the "racial undesirables" are so exaggerated that the main plot and the subplots lose all credibility. How stupid did Goebbels and Zerlett-Olfenius believe the German audience to be? The stereotype presentation of the bad guys and the good guys is apt for comedy — but not for a tragedy with propagandistic objectives.

What is "good propaganda," then? Simon Mills heads his chapter on the 1943 *Titanic* with a bon mot by actor-playwright Sir Noël Coward: "I don't like propaganda in the theatre unless it is disguised so brilliantly that the audience mistakes it for entertainment."[20] Brilliant propaganda is not the black-and-white presentation of good Germans and bad enemies, nor is it marching Hitler Youths looking proud and happy while singing the Horst Wessel Song. Brilliant propaganda is so subtle that one does not notice — taking it for entertainment, as Coward states. A comparison of German films produced during the war shows the difference. Didactic plays discrediting Jews, Slavs, and other non–Aryan people are easily seen through, and films with wonderfully brave, solid, and reliable Germans somehow do not convince. It is the films leaving a smile on one's face that are dangerous. For example, the 1941 film *U-Boote westwärts!* (*U-boat, Course West!*), a propaganda piece concocted to convince German youths to enroll in the submarine service, is still palatable to an audience today. Present-time viewers even negate that there is any propaganda at play, certainly not more than in English or American war films that were made at that time. A detailed analysis, though, unveils a propagandistic strategy that penetrates every single scene and works best where social and family values are imparted, using little children as highly convincing actors.[21] Though the film is officially banned as Nazi propaganda in Germany today, copies are easily available on the Internet, and user comments show that the mechanisms of subtle propaganda are at work today just as much as they were in 1941. Real propaganda is seductive, imparting an impression of "life as it is."

The failure of the black-and-white plot with its many clichés is only one reason why Goebbels' propagandistic retelling of the *Titanic* failed, even though it was met with great success in the countries where it was shown. The other important reason is that the anti–British line is not consistently carried through — and this is because the *Titanic* story is not apt for nationalist propaganda. Both the historical core and the myth built around the *Titanic* disaster are far too complex, even if the focus is laid on the paradigm of nation only. The *Titanic* passengers and crew cannot be sectionalized according to national stereotypes: It is impossible to divide the people on board the *Titanic* into non–German bad guys and Aryan good guys. The "good guys" in the 1943 production in fact are archetypes that need not necessarily be German: Jan and Anne could, according to their looks, just as well be Swedish or Norwegian (or even modest Slavonic farmers!), Hedi and her "Franzl" might actually come from Austria or Switzerland (and why shouldn't they have been good-humored English crew members?), Prof. Bergmann personifies the image of the cosmopolitan scholar, and Petersen — well, Petersen is no more than a caricature of "German" rectitude and sense of duty. And then, there inevitably turn up some positive characters who cannot help being English: Once disaster has struck, the English crew displays exemplary professionalism. The wireless operators are, in line with the *Titanic* myth, a paragon of selflessness (with an oft-named sentimental scene of Jack Phillips releasing his canary under the orchestral strain of "Nearer, My God, to Thee" a few minutes before the sinking); the musicians play their final song until the very end in this movie, too, and many passengers — whether English, German or of another nationality — simply behave with exemplary countenance and circumspection. In addition, there are some English passengers whose fate elicits sympathy, whether it is the elderly duchess in First Class, whose ill forebodings about the voyage did not help her to get a place in a lifeboat in good time after all, or the loyal friends Henry and Bobby, who resist Marcia's malicious attempts to split up their friendship and eventually escape on a self-made raft (incidentally saving Anne's life, too). Despite the attempt to suppress all pity for the financial sharks and their immoral wives, the film cannot avoid poignancy — and this is a universal poignancy, evoking sympathy for the victims of the *Titanic* regardless of their nationality.

Goebbels expected Zerlett-Olfenius and Selpin to produce an anti-

British film, directing the indignation of the audience in all the countries where the film was shown against greedy and ruthless England. In contrast, the Germans on board were to be shown as a paragon of virtue. This did not work. The propaganda is primarily anti-capitalist and not anti–British in a national sense. (It is not surprising that the film was a welcome asset for the Soviets, who allowed it to be run in Eastern German cinema after the war.) While the villains are the rich on board, the heroes are the poor — dutiful crew members, modest Third Class passengers, the stokers in the engine rooms. This is the first *Titanic* film to make a significant point about class differences, although the classes do not clash and the screenwriter even missed the chance to show how Third Class passengers were stopped by locked gates. Yet it is "the little people" who are the good guys (with the exception of the above-named racial undesirables), while there is very little positive to be said about the First Class passengers.

With its stereotype characters, the film can in fact be seen as a parable with a moral lesson on the cardinal vice of greed:

> And so the film treats the HMS [*sic*] *Titanic*, her collision with an iceberg and subsequent sinking, as an allegory for western capitalism, which, like the titular ocean liner, is bloated, accelerative and heading for crisis. The film makes this most explicit by using the upper and lower decks of the ship to highlight social stratification (the rich hobnob on the upper decks while the poor live in steerage compartments), whilst the *Titanic*'s sinking, which was due to the ship travelling too fast in order to break naval records, is shown to be the result of businessmen who were using the ship's lunge for the record books to drive up stock prices.[22]

If one accepts this allegorical character of the film, much of the awkwardness in the plot and the character treatment disappears. Villains like Ismay and Astor need not to be taken at face value, they are simply archetypes in a didactic play. And since the propaganda line in the film does not work as a vehicle for Nazi ideology anyway, the film can just be taken as a didactic entertainment using one of the most famous disasters of the 20th century in order to warn against the vice of ruthless greed. Thus, the 1943 *Titanic* is the only film that makes the hubris motif of the *Titanic* myth central in its design; all others reduce it to a little detail that is neither instrumental nor dominant in the tragedy of the *Titanic*.

The enthusiastic audiences of the 1940s and '50s obviously understood how the film was to be taken. They did not bother with the credibility of stereotype plots, and probably not with didactic messages about vice and virtue either, but they simply enjoyed the entertainment value and the good handicraft *Titanic* displayed. The film shows impressive sets, it has got a star cast with some excellent acting, and it offers some convincing moments of melodrama, tragedy, and comic relief. The editing is excellent at times, creating dramaturgical density in the moments before the collision, and some of the special effects in the flooding scenes were so successful that they were used again in *A Night to Remember* (1958). It is for these qualities that *Titanic* sometimes is shown on present-day German television and has been made available on DVD by Kino Video as well as in the Ufa Classics edition.

The question of propaganda has not completely been forgotten, though: While Kino Video presents the shorter after-war version without the anti–British trial scene at the end (thus ending effectively with the sinking of the ship), the Ufa Classics edition offers the full-length original version, including the final title card with the acrimonious accusation of British greed. (As a sort of counterbalance, the special features section on this DVD contains a short film about Nazi cinema and the propaganda aspects of *Titanic*.) Interestingly, the version shown on German television is a mixture of both: It does end with the court scene, thus white-washing the White Star Line and triumphant Ismay — but this is just followed by "The End" with the problematic title card missing. With all respect for authenticity, it is not in the interest of present-day German television channels to vilify England.

These varying solutions — complete cutting, cutting of the end-title, or authentic full version — reflect the importance of this final moment for the evaluation of the entire film:

> It is the end-title, however, that is crucial to any evaluation of the film as propaganda. If there were any question about its origins and intentions, the end-title removes all doubt. Like the caption of a cartoon or photograph, it encapsulates and specifies the message. In this case it refers directly to the injustice evident in the final scene: as the verdict of the inquiry is about to be announced, the German first officer says: "And now we will see if there is any justice." The answer of course was a resounding "no." The end-title then establishes the link between the injustice, the underlying materialism, and Britain.[23]

With the final title card being cut away, the anti–British impetus of the film has indeed been weakened. Not least, because the final trial scene is not all fictitious: The British Inquiry, taking place in London from May to July 1912, has generally been regarded as a whitewash, so that the 1943 *Titanic* film seems to simply state things "as they had been."

It is, however, a question of presentation: As Robert Peck notes in the above quotation, the final judgment of the court is dramatically highlighted by impeccable officer Petersen's remark that the jury's decision will show if there is any justice. With this juxtaposition, the British Inquiry's historical report is turned into a blatant demonstration of injustice and prevarication.[24] This is sealed by the final card, which turns the court scene into a bitter accusation of British greed and injustice. Without the card, the scene still remains bitter — but in a more general sense, as a universal accusation of a legal system that works at the service of the capitalist ruling class. If this statement simply is followed by the title "The End," this is a bitter morale palatable to any audience. The anti–English sting has been taken away.

To put it into a nutshell: The *Titanic* disaster can be reduced to a stereotype moral play — but it is not fit for propaganda. The myth is too complex to put the blame on one particular failure, the setting is multi-national, with the victims coming from many countries, and the disaster engenders general pity, even for those who — such as Captain Smith — definitely did have some responsibility for the collision with the iceberg.

Epilogue

There is one final instance of bitter irony in the 1943 film: Two years after production was finished, the ship on which the sinking scenes were filmed sank in the Baltic Sea. This time, the disaster was much more due to human error than the sinking of the *Titanic*: In the case of the former luxury liner *Cap Arcona*, the atrocities of the Nazi regime were combined with the horrors of war. The *Cap Arcona* was filled with thousands of prisoners (mainly Jews) from the concentration camp Neuengamme, whom the Nazis sought to transfer to Denmark in the final days of war. In a general attack on shipping in the Baltic Sea, the *Cap Arcona* was bombed by the Royal Air Force squadrons on May 3, 1945, and several thousand emaciated prisoners lost their lives, either drowning or freezing to death in the cold water — or being shot by SS guards who sought to prevent their escape. Thus, in several ways the sinking of the *Cap Arcona* with its involuntary, tormented passengers was much worse than the *Titanic* disaster. The 1943 film may help to remind viewers of this forgotten catastrophe.

5
Titanic (1953)
Myth Turned into Melodrama

Sometimes, a ship has to sink to put a marriage back on track. Or, as a viewer puts it:

> As the voyage begins, Clifton Webb and Barbara Stanwyck are in a shattering marriage, held together only by their son of about 12 years; this is the central theme. Oh, by the way, the *Titanic* strikes an iceberg, is sinking, and there aren't enough lifeboats for all. This motivates Webb and Stanwyck to rethink their lives and to reunite just in time to be permanently parted by the sinking.[1]

The story sounds banal. Nevertheless, Charles Brackett, Richard L. Breen and Walter Reisch received the Academy Award for their script. And they did deserve it.

The script is a model of classic proportions. The general growth of momentum and the climactic turning points are clearly discernable in the development of the main plot, while the subplots reflect, support and intensify the dominant storyline. This well-balanced structure is fleshed out by a strong main theme, which again is supported by every detail of the various subplots as well as the background setting. It just happens that the background setting is the sinking of the *Titanic*, which works in perfect symbiosis with the quite "un–*Titanic*" main plot. But *Titanic* is not the focus: It is a question of melodrama, not of disaster. *Titanic* enthusiasts with their demand for historical accuracy do often rage at director Jean Negulesco's Hollywood film. Yet if one accepts that historical accuracy is not the point here, *since the story is not at all that of the* Titanic, it is a perfectly functioning script, constituting the fundament for a strong film realization that combines a star cast with the high Hollywood standards of the 1950s.

The theme of the film is the sanctity of the American family — in a way, a film realization of one important aspect of the *Titanic* myth, namely "appropriate" gender roles and matrimonial devotion, as epitomized by the Straus couple. The main plot is a classic divorce and remarriage plot (though it neither comes to divorce nor to remarriage). The protagonists are Julia and Richard Sturges, an estranged American couple traveling on the *Titanic*. Having lived as Americans in European high society circles for many years, Julia seeks to take the children — 18-year-old Annette and 12-year-old Norman — to her childhood home in Michigan for good in order to escape hollow upper class life and to impart sound American values to them. Richard, a paragon of the Europeanized American, has found out about her plans, and they spend the first part of the voyage fighting about the children. A first climax is Julia's dramatic revelation that Norman is not Richard's son, prompting Richard to disown the boy who adores him as his father. As the *Titanic* collides with the iceberg and Richard at once finds out about the true situation, he assumes responsibility for his family again. In a melodramatic (though indeed quite moving) farewell scene, Julia and Richard rediscover and reconfirm their love for each other. As the lifeboat with Julia and her children is being lowered, young Norman in a chivalrous gesture secretly leaves his place to an elderly woman and steps back onto the ship, looking for his father. They are reunited just before the sinking; Richard declares his love and pride for Norman and openly acknowledges him as his son. They go down arm in arm, with all the remaining passengers on board singing "Nearer, My God, to Thee."

It is melodrama that is at the center of this *Titanic* film — history is not the point. Typically for 1950s Hollywood, historical detail is tailored to suit a film's storyline, resulting in a multitude of factual errors and anachronisms, which are neatly pointed out by *Titanic* experts on webpages and in the Internet Movie Database.[2] The *Titanic* is reduced to a mere vehicle for another theme: The sinking is the means by which upper middle-class nuclear family tensions are resolved.[3] Thus, Hollywood's first version of the *Titanic* story is nothing but a minor domestic drama set against an epic background.[4] However, the film does make this drama universal, since the script takes up the universal themes crystallized in the *Titanic* myth: gender, class, nation, race, religion. As Alan Finlayson and Richard Taylor point out, its script takes up central issues of the *Titanic* myth, namely the contrast between American and British values (the latter generalized as "European") and gender roles that start out being reversed and eventually are set back to "normal" in the course of the story's development.[5] These focal issues of conflict are played out on the basis of an implicit demonstration of Anglo-Saxon superiority and on the poignant background of the *Titanic* voyage and sinking. Thus, Hollywood's first *Titanic* production does indeed tackle the *Titanic* myth in its vital aspects, although at first sight it seems to cover it up with a melodramatic family story.

And it is a "modern" film, at least in terms of the 1950s: In its solution of the conflicts within the Sturges family, the 1953 *Titanic* reaffirms the values of its time, namely American middle-class values and traditional gender roles. In *Titanic* literature, this film is usually regarded on the background of its historical context, namely the "age of anxiety" with the Iron Curtain, the Cold War, the menace of global communism, and the atomic threat becoming a tangible reality: "The *Titanic* story becomes a metaphor for the destruction of a secure pre-war world.... It is a *Titanic* for the Cold War."[6] With the Old World lying in ruins and the British Empire beginning to crumble, the emphasis is put on the superiority of America and Americanism — this is exactly what is at stake in the conflict between Julia and Richard Sturges in the 1953 *Titanic*. At the same time, the gender roles in their relationship initially are reversed: a sign for universal disorder threatening society. Their conflict unfolds up to the climax. The sinking of the *Titanic* then is the catalyst to put things back into place and re-establish both the superiority of American values and the viability of traditional gender roles.

First Class with a Gender Conflict

The themes of class and nation are somewhat blurred in this film. Class is an important issue of discussion, but remains entirely on First Class level: It is a question of American versus European values, of an obsolete, rootless European high society (flirting with the attributes of old nobility) versus a sound and simple American lifestyle. Thus the class issue is reduced to the juxtaposition of two stereotypes, one being a caricature of European upper class life around 1912, the other a romantic ideal of true Americanism. Real class issues are completely blocked out: Third Class is used for staffage only, with short glimpses displaying the usual stereotypes of dance and joy for life. The poor Basque Uzcadum family (the name in itself is a parody of "outlandishness"), from which Richard Sturges presses a ticket to get onto the *Titanic* at Cherbourg, is a mere foil to first display the main character's arrogance and then, after the collision, his renewed sense of honor and responsibility.[7]

The focus is entirely set on First Class, and thus this film again applies the *Grand Hotel* format with various storylines developing partly independently, partly intertwined, in a splendid First Class setting. Indeed, the screenwriter made quite a point of stressing this setting: There are altogether four scenes in which the *Titanic* "jet set" is enumerated one by one — you really get the names!

1. opening scene:
   Titanic's cargo office with gratulatory gifts "Happy Maiden Voyage" to
   — the Astors
   — Benjamin Guggenheim
   — Captain Smith (in his time called the "millionaires' captain")
2. tender from Cherbourg with many famous First Class passengers on board:
   — the Astor couple
   — the Straus couple (who in reality boarded at Southampton)
   — the Widener family
   — Maude Young (= Margaret Brown)
   — fictitious First Class passengers: Julia Sturges and her children, friends from the European jet set, and social upstart Earl Meeker
3. First Class dining room: Richard Sturges enters and jovially greets
   — the Straus couple
   — the Widener couple
4. wireless office:
   Phillips and Bride discuss the First Class passengers' telegrams, naming
   — the Hays family
   — the Duff-Gordons
   — the countess of Rothes
   — Major Archibald Butt

This is the *Titanic*, there is no doubt: the staffage of famous First Class passengers ensures the "authenticity" of the setting. At the same time, these scenes clearly demonstrate where the Sturges family belongs: high society, with Julia feeling rather uneasy (she is quite happy with their remote board in the dining room, whereas her daughter Annette sulks about this socially unfortunate position), while Richard is all at home and ease.

While the class issue is more of a juxtaposition of clichés than a serious issue in the conflict between Julia and Richard, the gender issue, epitomized in the change of their relationship, is perfectly developed in the course of the voyage — Hollywood melodrama at its best, with the leading stars living entirely up to it. The first part of the script accumulates a series of confrontations between Julia and Richard, in which Julia — the active part — displays determination and strength:

	Date	*Locale*	*Subject of Discussion*
Confrontation 1	April 10 evening	dinner table	Julia taking the children to Michigan for good; marriage plans for Annette => American vs. European values

5. Titanic (1953)

	Date	Locale	Subject of Discussion
Confrontation 2	April 11 or 12 morning	cabin	full disclosure of Julia's plans, juxtaposition of Europe and America, Annette breaks with her mother
Confrontation 3	April 13 evening	cabin	Norman's future, revelation that he is not Richard's son

With Julia's highly dramatic revelation of Norman's true parentage — indeed the "high trump" Richard suspects her to have in hand — the roles finally begin to turn in the direction they belong (according to 1950s Hollywood standards). The series of energy-filled confrontations with Julia as a determined mother fighting for her children's future is followed by a series of colloquies that re-establish the traditional gender roles, with an increasingly meek and entreating Julia:

	Date	Locale	Subject of Discussion
Colloquy 1	April 13 evening	Promenade Deck	Julia explains about Norman, Richard breaks with her and disowns Norman
Colloquy 2	April 14 evening	Smoking Room	Julia entreats Richard to be kind to Norman until they separate
Collision as turning point: gender roles are restored			
Reunion	April 14 night	Boat Deck	reconciliation and declaration of love
Separated by destiny			

Both main characters display a clear development in the course of the plot: Richard, demonstratively snobbish and vain in the beginning (he openly disparages the Uzcadum family while trying to persuade them to sell him one of their tickets), develops into a man of integrity and strength as soon as he has learned about the true situation after the collision. Effeminate, artificial, and sulking about the defilement of his manly honor, he suddenly turns into a responsible and strong family man, taking care of his children (including Norman) and evincing an unexpected tenderness for his wife. His final words, melodramatic as they are, indeed are moving — not least due to actor Clifton Webb's ability to incarnate the role of the refined gentleman who retains composure and yet displays true emotion in the decisive moments of life:

> JULIA: Oh, Richard, where did we miss out on each other?—I beg your pardon, sir. I put you down as a useless man, somebody to lead a cotillion.
> RICHARD (*sighs*): After all, it was my major talent.
> JULIA: Oh, I'm sorry. Sorry about everything.
> RICHARD: We have no time to catalogue our regrets. All we can do is pretend twenty years didn't happen. [*staring wistfully into the night*] It's June again. You're walking under some elm trees in a white muslin dress. The loveliest

creature I ever laid eyes on. That summer, when I asked you to marry me, I pledged my eternal devotion. [*serious and tender*] I would consider it a great favor, Julia, if you would accept a restatement of that pledge.
[*Julia hugs and kisses him*]
JULIA: Oh, Richard, please don't go away. [*she cries and is taken away into a lifeboat*]

More melodrama than one can bear, seen from a 21st-century standpoint. But in the 1953 film, this is indeed the great scene — the moment of truth for the couple who has lived for almost twenty years in strife and increasing estrangement. That the climactic melodrama scene of the script has indeed been turned into the great scene of the film is due to the mastery of the actors, who were not Hollywood stars for nothing — and the screenwriters knew well that their script had to be imbued with this mastery to make a good film.

While Richard turns from the effeminate snob into the strong man, Julia is reduced from the hard, determined, and active mother to a state of distraught and passive helplessness. In short: She turns into a woman. This is, as Finlayson and Taylor conclude in their analysis quoting the study of Jackie Byars on gender roles in 1950s melodrama, exactly what American melodrama in that period was about:

> As women of all ages, races, marital and maternal statuses, and socio-economic classes flooded out of their homes and into the workplaces of America, the family structure began to change, previously sacrosanct gender roles began to alter, and struggles over the meaning of female and male became particularly evident in the cultural atmosphere.... [F]amily values became socially and culturally central to Americans, and Hollywood films interpreted and helped to make sense of this basic social institution symbolically deploying it across a panoply of permutations.[8]

Although gender roles are reversed in the case of the two main characters (Richard with his boutonnière and his love for clothes in contrast to the hardened, determinate Julia), the stereotypes regarded as "norm" are constantly affirmed throughout the film: There is no doubt that both parents' aim for Annette's life is a good marriage, while Norman is expected to grow up to a "proper man." Since Julia bases all her decisions on this aim, it is clear that her determinate, "unfeminine" attitude is an exception only, necessitated by the urge to save her children from becoming spoiled and effeminate "Europeans." In fact, the gender norm is never questioned, and the ship's collision with the subsequent "chance" to demonstrate masculine chivalry and feminine resignation into fate is the perfect means to reinstate the traditional gender roles and thus to resolve the family conflict. The *Titanic* disaster indeed demonstrates what the reversal of the "natural order" leads to.

Religion and Redemption

The "sanctity" of marriage and family as main theme of the film is strongly supported by a supplementary thematic line, namely religion. Notably, the original production title of the film was the famous hymn title "Nearer, My God, to Thee," with the hymn being turned into a symbol of religious acceptance and redemption at the end. The producers eventually decided to change the title. *Titanic*, though already used for the (little known) German production of 1943, would be much more appealing to a general audience than an overtly religious sounding title.[9] Nevertheless, the religious current is strong throughout the film. Building on the religious aspect of the *Titanic* myth, a tale of resignation into God's will and final redemption, the screenwriters used the disaster for an individual tale of redemption: Richard becomes a man in the crisis and "saves" the family (that is, his relation to Julia and to his son) by dying. In the end, he and his re-acknowledged son stand arm in arm and sing the famous hymn. Richard has redeemed himself and, in noble composure and stoic acceptance, finds peace in God.

His development and attitude are neatly reflected in two minor characters: Norman, too, grows up in the course of the voyage and proves his coming of age in a noble act of self-sacrifice (though Richard rightfully remarks that Norman's act reminds him of "those fool drummer boys who stayed on to play 'Last Retreat,'" thus underlining that Norman still is an innocent child and should not have made this decision). A somewhat darker counterpart is George Healey, the defrocked Catholic priest, who appears as a desperate drunkard throughout the first part of the voyage, but then, in the moment of need, heroically descends into hell (i.e., the boiler room with the boilers exploding) in order to give religious comfort to the stokers trapped there. This detail, by the way, is both a pretty variation on the *Titanic* myth and a noble gesture of "class awareness" on the part of Hollywood: The engineers and (less frequently) the stokers are often named as the little heroes of the sinking, who generated power to the last moment — but they are never granted a noteworthy part in any *Titanic* film. So the Hollywood melodrama at least makes a point that they do receive spiritual support in the hour of death. Their inconspicuous heroism is also underlined by an earlier scene in the engine room, with the chief engineer representing their sense of sacrifice:

> CAPT. SMITH: Can you still keep up steam?
> CHIEF: We'll give it a try, sir.
> CAPT. SMITH: Good. We need power for the Marconi instrument. And I want to keep the lights burning as long as possible. If there's a ship coming, she has to see us.

CHIEF: Right, sir.
CAPT. SMITH: I presume you know you may not make it out of here.
CHIEF: Yes, sir. That's the way of it sometimes.
CAPT. SMITH: Good luck.

On all levels, the 1953 *Titanic* is a story of noble self-sacrifice, in most cases with a religious undertone to it. In contrast to more recent *Titanic* films, there is no emphasis on the climax of the disaster, that is, the actual sinking and the rising panic of those who had no chance to survive. While the moments before the sinking are, as in most *Titanic* films, dramatized in a collage of quickly changing shots and mini-scenes, the overall time span between the collision and the sinking is stylized into a sort of parable. The 1953 *Titanic* is not a disaster film: It avoids panic at all costs.

The officers' realization that the ship is mortally wounded is not shown: Everybody seems to know at once that the *Titanic* will sink, and Captain Smith gives this information freely away to Richard (though, of course, with the stereotypical request not to break this news to other passengers). The film setting of these final hours is almost surrealistic: a theatre play staged on the various levels of the ship in neatly choreographed studio pictures. Except for a little commotion in Third Class — caused by the emigrants' lacking knowledge of English and not by outlandish panic — the passengers are perfectly calm. This composure culminates in the highly unrealistic scene before the sinking, with the passengers standing on the various decks and joining in the band's "Nearer, My God, to Thee." The end is merciful — no screaming panic and terrifying last moments as in Cameron's spectacle, but a final strong explosion causing the ship to go down at once. The singing stops and is followed by silence; there was no way that the stoic passengers would scream and shout in the icy water. This ending is not meant to be realistic: The period between the collision and the sinking is turned into a vehicle for reconciliation and thus for a solution of all conflicts, leading to a quasi-religious finale. With the collision as turning point — God's inscrutable will rather than His judgment — the story turns into a parable for exemplary behavior when destiny strikes. This stylization is, of course, strongly linked to the *Titanic* myth: The strong religious current of the film is inseparably bound to the notion of Anglo-Saxon superiority, exemplarily displayed by Richard's behavior (which is doubled by the composure of John Jacob Astor and the Straus couple) and the remaining passengers' affirmation of faith in the final scene.

The sinking is an act of God's supreme power, and paradoxically, it enables a happy though tearful end. Indeed, this film does not raise the question of fault and human error, although there is a half-hearted attempt at emphasizing the motif of the *Titanic* running at full speed.[10] Since the collision

Titanic (1953): Hollywood's sinking of the *Titanic* resembles a studio stage setting (Twentieth Century Fox).

and the sinking are indispensable to lead the main plot to a satisfying solution, they are presented as destiny and, in the final moments, handed over to the care of God.

The Subplots and Their Relation to the Main Plot

An analysis of the subplots and their relation to the main plot reveals the mastery of the script. Every subplot is linked to the main plot in a specific way, with the individual characters reflecting or contrasting the main characters Julia and Richard:

Subplot	Function	Theme	Character development

Annette and Giff	— romantic interest
	— Annette as
	 a) illustration of
	    Julia's assertions
	 b) parallel to Richard's
	    development
		love
		true values
		redemption
			coming of age (Annette)
			= conversion to true values
			= finding her true identity

Subplot	Function	Theme	Character development
Norman	positive parallel to Richard	honesty tragedy	coming of age
Priest	reflection of Richard's development	redemption	rediscovery of identity
Maude Young	positive counter-image to Julia (and to Richard)	straightness	—
Earl Meeker	counter-image to First Class passengers	hypocrisy	—
Basque family	instrumental in Richard's development	simplicity	—

The most conspicuous subplot is the love story between Annette and Giff, which supplies the romantic interest. In the case of Annette, the development is a coming of age — and, concomitantly, strong publicity for true American values. In the beginning, she indeed is the "arrogant little prig" her mother declares her to be, greeting an American (and thus English-speaking) friend on the tender in perfect French and ridiculing Giff as he displays his interest in her. Her haughtiness quickly begins to crumble, though: Feeling guilty about having taken her decision against her mother, she gracefully grants Giff a single dance to please Julia. As is to be expected, obligation quickly turns into pleasure. The next scene with Annette and Giff reveals that the roles have been switched. Now it is Giff with his 100 percent American attitude who is superior, and it is Annette who is feeling embarrassed, because she clearly does not know anything about contemporary American culture:

> ANNETTE: I guess it's of no importance, but I wanted to tell you something about last night.
> GIFF: No need to. You danced with me four times. That's more than I figured on.
> ANNETTE: No, I mean the way I walked off without saying anything. It wasn't very adult of me, and I believe in being adult.
> GIFF: Forget it. You did your bit, only I kind of figured you were having a good time.
> ANNETTE: To be frank, I was!
> GIFF: So you left me standing right in the middle of the floor?
> ANNETTE: That's just it! I didn't know what to do when the orchestra started playing that funny dance! What do they call it?
> GIFF: The Navajo Rag?
> ANNETTE: That's the one. I'd never heard it before.
> GIFF: Never heard it before? Where have you been? Locked up in some art gallery? Why, that's the hottest jig the kids do!

5. Titanic (1953)

Annette's haughty European superiority is turned into embarrassing backwoodness. The refined American young lady, in her element at a dinner with the Metternichs, has no clue what "the kids do" in the land of progress — but she is hungry to learn, and learn she does quickly. Giff teaches her the Navajo Rag right on the ship's deck, and her heart melts. Shortly before the collision, a parallel scene then doubles the famous dance scene on the deck: Annette joins the American students in their singing and painfully realizes that she does not know any of their songs, which stand for vigorous American joy of living — a double contrast both to Annette's upper-class education and to the impending disaster. Thus, Annette makes visible what Julia asserts in her arguments with Richard: Encrusted European culture is going down, and the future lies in the simple, straightforward life of the American middle class. This illustrative function is supplemented by a dynamic function: Annette's development, which is both a coming of age and a discovery of her true identity, runs parallel to Richard's development. In a way, Annette, too, is redeemed, namely from getting lost in a dying, obsolete, non–American culture.[11]

Giff, in contrast, is a stereotypical figure with no character development: He, the young tennis star (a conflation of two well-known tennis players on board the *Titanic*, who traveled First Class and survived the disaster[12]), is the paragon of young American vigor, and his cultural "superiority" is never questioned. Since his brashness at the Sturgeses' arrival is counterbalanced by a later scene with Julia on deck, where Giff displays exquisite courtesy and good manners, he does by no means appear as an uncouth counter-image to Annette's European refinement. Instead, he represents sound American virtue, exactly the "nice boy" Julia desires for her daughter. Of course, Giff does survive, by the stock dramatic device for young men getting honorably saved from the *Titanic*: While helping to untangle the ropes of a lifeboat — in a dangerous stunt, of course — he falls down into the boat, gets injured and thus saves both his life and his honor as a gentleman. He and Annette will be reunited on the *Carpathia*: The perfect young American couple survives, while *Titanic* goes down with old Europe.

The significance of this main subplot is seen in the script's structure. The proportions of the award-winning script are classic: a three-act structure with the first climax being the dramatic revelation that Norman is not Richard's son. This climactic moment leads into the development of the second act with its increasing momentum. The two focus points in this act are also clearly seen and relate to the overall development: On the one hand, Richard decides to disown Norman, on the other the collision takes place, which then leads to the climactic moment of truth, the melodramatic reconciliation of

Julia and Richard, immediately followed by their separation. The third act is a dense accumulation of events: Norman stepping out of the lifeboat, people getting separated (and, in case of those remaining on the ship, condemned to death), the redemption of the priest, Giff being saved, Richard acknowledging Norman — and then the sinking as the final climax. It is remarkable that the halfway point — or point of no return — approximately at the middle of the script is *not* part of the main plot, but a decisive moment in the main subplot: Having finally won Annette's heart, Giff tosses his cap overboard with a whoop — a moment of overwhelmed joy. His cap lands in the water between chunks of ice. Thus, Giff's love and zest for life are juxtaposed, without his knowing, by the image of impending death. A remarkable moment of dramatic irony, and indeed a point of no return: While the relationship between Annette and Giff is developing towards consummation, the ship bearing them steams towards disaster.

The other subplots are less elaborate; after all, they do not have to supply the indispensable love interest. Norman is a young and innocent variation on Richard's development. Like Richard, he does turn into a man, though it is clear that he should have remained the child he is and have saved his young life. However, Norman is the essential catalyst for the main plot: He spins off the decisive development in the relationship between Julia and Richard (from shock and rejection to final reconciliation), and he takes Richard's development to perfection, prompting him with his noble gesture of self-sacrifice to overcome his ridiculous wounded male ego and to set his priority on true love and loyalty instead. Without Norman, Richard's development would have been incomplete.

The defrocked priest George Healey, in contrast, reflects Richard's story of redemption in a much darker hue, but at the same time emphasizes its religious side. There is not much of a character development, since Healey simply switches from a drunken loser into a responsible man. He rediscovers his identity at the moment of disaster. At least, he is good for some of the film's most intelligent repartees. When Richard leaves the Smoking Room right after the collision and meets the priest on deck, Healey points the iceberg out to him:

>   RICHARD: Did we hit it?
>   HEALEY: No, sir. It hit us.

After the first mighty boiler explosion, coughing stokers come up from the engine room. Healey asks if there still are men down there. When one of the stokers confirms this, Healey brushes past him to go down:

>   STOKER: For God's sake, mister, don't go in there!
>   HEALEY: For God's sake, I am going in.

The other minor characters are even less developed: They are stock characters standing for fixed attitudes and thus, in a way, representing the microcosm of the *Titanic* in this otherwise so First Class–oriented film. However, they still have their functions in the development and elaboration of the main plot.

Maude Young, representing the historical character of "Molly" Brown, lines up perfectly with the needs of the script. Having developed into a "symbol of a triumphant nation"[13] since the 1930s, "Molly" Brown alias Maude Young incarnates the values Julia so clearly advocates. Although Julia with her refined attitude would probably not display her Americanness so brashly, Maude in fact is what Julia stands for: A woman with sound virtues, straightforward, upright and firm in her values. Like Julia, she has masculine character traits: At first, in the role of a persistent card player (highly questionable for a woman according to the code of behavior), and then, of course, by her usual *Titanic* attribute of being the strong lady in Lifeboat 6. At the same time (again like Julia), she does display somewhat motherly feelings, though hidden under her tough outside. Thus, she does not hesitate to confront Richard with hard words when he sends crestfallen Norman away: "He certainly clouded up. A word'll do it faster than a hickory stick any time." Primarily, however, she stands for persistence and unsinkable strength: Historically famous, she keeps the spirits up in Lifeboat 6, induces the other women to keep warm by rowing — and even uncovers the notorious coward Earl Meeker, who has saved his life by dressing up like a woman. This is, of course, the historical legend of the First Class coward cheating himself to a place in a lifeboat; in reality, it was two young Third Class passengers who spontaneously used their chance of being taken for women due to some clothing around their head, and it was certainly not Margaret Tobin Brown who uncovered their "fraud." Though Maude Young alias "Molly" Brown displays the stereotypical brashness, she does also incarnate an important issue of the film, namely sound American virtue, which can be displayed by women just as well as by men, as long as they have grown up in the healthy surroundings of an American middle-class home.

Earl Meeker is another stereotype, not so much of the *Titanic* myth, but generally in literature and theater: the cowardly upstart, who seeks his own advantage only in whatever situation. In his pursuit of influence and riches, he is a counter-image to the entire First Class: He lacks the nobility and character of a John Jacob Astor (with whom he tries to ingratiate himself), he has none of Richard Sturges' social grace, he has none of the self-confidence and firm standpoint of Maude Young alias "Molly" Brown. Generally in drama, this archetype is used as a foil to give the main characters a stronger profile; in the 1953 *Titanic*, he is conveniently used for the image of the coward in the lifeboat.

The third subplot using characters as a foil for the main characters is the fate of the Basque family. They are instrumental in Richard's development: At Cherbourg, they are used to display his arrogance and disdain for lower class foreigners; in the course of the voyage, Richard can at least show that he is a man of honor, true to his word, preparing the promised estate agreement for Mrs. Uzcadum to sign—and in the end, the poor family serves to show that he takes responsibility, even under extreme circumstances, making sure that the entire Basque family is saved even *before* he seats his own family in a lifeboat. As mere means and foil for the development of the main character, the family is not given a story of their own. They offer the stereotypical image of Third Class simplicity and credulity, nothing more.

The Third Class passengers thus are used as a mere staffage in this film, not even with a minor plot allowing some characterization and development. The same applies to the crew. They represent the stereotype of dutiful officers, with Captain Smith giving quite a literal representation of the legend that developed around the real captain after the sinking: stoical, restrained, dutiful, a man of inner nobility. His insistence upon full speed is taken up as motif, yet it is not directed against him as a reproach. This does, in fact, reflect the historical assessment of his conduct as captain in the 1912 inquiries. In the 1953 film, he as captain is singled out quite naturally amongst the officers (accordingly, his role was filled by film star Brian Aherne), but there is one more detail in the film that underlines his character and his personal tragedy. Right at the opening of the film, Captain Smith receives a parcel with an old, scraggly British ensign, reminding him of his first voyage. The ensign is hoisted—an image both of Smith's adherence to good old seafaring tradition and to his Britishness. This little detail arches the entire film: In the moment before the sinking, just as the orchestra begins to play the hymn, the ensign is shown fluttering in the night. It does not matter that this is one more of the many factual errors in the film: The meaning of this shot is symbolic, showing the decline of old, traditional England, while the American virtues—so strongly promoted throughout the film—survive. And this detail is linked to the religious theme: Like the passengers singing "Nearer, My God, to Thee," the British ship dies with dignity, holding up its banner until the last moment. As a whole, the crew members are depicted as the little heroes of the background story: efficient officers, loyal musicians, and the engineers stoically accepting their fate. They are there to provide the infrastructure for the First Class setting, in which the real drama unfolds.

The same is to be said for the historical characters: the Astors, the Wideners, and the Strauses are used to display the Sturges family's status and cosmopolitanism, no more. However, the screenwriters deftly used some of the motives offered by the historical *Titanic* story to anchor their fictional characters in the background story. As mentioned above, the First Class tennis stars, who are reflected in young and healthy Giff Rogers, the gamblers in the Smoking Room, who are functionalized as a means for Richard to take demonstrative distance from his family, Father Thomas Byles, who is reproduced in a varied version in Catholic priest George Healey, praying with the most helpless victims just before the sinking. Not least, there is also the motif of the boy who decided to stay on the sinking ship because he wanted to be taken as a man: Alfred "Alfie" Rush from Kent, traveling Third Class, had turned 16 on the very day of the sinking. When he was offered a chance to go with the women, he declined, preferring to stay with the men.[14] Norman is just 12, but the long trousers motif in the film displays his ardent desire of being counted as a "man"— and consequently, he stays and dies.

Thus, despite its entirely fictional main plot and despite its multitude of anachronisms and factual errors, the 1953 *Titanic* is closer to the historical event than one would expect. The most notorious error of the film, by the way, was not caused by ignorance or lack of sense for continuity: Of course, the ship was hit on the starboard side, and in the film it is also approaching the iceberg in the correct way. Simon Mills explains why the iceberg then, illogically, is seen cutting into the ship's port side:

> Whilst cutting together this particular sequence the editors found themselves having to perpetrate a subtle but significant historical alteration in order to get themselves out of a hole. The problem stemmed from the fact that for the entire film the *Titanic* had moved across the screen from right to left, and when it came to filming the collision sequence it was technically impossible to match the wide angle shot of the *Titanic* moving along the base of the iceberg with the underwater shot of the iceberg tearing the gash in the hull. If the filmmakers had abided by the historical facts then, for the few seconds that the underwater shot was on the screen, the hull would have had to move from left to right in order to correctly show the starboard side. While this may have been historically correct, in filmmaking terms it would have been totally unacceptable because it would have interrupted the flow of the sequence, and so the producers simply took license and filmed the iceberg slicing into the port side of the hull instead.[15]

Later *Titanic* film producers, with their increasing fetishism of authenticity, would never have allowed this blatant deviation from reality — but in 1950s Hollywood, film art was still allowed to dominate over (attempted) authenticity.

Music, of course, is another point of disagreement. The end with all the passengers singing "Nearer, My God, to Thee" is anything but realistic. But it is not meant to be so. As shown above, the final hours of the *Titanic* are conceived like a parable, resolving the tensions and leading to redemption.

The general resignation into God's will is part of this parable; again, the script takes up an important aspect of the *Titanic* myth and uses it to its own ends. This symbolic function of the final hymn is underlined by the general use of music: Strikingly, this high-strung melodrama does not use music — highly unusual for the genre at this time. No sweeping violins to underline Annette and Giff's first kiss, no thundering brass to intensify the dramatic moments of the collision and the sinking. The score of the 1953 film is characterized by silence. After the opening credits, leading with a fanfare into the opening image of the *Titanic* at sea, there simply is no music, except for the diegetic music of the *Titanic*'s band (which, fictitiously, is a large orchestra with a wind and brass section). Only at one point does non-diegetic background music underline the dramatic development: As the iceberg is spotted, high violins set in and keep their shrill tension throughout the entire collision scene, becoming so intense that they eventually sound like an alarm. The rest is silence. But this silence only regards music: A fictitious alarm overtakes the role of the dramatic score — a repetitive, increasingly enervating alarm signal, anachronistic and disturbing. This device may have been influenced by the German 1943 film, which had a similar, un-authentic alarm signal going on throughout the manning of the lifeboats. At the same time, it is a targeted dramaturgical technique: The alarm signal is used in film to catch the audience's attention and make them aware of impending danger, etching into the spectator's consciousness.[16]

The use of sound and music indeed is remarkable. The silence throughout the film, but especially after the collision, is eerie; there is no music to lull us into the melodrama of the plot. In this point, director Jean Negulesco negated the convention of the genre, and thus makes the drama displayed much more intense. Even the solemn hymn, played by an entire orchestra, is diegetic, although it helps to turn the sinking into a metaphysical scene of redemption. After the sinking, in the epilogue showing the lifeboats drifting between icebergs, the hymn is taken up again, and this time it is turned into the grand musical sweep that has been missing throughout. Generally, though, music is relinquished in this drama, and by this, the drama of personal relations appears to be intensified.

As Steven Biel shows in his cultural historical analysis, the myth of the *Titanic* is essentially conservative. Modernity is checked, hubris is punished, traditional values prevail. This is entirely in line with the point of the 1953 *Titanic* script: The traditionalist view on gender roles, on American national superiority and the recommendation of sound middle-class values, all this imbued with a strong religious spirit, link up perfectly with the *Titanic* myth. The 1953 film perfectly matches Biel's general description of the myth as a moral lesson:

Since manliness and character were synonymous, the disaster was seen as a transformative moment in which luxury and effeminacy were simultaneously stripped away and the "true" nature of things was restored.... The *Titanic* destroyed veneers, brought men back to elemental reality, showed in the face of death how life ought to be lived. It also demonstrated the compatibility of Christianity and masculinity. ... Representing the first-cabin passengers as, in their final hour, men of Christian character made modernity more palatable by demonstrating the durability of older values. ... Part Christian conversion narrative and part knightly adventure story, the conventional version of the disaster provided closure by showing how the ruling class redeemed itself when put to the test and, more broadly, how modernity was traditional after all.[17]

It is almost uncanny: The Hollywood story of the early 1950s corresponds exactly to what Biel extracted from 1912 sermons on the disaster. Had American society, whose values are so clearly reflected in the telling tales of popular culture, retained its traditional course throughout forty years and two World Wars? As Biel deducts from the representation and treatment of the disaster in 1912 publications, sermons and retellings, the story of the *Titanic* was turned into a tale of redemption — a parable of the natural goodness of class, racial, ethnic and gender hierarchies.[18] This is exactly what the 1953 film presents. The class, ethnic, and gender distinctions are taken as given — the Third Class Basque family gracefully accepts Richard's pressing and derogative remarks about them and their like, the traditional gender roles, as mentioned above, are cemented, and the story to a considerable extent is about redeeming Julia and Richard from the unnatural roles they have assumed. The sinking of the *Titanic* does not upset contemporary society, it puts it back into place — with the mythic hymn sealing the "happy end":

> Where, in some renditions, the fateful collision stands for the underlying tensions of society or civilisation, literally turning upside down a world that was already metaphorically so, here the sinking constitutes the confrontation that puts things the right way up. By the end Julia has prostrated herself before her husband and he has recalled the days when his sexuality was lacking an apparent ambivalence. When death confronts, things are made plain and it is time for women to cry and men to die.[19]

Since this thoroughly conservative interpretation lies at the heart of the *Titanic* myth as it developed right at the moment of the sinking, the 1953 Hollywood film does have much more to do with *Titanic* than is generally believed and accepted.

There is no doubt, though, that this is an all–American version of the tragedy, tailor-made to the taste of Hollywood's audience. In fact, none of the British passengers is in any way highlighted in the script; even the most prominent British characters of the myth, Ismay and Andrews, are missing.

Negulesco's *Titanic* certainly is not meant to vilify the English; they simply do not play a role of their own, which implies, along with the argumentation of the script, that their age is past. This is exemplified by the personal tragedy of Captain Smith, the only British character playing a conspicuous role in the script, with the scraggly ensign as symbol for old England's decline.

Titanic was meant to impress an American audience, and it was conceived as a media event of "titanic" dimensions: TITANIC IN EMOTION! TITANIC IN SPECTACLE! TITANIC IN CLIMAX! TITANIC IN CAST! THE MOTION PICTURE AS OVERPOWERING AS ITS NAME!, as the tagline puts it. Accordingly, Twentieth Century Fox invested quite a lot in the production. Charles Brackett, Richard L. Breen and Walter Reisch were high-profiled screenwriters of their time, and Negulesco was at the peak of his success with Hollywood melodramas and light romantic comedies when he was asked to direct the film.[20] This excellent team was combined with an all-star cast: Barbara Stanwyck (Julia), Clifton Webb (Richard), the young Robert Wagner (Giff), Audrey Dalton (Annette), Richard Basehart (the priest), and Brian Aherne (Captain Smith). In this stylized drama of emotions, each of them quite lives up to their reputation as Hollywood stars. In most scenes, their acting is excellent, if not necessarily to the taste of present-day audiences. But it is classic melodrama they act, and in this genre, their performance is immaculate.

In a way, the 1953 *Titanic* film was a "routine" Hollywood production, focusing on a standard Hollywood theme in the guise of melodrama rather than on the story of the *Titanic* itself. Nevertheless, the film is closely interconnected with central aspects of the *Titanic* myth: the story of the *Titanic* is used for a moral lesson, teaching the conservative values of an American middle-class society with clearly fixed roles of gender, class and nation. The popular art of Hollywood film thus takes up a much older tradition:

> Hollywood movies, against varying backdrops and fantastical landscapes, place the dramas of us all — emotional conflicts, conflicting desires and clashing demands of a prosaic sort — at the centre of their world-view. In providing a context for the playing out of these troublesome realities, cinema takes on the old bardic function of story-telling, allowing us to consider at a grander level the banalities that more usually preoccupy us. In so doing cinema becomes not only entertainment but also a vehicle for moral instruction.[21]

The *Titanic* disaster is both the perfect background and the necessary catalyst for the moral drama of the Hollywood film. The sinking is the watershed where lovers are separated, families are broken up, and in this tragic process, the true values of family life and matrimonial love are rediscovered and reconfirmed. Thus, the 1953 melodrama is much closer to the core of the *Titanic* tale than most viewers believe.

6

A Night to Remember (1958)
The "Real Story"

In today's viewer comments, the 1958 film *A Night to Remember* receives highest praise. Superlatives like "one of the best historical films ever made" or "by far and away the most definitive and honest telling" of the *Titanic* disaster abound.[1] Many viewers draw comparisons with the 1997 Cameron film, almost always to the disadvantage of the latter. Others remark correctly that it is actually not possible to compare the two: large-scale Hollywood epic versus British docudrama, love story versus disaster narrative, color versus black-and-white, and then the stark contrast between the aesthetics and values of two entirely different periods in film history. If there shall be comparison, it makes more sense to compare the 1953 and the 1958 *Titanic* films, since they come from the same period. In their dissimilarity they highlight the fundamentally different approaches to the *Titanic* disaster in film: In the Hollywood production, it is melodrama, love, and family that is the focus; the disaster only offers the background and necessary catalyst for the family tensions to resolve. In *A Night to Remember*, it is the disaster itself that is the focus; the ship is the star.

The Main Plot: The Ship as Star

The trigger and the basis for William MacQuitty's film production was the publication of Walter Lord's 1955 novel *A Night to Remember*. MacQuitty, who as a boy had witnessed the *Titanic*'s launch, made sure to purchase the rights as soon as the British edition came out in 1956, and secured the services of scriptwriter Eric Ambler and director Roy Ward Baker. Based on Lord's novel, the script was from the start conceived as a multi-perspective kaleidoscope focusing on the final hours of the *Titanic*. It is characterized by the same fast pace and multiplicity of ever-changing perspectives that the novel displays — an almost confusing mass of scenes, shots and shortest impressions, adding up to the mosaic of the full-scale disaster. Ambler and Baker took the treasure of details offered by Lord and simply translated it into the medium that already shines through in the book: a highly visual representation of the fateful voyage, in which every detail seems to contribute to a relentless journey towards disaster.

This basis set the stage for an unusual cinematic approach: There is no great love story, there is no one focus besides the story of the *Titanic*. This story (that is, the condensed voyage up to the collision and then, in enlargement, the hours of the sinking), is loosely held together by a few "human threads," but none of the characters in the film dominates so much that they could be called "a star." None except Second Officer Lightoller (Kenneth More) — who, however, is depicted as a paragon of modesty and professionalism and thus not a star, but a lead role, a "*primus inter pares* at best," as producer, screenwriter and director agreed.[2] It is the *Titanic* herself and her tragic story that are the focus of the film.

This restraint in terms of film drama is part of the documentary aesthetics in *A Night to Remember*. It is the aim of this film to show that the disaster is story enough, that it offers more than sufficient emotion for an entire film to work. Thus, the story itself turns into the cinematic "*Titanic* code," both in its line and in its details. The film simply builds on the classic narrative rhythm inherent in the *Titanic* story: from serene innocence via a slow awakening and increasing inquietude to cruel disaster. In the end, resigned peace and silent mourning to the sounds of "Nearer, My God, to Thee." The script is strictly linear. After the first climax, namely the collision (occurring exactly where the first climax in a script with classic proportions should be), the development is episodic throughout, offering as many glimpses into the ship's stratified cosmos as possible.

Realism is at the heart of *A Night to Remember*; it was, in fact, the central issue of the film's marketing campaign.[3] Every means available aims at "authenticity": Lord's documentary novel as basis for the script, with the integration of numerous testimonies of survivors; extensive historical research; experienced advisers such as Fourth Officer Boxhall (who had survived the *Titanic* disaster), an ex-commodore of the Cunard Line, and the late officer Lightoller's son instructing actor Kenneth More how to play his father; the deliberate choice of black and white instead of color; the general documentary style of the entire film. The result is a "truly British film," praised for its unpretentious, restrained style and the overall "rare quality of integrity."[4]

6. A Night to Remember *(1958)*

As Sarah Street underlines, technology plays an important role in the film's aesthetic realism.[5] On the one hand, the ship's stratified spatial organization has become a major asset in this film, reflecting Edwardian class society. This topos in the *Titanic* myth had never been used consequently in film before, although it offers the perfect cinematic means to show the ship as a microcosm of society. Yet earlier films had not used the class issue of the *Titanic* myth much at all, focusing entirely on First Class with — perhaps — a few touches of folksy life in Third Class. In *A Night to Remember*, in turn, class has become the focal theme of the entire script. The *Titanic* with her clearly divided structure was perfect to highlight this issue.

However, the importance of technology is by no means restricted to the structure of the ship. The film convincingly imparts the historical fascination with technical prowess. Thus, the opening scenes expose the *Titanic* in all her grandeur, and throughout the film, there is a remarkably high number of scenes in the engine rooms. A modernistic touch is added as the *Titanic* sets out on her maiden voyage: Instead of sweeping film music, a veritable hooting concert accompanies cross-cut images of the enormous funnels — musique concrète à la *Titanic*. This is not the only place in the film where sound design replaces music: In a way, the film displays a contained homage to technology — the very instance that would become the *Titanic*'s doom. For the omniscient audience, these opening scenes of maritime grandeur have a poignant quality. Just as the bottle breaks in the fictitious christening of the splendid ship, the ship will break as it meets the iceberg on its maiden voyage.

Technology in *A Night to Remember* does have a succinct touch of the grandiose. For all the documentary aesthetics of *A Night to Remember*, spectacle was indeed an issue in the 1958 production. As Street emphasizes:

> Although Walter Lord's book had been a major success, the film relied on the assumption that people still had an insatiable curiosity about how the disaster occurred. As the reviewer in the American magazine *Saturday Review* commented: "A large part of the audience has a passionate interest in just how something happened."[6]

This point is the very secret of the disaster film genre: The climax is the disaster, the tickling moment to see how a tsunami breaks over an entire town, how a tornado whirls up cars and people, how giant rocks rain from heaven as a volcano breaks out. No description on paper can make up for the sensation to *see* and *hear*. This is why the film version of *A Night to Remember*, although so close to Lord's famous novel, had such an impact and somehow sealed the conviction that *all this* had happened on April 14 and 15, 1912, *exactly* as shown in the film.

A Night to Remember is the first film to go into great detail about the sinking. It sets the standard for the films to come: a kaleidoscope of shots and short scenes, offering a comprehensive impression of the disaster in its unfathomable dimension and grandeur. The final agony is set in motion with "Nearer, My God, to Thee." As with many other details in *A Night to Remember*, James Cameron would later adopt the same technique to turn this allegedly final song into a statement of moving humanity: After Captain Smith's release from duty, the musicians end their last piece of light-hearted music, Wallace Hartley courteously bows to them with kind words ("It's the end, boys. We've done our duty. We can go now"), the men turn around to go, Hartley stays, sets the violin to his chin and, all by himself, begins with the (British) tune of the hymn. The musicians turn, hesitate, come back with their instruments, and one by one set in with a harmonization of the tune, until they all play together again. "We can go now," as Hartley said, and so they stay on to play: They have nowhere else to go — except to God. The cellist begins to sing, the hymn turns into a combination of diegetic and non-diegetic music, resounding over the water, stirring those who sit in the boats. Music as a prelude to the final disaster.

And then the end sets in. The ship rises out of the water, Captain Smith has his last moments on the bridge, the bow goes down, the collapsibles are swept away, desperate people rush towards the stern, people fight in the water. Andrews stoically waits in the Smoking Room, water breaks into the First Class dining room, bread loaves fall down, dishes break, people crowd and scream on the stern, the survivors in the lifeboats look on in silent dismay. The stern rises higher and higher, people jump, a falling funnel smashes people in the water, the ship moves relentlessly down. The people in the lifeboats begin to pray, muttering in English, Polish, Hebrew, Swedish. The water comes up to the decks, people scream and cling to anything they can hold on to. And then the *Titanic* disappears, with a cloud of water gushing up.

It is a terrifying sequence, and it really fulfills its function: a many-faceted impression of "how it really was."

The rest, however, is not silence. For the first time in film, *A Night to Remember* takes up an important realistic detail from the historical testimonies: the cries of hundreds dying in the water. According to many witnesses, this great, universal cry, a "cry that clamored for its own destruction" (as described by survivor Lawrence Beesley), was one of the most traumatizing experiences of the night.[7] Second Officer Charles Lightoller would write, "I never allowed my thoughts to dwell on them, and there are some that would be alive and well to-day had they just determined to erase from their minds all memory of those ghastly moments, or at least until time had somewhat dimmed the memory of that awful tragedy."[8] Director Roy Baker was the first to take this

A Night to Remember (1958): For the first time, more realistic scenes of the final moments are offered in a *Titanic* film (Rank Organisation).

traumatic experience up in film and translate it into sound. Thus, in *A Night to Remember* the "star" *Titanic* sinks with the entire outrage of human desperation.

Social Microcosm: Class as Main Theme

The lack of a clear (human) star is a decisive aspect of the film's documentary aesthetics. At the same time, this multi-faceted stance is part of the film's strong focus on class. As Sarah Street emphasizes, *A Night to Remember* deliberately refuses to offer sustained character portraits.[9] In contrast to Lord's novel, there are a few characters who are followed through, but in no case — excepting Lightoller — are they given enough room and attention to really develop into rounded personalities. Instead, they can be regarded as "typages," that is, characters types of little individuality representing a group — in the case of *Titanic*, their respective class.[10] These character types are unmistakably exposed at the beginning of the film; in varying proportion, they can be followed through to the very end:

Type	*Characters*	*Scene*
Crew (professional middle class)	Officer Lightoller with wife	train journey
Short scene in the White Star office, presenting supplies and number of passengers		
First Class	Lord and Lady Richard	departure from a mansion in a coach
Second Class	honeymooners	departure from a prosperous middle-class home in a car
Third Class	Irish emigrants, priest and village people	departure from their village on a horse cart
Crew (professional middle class)	Officer Lightoller with his wife	farewell in Lightoller's home

The film starts with a prologue: the fictitious christening of the *Titanic* followed by the launch. Then the credits are given before a dramatically lighted seascape with equally dramatic music, and then, finally, the real exposition starts, as laid down in the table: a series of small preparatory scenes before the *Titanic* sets out on its voyage, scenes that serve to expose the class system and the "typages" who will represent the various classes and spheres throughout the film. The farewell scenes of the three passenger classes follow in immediate succession; they are clearly devised as vignettes presenting the types, their

6. A Night to Remember *(1958)* 135

standing (mansion — house — cottage; coach — car — horse cart), and their stereotypical surroundings (countryside — town — village; the Irish emigrants are, of course, seen off by a Catholic priest). The exposition of the three classes is framed by two scenes with Second Officer Lightoller, who both represents the crew and the professional middle class. The class types will be followed throughout the film, offering glimpses into the ship's various classes, their locales and their lifestyles. Thus, class is a constant issue throughout.

In contrast to all other films before, First Class fares worst in *A Night to Remember*. This class is represented by an aristocratic English couple, doubtlessly an allusion to Sir Cosmo and Lady Lucile Duff-Gordon, who had to defend themselves in 1912 for having escaped in a lifeboat filled with only a quarter of its capacity and for having prevented the crew members in the boat from turning back to save some of the victims in the water. In *A Night to Remember*, they appear as Sir and Lady Richard, aloof and arrogant. Their contempt for their surroundings is reflected in their servants' cynical remark on the workhouse children who give their lord and ladyship an enthusiastic farewell: "The workhouse kids — making sure of their Christmas turkey from the home farm." Scriptwriter Ambler did not give this couple a personality at all; they only fulfill the function of representing First Class. Correspondingly, the First Class interiors of the *Titanic* are by no means highlighted as much as they are in the other films (although MacQuitty took great pains with excellent sets): They are background, no more.[11] The famous First Class interiors are functionalized: They make a fine foil to highlight Second Officer Lightoller's professional care for the ship and Captain Smith's social interaction with the millionaires. Yet there is no subplot that would give any First Class passenger an individuality. The aristocratic couple in fact appears like a caricature. In his 1943 propaganda *Titanic* film, Joseph Goebbels could well have made use of this stereotype of aristocracy to demonstrate the arrogance of British upper class.

The presentation of Third Class works with stereotypes, too. The poor Irish emigrants, who are so affectionately seen off by their priest and the village community, offer the stock-in-trade *joie de vivre* that has turned into a must for *Titanic* films. There is, of course, a dance scene in the Third Class common room, with the vigorous Patrick Murphy singing "I'm Off to Philadelphia in the Morning," followed by a shy love interest starting to blossom between Patrick and a young Polish emigrant.[12] The focus on the Irish emigrants is new; it will be taken up, just like the stock motifs of folksy music-making, dance and flirtation, in the three major *Titanic* films to come. In the course of the evacuation, the desperate situation in Third Class is highlighted several times. Building on the testimonies of survivors, *A Night to Remember* again sets the matrix for the films to come: A little group finds its illegal way through Second and First Class, another ends at a gate and breaks it open (with a scandalized steward yelling at them), yet the mass is patiently waiting in rising anxiety. At this point, the decent class criticism of the film is underlined: As the crowded Third Class common room is shown, with nervous people waiting at the stairs, dramatic music sets in. The scene is repeated — one of the few moments in the film where film music is used at all. Here, it underlines the desperate situation of those whom nobody cares for. In the end, though, there is a little ray of hope for this lost class: Patrick survives, and so does his Polish girl friend. Is there a future for them?

The most profiled "class type" is the Second Class Clarke couple. That is, middle class and therefore the very class that is the focus of the entire film. The newlyweds are charming, they are in love — and they stay together. With regard to the historical *Titanic* story, the fictitious couple fuses several historical personages: They represent the various honeymooners who were on the *Titanic*, they voice the Straus couple's oath of loyalty, and they reflect the option of those couples on the *Titanic* who did not have a child to care for and therefore could take the decision to stay together till death.[13] The lighthearted couple offers a miniature representation of the *Titanic* story: a splendid outset with brilliant prospects for a happy future, innocent gaiety on the ship, then the shocking realization of the inevitable, finally courageous resignation into God's will, going into death with their heads held high.[14] Young Mrs. Clarke's decision is more tragic than that of Ida Straus: She has yet her entire life before her. Where Ida Straus said, "We have lived together for many years," the honeymooner states, "We started out together"— and then concludes, "and we'll finish together." This is the inner grandness of a young middle-class woman. In the retained emotionality of the dialogue, her composure is presented as the nobility of the modest middle-class people rather than as a rousing theme of love.

These three types, hardly personalized, hardly profiled, are continually cross-cut throughout the film, offering an image of the *Titanic* microcosm. As the crisis begins to mount, however, the class divisions begin to break down, most graphically indicated in the broken gate to First Class. The sinking of the *Titanic* symbolizes the end of clearly structured Edwardian society.[15]

The Ideal of British Middle-Class Virtue

William MacQuitty and Eric Ambler emphasized that their display of the class system was not meant as critique: "We had no political agenda....

6. A Night to Remember (1958)

What I tried to demonstrate was that these class attitudes were accepted by the whole population from top to bottom. It was never an attempt to critique."[16] Nevertheless, *A Night to Remember* does have a distinct political message, reflecting the context of England in the 1950s. It is the middle-class people who are the true heroes of this film. After the traumatic experience of the Second World War, with the British Empire beginning to dissolve and the Cold War tensions menacing England, the *Titanic* disaster represents the downfall of a clearly structured world — and the rise of a new, modest, professional class that was about to become the driving force in the country.[17] Just as in earlier films, the ideological, conservative elements of the *Titanic* myth — chivalry, marriage, religion — all are affirmed, but this time they pertain to the middle class.

The plea for middle-class virtues is personified in the crew, with Second Officer Lightoller as paragon of integrity and reliability. Many of the short scenes in the kaleidoscope of *A Night to Remember* serve to demonstrate the crew's efficiency and conscientiousness. The men in the engine rooms are reliable and courageous, the wireless officers incarnate a self-sacrificing sense of duty, Chief Baker Joughin leaves his place in a lifeboat to a mother who would otherwise be separated from her child, ship architect Andrews from Harland & Wolff is for the first time in *Titanic* films shown as a paragon of dedication and gentleness, and the restaurant staff is singled out by a moving episode during the final moments of the ship, in which the elderly chief waiter protects a little orphaned Third Class boy and affectionately comforts him in the face of death.

It is, however, Second Officer Lightoller who subsumes the ideal of professional middle-class virtue. Lightoller is everywhere. He opens the film, displaying an exquisite sense of humor. Both in social circles (the train compartment) and in his affectionate home, his conduct is flawless, until the very end. There are several historical reasons why Ambler singled out this officer to become the leading character in the *Titanic* tale. According to the testimonies, Lightoller's conduct was unblemished, quite in contrast to some crew members, such as Quartermaster Hichens with his pathetic reign over Lifeboat 6.[18] In both inquiries after the disaster, Lightoller played a central role as witness. And, above all, he was the surviving senior officer and thus ennobled by his rank.

A Night to Remember, though, deletes even the slightest suspicion that Charles Herbert Lightoller might have been interested in rank. In the fictitious farewell scene with his wife, he underlines that he does not at all mind having been graded down to be Second Officer at the last minute, whereas he originally should have been First Officer on the *Titanic*'s maiden voyage.[19] Instead, the scene displays his humor, love and tenderness — the only private scene granted to any of the *Titanic*'s crew members in the film. Lightoller's devotion to his wife will later be hinted at again, as he regards her picture in his bunk. Otherwise, he is the professional man from the ground up. And he is everywhere. It is Lightoller who checks the decks and the lifeboats after change of watch, it is he who reassuringly chats with the First Class passengers (of course firmly rejecting the repeated offer to take a drink), it is he who warns the Smoking Room steward to keep an eye on a known gambler so that the *Titanic* does not "get a bad name." And it is he who is the rock in the increasing turbulence of the evacuation. Everything known about the crew's efforts in saving as many passengers as possible is projected on Lightoller: It is he who is harassed by Ismay's clumsy efforts to help and finally rebukes him with the authority of the expert, it is he who gently forces hesitating ladies into lifeboats, who drags cowardly men out of the boats, who shoots into the air to quell a panic. In all this turmoil, he retains his golden heart: He knows about the inner tragedy of a First Class passenger carrying his little son to a boat, he is dismayed to observe people in hysterical fits, he is stunned as he watches a stoker jump into the water and die, and even as he himself fights in the icy water, he gives orders that help others find their way to a boat. In the end, it is Lightoller who — historically correct — keeps order on the fragile little raft constituted by the upturned Collapsible B. Without his experience as a seaman and his authority as an officer, the two dozen men on this miniwreck would never have survived the night.

It is here in the 1958 film that Lightoller becomes philosophical. Walter Lord's nostalgic musings about the meaning of the *Titanic* disaster are put into his mouth:

> GRACIE: Will that be the *Carpathia*? [*Lightoller nods*] Aren't you glad to see her?
> LIGHTOLLER: Yes, I'm glad. But then I'm still alive.
> GRACIE: If only she'd been nearer.
> LIGHTOLLER: There are quite a lot of ifs, aren't there, colonel? If we'd been steaming a few knots slower or if we'd sighted that berg a few seconds earlier, we might not even have struck. If we'd carried enough lifeboats for the size of the ship, instead of just enough to meet regulations, things would have been different again, wouldn't they?
> GRACIE: Maybe. But you have nothing to reproach yourself with. You've done all any man could and more. You're not ... [*looks up*] I was going to say, "You're not *God*, Mr. Lightoller."
> LIGHTOLLER: No seaman ever thinks he is. I've been at sea since I was a boy. I've been in sail. I've even been shipwrecked before. I know what the sea can do. But this is different.
> GRACIE: Because we hit an iceberg?

6. A Night to Remember *(1958)*

LIGHTOLLER: No. Because we were so *sure*. Because, even though it's happened, it's still unbelievable.... I don't think I'll ever feel sure again. About anything.

According to Lord's famous musings, the sinking of the *Titanic* meant the end of an era, of a better, more secure and more serene age. In the film, it is Second Officer Lightoller who becomes the mouthpiece for this nostalgic interpretation, providing it with an air of "authenticity."

Second Officer Lightoller is the hero of this *Titanic* film. Yet it is part of the film and its message that this hero is modest. No great emotions, no great gestures, no tragic stance. Professionalism and reliability are the key words. A realistic hero in a realistic *Titanic* tale.

And this sort of heroism is entirely British. Besides class, *nation* plays a primary role in *A Night to Remember*. Captain Smith does not exhort the passengers and crew to "be British," as legend has it — but this appeal actually resounds throughout the entire film. Jeffrey Richards regards *A Night to Remember* as "almost a British riposte to Fox's 1953 *Titanic*," referring to the marginal role the American passengers play (with the telling exception of "Molly" Brown).[20] In fact, many of the composite characters (that is, fictional characters that unite several traits of the historical passengers) are depicted as British. Yet it is not a question of individuals being British: It is the British spirit that permeates the film—"a British film made by British artists for a British audience," as director Roy Baker put it.[21]

A Night to Remember is a plea for British values, for the stereotype of a British national character, as seen and defined in the 1950s: sense of humor, sense of duty, stoicism, tolerance, and a sense of individualism that in the war was mitigated by the necessity of a sense for community.[22] In British film, the war experience actually prepared the style of documentary authenticity so typical in the years after the war. Understatement and "authenticity," a focus on "British life and character"—and certainly not melodrama. "Involved rather than spectacular," as Richards puts it in his analysis of *A Night to Remember*.[23] The film was duly praised for its Englishness, its realism and its emotional restraint—which must by no means be confused with a lack of emotion.

Second Officer Lightoller subsumes all the values regarded as British: good nature, decisiveness, an imperturbable sense of duty, and a natural, almost elegant authority. (The fine officer's uniform—a civil uniform and not a soldier's—does help a great deal in this respect.) In the end he is strong and infallibly reliable, visually symbolized in the rustic woolen sweater he wears rather than his uniform. Duty is, in fact, a continuing theme in the film, boosted by the historical facts of the *Titanic* theme: Phillips who remains at his post after he has been released, the musicians, the faithful engineers, and the overall concern of the officers with the burden of command and the responsibility for the ship.

Duty is attenuated by another deeply British characteristic: humor and irony.[24] Lightoller displays his sense of humor in the very first scenes. In fact, the film is infused with humoristic scenes and little ironic shots. Partly, this is dramatic irony, adding little twinges of poignancy: the blessing at the *Titanic*'s christening, the doctor's toast to good health (just before the collision), and the many little shots based on the historical irony of fate, such as the officer on the *Californian* who attempts to learn about telegraphy but does not understand the *Titanic*'s urgent CQD, the waiters in the dining room supposing that the ship has thrown a propeller blade ("We'll be going back to Belfast — you see!"), the football game with ice chunks on the Third Class deck. Or the ironic juxtaposition of four mini-scenes radiating entire peace and innocence: Bruce Ismay asleep; a tongue-in-cheek love affair hinted at in First Class; a beautifully dressed First Class passenger looking tenderly after her children; a rocking horse in the (fictitious) children's playroom. These four vignettes of peacefulness are immediately followed by the collision.

But it is also the fictional repartees that impart a sense of decent British irony. First Class passenger Lucas remarks to Mr. Andrews after he has been informed about the lack of lifeboats: "I take it you and I might both be in the same boat later." Or Chief Engineer Joseph Bell to his fellow engineers, after he has been told that the situation is critical, but they must under all circumstances keep electricity going: "Er, if any of you feel like praying, you'd better go ahead. The rest can join me in a cup of tea." It is this sense of humor, this noble distance to one's self that again underlines the heroism of the common people.

In addition, *A Night to Remember* contains a surprising number of simply humoristic scenes, even in the course of the evacuation. The very opening scene in the train compartment builds on a humoristic twist; it is followed by countless little incidents that make the audience smile — despite the disaster looming over the ship. A special episode is the fate of Chief Baker Charles Joughin. He has been granted a little monument in this *Titanic* film: His miraculous survival, probably helped by a considerable dose of alcohol, is turned into one of the many minor plots of this *Titanic* kaleidoscope. Joughin is made a paragon of common sense, who even in the minutes of the sinking displays a sense of humor and humanity. He does survive, even though he has to stay in the water for a span of time that would have killed other people. This is historically correct. But it is also a cinematic stereotype: In a surprising number of films featuring maritime disasters, it is the cook — usually a humoristic figure — who eventually survives.[25] In the *Titanic* story, it was the chief baker who survived, staying at the very end of the stern until the last moment and then enduring the icy hell of the Atlantic.

The humor in *A Night to Remember* is charming; in its restraint it is deeply moving. A sort of "nevertheless": despite disaster, there is still a determination to smile, a discreet, very British power of endurance.

Gender and Religion

The other dominant aspects of the *Titanic* myth, gender, race, and religion, play a minor, albeit perceptible role. Gender is not focused on in its conflicting relation between male and female. Yet the film does offer an overwhelming endorsement of marriage, as Jeffrey Richards puts it,[26] and thus clearly advocates a traditional model of gender roles. The Lightoller couple is presented as an exemplary relationship between husband and wife, the Second Class honeymooners incarnate the Ida Straus message of loyalty till death, and the Straus couple itself is presented in all their poignancy.

And then there is the Lucas family. Another mini-plot is constituted by a fictitious First Class family which combines aspects of the historical Ryerson family and the young Smith couple. As fictional Robert Lucas hears the truth from Andrews, he calmly explains the situation to his wife and asks her to get their three children ready — of course not letting her know that he himself has no chance to survive. Yet his casual conclusion, "I think we should do what the captain says," takes the message home to her. Her "Very well, Robert" is an example of perfect composure. On the Boat Deck, however, Liz Lucas becomes disconcerted by the hysterical fits of other wives and begins to grasp the true dimension of what is happening. Her sudden decision to stay leads to the quotation of historical passenger Lucian Smith's words, with some fictional elaboration due to the family situation of the Lucas couple[27]:

> ROBERT: My dear, I never expected to ask you to obey me, but this is one time you must. It's only a matter of form for you and the children to go first. Everyone here will be quite safe.
> LIZ: Is that the truth?
> ROBERT: Certainly it is.

A wife has to obey her husband. By 1912, this ancient rule of gender relations had become reduced to a tacit principle, but the *Titanic* situation made it necessary for Lucian Smith to utter these words. In their solemnity, they are gratefully taken up in *A Night to Remember*. Thus, the traditional gender roles are confirmed in the most poignant way.[28]

The solemn endorsement of marriage also contributes to the religious dimension present in *A Night to Remember*. Religion has a consolatory role throughout the film. The script reverberates with "God bless you": Smith's final admonishment to passengers and crew; the poignant — and historical — words of the swimmer, who is denied entry onto the overloaded Collapsible B and thus condemned to die; several instances where prayer is recommended.[29] It is not only "Nearer, My God, to Thee" that accompanies the ship's last minutes, but also the Lord's Prayer, both at the stern and in the lifeboats, as well as prayers uttered in various languages including Hebrew (thus representing even another religion). The penultimate scene of the film is the historical memorial service on the *Carpathia*, which shows the survivors in shock and mourning, and includes a long, fully cited prayer.

The final shot assures the audience that the *Titanic* victims' "sacrifice was not in vain," listing the amendments implemented after the *Titanic* disaster to provide greater safety at sea.[30] Thus, the victims are given the role of martyrs — an attitude that is suggested in Lord's novel and was soon taken up by *Titanic* enthusiasts worldwide.[31] The background music to this shot is an orchestral version of "Nearer, My God, to Thee": a gentle requiem for those who sacrificed their life, making the sea lanes "safe for the peoples of the world."

The end thus gives religious comfort, fully in line with the *Titanic* myth: the tragedy leads to redemption, a gentle resignation into God's will.

Tellingly, the Old Testament aspect of religion in the *Titanic* myth, that is, punishment for hubris, is completely taken back in *A Night to Remember*. On the one hand, there is the distinct admiration for technology, which contradicts the 1912 topos of human hubris as expressed in uncritical confidence in technological progress. Hubris is hinted at once in the opening compartment scene (the *Titanic* is praised as "symbol of man's final victory over nature and the elements"), but then this subject is dropped: Technology is not depicted as problematic in *A Night to Remember*.

On the other hand, the confidence in the *Titanic* being "unsinkable" does not play any role in this film. It is used as a First Class passenger remark for dramatic irony, but not as fatal overconfidence on part of the White Star Line. Thus, the common reproach against Bruce Ismay, which played such an important role both in 1912 and in later film adaptations, has been completely omitted in the British film. In *A Night to Remember*, Ismay is acquitted. There is no word that he would have wanted the *Titanic* to go at high speed in dangerous waters, on the contrary:

Ismay, Smith and Thomas Andrews on the bridge, right before departure
ISMAY: We should arrive, er ... let's see ... Wednesday morning.

6. A Night to Remember (1958) 143

SMITH: Oh, we might do better than that.
ANDREWS (*to Ismay*): Not out for a fast run this trip, are you?
ISMAY: Oh, no, no, no, nothing like that.
ANDREWS: You'll do better when the engines have settled down.
ISMAY: Yeah. [*to Smith*] Naturally, captain, you'll use your own judgment.
    [*Laughs*] I'm just an ordinary passenger on this trip.

An early arrival, which the historical Bruce Ismay (according to several witnesses) had hoped for (he denied this in the inquiries), is not envisioned in *A Night to Remember*. Instead, the utmost priority is safety, as confirmed by Ismay and Captain Smith in the First Class dining room — a beautiful image of responsibility, which unfortunately had nothing to do with the realities of competition in the transatlantic traffic.

Ismay is generally depicted in a favorable light: He leaves the responsibility for the ship to the captain (thus confirming the image he presented at the inquiries: that he was a passenger, nothing more), he is struck as he is informed about the situation after the collision (here, his belief "but the ship cannot sink" is stated at least once, but then he thinks at once practically, referring to the limited number of lifeboats), his clumsy attempts to help are somewhat moving, and in the end, in the lifeboat, his despair is so convincing that the spectator feels sympathy for him. Bruce Ismay is by no means a villain in *A Night to Remember*— he is another tragic character in the general tragedy of the *Titanic*.

The "Titanic *Code*": *Authenticity and Nostalgia*

This attempt to grant justice to historical Bruce Ismay is part of the general aim to show as many perspectives as possible, in a *neutral* vein, focusing entirely on the "authentic." The *Titanic* kaleidoscope of *A Night to Remember* involves — following Lord's novel — as many historical characters and instances as possible. They are by no means all presented by name (in several cases their identity even had to be disguised in order to avoid libel suits[32]), yet they form the fabric of "the real story." They are (almost) all there: the gamblers, the Irish emigrants, "Molly" Brown as comic relief (her name is, however, not given), the Duff-Gordons (alias Sir and Lady Richard), the Straus couple, Benjamin Guggenheim and his valet, Edith Russell and her lucky pig, Thomas W. Stead reading in the Smoking Room, Edith Evans relinquishing her place in a lifeboat. In addition, composite characters are created, uniting traits from historical passengers such as the Ryersons, Smiths and the various honeymoon couples. Conspicuously, though, the American Astor couple is not present.

The crew is equally used as cabinet for authenticity. For the first time in *Titanic* film productions, engineers and stokers are turned into characters; Chief Baker Joughin plays a little role of his own, and several scenes with wireless operators Jack Phillips and Harold Bride presenting various details named in the 1912 inquiries (such as the *Mesaba* ice warning being spiked) set the standard for future *Titanic* films. The officers, however, are sacrificed in order to profile Second Officer Lightoller: They are but supernumeraries and do not have a personality of their own. First Officer Murdoch reacts like a dumbfounded idiot in the moment of the collision and not in the professional way that he historically did, Captain Smith is a rather weak figure, and Chief Officer Wilde is only mentioned once; he does not even figure in person.[33]

The "authenticity" of the characters is supplemented with the "authenticity" of the incidents in the hours of the sinking. Following Lord's matrix, the film integrates countless little episodes that make up the "historical" mosaic of the *Titanic* disaster. For the first time, panic becomes a major issue in a *Titanic* film. Several scenes with hysterically screaming women do in fact distort the historical evidence, whereas the rising anxiety in the Third Class is masterly depicted. As witnessed by Archibald Gracie, who went down with the ship, but then found refuge on Collapsible B, the great mass of the Third Class passengers floods out onto the Boat Deck just when it is too late. For the first time in *Titanic* film productions, *A Night to Remember* depicts how the masses in rising panic flee from the upcoming water to the stern, thus giving a somewhat realistic impression of the human agony in the final minutes of the *Titanic*.

Other scenes help to turn legends into "reality": the jokes about ice in the First Class Smoking Room, the briefing with Thomas Andrews in the chart room, the "gash 300 feet long," the famous issue of the CQD signal and Bride's later suggestion to "try" the new signal SOS, or Jack Phillips's anger about the allegedly stupid wireless operator on the German ship *Frankfurt*.

A new, historical feature: The two other ships that are involved. Together with the *Titanic*, they form a tragic triangle: at the top the *Titanic* in dire straits, in immediate vicinity the *Californian*, whose officers do not understand her cries for help, and, too far away to be in time, the *Carpathia*, whose captain does everything to help the *Titanic*. Were it not for Lord's novel and the film version *A Night to Remember*, the *Californian* and her unfortunate captain Stanley Lord would have been forgotten today. The 1958 film includes this issue for the first time, taking the wonderful opportunity for dramatic irony: watchful officers on a nearby vessel who notice both the rockets and

6. A Night to Remember *(1958)* 145

the queer list of the ship at the horizon, without being able to make sense of the signs; the sleepy captain, who is informed about the white rockets but does (correctly) not interpret them as distress signals; the wireless operator Cyril Evans who has just gone to bed as the CQD of the *Titanic* comes through; and Third Officer Charles Victor Groves who hears the distress signal but is not experienced enough in the Morse code to be able to make sense of it. All these details are historical; in film, they offer the tremendous opportunity to create suspense and irony. Until today, viewers admit that they could not help hoping that the *Californian* would still get the message.[34] Captain Lord, however, was irrevocably made the scapegoat in public perception due to this film — although it is proved that he could in no way have helped the *Titanic*, even if the latter's distress signals had been unmistakable.[35]

The *Carpathia*, in turn, is "the good ship." The film underlines the point that Lord made both in his 1955 novel and in his later publication *The Night Goes On* (1986): Captain Rostron is a paragon of dutifulness and humanity.[36] As he is informed by wireless operator Harold Cottam that the *Titanic* has sent CQD and is sinking, he immediately gives the order to change the course of the *Carpathia*—and only then asks Cottam for a confirmation of the message. In another scene, he gives meticulous orders to prepare everything to take up survivors and to invest every quantum of energy to heighten the speed of his ship; his impatience to help turns into agony. Another new feature in *Titanic* film history is the post-disaster activity on the *Carpathia*. In all films to come, these scenes will be taken up to contextualize the disaster and give the surviving main characters a story to continue.

Thus, with the inclusion of the *Californian* and the *Carpathia*, a more realistic situation of the "night to remember" is given: The *Titanic* was by no means alone in the night of April 14. But again, it was an unfortunate constellation of coincidences and facts that precluded the salvation of some 1,500 people.

The many historical incidents and characters, mostly but short impressions and vignettes, set the standard for all *Titanic* films to come. In *A Night to Remember*, we meet all the motifs that would become stock-in-trade — the "*Titanic* code" in its combination of the historical storyline, individual scenes, and the well-known characters.

The trend-setting function of this code equally applies to the overall atmosphere of the film. As in Lord's novel, the pursuit of "authenticity" is inseparably linked with nostalgia; both elements will from now on become paramount in *Titanic* films. Many little details, both historical and fictional, create a wistful atmosphere: the good-natured gambler, who leaves a message to his sister and answers with a blessing as he is pushed away from Collapsible

B, the half-grown lift boys left to themselves (to die in the sinking), the children's playroom with the rocking horse (in the last shot of the film, it is seen floating in the water, followed by the notorious life buoy with the name "*Titanic*"), and the many scenes with little, common people, whose sense of duty, loyalty and courage in the face of death turns into a poignant plea to remember the countless forgotten heroes of this great disaster.[37] In its restrained emotion, its deep seriousness combined with a decent sense of humor, *A Night to Remember* offers a deeply moving version of the *Titanic* tale. The film translates Lord's nostalgia for a better world into emotion without melodrama, thus giving the impression of a better world that really existed and went down with the *Titanic*.

A Night to Remember is a master narrative, and it was used as such by every single director who would later accept the challenge to tackle *Titanic*. The narrative technique is indeed impressive. It is amazing how much information is conveyed within single shots and mini-scenes: The film achieves a dramatic density that would remain unequaled in later *Titanic* films. It is the art of the casual, of dramatic irony, and of perfect pacing. Igenlode Wordsmith summarizes this feat of *A Night to Remember* in a concise way:

> One of the most impressive things about this film is the almost flawless way in which large amounts of information are conveyed — and vast numbers of characters introduced — without any sense of strain or visible exposition. The *Titanic*'s colossal size and provisioning requirements, her status as a national icon of pride, the proportions and variety of her passenger list, all are mentioned naturally and concisely within the first few minutes; the characters on the whole are not established by name, but only by role....
> But the great art of this film lies in its use of tiny, effective details to conjure atmosphere or to make a point. A toy pig grabbed: a jewelry-box abandoned. A wry line of dialogue: "Anyone who feels like it can pray — or you can all come and have a cup of tea." A lapping rim of black-scummed water at the foot of the companionway. A hand silently slipping from its death-grip on an upturned keel... Within its emotional compass, the picture seldom or never puts a foot wrong. Every point is made quietly, by implication, not hammered into the audience, and is all the more telling for that. The mood shifts very gradually from the humour and optimistic warmth of the voyage opening to the clawing terror of the ship's last moments and the icy drained dark of the night; the pacing is almost perfect. The film need not be a moment longer, and could scarcely last a moment less. It draws upon the greatest traditions of British cinema — the documentary, the intelligent script, the ensemble cast, the emotional intensity — and in many ways encapsulates them all.[38]

Critical reception in England was enthusiastic.[39] *A Night to Remember* was praised for its authenticity, its documentary realism, its truly literary quality, its decent sense of humor, and its fine representation of the characters. In the U.S., reception was more mixed: American audiences missed the melodrama they were used to, rejecting the docudrama format of the film. Critics nevertheless acknowledged its achievement: *A Night to Remember* was awarded the 1958 Golden Globe Award in the category Best English Language Foreign Film.

In general, though, its reception reflected the differences in how the *Titanic* story was treated and how its myth was translated in the 1953 and 1958 productions. While the 1953 *Titanic* offered a grand-scale Hollywood melodrama, *A Night to Remember* is the truly *British Titanic* film. Due to its excellent quality and its ardent adherence to "authenticity" and realism, it created a code for the *Titanic* films to come. Producing a *Titanic* film was no longer thinkable without a close look at *A Night to Remember*.

7

S.O.S. Titanic (1979)
Great in Detail, Weak in Plot

The American television production *S.O.S. Titanic* (director: William Hale) ambitiously continues what was started with *A Night to Remember*: a minute-to-minute reconstruction of the *Titanic* story, using as many historical passengers and incidents as possible. This time, however, it is the entire voyage that is covered and not just the decisive hours between the collision and the sinking.

This is not the only difference, though: In *A Night to Remember*, the focus remains on the ship, and there is only a very restrained attempt to provide additional fictional details for the lives and personalities of the historical characters. *S.O.S. Titanic*, in contrast, shifts the focus and develops the personal stories of the passengers. The result is a television drama with invented relations and details about the passengers, turning some of the historical characters into soap opera–type protagonists whose lives are highlighted on the canvas of a disastrous event. *S.O.S. Titanic* appears as a hybrid between a docudrama and a multi-plotted television drama, constructed out of the ingredients offered by the *Titanic* code. Dramatically, the result is unconvincing. At the same time, *S.O.S. Titanic* gives insight into an unequaled wealth of *Titanic* details, covering more aspects of the ship, its spaces and its people than any other *Titanic* film, with many impressive, poignant, and even humoristic moments. It offers the *Titanic* code, exploited to its fullest, and in its original version, it indeed is a pleasure to watch.

The Frame Structure and Its Significance for Characterization

It is amazing how much a film can change if some of its scenes are shifted around. *S.O.S. Titanic*, the first film to depict the *Titanic* disaster in color, exists in two versions: the original 150-minute television version, broadcast as a mini-series on ABC in September 1979, and a 103-minute theatrical version shown in Australia and various European countries in 1980–81; the latter is available as DVD and sometimes broadcast on cable television up to today. The original television version is longer — but, more importantly, it tells a different story. Instead of just cutting a few scenes and shots to make the story more concentrated, the producers shifted some of the central episodes and thus changed the entire focus of the film.

The shorter theatrical version offers the usual, linear *Titanic* storyline, sometimes embarrassing in the attempt at providing comic relief, sometimes bland as to the depiction of historical characters and their love interests. The original television version, in contrast, is based on an unusual perspective, never before used in film: the experience and recollections of J. Bruce Ismay, director of the White Star Line, whose life was destroyed by the *Titanic* disaster, although — or rather because — he survived.

In order to focus on this perspective, the linear narrative was broken up in the original television version: Scenes on the *Carpathia* constitute a framework into which the retrospective narrative of the *Titanic*'s aborted voyage is inserted as a flashback initiated by Ismay's desperate musings. The large amount of time taken up by the voyage does, of course, give the film the usual character of the traditional *Titanic* narrative. However, the comparison between the linear stock-in-trade narration (as offered by the theatrical version of *S.O.S. Titanic*) and the original television version (available on YouTube only) shows how important the use of the *Carpathia* scenes as a framework for the *Titanic* narrative is: To start with the tragic end supplies some of the main characters shown in the main narrative with an emotional depth that they do not have in the linear theatrical version.

It is the representation of Bruce Ismay and Madeleine Astor that mainly profits from the dramatic device of starting with the end. The plot of *S.O.S. Titanic* sets a certain focus both on the director of the White Star Line and on the Astor couple. In the shortened, linear version of the film it is conspicuous — at least to *Titanic* experts — that Ismay is not depicted as the arrogant capitalist (as in the 1943 film and the two *Titanic* films of the 1990s). Both in accordance with the data from the 1912 inquiries and his depiction in *A Night to Remember*, *S.O.S. Titanic* offers a balanced view of Ismay's role and behavior on the *Titanic*.

Thus, it is Captain Smith and not Ismay who decides that speed will not be reduced despite the ice warnings:

> *Captain Smith shows Ismay the ice warning from the* Baltic *in presence of other officers.*[1]

ISMAY: You have any plans to alter speed or course?
SMITH: I never have in the past. The position as you know is the same as with every large ship sailing this route. So long as the weather is clear and visibility good — full speed ahead. Put the days behind you as rapidly as possible. I have lived by that and never encountered the slightest difficulty. Uh, have you anything in mind different, uh, for the *Titanic*?
ISMAY: Certainly not. I and the company have always had utmost confidence in your judgment. Of course we should be sorry not to arrive in New York on schedule — but please, carry on as if I weren't even on board!

Though Ismay is — at least rhetorically — given a word to say in the matter, he relinquishes meddling with the captain's decision. Interestingly, the shortened theatrical version clearly underlines the issue of speed by intercutting the kaleidoscope of scenes on board with repeated shots of the engine room, featuring an open boiler hatch and the signal "Full," that is, "full speed ahead." These intermittent shots are almost completely missing in the original television version; it is only immediately before the collision that the "Full" sign is twice shown as dramatic contrast to the joyful party in Third Class. Instead, the original version puts the emphasis on fate in form of superior, indifferent nature by intercutting several times the ominous image of icebergs at night, underlaid with a menacing drone and the icy sound of wind.

Thus, in *S.O.S. Titanic* blame is taken away from Ismay, offering a more friendly portrayal of the White Star president instead. In addition, Ismay is shown as a man deeply disturbed by the catastrophe, a man trying to help where he can — and eventually failing in his double role as responsible director and simple passenger. This dilemma reflects Ismay's strategy of defense in the 1912 inquiries: It was of utmost importance to him and his company that he had been "a passenger only" and in no way meddled with the navigation of the *Titanic*. In *S.O.S. Titanic*, this professional dilemma is translated into a personal predicament, bestowing sympathy on a man who has been shown entirely broken at the beginning of the film, with his words and behavior corresponding to the historical documentation. It is obvious from the last scene granted to him that he is on the verge of insanity. This is underlined by an uncanny, somewhat perturbed theme in the violins played in connection with the first menace of ice, the *Carpathia* rescue scenes featuring Ismay and, tellingly, at the very moment he realizes that he is no more than a helpless passenger in the face of disaster.[2]

Without the framework on the *Carpathia*, this generally positive characterization is much weaker. Only *Titanic* connoisseurs will realize that the negative facets of the stock-in-trade characterization of Bruce Ismay are missing. In the original television version, in contrast, his positive depiction is programmatic. It is Ismay who turns out to be the focal character in the intro-

7. S.O.S. Titanic *(1979)*

S.O.S. Titanic (1979): "FULL" speed ahead as visual leitmotif to create suspense before the collision (EMI Films).

ductory sequence on the *Carpathia*, and it is he who opens up the flashback onto the voyage, with an explicit indication that his recollections lead us back to the splendid outset of the *Titanic*. However, the focus does not lie on Ismay right from the start: Only after the *Carpathia* has reached the position of the sinking and the first, haggard survivors have boarded the vessel, is it Ismay who eventually becomes the central person that creates the link to the *Titanic*'s splendid past. As the *Carpathia* plows through the water, having taken course towards New York, Ismay stands alone on the deck, refusing all help and comfort offered by the ship surgeon. On the brink of insanity, he points out something in the water. The doctor's appeasing answer, "It's only a bit of flotsam, sir ... a few deckchairs by the look of it," sets off a process of thought and remembrance in Ismay:

> *Camera closing in larger and larger on Ismay's face.*
> ISMAY (*helplessly*): That's all....
> SURGEON: All I can see, sir.
> ISMAY: [*long pause*] A few chairs. All that beauty. All that strength. Power. Grace. [*chuckles almost insanely*] A few chairs! [*chairs are shown floating on the water*] So much gaiety.
> *Sudden transition into the main narrative:*
> *Brilliant band music sets in, the Grand Staircase on the* Titanic *is shown; the long flashback begins.*

After this introduction in the television version, it is not surprising that Ismay as privileged passenger on the *Titanic* is depicted more sympathetically than in other *Titanic* films: It is *his* recollections that are represented in the main narrative. The opening sequence of the main narrative is created through Ismay's mind: We see him proudly presenting the luxuries of the *Titanic* to his wife and son, chatting amiably with Thomas Andrews and John Jacob Astor. In these casual scenes he is presented as a happy, cordial, rightfully proud man; a gentleman at the peak of his fine career.

The narrative frame is not that narrow, though: Ismay's recollections immediately mingle with numerous other scenes on board the *Titanic* that he himself cannot have witnessed. Thus, in seamless transition from personal recollection to cinematic narrative, we get a kaleidoscope of narrative strands and insights into the various spheres of the ship. Nevertheless, the introduction shapes our understanding of the film: The *Titanic* story is entangled with the fate of a tragic person, based on the scarce reliable facts and on Ismay's own testimony at the inquiries. That Ismay is shown as a man who loves life, who enjoys the beauty of his ship, who laughs and dances with the other passengers and then breaks down completely in the course of the disaster bestows credibility and a specifically poignant note upon this representation of an historical character who all too often has been misused to supply film scripts with the desired part of an arrogant, unscrupulous villain.

Ismay is not the only protagonist who is turned into a more rounded character than usual due to the opening of the film with the scenes on the *Carpathia*. The first survivor to dare step out and climb the ladder to the deck of the *Carpathia* is Madeleine Astor.[3] It is she who is taken up by an officer and, upon his question about the *Titanic*, utters the single word, "Gone." Since the opening sequence combines both the first call for help received by the *Carpathia* in the middle of the night and then the early-morning arrival at the position of the sinking, without any trace of the ship that Captain Rostron expected to meet, Madeleine Astor officially seals the *Titanic*'s fate at the outset of the film.

With this tragic opening, the characterization of Madeleine Astor is put into a more positive light than in the linear theatrical version. In the main part of the film she appears to be a naïve, childish person, somewhat unsuccessfully trying to convince her husband of her deeply felt love for him. John Jacob Astor and his young wife are the couple who most consistently represents the First Class in *S.O.S. Titanic*. Screenwriter James Costigan — rather unsuccessfully — tried to imbue the famous couple with a shade of tragedy due to the social scandal Astor's divorce and remarriage had caused. Thus, the Astor scenes in the main narrative focus on the repeated reassurance of their love for each other, with Madeleine appearing as the innocent and helpless young wife who suffers from the social contempt her husband is exposed to. For the most part, the Astor scenes are simply embarrassing. The tragic end in the theatrical version does not help much to counterbalance this impression, which has been built up throughout the entire film. The original version, in contrast, opening with Madeleine as victim and involuntary harbinger of horrible loss of life, does set her into a more sympathetic light, providing dramatic irony in every scene during the voyage where she innocently enjoys life and love at the side of her husband.

In the original version, Madeleine also has the last word: Her answer to the well-meant, yet useless comfort that *Carpathia* passenger Mrs. Ogden tries to offer (again, an historical fact) is, "No coffee. No God either. God went down with the *Titanic*"—and these are the last words of the film.[4] At the same time, they offer the final comment on the floating deck chairs that are shown once again as the last traces of the *Titanic* and her passengers. In a way, the fate of the *Titanic* means a coming of age of the naïve millionaire wife. In contrast to James Cameron's Rose, though, Madeleine does not travel towards a new, liberated life and a land of opportunities, but towards an unknown fate without the man she had loved.

Strictly Historical: The Representation of the Various Social Spheres

Within the narrative framework, the main narrative, unfolding on the four-day voyage, adds many more strands to the plot. The most interesting aspect of this *Titanic* film is that it offers ample insight into spheres of the ship that have been ignored so far in *Titanic* filmmaking. All classes as well as various spheres within the crew are given their own little scenes, and some of them are represented with plots of their own. For the first time, some of the historical stewardesses step out of the historical canvas with a personality of their own; for the first time, invisible servants such as the boot cleaners are shown at work. It is not only the three-class structure, but indeed the comprehensive microcosm constituted by the ship that is depicted in countless little shots and scenes. Altogether, the social and professional structure of the *Titanic* is reconstructed in more detail than in any other *Titanic* film.

Most strikingly, an important strand harks back to the 1912 book by Second Class passenger Lawrence Beesley, who plays a role as one of the main characters in *S.O.S. Titanic*. As in *A Night to Remember*, Second Class finally is given a plot of its own. Yet whereas the Clarke couple in the 1958 film was fictitious, a "typage" for middle class, *S.O.S. Titanic* uses the most famous historical passenger from Second Class, providing him with a fitting love interest. Thus, Englishman Beesley and American teacher Leigh Goodwin — a fictitious character based on Beesley's original reference to a female American teacher with a pince-nez[5] — represent the sphere of Second Class, including the typical middle-class space of the library for Second Class. Their rather pathetic and eventually aborted romantic affair is one of the weaker parts of the film.

However, Beesley and the American teacher play a key role in the film's discussion of the class issue. James Costigan functionalized this Second Class couple to insert an explicit reflection on the ship as microcosm of the Edwardian class system, simultaneously juxtaposing British and American values:

> *Leigh Goodwin and Lawrence Beesley are standing on the Second Class deck.*
> GOODWIN: This ship is the microcosm of the British social system — a maze of barriers erected to keep *them* [*points to the Third Class passengers*] from getting where *we* are and to keep *us* from getting where *they* are [*points to the First Class deck*].
> BEESLEY: Yes, but it's not social, is it? It's purely economic. Any rich upstart can get his pick of accommodation up there [*points to the First Class deck*] and any nobleman short of funds might find himself traveling down there! So, in a sense, the thing is constructed on the American principle of equal opportunity based on the ability to pay.

Typically, there is no evaluation of the class system and its implication of social and national values in this conversation; the system is taken as a given. It is only after the disaster, on the *Carpathia*, that the fatal complacency of the upper class will become subject of their discussion. With their reflective conversations, Beesley and his shipboard acquaintance act as a sort of Greek chorus both throughout the main narrative and in the epilogue on the *Carpathia*, commenting on the tragic event and its meaning for their attitude to life.

It is a special feature of *S.O.S. Titanic* that the class differences, so central in the *Titanic* myth and omnipresent in *Titanic* lore and scholarship, are made an explicit point of discussion in the film. In all other films, class differences are implicit, although quite visible in the contrast between the chances passengers in the First and in the Third Class had for survival. *S.O.S. Titanic* explicitly voices the conspicuous similarity between the *Titanic*'s structure and the British social system, thus preparing the audience for the consequences this structure will have in the sinking.

In order to offer more tangible insights into life of the various classes on the ship, each of the classes is represented by a couple in love. The focus in First Class lies on the Astor couple (although the honeymooners Daniel and

Mary Marvin as well as the Harris couple are shown in several scenes, too). Beesley and his fictitious love interest represent Second Class, and in Third Class, two historical passengers are coupled — conveniently, one of them died, and the other is not known by name.

In comparison with other films, Third Class receives an unusual degree of attention. On the one hand, the Third Class passengers are stereotypically depicted as the poor but happy lot, with lots of Irish music and dancing — again, *S.O.S. Titanic* takes up the cue from *A Night to Remember* and elaborates it amply, with two evening dance parties in the Third Class common room and a slowly developing love story between two historical characters. On the other hand, though, the historical Third Class passengers appear much more as rounded, realistic personages than the stereotypes presented in other films.

Costigan did indeed make the most out of the historical data: Individual groups of Third Class passengers are highlighted, integrating as many people as possible. Tellingly, all the Third Class passengers depicted as more rounded characters are Irish; the focus on the Irish group in this class that was first found in *A Night to Remember* now has become programmatic. *S.O.S. Titanic* is the only film that shows the transfer of the tender from Queenstown to the *Titanic*, featuring the Irish airs that Third Class passenger Eugene Patrick Daly played during the short passage.[6] On the ship, a sort of balance between the sexes is created as they take possession of their cabins. The "three Kates" (historical passengers Kate Gilnagh, Kate Murphy, Katie Mullen) and Kate Murphy's sister Mary are struck by the relative comfort of their modest four-bunk cabin; in their chatting they disclose some of the documented details about the *Titanic* accommodation and routines.[7] At the same time a group of young men, consisting of the historical characters Martin Gallagher, Daniel Buckley, David Charters, and James Farrell, check into their cabin, exchanging opinions about their homeland Ireland. Later, these groups are shown in various scenes and begin to mix in the Third Class dancing — of course, with humoristic little scenes of flirtation and the development of a more serious love affair. After the collision, the four young men conflate several historical Third Class men that led women up to the Boat Deck, breaking down a locked gate and resisting the stewards' attempts to keep them down. The women eventually are let through due to Farrell's historical exhortation, "For God's sake, man, let the girls pass to the boats, at least!"

Irishman Martin Gallagher, who died in the sinking, was used by screenwriter Costigan to develop the third love plot in the film. In order to construct a fictitious Third Class love story, Costigan brought Gallagher together with the unnamed beauty named in Beesley's book: "Among the Irish group was one girl of really remarkable beauty, black hair and deep violet eyes with long lashes, and perfectly shaped features, and quite young, no more than eighteen or twenty; I think she lost no relatives on the *Titanic*."[8] In *S.O.S. Titanic*, this young lady is a fair-haired Irish girl remaining just as anonymous and enigmatic as in Beesley's description: We never learn her name; and though she is allowed many inscrutable and wistful glances in her acting, she never says a word, except for her single, first and last utterance near the end of the film, namely her beloved's name at the moment of the sinking. Their love story is a cliché, love at first sight, yet it conveniently introduces the third love plot in the drama.

Another important Third Class passenger is Gallagher's companion Daniel Buckley: *S.O.S. Titanic* is the only film that actually identifies the legendary man who escaped in women's clothes. In *A Night to Remember* this passenger is equally presented as a frightened and embarrassed Third Class youth, but his name is not given. The other films, in contrast, adopt the famous 1912 legend, assigning this compromising role to a cowardly First Class passenger and thus underlining the code of honor that was claimed for men in late Edwardian times.[9] Costigan, in turn, stuck to the documented truth: Irish Third Class passenger Daniel Buckley did indeed escape with a shawl over this head handed to him by a woman in Lifeboat 13, while other men who had entered the same boat were dragged out again.[10] In *S.O.S. Titanic* this escape is depicted as what it was: a spontaneous act of a frightened youngster, assisted by a natural gesture of help on part of a female passenger — certainly not a cowardly disregard of the code of honor that the First Class "gentlemen" adhered to.[11]

The Third Class scenes and characters thus have several functions in the film:

1. they add an Irish touch and folksy liveliness to the main narrative;
2. they offer a rich staffage of otherwise never-shown historical characters and combine them into groups linked by love and friendship;
3. they provide the background of "the people" on a ship divided into clearly separate social spheres and in a narrative focusing on representative individuals from the three classes.

There are further spheres of the ship, otherwise never shown, that receive short scenes or individual strands in the plot. The engine rooms are frequently shown. The emphasis, though, is put on the machines and not on the men: the mighty engines, revolving like giant organisms, are turned into icons of technical prowess. An innovative addition are insights into the work places of other crew members, such as the laundry and the boot cleaners' office. Luxurious extras as the gymnasium and the Turkish Bath are equally presented, the latter with a lengthy scene in the original television version serving for comic relief. The Café Parisien, the Verandah Café, the First Class dining room and various staterooms as well as the Third Class cabins and common room offer the standard locales, but due to the attention given to Second Class, the audience also gets an insight into the more modest "middle-class" corridors. For *Titanic* lovers, this film thus offers an unequaled spectrum of insights into the microcosm of the ship.

S.O.S. Titanic is special in that it fills its scenes with many identifiable historical characters who perfectly fit into the setting as supernumeraries with single lines or no words at all, yet clearly can be identified by those familiar with the historical material. Besides the stock-in-trade characters from First Class and crew, several Second and Third Class protagonists as well as historical characters on the *Carpathia* can immediately be identified by name:

First Class: Astor couple (John Jacob and Madeleine Astor)
Margaret Tobin Brown (as "Molly" Brown)
Emma Bucknell
Marvin couple (Daniel and Mary Marvin)
Harris couple (Irene "René" and Henry Harris)
Lucy Noël Martha Dyer-Edwards, Countess of Rothes
Benjamin Guggenheim
Straus couple (Isidor and Ida Straus)
John Borland "Jack" Thayer, Jr.
Milton Long
[Edith Russell] represented by her "lucky" musical pig
Thomas Andrews (ship architect)
J. Bruce Ismay (White Star president)

Second Class: Lawrence Beesley (with fictitious love affair)
American teacher (with fictitious love affair)
Father Thomas Byles
Michel Navratil (traveling as "Louis M. Hoffman") and his two boys Lolo (Michel Navratil) and Momon (Edmond Roger Navratil)

Third Class: Daniel Buckley
Martin Gallagher (with fictitious love affair)
James Farrell
David Charters
Kate Gilnagh
Kate Mullins
Kate Murphy

	Mary Murphy
	Bridget Bradley
	Mary Agatha Glynn
	nameless Irish beauty (with fictitious love affair)
	Olaus Abelseth and relatives
Crew:	Captain Edward John Smith
	Officers Wilde, Murdoch, Lightoller, Pitman, Boxhall, Lowe, Moody
	Master-at-arms Thomas W. King
	Quartermaster Robert Hichens
	Lookouts Archie Jewell, George Symons, Frederick Fleet, Reginald Lee
	Wireless operators John George "Jack" Phillips and Harold Bride
	First Class Stewardess Mary Sloan
	First Class Stewardess Violet Jessop (here depicted as an elderly woman)
	Second Class Steward John Hardy
	Third Class Steward John Hart
	Lift attendant Alfred King ("Alfie," here depicted as a child)
	Library Steward Thomas Kellard
	Gymnasium Steward Thomas McCawley
	Chief Boot Cleaner Sydney Frederick Stebbings
	Assistant Boot Cleaner Edward John Guy
	Bugler Peter Fletcher (here depicted as a boy)
	Chief Baker Charles John Joughin
	Band leader Wallace Hartley and seven musicians
	Chief Engineer Joseph Bell
	Leading Fireman Frederick Barrett
Carpathia:	Captain Arthur Rostron
	Officers Hankinson, Dean, Bisset, Rees, Barnish
	Wireless operator Harold Thomas Cottam
	First Class Surgeon Dr. Frank E. McGee
	Passenger Mrs. Louis M. Ogden

In addition, there are countless historical characters who appear without their names, and without a line — yet they form the "authentic" canvas of the drama on the *Titanic*. Interestingly, the *Californian* is entirely omitted, despite the effort at encompassing historical correctness. Did the producers not agree with the public image of Captain Stanley Lord as scapegoat — or was it a question of overlength that made them omit the important part of the indifferent ship?

Some of the historical characters are used to provide the famous and popular scenes of the *Titanic* code, such as Guggenheim's farewell (in an intelligent "deconstruction" of its noble stance[12]) and Ida Straus's oath of loyalty to her husband. Others constitute secondary characters with mini-subplots (e.g., the Marvin and Harris couples[13]) or background staffage during the sinking that yet can be historically traced, such as Jack Thayer and Milton Long jumping off the ship together, the intoxicated baker Charles John Joughin, or the French-speaking Michel Navratil, who, having kidnapped his two little sons after an unfortunate divorce, put them into a lifeboat and then died in the sinking.[14] Some of the "staffage" characters are used with dramatic license: The Countess of Rothes is transformed into an enigmatic, seductive character (with a rather ridiculous scene serving for comic relief in the Turkish Bath), while 59-year-old Emma Bucknell (who historically embarked together with Margaret Brown at Cherbourg and told her about her "evil forebodings") has been turned into a matron and humoristic sparring partner for her travel mate, profiling the comic relief that the "Molly" Brown scenes supply. These scenes are the most embarrassing part of the film, with an elderly "Molly" Brown making herself the clown of the First Class. Again, the original television version with its *Carpathia* framing helps to offset the thoroughly awkward representation of the prominent millionairess and human rights activist Margaret Brown, showing her (historically correctly!) as a more sympathetic, caring character on the *Carpathia*. For the first and only time in a *Titanic* film, Margaret's name is explicitly discussed: Her friends keep calling her "Maggie" (which was Margaret Brown's preferred name as a young girl), while she keeps admonishing them that she prefers to be called "Molly." It's a fictitious detail, not really as funny in its effect as it probably was meant to be, but it re-establishes an historical feature, namely the correct name of Margaret Brown.

Another rather embarrassing strand in *S.O.S. Titanic* is the peculiar relationship between ship architect Thomas Andrews, who is, as in *A Night to Remember*, depicted as an impeccable and diligent character, and stewardess Mary Sloan, whose conduct oscillates between empathy and clumsy attempts at seduction. These scenes may reflect an endeavor at translating the crew's positive image of Andrews into film drama: While the historical Mary Sloan testified about the gentlemanly care Andrews had shown towards her at some instances during the sinking, Violet Jessop's testimony expresses open admiration.[15] Besides, Jessop also mentioned Andrews' love for Ireland and his homesickness, which are the starting point of his friendly relationship with Irish stewardess Mary Sloan in the film.

In general, the poetic license which Costigan has taken in the treatment of the historical characters is disputable. The three love stories and the half-hearted flirting between Sloan and Andrews are all embarrassing or pathetic, the comic relief is exaggerated, and the scenes up to the collision teem with stereotypical hints at danger, sinking, and ships not arriving in port. An unforgivable error is the date April 12, 1912, for the last day of the maiden voyage; *Titanic* experts will also cringe at the *Carpathia*'s Captain Rostron yelling hectic orders as the lifeboats arrive, while a great deal of his reputation has in fact been based on his meticulous and circumspect preparation of every detail already on the way to the site of the sinking.

Problems of Plot—Nevertheless an Impressive Film

The greatest problem of the film, though, is the design and development of the plot. Classic film drama focuses on a main plot with several subplots, one of which may again be regarded as main subplot. *S.O.S. Titanic* offers a peculiar mixture of this classic design and a loose episodic structure—a mixture which does not really work.

What is the main story in *S.O.S. Titanic*? The theme certainly is the *Titanic* disaster. It clearly is an important objective of the script to focus on this theme and use many historical details to represent it. Yet in the case of the television production, history was not regarded as sufficient to constitute a convincing film drama; fictional plots had to be added. Accordingly, Costigan tried to embellish the historical story of the ship disaster with human interest strands. While *A Night to Remember* uses "typages" that represent their class, yet do not individually develop a life of their own, in *S.O.S. Titanic* every class, even the crew, must be provided with a (half-hearted) love story; and fictitious episodes—such as the humoristic Turkish Bath scene—are supposed to add extra variety. The result is dramatic failure. On the one hand, it clearly was a mistake to try and imbue the historical characters with some additional drama. On the other hand, the technique of multi-plotting on the basis of a linear event eventually fails, since the individual plots lack coherence and dramatic momentum.

Multi-plotting actually is a technique frequently and successfully used in television drama series. Several main characters are brought together in an ensemble piece, each having their own story to tell. This is very much the case in the television production *S.O.S. Titanic*: The most conspicuous plots are the three love stories, and maybe also the somewhat awkward relationship between Thomas Andrews and stewardess Mary Sloan. Which of the stories is set into focus, though? It is impossible to tell. In the original television version with the frame narrative on the *Carpathia*, there is an additional focus on Bruce Ismay, whose tragedy might be seen as a central theme running parallel to the tragedy of the *Titanic* in the main narrative. Yet this thread is not strong enough to be recognized as main plot, since it almost totally disappears in the main narrative. And in the theatrical version, where the main narrative is not introduced through Ismay's flashback, the emphasis on his character is entirely lost.

Accordingly, there is no main plot among the human interest strands. The "main plot" remains the *Titanic* disaster, with several subordinated strands unfolding throughout the voyage. Yet in contrast to *A Night to Remember*, the relationship between main plot and subplots remains awkward throughout. In *A Night to Remember* the subplots do not depend on the individual development of the three couples. The couples represent the concepts of class, but do not constitute a significant drama of their own. Due to this unusual conception, the subplots do not compete with the main plot, the sinking of the *Titanic*, but *support* it. The amorous subplots in *S.O.S. Titanic*, in contrast, are conceived as individual love stories that develop on the *Titanic*. Yet although the setting for this multiple-plot structure seems to come right out of the textbook (the plots take place in a single restricted environment and over a short time span), none of these subordinated strands assumes a convincing profile that could qualify it as a real plot. Since the general focus remains the *Titanic* story itself, with countless little episodes contributing to as full an image of life on the ship as possible, the love stories actually turn out as rivaling mini-plots that drown in the kaleidoscope of unrelated mini-scenes. Their position remains ambiguous: They are supposed to offer strands of their own, yet are too weak and too much integrated into the colorful kaleidoscope to be able to stand alone. None of them displays a convincing development; in the worst case, the gradually developing personal relationship is aborted, as in the case of Lawrence Beesley and the American teacher. Martin Gallagher's romance might be seen as a complete set-piece of the type "boy finds girl, boy loses girl" (and, concomitantly, his life). But with a girl just throwing wistful glances without ever uttering a word, the dramatic potential in such a story is limited.

By trying to imbue a few historical characters and facts with theatrical life, Costigan created a badly connected patchwork of episodes lacking dramatic life. The only real and well-proven story in the film, the voyage and sinking of the *Titanic*, does not help to solve the problem. In contrast to *A Night to Remember*, the main story is reduced to a canvas for the uneventful mini-stories and scenes on board. Besides the lack of dramatic momentum in the individual strands, there is also a lack of overall structure. The linking of the strands to one thematic idea — the problem of love in a heterosexual relationship as dominating theme on the ship — is too general, and their linking to the actual theme — the *Titanic* disaster — is too weak to be convincing.

The story itself mainly constitutes a painful recollection of the *Titanic* disaster. It is constructed as such in the original television version with its flashback technique and a setting in gentle, muted colors. Thus, it takes up the motif of nostalgia that so strongly and convincingly permeated *A Night to Remember*. Yet a sad and wistful recollection alone simply does not work for a lengthy film drama. The main problems of the script of *S.O.S. Titanic* therefore are a weak presentation of the main plot, a general indecision about the relation between main plot and subplots and a lack of convincing connections between the two.

Yet despite these structural and dramatic weaknesses, the film is a pleasure to watch. It displays a considerable number of new aspects and is generally characterized by a profound approach to the historical disaster and its impact on the people involved.

Titanic enthusiasts will love the sheer wealth of historical detail that is well integrated into the narrative and its setting. They will, in turn, loathe the fictional distortion of some of the historical characters as well as some of the scenes serving as comic relief, which are rather awkward if not openly tasteless. The titles of user reviews accordingly vary from "One of the most authentic *Titanic* movies ever made" to "Just horrible compared to *Titanic* [1997 version] or *A Night to Remember*."[16] A more detailed analysis, though, discloses the many positive aspects of this film. There are several aspects that make *S.O.S. Titanic* stand out from other *Titanic* productions:

- for the first time in a *Titanic* film, Second Class receives a considerable share of attention (including some glimpses of the Second Class interiors);
- Lawrence Beesley's book is used as a source and a basis for inspiration;
- the ship's class system is explicitly discussed;
- historical characters and spheres of the ship that have never been shown in *Titanic* films before are integrated;
- the *Titanic*'s strong "Irish connection" is exposed on an unprecedented scale and — singularly among the *Titanic* films — not only in Third Class;
- a certain emphasis is put on a less biased interpretation of Bruce Ismay's experience and feelings about the disaster;

- for the first time the victualling crew receives a share of attention;
- for the first time the survivors' situation on the *Carpathia* is shown in more detail;
- the motif of hubris is translated into a juxtaposition of life on the ship and superior, indifferent nature;
- no other film, excepting James Cameron's *Titanic*, has such a remarkable musical score.[17]

The Second Class plot with Lawrence Beesley and the explicit discussion of class differences takes the class issue one step further than in *A Night to Remember*. For the first time, clear criticism is expressed in light of the — neatly separated — survivor groups on the *Carpathia*. This criticism, voiced by Beesley and the American teacher, offers a moral especially aimed at the First Class passengers, whose world of complacent self-reliance has been shaken:

> BEESLEY: Shall we ever be able to look at the world in quite the same way?
> GOODWIN: I'll never see it as safe and snug if that's what you mean.
> BEESLEY: None of us will. [*looking down to the Third Class survivors*] They never did, of course. For them, it's always been unjust. In a way one might almost envy them the fact that they have no illusions to be disabused of. But they — [*looking up to the First Class, with a sign "First Class Only. No Admittance" being shown hanging on a chain*] I should think that they, especially, had a shocking glimpse of the underside of things. The *Titanic* was a way of life designed especially for them: safe — snug — teeming with creature comforts. And it's crumbled under them.

This is much more than Walter Lord's nostalgic "the world will never be again what it was." Beesley's (fictional) words are an incisive analysis of what *Titanic* meant to those who could afford a safe, snug world — and how this myth has been destroyed for them, forever. The various shots of the passengers underlying these words are poignant — not least, because there is also a positive scene of survivor children making faces and laughing while Beesley talks: The great "nevertheless" of life. Yet Beesley's critical stance towards First Class is attenuated by the heartrending scene that follows: Here the richest of the rich are shown, formerly naïve millionairess Madeleine Astor, life-loving Mary Marvin, innocuous René Harris — three well-dressed women, staring emptily into the air, utterly destroyed through their experience. Their mourning is ennobled through the contrast with well-meaning, chattering *Carpathia* passenger Mrs. Ogden:

> MRS. OGDEN: I know how I'd feel in that place. And believe me my heart goes out unto all of you. But you've got to go on living. You just have to say to yourself, "It was God's will!" Whatever you do, you must never lose

faith in the infinite wisdom and mercy of the Lord. [*gently to Madeleine Astor*] Coffee, hmm?

MRS. ASTOR: No coffee.... No God either. God went down with the *Titanic*.

The privileged First Class ladies certainly have learned their lesson. Madeleine Astor, appearing so naïve and shallow in the main narrative, is elevated to a tragic stance through her final word that closes the entire film. "God went down with the *Titanic*": a powerful statement epitomizing the survivors' state of mind.

No other *Titanic* film actually took pains to show the aftermath as it was: a ship of widows, stupor and trauma, utter desperation. Not so much in words, but in its technique of showing a multitude of details, shots and little scenes, *S.O.S. Titanic* powerfully imparts what the disaster meant to those involved.

Another feature that is uniquely highlighted in *S.O.S. Titanic* is human hubris. In an unusual manner, the famous motif is not introduced through repeated remarks that the *Titanic* is unsinkable. Rather, it has been translated into a juxtaposition of innocent life on the ship and superior, indifferent nature: an ice field with menacing, jagged bergs and sheets of ice not only forms the visual frame at the beginning and the end, but is also intercut again and again as "memento" shot while on the *Titanic* entertainment and gaiety prevail. In fact, these repeated shots of awe-inspiring, indifferent and deadly

A forgotten baby in the flooding Third Class corridors: *S.O.S. Titanic* is rich with poignant details (EMI Films).

nature might reflect a famous passage from Lawrence Beesley's book (after all, a main source for the script), in which the horror and the beauty of the gorgeous bergs are described:

> Looking towards the *Carpathia* in the faint light, we saw what seemed to be two large fully rigged sailing ships near the horizon, with all sails set, standing up near her.... But in a few minutes more the light shone on them and they stood revealed as huge icebergs, peaked in a way that readily suggested a ship. When the sun rose higher, it turned them pink, and sinister as they looked towering like rugged white peaks of rock out of the sea, and terrible as was the disaster one of them had caused, there was an awful beauty about them which could not be overlooked. Later, when the sun came above the horizon, they sparkled and glittered in its rays; deadly white, like frozen snow rather than translucent ice.[18]

This awful beauty is reflected in the film, yet it is used as a menace and a memento, warning mankind that nature is superior.[19] The sound of icy wind contributes to this impression, especially when juxtaposed with the trustful singing of the hymn "Eternal Father, Strong to Save" or, even stronger as a statement, with the light dance music in the Café Parisien.[20] These shots, intercut again and again into the celebratory part of the voyage, imbue a sense of destiny, very much like in Thomas Hardy's poem "The Convergence of the Twain." Human hubris is not explicitly named in *S.O.S. Titanic*, yet the images of indifferent nature make it clear who will be the more powerful.

Finally, there is also an interesting sense of self-irony in this film. Although the excessive adherence to historical detail can be regarded as a celebration of the *Titanic* story, the filmmakers clearly rejected an unreflected adoption of all of its legends. There is, of course, the Straus scene, there are the many stereotypes in First and Third Class and the diligent crew. Yet there are also instances that deconstruct the myth. Most conspicuously, these are the many comic relief scenes that at the same time add an ironic comment, such as the Turkish Bath sequence or "Molly" Brown's overdone behavior. An explicit deconstruction of a popular legend is Benjamin Guggenheim's famous farewell, whose formulation has tellingly been altered. Guggenheim does not declare his chivalrous decision to die like a gentleman in the adequate surroundings of the First Class interiors; instead, he is standing on the Boat Deck and gives his legacy to a woman being lowered in a lifeboat (probably his mistress Léontine Pauline Aubart):

> If, by any chance, I should not be on the list of survivors, tell my wife that the last time you saw me I was wearing my English dinner jacket. I was prepared to die like a gentleman. It'll make a nice story for her to tell her friends.

Not First Class nobility, but a good story to entertain friends at the tea party — *S.O.S. Titanic* almost sarcastically deconstructs the legend, reflecting the social function of the famous statements in the ensuing *Titanic* myth. A close viewing of the film shows again and again how the myth intentionally is being challenged with ironic little scenes.[21] This is, indeed, a meta-reflection: the film humorously mocks the legends that it puts to use itself. Yet in the end, this is a deeply human sense of humor, the same sort (in coarser guise) as in *A Night to Remember*: the little ironies do in no way reduce the poignancy of the human drama unfolding on the *Titanic*.

For all its weaknesses and exaggerations, *S.O.S. Titanic* has many qualities that put it among the best of the *Titanic* films. Despite its many ironies, *S.O.S. Titanic* conveys a deep sense of tragedy, especially in its original version with the frame on the *Carpathia*. Although clichés are used, the atmosphere on the ship and during the various stages of the voyage and the disaster is well conveyed.[22] The setting displays a striking sense for detail, not only with regard to the historical facts, but also in the dramatization of the sinking: The image of a lost and forgotten baby, sitting helplessly amongst a panicking crowd in a flooding Third Class corridor, probably is one of the most poignant shots in all *Titanic* productions. No other film does so consistently impair the sense of tragic destiny by juxtaposing the splendid life on the *Titanic* with recurrent shots of sublime, superior nature. Whatever critics of *S.O.S. Titanic* may say, the film is definitely worth watching, and due to its many unusual features it must be regarded as an important, individualized contribution to the translation of the *Titanic* disaster into film.

8

Titanic (1996)
Poor Plots with an Impressive Disaster

Did James Cameron find inspiration in a television production — or did someone get hold of Cameron's script during the blockbuster's production, rip it off, rush it into production and present it as the great *Titanic* film exactly one year before Cameron's film came out? Many viewers surmise that the 1996 mini-series produced by American Zoetrope (director: Robert Lieberman) was a rush job profiting from the *Titanic* hype that had grown around Cameron's production since word had been spread that this was going to be a *Titanic* movie — and a big one.[1] The 1996 television production and Cameron's mega-hit indeed have much in common:

- a story of love made impossible by destiny (i.e., the sinking of the *Titanic*)
- a young and open-hearted Third Class hero falling in love with another passenger
- a focus on the luxury and beauties of First Class — blazing colors, beautiful costumes, a conspicuous focus on the excellent food served
- a First Class lady deciding to give up her safe life in the upper class circles and start a new, more adventurous life with her lover[2]
- the contrast of extensive dance scenes in First and Third Class
- First Officer Murdoch shooting men in panic and then committing suicide
- Lifeboat 14 returning to save some of the victims in the water
- the famous "female lover lowered down in lifeboat" perspective
- an astounding correspondence of visual details and wordings throughout the film
- an astounding correspondence of the collision scenes

Striking as the number of close correspondences may seem, none of these elements are really something new in the history of the *Titanic* myth in film. *Titanic* films abound with stories of star-crossed love; they all use the splendid First Class interiors; from 1943 onwards, dance scenes in First Class and Third Class are contrasted in all major *Titanic* productions; the perspective of the woman looking up to her beloved while being lowered in a lifeboat is found in the 1943 film, and the legend of an officer shooting panicking passengers was integrated into fictional versions of the *Titanic* story right from 1912 onwards.

Quite generally then, the 1996 mini-series must be seen as a logical continuation of the cinematic *Titanic* code: a *Titanic* tale that includes as much historical (and legendary) detail as possible, while avoiding some of the problems that the 1979 television production had. The quasi-historical love stories of *S.O.S. Titanic*, disseminated over the ship's three classes, had proven too weak: It is problematic to imbue the historical *Titanic* passengers with a life they did not have. Accordingly, the love stories in the 1996 production have been turned fictional again. Desiring to make use of the stereotypical contrast between First Class and Third Class, television screenwriters Ross LaManna and Joyce Eliason still retained the double structure of two contrasting love stories, while Cameron would choose to combine the threads in an impossible twist — poor but honest Third Class boy meets spoiled First Class girl in need of redemption from her class. Though melodramatic enough, the 1996 love stories still are more realistic: a rekindled love made impossible by destiny in First Class, and a newly growing love interest in Third Class with the two lovers surviving and having a future together. Thus, the class barriers are retained — not quite as romantic as Cameron, but somewhat more plausible. Jamie Pierce, the young Third Class hero, does indeed resemble Cameron's Jack Dawson — but then, how much variation would there be for a young, aspiring hero of this kind? At least the 1996 hero is not as much of a stereotype as Jack Dawson: Starting off as a (still likable) thief, Jamie Pierce is allowed some character development, and of course, it is his pure love for Aase that turns him into an honest man. However, since this development is so stereotypical and overblown (seasoned with pathetic declarations of starting a new, honest life due to his love for Aase), it offers not much more credibility than the impeccable hero of the Cameron film.

Yet despite the general adherence to the *Titanic* code, a few scenes in the 1996 mini-series do indeed correspond to Cameron's film to an astounding degree, up to visual details and wording in statements that are non-historical and therefore not taken from a generally accessible source — such as Murdoch's desperate muttering before the collision, "Come on ... come on! Turn, you whore! Turn!" which in the 1997 film appears as "Come on! Come on! Come on! *Turn!*" or Bride's joking remark "Ain't that lovely? Music to drown by!" in the 1996 production, which is then found again as a class-conscious statement of Jack Dawson's friend Tommy Ryan in the Cameron movie, "Music to drown by, now I know I'm in First Class!" Another surprising correspondence is the blackening of the screen as the *Titanic* leaves Southampton, an impressive visual device to illustrate the overwhelming size and power of the ocean liner. Mere numbers do not arouse the imagination: It is the almost shocking visual impression of the enormous bow blinding out the surrounding world that makes us understand what the size of the *Titanic* actually means. Is the congruence of this effective visual device really coincidence?

It will be impossible to say if the screenwriters of the television production somehow copied out of Cameron's script or if Cameron let himself be inspired by the television production in some details.[3] Indeed, it is not important. The 1996 television production and the 1997 Hollywood blockbuster are two different versions of the *Titanic* disaster, and they add quite different facets to the myth and its use in cinema. Thus, each deserves discussion in its own right.

Structure and Plots

The television mini-series covers the entire voyage of the *Titanic* and ends with scenes on the *Carpathia* and the subsequent arrival of the survivors in New York. It is indeed the first film version that actually follows the surviving passengers up to port. Otherwise, the mini-series follows the model of the earlier films: After an introductory sequence using footage of the launch and a fictional scene before departure, the main part of the film covers the entire voyage of the *Titanic*, with the collision being the decisive turning point between the first, celebratory and the second, tragic sequence. The two parts of the production are structured as follows, with the voyage and the famous hours between the collision and the sinking being the clear focus of the production:

Part I:
1. Opening credits (with sepia pictures of the construction, the launch and the *Titanic* leaving port)
2. Prologue in England:
   Alice Cleaver's nightmare and her hiring by the Allison family
3. **Departure and voyage = main part** (75 percent)
4. Collision (ending with a cliffhanger a few minutes after the collision)

Part II:
1. Opening credits
2. **Time span between 11:45 A.M. and the sinking = main part** (65 percent)
3. In the lifeboats
4. Survivors on the *Carpathia*
5. Epilogue: Arrival in New York (happy end for several plots)

The dramaturgical principle corresponds to *A Night to Remember* and *S.O.S. Titanic*: The ship is shown as a microcosm with many events happening at the same time in the different classes and spheres. The technical means to provide this impression are, like in the earlier productions, multiple-plotting and the montage of many different scenes and shots, especially right before the collision and then in the period until the sinking. This kaleidoscope of impressions is supplemented by shots on the *Californian* and the *Carpathia* to give as comprehensible a picture of the events in the night of April 14–15 as possible. Added are scenes on the *Carpathia* and at the arrival in New York. The film thus offers a horizontal time span from April 9 to April 18, 1912, and a vertical enlargement of a few events during the voyage and the night of the disaster.

It is a new feature in *Titanic* films that the scenes in the lifeboats are so extensively shown, mixing historical scenes with fictional additions (thus, the villain Doonan is finally done away with).[4] It is also a novelty that the survivors on the *Carpathia* are shown with more elaborate scenes; this is used as a device to accuse *Titanic* passengers who only thought of themselves (the arrogant Foley couple being a caricature version of the Duff-Gordons), to integrate the poignant historical line "I wouldn't have left him if I had known there weren't enough boats,"[5] and, at least one comforting, though fictitious moment, to reunite the lovers Jamie and Aase. In addition, Margaret Brown (figuring as the notorious "Molly") is shown in an historically correct way, namely caring for Third Class survivors in need. The two parts of the series are arched by the Alice Cleaver story, with the somewhat ironic ending that nurse Alice does save a baby in danger of drowning, but thereby involuntarily condemns her employer's family to die in the sinking.

The script has a multiple-plot structure, with three strands being the dominant plots:

	Main characters	*Theme*	*Sphere*
Plot 1	Isabella and Wynn	star-crossed love; coming of age (Isabella)	First Class
Plot 2	Jamie and Aase (linked up with Doonan)	love; crime; coming of age (Jamie)	Third Class / crew

	Main characters	Theme	Sphere
Plot 3	Alice Cleaver and the Allison Family	ill fate and its forebodings	First Class (servant)

While the first two plots build on fictional characters and provide fictional love stories (seasoned with a ridiculously overblown criminal plot in the case of the Third Class love story), the Alice Cleaver plot actually takes up one of the unexplored fates of real *Titanic* passengers that has never been treated in film before. Alice Cleaver boarded the *Titanic* as the nurse of the Allison family, in charge of two-year-old Loraine and her infant brother Trevor. Loraine was the only child in First Class who did not survive the sinking. According to the testimony of Major Peuchen, her mother Bess Allison had already been sitting in a lifeboat with her little daughter when she left it again in search for her husband. The relatives of the Allisons, though, surmised that Alice Cleaver had taken Trevor with her into Lifeboat 11 without informing the parents, so that Bess and Hudson Allison stayed with Loraine on the ship to search for their son.[6] Taking up the latter theory, the film offers a possible explanation for the perishing of the Allison family, additionally building on the incorrect assumption that the nurse Alice Catherine Cleaver was identical with Alice Mary Cleaver, who allegedly had killed her child in 1909.[7] The character of Alice thus is represented as a psychically overwrought young woman, constantly on the verge of panic, who realizes at once after the collision that the ship is sinking and grabs little Trevor to save at least this baby (having killed her own child in a state of aberration and despair). This gives further opportunity to integrate a famous aspect of the *Titanic* myth into this storyline, namely the many documented forebodings of the disaster: The film starts with Alice's nightmare of a drowned baby, right before Alice is hired by the Allison family to accompany them as nurse on the *Titanic*, and this nightmare becomes a sort of leitmotif up to the sinking. In Southampton, a blind preacher is added, summoning the passengers to repent and prophesying "shrieks and crying and moaning" to those who board the ship. As is to be expected, this specific theme, the manifold premonitions of the sinking, does not really work: It is just too much for an audience who knows anyway what will happen. Alice Cleaver with her constant wailing and sulking is getting not only on the Allisons' nerves, but also on the audience's nerves. The explanation of the Allisons' fate is plausible, but it could have been turned into much better drama.

The other two main plots are equally melodramatic. The First Class love story presents a stereotype of star-crossed lovers. A married woman with her husband and a twelve-year-old daughter waiting for her in New York, beautiful Isabella Paradine meets her former lover Wynn Park again on the *Titanic*.

It turns out that he has booked a cabin (of course right opposite her stateroom) with the intention to force a meeting and a clarification why she left him many years ago. The inevitable happens: Isabella realizes that she still loves him, they make love, and she decides — on the evening of April 14 — that she will stay with him and take her daughter along to Bolivia, where he has purchased mines. Shortly before the collision, she sends a telegram to her husband informing him about the situation. Isabella and Wynn are inevitably separated, and right before the lifeboat is lowered, she admits that her daughter is his child. She does see him again — as a corpse on the *Carpathia*.[8] Against Isabella's expectations, her husband and her daughter still expect her in New York: miraculously, the telegram never arrived. With this scene, the film ends on a somewhat happy note (though it is up to Isabella how she will live with her husband after her experiences on the *Titanic*). The story does not convince; the melodrama in the 1953 *Titanic* film is by far superior. It never becomes clear why Isabella actually ditched Wynn Park — after all, he seems to be quite wealthy, so why should she have chosen her much older husband as safe harbor when she was pregnant with Wynn's child?

The Third Class plot is played out on a somewhat darker note, although Jamie Pierce is the fair-haired young hero who eventually overcomes all obstacles. He is an admittedly rather innocuous little thief who gets on board by stealing a ticket. Instrumental in this feat is the exaggeratedly evil steward Simon Doonan, who forces Jamie to become an accomplice in his plan to steal the First Class passengers' jewelry. On board the *Titanic*, Jamie falls in love with Aase, a Danish religious convert who eventually manages to convert Jamie to becoming the good character he essentially is. Their love story builds on a gradually developing relationship that, right before collision, becomes dramatic: Doonan rapes Aase in the (fictitious) Third Class shower; Jamie saves her by taking her to a lifeboat; after the sinking, Doonan is disclosed right in Aase's boot (he is the guy escaping in women's clothes this time); Doonan gets killed, Aase almost gets killed; and in the end, Aase and Jamie are happily reunited on the *Carpathia*, with the shining prospect of a new life together in California (where Jamie incidentally wants to go into the film business). With Jamie's conversion to being a good guy, this plot is actually a coming-of-age story, but one never gets the impression of him becoming adult. Aase is a stereotype of innocence and purity, which cannot be destroyed by the rape (though she of course feels defiled). And Doonan is just a caricature. Thus, the plot with all its stereotypes — including the familiar stunt number which leads to Jamie being saved by falling into a lifeboat — does not convince either.

8. Titanic *(1996)*

The interesting points about this film are the highlighting of the Allison family's fate (however poorly represented) and the epilogue that for the first time takes the surviving passengers beyond the *Carpathia* and shows their arrival in New York — which, paradoxically, leaves the audience with a feeling of a happy ending, since the main strands of the drama on the ship lead to a somewhat positive outcome. In addition, Third Class receives more attention than in all previous films. On the one hand, the love story between Jamie and Aase is developed into a main plot (and thus highlighted much stronger than the corresponding Third Class romance in *S.O.S. Titanic*), on the other, the fate of the strongly religious Jack family is shown as a subsidiary plot, constituting a reflection of the historical Goodwin family, who perished with all children.

A special point is the close interlinking of the three plots with the collision — though this seems to be a little bit over the top. A few moments before the collision,

- Isabella sends her divorce telegram to her loyal husband;
- Aase is raped by evil Simon Doonan (foreboding how the maiden ship will be raped by the iceberg in just a few minutes?);
- Alice Cleaver is uncovered as a murderess by the Astors' maid.

It is actually a fine dramaturgical technique to link the plots so closely to the disaster of the *Titanic*, which is the precondition for the fictitious strands to fully unfold — but is it the point of the scriptwriters that the personal failures of our main protagonists lead up to the collision as a sort of divine judgment?

The other historical characters and motifs are, as usual, mostly used for staffage. Fictitious Hazel Foley garrulously presents us with the *Titanic* jet set in one of the first scenes: the Astors, the Wideners, the Strauses, Benjamin Guggenheim with his French mistress Léontine Pauline Aubart (the first time his mistress is presented in a *Titanic* film), and the notorious "Molly" Brown, who is represented as usual, namely as the *nouveau-riche enfant terrible* of the upper crust. Captain Smith and Bruce Ismay are granted a few more scenes in order to introduce the stock motifs: While Smith is simply depicted in his function as captain (slightly more active than in other *Titanic* films), Ismay for the first time since 1943 emerges as a villain, namely as the greedy capitalist insisting on a higher speed against the captain's better judgment in a fictitious competition for the Blue Riband. Yet in the multiplicity of subplots and scenes, this stock-in-trade motif of the *Titanic* myth simply drowns. Interestingly, ship architect Thomas Andrews is entirely missing in this film: Captain Smith is given his lines about the condition of the ship after the collision and is thus provided with more authority. The officers are, of course, all there, just as the wireless operators Phillips and Bride with their historical lines. Phillips is given a moving exit as he dies of exposure and exhaustion on the upturned Collapsible B.[9] The crew and the captains of the *Californian* and the *Carpathia* are represented as usual according to the available documentation.

Among this historical menagerie, Madeleine Astor is singled out by becoming Isabella's confidante. As usual in *Titanic* films, she looks much older than the eighteen-year-old girl she was, but her role is conceived as an actually well-fitting supportive part in the First Class romance, again with a sort of happy end at her arrival in New York (despite her fears and expectancy, she is met by John Jacob Astor's sons).

Striving for Authenticity: Historical Motifs

With the 1958 and 1979 films as forerunners, the 1996 television mini-series clearly was bound to the *Titanic* code. While the earlier films used Walter Lord's documentary novel as well as the early publications of survivors as matrix, the 1996 production had yet more literature to build on, since the discovery of the wreck in 1985 had sparked a new wave of *Titanic* studies. Accordingly, for the first time in *Titanic* film, there is no word of the infamous "300-foot gash" that allegedly had been slit into the starboard side of the *Titanic*, but the hull plates are pressed in at the collision, with the rivets giving way, which based on the examination of the wreck, is thought to be the nature of the damage.[10] Other historical motifs have been used in earlier films: the cancellation of the boat drill because of the Sunday service, the missing binoculars, various ice warnings (with the *Baltic* ice warning that Ismay put into his pocket, the *Mesaba* warning that never reached the bridge, and the late night warning from the *Californian*, which overstressed Phillips cut off), passengers playing with the ice on the deck, wireless operators Bride and Phillips joking about the SOS signal, the white rockets, various scenes on the *Californian* and the *Carpathia*, Captain Rostron's immediate reaction to the distress call. In addition, there are the historically based standard scenes in the hours before the sinking:

- Ismay's meddling and his argument with Fifth Officer Lowe
- Margaret Brown helping with the passengers and being forced herself into Lifeboat 6
- Second Officer Lightoller trying to deny 13-year-old John Ryerson access to Lifeboat 4, eventually giving in to Arthur Ryerson's protest, but then allowing no more boys into the lifeboats

- John Jacob Astor's farewell to his wife
- the Straus scene
- Third Class passengers being stopped by locked gates, one gate being broken down
- a stoker trying to steal Jack Phillips's life jacket

The collision scene offers the usual collage of shots from various parts of the ship and the standard lines of the lookouts and the officers on the bridge; the muttered curses of First Officer William Murdoch are fictitious. The dramatic irony of the Third Class passengers playing football with pieces of ice is used for quite a successful cliffhanger ending to the first part of the series: "Molly" Brown, brash as ever, claims, "After all, this tin tub's unsinkable!," and then puts her brandy glass onto one of the deck's superstructures; after she and the other card players have returned to their game, the glass slowly slides to the side due to the slight but ominous list of the ship, and finally is shattered. The tragedy takes its course while the passengers still think this is a joke.

A few historical motives are added that had not received attention in earlier films, for instance the reason why the Third Class gates are locked (namely U.S. immigration law). It is fictitious, though, and part of the villain plot, that a crew member (here: Simon Doonan) actually locked in the Third Class passengers with the intention to let them drown. "New" historical motifs are the ship breaking in two just before the sinking and Lifeboat 14 with Fifth Officer Lowe going back to rescue some of the victims. However, the film does not really make much of the sensational novelty that the ship indeed had broken in two pieces before the final plunge (one of the contested issues since 1912 that was solved only by the discovery of the wreck[11]). The splitting of the decks turns out to be a single, inconspicuous instant in the montage of the multiple final moments, hardly noticeable to viewers who do not know the story of the *Titanic*. The stern falling back onto the water, one of the most dramatic moments in the Cameron film, is not seen at all; the producers gave away one of the most sensational visual aspects of the disaster. James Cameron, in turn, would go right for this effect.

To the historical motifs, some aspects of the myth are added, thereby consolidating these aspects as part of "the real story." A stock motif is speed. For the first time in *Titanic* movies, a desired competition with the *Lusitania* is named, which — according to the technical facts — is just as unrealistic as president Ismay climbing down into the boiler room and personally giving the order to fire up more boilers to increase speed.[12] A rather charming instant of legend is the famous joke "I asked for ice, but this is ridiculous!" erroneously

Titanic (1996): A telling list of a crystal glass is used as cliffhanger in the miniseries (Konigsberg/Sanitsky in association with American Zoetrope and Hallmark Entertainment).

attributed to John Jacob Astor in *Titanic* tales — in the 1996 production, this joke helps to give Astor a more human touch, lacking in most *Titanic* films.[13] Another novelty in *Titanic* films, the legend about First Officer Murdoch shooting first a desperate man and then himself, is taken up — with almost exactly the same gestures and wording that are featured in the Cameron film. Surprisingly, the emotional potential of "Nearer, My God, to Thee" is hardly put to use: As Smith releases the musicians and they voluntarily take up their instruments again, they do play some more serious music, but not the famous melody of the "Nearer, My God, to Thee." A little later, in the general chaos of the sinking, the hymn eventually reverberates, just as a few notes of the waltz "Songe d'Automne" — yet only *Titanic* experts will notice this allusion to a famous mystery of the *Titanic* myth.[14] Smith's legendary call "Be British!" equally drowns in the turmoil on the deck.

The forebodings are, as stated above, a rather problematic feature. To make the historical premonitions and prophecies of the *Titanic* disaster work in a serious feature film, it takes an excellent dramaturgy and excellent acting.

The television script and the overwrought acting of Felicity Waterman alias Alice Cleaver lack this quality.

Interestingly, the traditional categories of the *Titanic* myth are almost entirely blinded out in this production. The issue of class, so important in the 1958 and 1979 films, is reduced to its very minimum, namely the social structure of the ship, without any effort at reflection. Gender roles are not questioned, but cemented in stereotype love affairs, and the discussion of nation and race is entirely relinquished (it is not even the infamous "Latins" who try to storm a lifeboat, but stokers from the social underworld of the ship). Religion, in turn, plays a somewhat curious role: Partly it figures as *couleur locale* in the Third Class plot, but, above all, as an almost metaphysical elevation of the dramatic last moments of the *Titanic*. While the negligence of the controversial aspects in the main categories of gender, class, and nation reflects the low budget and hasty production of this series, it is this final elevation that most clearly turns the 1996 *Titanic* into a film worth seeing.

The Climax

It is easy to condemn this television production, but it is not fair. Considering the low budget, the extremely short production time and, accordingly, bad shooting conditions, the screenwriters, the director, the technical cast and the actors did an amazingly good job. Except for clearly recognizable CGI (computer generated imagery) in a few shots (especially the *Titanic* on the ocean and the *Carpathia* arriving in New York), the special effects are much better than what could be expected of a low-budget television production. The sets, though impaired by the general lack of time and additional damage exacted throughout the shooting, display a great sense for detail and authenticity. Many of the First Class interiors are clearly modeled after the original locales, and in the sinking, details are displayed that have become famous since the discovery of the wreck and thus give the impression of "the real story": for example, the cherub at the foot of the Grand Staircase, which is highlighted in the sinking. Since a corresponding bronze figure was retrieved from the bottom of the ocean in 1987, its picture has become well-known from many publications.[15] The cinematic sinking thus explicitly refers to one of the icons of the specific poignancy in the *Titanic* tale, namely beauty and love for life thrown into a dark and cold abyss, lying there in silence and darkness, waiting for redemption.

The sinking is indeed one of the most remarkable sequences of the film.

Titanic (1996): Since its retrieval from the depths, the bronze cherub from the Grand Staircase has become a warrant of authenticity (Konigsberg/Sanitsky in association with American Zoetrope and Hallmark Entertainment).

The television production relinquished a dramatic, moment-for-moment representation of the final minutes. This would have been impossible budget-wise and would have resulted in a poor, unsatisfying rip-off of the real disaster. Thus, the filmmakers chose another solution: a pastiche of overlaid images in slow motion whose dream-like quality is supported by the sound of distant screams and by the music that spans the entire sequence. Many viewers have been disappointed by this sinking, taking it for a cheap, pseudo-dramatic solution, a pathetic chaos that avoids the cinematic effort of a realistic-looking process. However, the point is not primarily keeping the budget down (though this doubtlessly played a decisive role). To take the sinking out of cinematic realism is to turn it into something "larger than life," just as the use of visuals and sound implies. The combination of slow-motion, muffled or entirely suppressed sound, and a dominant musical score is a typical device to elevate an event beyond its immediate impact; the disaster becomes universal, a nightmarish vision of man perishing due to human error, to arrogant recklessness, to the essential destitution of mankind. It is the universal Flood Myth, transferred onto an early 20th-century ship.[16] This implication of a quasi-religious global event is heightened by the fact that the Lord's Prayer, a diegetic element of the last scene on the deck (in fact, prayed by the deeply religious Jack family after they have realized that they will not be saved), leads over into this montage and then into the music.

The sequence takes but three minutes. Yet it is universal, encompassing the entire ship and the horrified onlookers in the lifeboats — *theatrum mundi*, the stage of a perishing world, comprised in a series of kaleidoscopic shots, some featuring the main characters, others representing the collective dimension of the disaster:

- stokers in the engine room, water floods in
- Third Class passengers run through First Class corridors
- First Class dining room topples into chaos
- dishes in the kitchen crash down
- people jump from the deck into the water
- the stern rises out of the water
- Ismay buries his face in his hands in utter despair
- people swim in the water
- the great wave rushes over the Boat Deck[17]
- the Grand Staircase floods
- people perish in the flooding First Class corridors
- people are swept off the flooding deck
- the stokers perish
- terrified survivors row and wail in the lifeboats
- a little boy cries
- a couple on the deck clings to each other in terror
- Third Class passengers climb for the stern
- Wynn Park on the deck in resignation
- people cling to the railings of the ever-steeper deck
- injured Jamie in a nightmarish stupor
- the stern rises higher and higher, the lights still burning
- masses of people cling to the railings
- Aase stares in horror from the lifeboat
- people slide off the deck
- the ship breaks into two pieces, explosions, the light goes out
- Officer Lowe stares in horror from the lifeboat
- a little Italian boy in a lifeboat wails for his father
- the wood on the deck splinters
- Alice Cleaver screams in despair

- the plate "S.S. *Titanic*" on the lifeboat's side
- a funnel crashes into the water
- "Molly" Brown in awed contemplation
- the bow part plunges down into the depths (underwater vision)
- Isabella and Aase stare in silent horror
- the stern goes down and disappears
- Isabella and Aase in painful resignation — a musical cadence ends the sequence

These multiple impressions, overlapping into each other, represent what *Titanic* stands for: immeasurable suffering, individual and collective, not only encompassing the passengers, but also their families worldwide. In short: the suffering of mankind.

The auditory leitmotif of this scene is not the music, it is the scream — a *Titanic* version of Edvard Munch's famous 1893 expressionist painting. Screams abound in the echoing sound design of this nightmare sequence: the multiple screams of the passengers, individual screams of individual victims, the heartrending wailing of a little boy after his father, and the endless howl of Alice Cleaver as the ship finally goes down. The other sound effects, sounds of violence and death, equally resounding from a far, timeless distance, are subjected to this manifold scream. The music elevates the events to a higher level — but it never can muffle the scream.

The *Titanic* disaster is far from being the worst disaster that ever happened on sea — even in peace times. This sequence translates into film the process of an historical event being transformed into myth. The overabundance of terrifying impressions, the agony of those who run for their life, the reactions of the horrified onlookers, the dream-like slow motion and the distancing of realistic sound illustrate how the event has been perceived by a general public: an event looked upon through a magnifying glass, turned into an emblem for the tribulations of a century. The film montage integrates us, the audience, into this mode of perception. It is therefore that this sequence — although the tragic music is no more than a stereotypical synthesizer score — has got such a strong effect: It encapsulates the myth of the *Titanic* into three minutes of film.

Nevertheless, the universalized disaster remains linked to the rest of the film — and again, this contributes to the poignancy of the sequence. We see Ismay in deepest despair — his deadly ambition to win a record is forgotten and forgiven. We see Wynn Park in dignified resignation. Yet above all, we see the survivors in the lifeboats, forever marked by this horrible vision. While Jamie lies in a nightmarish stupor, the other characters whom we have become familiar with throughout the film experience every single moment of the sinking in full consciousness and in horror.

The 1996 *Titanic* does have its qualities. These three minutes, a highly viable alternative to the ultra-realistic reconstruction of James Cameron, belong to the special moments in cinematic *Titanic* legacy. And this is not the only achievement of the mini-series. The sense for detail, the exquisite costumes, a few excellent scene transitions and a general competent hand in developing the individual plots contribute to the overall good effect this film has. Although the plots are dramaturgically not the most realistic, and although some of the main characters appear as stereotypes (or simply as enervating), there is some good acting and a growing poignancy throughout the second part of the film. The sinking, the endless hours in the lifeboats, and the painful scenes on the *Carpathia* make the story come alive — and it is not the story of star-crossed lovers or innocence prevailing, but it is the story of the *Titanic* that finally has become the focus of the film. Even the "happy end" in New York cannot undo this, on the contrary: Although the individual plots somehow all end on a happy note (Isabella winning her family back, Jamie and Aase walking into a sunny Californian future, and even Alice Cleaver turning herself into a media heroine), the universal mourning cannot be undone. The final title card relates the usual calculation, "705 were saved, 1,523 perished"—a stock device in *Titanic* films. Nevertheless, this title card seems to have a special function in this film. It keeps the *Titanic* story in focus, regardless of the comforting little scenes that let the film end at the Cunard pier. A viewer writes, "It makes you feel warm and happy in the end"[18]— yet it is a bittersweet happiness. The film is not a melodrama that needed a ship to sink in order to get to a happy family ending. The ship and its victims remain present in every moment of the end. Somehow, the filmmakers succeeded in integrating a few rather mediocre plots into a real tragedy — and then they let this tragedy prevail.

9

James Cameron's *Titanic* (1997)

No event, not even the discovery of the wreck, has brought the *Titanic* story and its myth so powerfully back into collective consciousness as James Cameron's *Titanic*. It is general knowledge that the film budget went up to $200 million (some do also know that Cameron at a critical point offered to reassign his own profit participation back to the film company in order to be able to finish the film[1]), that it won eleven Academy Awards, that it grossed over $600 million in the U.S. and over $1.8 billion worldwide. Up to Cameron's *Avatar* (2009), *Titanic* was the most successful film in history. If the word "Titanic" is uttered today, most people will think of Cameron's movie — and not of the historical ship.

A less conspicuous indicator of the film's tremendous success is the fact that it was immediately turned into a subject of scholarly interest. In the age of postmodernist cultural studies, the popular film proved the perfect "text" for analysis according to postmodernist master categories: class, race, gender, nation, genre, strategy of popular culture and the media, as well as various aspects of postmodern *Zeitgeist*— not least, just in time, millennial fears. The film can today be studied as a textbook example for contemporary cultural analysis of a work of popular art. Insightful essays have been written on[2]:

- gender aspects (especially in the film, but also analyzing the audience)
- class, both in 1912 and in contemporary American society
- nation and race
- genre (adventure-action; romance; disaster; heritage; rites of passage film; mixing of genres; and the blockbuster as a new meta-genre)
- postmodernist aesthetics as expressed in *Titanic*
- the role and treatment of history and memory

- the 1990s *Zeitgeist*: nostalgia; survivalism and the millennial myth; contemporary class mythologies
- the music in the film
- the mass media negotiation of the film
- the reception of the film (with a special focus on teenage girls' fandom)

These studies offer an impressive kaleidoscope of the complexities of modern film art and its reception. As implied in the title of the anthology *Titanic. Anatomy of a Blockbuster* (1999), the film has been dissected in its many aspects. The script is certainly not the best and the story contains numerous kitsch elements and clichés — but the film as "cultural phenomenon" cannot be ignored and demands careful cultural readings.

There is one missing link in almost all of these studies: They focus on *Titanic* as a modern phenomenon, on a "text" reflecting the culture of the 1990s — but they forget to tie up the aspects they discuss with the cultural historical *Titanic* myth and its expression in ten feature films up to the 1996 mini-series *Titanic*. Thus, the film is isolated from the tradition it builds on.

Titanic may indeed be a postmodern "text" but just as any work of postmodern art, it is not without historical fundament, not without artistic tradition. On the contrary: In his careful, detailed analysis of the entire film, David M. Lubin unfolds the incredible richness of motivic allusions and continuities found in Cameron's blockbuster, quoting both ancient myths and popular models in film history.[3] Cameron knows his art, and he has obviously watched uncountable films and read innumerable books. As Lubin shows, almost every instance of the film can somehow be connected with a forerunner, with images and scenes from a cinematic or a literary tradition. In several cases these are traditions of the *Titanic* myth and its earlier cinematic translations, but there are many more links to general motifs and subjects of Western literature and art.

Cameron certainly did not sit down and put these bricks together like a Lego house: It is a sign of his talent and art as storyteller that first the script and then the film offer a coherent, self-contained story, whose persuasive power is founded on an unusual density of classic allusions and traditional images that have been transferred to a new context, working as a story in its own right. But it is not alone Cameron's experience and talent as a screenwriter and director: A considerable part of the script's strength as a perfect Hollywood tale lies in the aptness of the *Titanic* story for dramatization and in the dominating categories of the *Titanic* myth, that — as in earlier films — render this specific historical event into the perfect fabric for storytelling.

In Cameron's *Titanic*, the categories and earlier dramatizations of the *Titanic* myth merge with cultural categories that became dominant in postmodernist thought and discourse. There are many reasons why *Titanic* became *the* film event of the 1990s. Certainly not least among them is the fact that some of the central aspects of the *Titanic* disaster, which began to dominate the discourse on the event right in 1912, perfectly link up with the central concerns of postmodern society and their discussion in the media, in popular forums (most important the Internet), and in scholarly analysis. The 1997 *Titanic* somehow addressed everyone, on a global basis.

The Main Categories of the Titanic *Myth and Their Treatment in Cameron's* Titanic

Interesting insights are yielded if the film is analyzed along the "classic" categories gender, class, nation, race and religion. On the surface level, *Titanic* appears to be 100 percent politically correct: a feminist coming-of-age narrative, a plea for a classless society, a strong restatement of the American Dream. The audience, emotionally involved with the main character Rose, who tells the story of her coming of age in the course of the *Titanic* disaster, leaves the cinema feeling good. After all, our dreams and ideals have been reconfirmed and somewhat purified in the catharsis of the disaster. This is contemporary Hollywood at its best — yet it is nothing but a dream.

The frame narrative is set in the present day (1996) on the research ship *Keldysh*, which has been chartered by a team of treasure hunters. They hope to salvage a safe from the wreck of the *Titanic* that they expect to contain a diamond of tremendous worth, the Heart of the Ocean. As their futile attempt is shown on television, an aged lady contacts them; it turns out that she was on the *Titanic* in 1912 and survived the disaster, beginning a new life under a new name after her arrival in New York. In flashbacks, she tells the main story, which is both the story of her first love and the story of the *Titanic*. Rose DeWitt Bukater, a spoiled upper class girl, is about to be forced into marriage with the rich villain Cal Hockley. The pair is traveling on the *Titanic*, with the wedding scheduled to take place after their arrival in the United States. Desperate Rose attempts to jump to her death from the stern of the *Titanic*, yet is saved by bohemian and artist Jack Dawson, who had won a Third Class ticket in a poker game just before departure. They do, of course, fall in love, and right before the collision Rose decides to break with her class conventions and begin a new life with Jack after arrival in New York. Her plans are marred since the ship sinks. After a considerable amount of action on the sinking *Titanic*, the lovers are among those who cling to the stern in the last moment and go down with the ship. In the water, Jack puts Rose on a floating door. Dying in the icy water, he makes her promise never to give up. Fortified by this promise, Rose snatches the whistle of a dead officer, draws attention to herself, and is saved by the single lifeboat that returned. On the *Carpathia*, she avoids the First Class passengers and declares her name to be Rose Dawson. In the end, back in present time on the *Keldysh*, it turns out that she unknowingly had saved the precious diamond in the pocket of her coat; she never made use of it throughout her rich, adventurous life as an actress. Now, at the age of 101, she drops it overboard to the site of the wreck. The film ends with her dream that she enters the wreck, resplendent in rejuvenated beauty, and as a youthful bride is eventually reunited with young Jack on the Grand Staircase, while the lost passengers of all classes applaud in perfect harmony. Although it is eventually left open, the context implies that this vision is not just a dream, but stands for old Rose's death and thus for her return to an eternal, paradisiac *Titanic*.

Despite its persuasive visions of classlessness and emancipation, there is not much about political correctness and a truly political message in *Titanic*. Instead, the film gathers a considerable part of its strength from popular stereotypes that are sold as a story of success. The category gender, central to the *Titanic* myth right from the start, is reduced to the central love story resulting in Rose's emancipation from the fetters of her class. From a Hollywood standpoint, the love story was essential to "sell" the disaster. As Cameron stated:

> I thought it was not artistically interesting to just follow a bunch of historical characters, never really getting involved in the event at an emotional level. I figured the best way to get in touch with the emotion of the event would be to take one set of characters and tell the story as a love story — because only by telling it as a love story can you appreciate the loss of separation and the loss caused by death.[4]

The disaster thus is translated into human terms. At the same time, it invests the personal love story with a mythic dimension.[5]

The category of gender is, however, entirely individualized in Cameron's *Titanic*. In contrast to earlier films, the decisive motto "women and children first" hardly plays a role in the *Titanic* blockbuster. Except for the extended separation of Rose and her lover, there are but a few fleeting moments where the pain of separation in the course of the evacuation becomes visible at all.[6] Both in the historical *Titanic* story and in the myth, this conscious separation of lovers and families was regarded as one of the most painful aspects of the disaster; it was taken up in most of the *Titanic* films up to Cameron's (most conspicuously with families being torn apart in the 1953 and 1958 films). Cameron, however, chose to relinquish such emotional competition to the central love story. The aspect of "gender" primarily focuses on Rose and her development, with Rose being used as representative of the general role of upper class women in late Edwardian society:

> RUTH: Your father left us nothing but a legacy of bad depths hidden by a good name. That name is the only card we have to play. I don't understand you. It is a fine match with Hockley. It will ensure our survival.
> ROSE: How can you put this on my shoulders?
> RUTH: Why are you being so selfish?
> ROSE: *I'm* being selfish??
> RUTH: Do you want to see me working as a seamstress? Is that what you want? To see our fine things sold at auction? Our memories scattered to the winds? [*starts to cry*]
> ROSE: It's so unfair.
> RUTH: Of course it's unfair. We're women. Our choices are never easy.
> *Ruth takes Rose's face into her hands, kisses her gently, then laces the corset tightly.*

As symbolized in the telling act of Rose's luscious body being tightly laced up in a corset by her mother, Rose does indeed epitomize the role of the refined Edwardian woman — at least, she is supposed to do so.[7] She is depicted as paragon of the upper class belle who has to accept the role assigned to her. It is her rebellious spirit that became so appealing to the audience of the late 1990s: a beautiful young woman breaking the fetters of her class and liberating herself to become a "free individual" and thus a female incarnation of the American Dream. This is indeed a new version of the traditional *Titanic* tale: Instead of female meekness, female independence is advocated, instead of matrimonial loyalty unto death (that is, the Straus couple), love's insurmountable strength in the struggle for survival is recommended. According to this modern reinterpretation of gender roles on the *Titanic*, Rose's jump from the lifeboat back onto the ship to join her lover is but logical. The childlike contract of the two lovers, "You jump — I jump," has replaced Ida Straus's more dignified "Where you go, I go."

The *Titanic* audience loved this modern tale of female emancipation. It is no coincidence that teenage girls and young women constituted the most important segment of the worldwide *Titanic* fan community (the particular attractiveness of film star Leonardo DiCaprio as Rose's redeemer did, of course, enforce the message). But it is by no means a true story of emancipation but only a "virtual feminism," a "costless liberation brought to you by a devoted, selfless, charming, funny, incredibly handsome lover," as film critic Katha Pollitt put it.[8] For Rose, "liberty" has always been an affordable commodity, up to the end of her rich and fulfilled life. As can be seen in the short retrospective presented by Rose's photographs just before the film ends with her dying dream, she continued to lead a privileged life after the *Titanic* disaster: She could afford to be adventurous, to fly planes, to ride horses and elephants, to catch giant fish. Sean Redmond points out that the photographs "reference her as a mobile, privileged white woman."[9] Rose may have earned the money necessary for these adventurous luxuries, but we are never told how, except for a short allusion that she had worked as an actress.[10]

Let us consider her story realistically: What happened after Rose DeWitt Bukater alias Dawson, who in the sinking had consciously renounced her class affiliation and all privileges, left the *Carpathia* in New York? She had nothing but a rather expensive (yet doubtlessly ruined) gown and a rather expensive coat on her body — plus a tremendously precious diamond which, however, she never turned into cash (underlining her independence from upper class riches and privileges). How did she then, a woman without financial means, start a new life in New York? Desiring to remain anonymous, she would certainly not have made use of Margaret Brown's support for the destitute Third Class passengers nor of the Titanic Relief Fund. Having become interested in the question of female liberty and thus emancipation, did Rose then take part in the suffragettes' movement, which was at its highest right in the spring of 1912? On May 4 of the same year, the very day of John Jacob Astor's spectacular funeral, there was the largest ever demonstration of suffragettes in New York — would Rose DeWitt Bukater alias Dawson have participated in such a political demonstration for women's rights? Hardly. Cameron's fairy tale of female liberation leaves out the aspects of everyday life and hardship. The feminism displayed in the Hollywood tale is "safe, sanitised, liberal,"[11] it is a virtual feminism retaining the old, patriarchal patterns where convenient. After all, Rose did not at all object to Jack's individual version of "women first": As the two lovers struggle in the water, she naturally accepts his chivalrous gesture to put her on a piece of flotsam that will not hold them both. Instead of seeking some other floating device for himself, he stays with her, freezing to death in the icy water. Alexandra Keller's conclusion hits the mark:

> Cameron's version of femininity, proposed in the figure of the take-no-prisoners woman, may be atypical for Hollywood but ultimately does not disturb its patriarchal imperative. In this it is eminently nonthreatening, therefore consumable, and therefore popular.... *Titanic*'s politics fit its blockbuster profile.[12]

The same must be said for the category of class. Cameron's *Titanic* makes a point of being politically correct in class matters. For the first time in a *Titanic* film, the central love story is a cross-class relation. In the earlier films, love stories on the *Titanic* unfolded entirely in First Class; in a next step (from *A Night to Remember* onwards), the lower classes were allowed their own amorous subplots, but the various love stories remained neatly separated according to the ship's class barriers. Cameron only took the final step in the pattern, (apparently) breaking down these barriers by coupling a Third Class passenger with a First Class beauty. In the tradition of storytelling, there is nothing original about this: It is the ancient fairy tale pattern of the swineherd and the princess, with the latter having to be redeemed by a poor but independent and adventurous young man. It was logical that this pattern one day had to be applied to the *Titanic* story with its architecturally fixed class categories.

However, the apparent subversion of the rigid Edwardian class structure is just as delusive as the apparent feminism in the coming-of-age tale. First, Jack Dawson is by no means a true representative of Third Class. He is marked as "the Other" in several ways, an entirely autonomous individual, who — without any problems — transcends the social space assigned to the various classes.[13] (Has anyone ever asked how he and his friend Fabrizio — and later he and his beloved Rose — managed to freely roam around the *Titanic*'s bow and step on the railing to play "King of the World"? This section of the ship was not open to passengers at all.) In his general mobility, Jack is a living symbol of the American Dream[14] — model to Rose, who will later emulate his mobility and thus turn into a female version of the same dream. Jack is not impoverished; his economic insecurity is voluntary (and probably just temporary), his life is a bohemian adventure and not a lower class struggle for survival. He gladly mixes with Third Class, having all kinds of international friends and going along in their dances (even though he does not know the steps, but does of course get them right instinctively). Yet in fact, he is free to move where he wants, even in First Class, turning into the perfect "gentleman" just by appropriating the superficial cultural signifiers of privilege: a perfectly fitting dinner jacket, the gallant kiss on the hand that he has "seen in a nickelodeon," and appropriate eating manners which he learns through a single stage direction by sympathetic upstart "Molly" Brown. In fact, Jack is a sort of classless "superman," and certainly not an advocate for Third Class, though he incidentally travels on the *Titanic* with a Third Class ticket. Rose's romance with him therefore hardly is cross-class, but rather a redemption tale coupling a female in distress with a somewhat superhuman being who exactly fulfills her need. It is not a coincidence that the story Rose tells is *her* coming of age, while there is no development at all in the perfect and unchangeable Jack.

Yet the class issue of *Titanic* is delusive also on a larger plane. Laurie Ouellette has pointed out that "rather than triggering class consciousness or resistance, the film actually works in the *opposite* direction by mystifying the causes and continuities of inequalities."[15] *Titanic* promotes several aspects belonging to the myths of a classless American society: the central idea that class is "un-American," the idea that class is only temporary and can be transcended, the notion that class only is a superficial aspect in society, and the romantic concept that "true love" exists independent of class relations.[16]

Throughout the film, class is coded as superficial and easily transcendable. For people like Jack — who, tellingly, is the driving force in the historical episode of Third Class men breaking down a locked gate — there are no class barriers, they have access to all strata within society. *Titanic* offers a romantic fantasy of anyone being able to cross class, since class is depicted as divorced from the decisive factor of economics, of education, of birth and upbringing. In reality, *Titanic* heavily promotes First Class culture, creating the illusion that anyone could take part in its privileges. Although on the surface, this First Class culture is linked to the past and therefore goes down with the ship, old Rose still represents a privileged class who can afford an adventurous life, a house of their own, a creative hobby like pottery, and even a housekeeper. (Does old Rose pay her granddaughter Lizzy for her work — or does Lizzy have another job to make ends meet?)

In fact, priority is clearly set on First Class throughout the entire film.[17] Naturally — and typically for *Titanic* films, reflecting the emphasis in the publicity for the luxurious ship back in 1911–12 — the splendid interiors of First Class are put to prominent use, with a special emphasis on the Grand Staircase as space of meeting, conflict and (cultivated) transgression of class limits. Thus, Rose takes her decision to leave her social space and join the Third Class party on the staircase right under the famous clock; Jack practices his entry into First Class habits waiting at the foot of the stairs; Cal later hunts the lovers down the stairs until they end up in the half-flooded Third Class corridors; and in the sinking sequence, the flooded Grand Staircase and glass dome are seen with a fairy-like drowned First Class lady floating in the water: In death, all class distinctions are nullified. In *Titanic*, First Class is turned into a blazing celebration of luxury and beauty. The dinner scene, with its meticulous reconstruction of all details of the dishes, the cutlery, and the rich sequence of exquisite courses, was the first-rated favorite among the test screening audience[18]: Its splendor quite clearly proved attractive to modern viewers who — realistically seen — hardly ever have the privilege to enjoy comparable luxury.[19]

In fact, the entire love affair between Jack and Rose unfolds within the luxury of First Class: Their first meetings take place on the First Class deck, Jack gets his chance to prove his cosmopolitan manners in the First Class dining room, he is later allowed into Rose's luxury suite and has his first erotic encounter with her there, drawing her as a nude. Even the consummation of their love takes place in the First Class space of a luxurious car (whose transport from Europe to the U.S. only could be afforded by a First Class passenger[20]). Where else should these erotic encounters have taken place? Third Class accommodation certainly did not allow for amorous privacy. Thus, the love story was bound to be a First Class story, with the exotic element of a Third Class lover.

The same is true for the rest of Third Class: The Third Class party as the only larger sequence in Third Class is nothing but an injection of folksy energy, showing Rose what she could get if she let go of her stiff upper class life. In the development of the love affair, this scene is an impetus, nothing more. Apart from this, the audience would hardly have enjoyed a long-term development of their love relationship in the down-to-earth, loud and brash environments of Third Class. The quiet luxury of the suite, Rose's ethereal gowns and her perfect makeup do not quite make a point for "political correctness" with regard to class — but they fulfill the Hollywood code.

The viewer is encouraged to enjoy the splendor and thus the privileges of the upper class. At the same time, the film promotes the illusion that class does not really count and can be transcended, as symbolized by Jack's class mobility during the voyage on the *Titanic* and by Rose in the later development of her life. The ship with its rigid class hierarchy is displayed as an un–American space; the rich American passengers (almost exclusively characterized as arrogant and shallow) appear as caricatures of an obsolete European aristocratic tradition that will go down with the ship.[21] In turn, a dream image — in fact, the American Dream — of a new, classless American society is constructed. It is, as can be seen in the unrealistic, idealized person of Jack or in the fragmentary biography of Rose, just an illusion. But it works perfectly for a blockbuster. As in fairy tale, the cross-class love story is but a symbol and remains within the closed world of the story, without any relation to the real world of the reader and viewer.

Accordingly, *Titanic* works with class stereotypes throughout: lucid, splendid, yet stiff upper class versus dark, bodily, down-to-earth and life-affirming Third Class. *Titanic* leaves the audience with the satisfactory impression that one can have both, through a process of costless liberation. Thus, the popular myth of the United States as a classless society is confirmed, the timeless validity of the American Dream is — in beautiful settings and colors — once more propounded, and the uncomfortable realities of a political class struggle are reduced to a convenient prop in a fairy tale romance. The end — which will be analyzed in more detail — offers a paradisiac vision of all classes being united in the eternal beauty of an immortal (First Class) *Titanic*.

Class, a central aspect in the *Titanic* myth, indeed plays an important role in Cameron's tale, yet it is trivialized and functionalized, curtailed to a convenient means to advance the main plot. Both in gender and class, the film in fact capitalizes on false politics:

> Given how much Cameron has spent on the film (a fact which virtually every audience member would have known), and given that the final act of narrative closure is one in which Rose performs an act of waste [throwing the diamond into the sea] that is only the prerogative of the very, very rich, the audience is, for a very small fee [that is, the movie ticket], made momentary shareholders in this upper-class ethos, while still being allowed the moral high ground of those in steerage.[22]

The aspect of nation in Cameron's *Titanic* is strongly linked up with the way class is treated. *Titanic* displays two ways of being "American": an obsolete, Europeanized American society which is doomed to drown, and the "New America," a modern nation-civilization that releases the individual from the class and gender oppression inherited from European tradition.[23] Rose's arrival in New York—of course with the Statue of Liberty figuring conspicuously, albeit incorrectly, as the *Carpathia* enters the harbor—thus appears as a "moment of symbolic rebirth."[24] Like a newborn child, Rose has nothing as she enters into the New World (excepting the diamond which she will not put to use), and she is soaked as though she had come out of amniotic fluid. A new life has been given to her. As shown above, though, the vision of "New America" (or, the American Dream) put forth by Cameron's *Titanic* is utopian, leaving out the dreary details of reality.

The British, in turn, play no role whatsoever in Cameron's film. They are inconspicuous professionals, the captain, the officers, the engineers, ship architect Andrews. In fact, Cameron simply uses the stereotypes presented in earlier films: a well-meaning, sociable, but rather helpless Captain Smith, professional yet still insufficient officers, the gentle but altogether passive Mr. Andrews. Andrews, at least, is integrated into the main plot through his three short conversations with Rose that give her the vital information about the lack of lifeboats. Thus, he is the only British staff member who has a certain functional role in the main plot—and it is, of course, Rose who is the last person to see him in his historical pose standing before the painting in the Smoking Room. Nevertheless, Andrews remains a vignette of dutiful, yet overall passive British kindness; his historically based abstinence from fighting for his own survival perfectly fits into this image. Cameron could have fleshed out these historical stereotypes of notable British characters on the *Titanic*. Yet as stated above, it was not his desire to "follow a bunch of historical characters," who, in his opinion, would not give opportunity for the emotional involvement he sought to create.[25] Not even Bruce Ismay plays a significant role in the script; Cameron did not take advantage of Ismay's oft-quoted "act of cowardice," which would not have contributed anything to the main plot.

In contrast, it is the Irish who become the one non–American nation of greater significance in Cameron's movie. In *Titanic* films, this is nothing new: A special focus on the Irish emigrants started with *A Night to Remember* and was intensified in *S.O.S. Titanic*, with several historical Irish passengers being highlighted both before and after the collision. In Cameron's film, however, "Irishness" achieves a new status. As Kevin J. Donnelly points out, Irish culture has got a structural and symbolic function in *Titanic*, corresponding in detail to the international commodification of Irish culture through the Riverdance shows, Irish pubs and Irish music bands.[26] Irishness codes both "the mystical" and "the primitive" in a positive sense: an atavistic form of being, close to nature, life-loving and life-affirming.[27] As a commodity, Irishness is musicalized, emotional, celebratory — just what Cameron offers in the famous Third Class party, the perfect counter-image to stiff and "denatured" upper class.

Paradoxically, Irish protagonists figure much stronger in the earlier *Titanic* films of 1958 and 1979, where they form a group with their own little plots and love affairs. In Cameron's *Titanic*, only one Irish character is given a marginal role for himself, Third Class passenger Tommy Ryan, who becomes friends with Jack and Fabrizio. Jack is *not* Irish, although he is often regarded and described as such: He boards at Southampton, comes originally from the United States (Chippewa Falls, Wisconsin) and has traveled widely in America and Europe. His friend and traveling companion is an Italian; it is only on the *Titanic* where Jack meets Irish fellow passengers and eventually learns to dance their jig. Nevertheless, Jack and the liberal, bohemian culture that he incarnates become closely linked up with Irishness in *Titanic*. It is music that provides this link: As early as in Southampton, Jack and his zeal for life are combined with fast-beat Irish music, as he and Fabrizio run to catch the ship. This kinetic folk music — fulfilling, as Donnelly observes, the same energizing function as rock music in action scenes[28] — returns as Jack and Rose flee from Cal's henchman Lovejoy and, like fairy spirits from another world, exuberantly reel through the blasting hell of the engine rooms. Thus, Jack is associated with the free and earthbound spirit of traditional music and traditional culture — another cliché that has nothing to do with the realities of Third Class and Irish emigration in 1912.

It is, however, not these particular scenes, but rather the general score that gives a particular feel of "Irishness" to the entire film. As in earlier films, composer James Horner uses Irish instrumentation and musical style as a "universal" symbol of emotion and sentiment.[29] The pastoral sound with strings playing rustic and lyrical melodies, the fast and rhythmic jigs and reels, and the idiomatic sound of the Irish uilleann pipe create a distinctive "Irish accent," which is found in large parts of the score. Instead of prominently featuring Irish passengers, Cameron and his film composer chose to permeate the entire movie with an Irish or, more generally, a Celtic quality. The music gives the film an overall tone of wistfulness, the sonic image of a lost, (allegedly) more pure and innocent world — thus tying up perfectly with a central aspect of the *Titanic* myth, in which nostalgia has played an ever increasing role. In Cameron's *Titanic*, the music, the wreck, the story of the disaster, and a long-lost, yet enduring love, form a singular, emotional unity:

> *Titanic*'s "Irishness" works as a signifier of difference, and precisely as a signifier of power relations, enhanced by its musical overtones.... The film's Irish-inspired music marks a spectral presence, one that charms the audience. The disaster is abhorrent and music acts as a talisman against the bane and terror.[30]

The saddened wistfulness — most strikingly found in the uilleann's lament at the beginning of Dion's theme song — is counterbalanced by the energetic quality of the Irish dances: The commodified Irish music in *Titanic* imparts the impression that the sought-after "freedom" and thus the "New America" personified by Jack and Rose can come through affiliating with the "Irish" qualities of the zealous, earthbound, and energetic lifestyle allegedly found in Third Class.

Thus, the "Irish-imbued" music reconfirms the double link that generated the overwhelming success of *Titanic*: a strong, persuasive combination of the *Titanic* myth with the immediate concerns and *Zeitgeist* of the 1990s. In its wistfulness, the score is closely bound up with the sense of nostalgia that has characterized the *Titanic* myth and code since the 1950s. On the other hand, the score with its Celtic touch and the alluring vocals reflects the success of New Age music in the 1980s and 1990s. The dominant "Irish touch" in *Titanic* again displays how Cameron successfully reprocessed and marketed the *Titanic* myth to the taste of his present-day audience.

Religion, the fourth dominant category in the *Titanic* myth, is strikingly absent in Cameron's version. Accordingly, there is not a single study to be found on the aspect of religiosity in *Titanic*. Christian religion, important as it is in the original myth, has been almost entirely blinded out in Cameron's film — or rather, it has been (fittingly) substituted by the postmodernist *Zeitgeist* of the 1990s.

There are a few instances where Christian religion is hinted at in the film. Tellingly, these are stereotypes with no significance for the plot or the main characters' attitude. And tellingly, Christian religion fares rather poorly in these scenes. The band's playing of "Nearer, My God, to Thee" is used as an emotional set-piece in the increasing chaos of the evacuation. The scene of the brave and noble musicians — finally a convincing image of "true Britishness" — is moving, yet it is not more than a replica of the corresponding scene from *A Night to Remember* (including the gradual harmonization of the hymn as the musicians turn back to join into the band leader's lonely tune). The hymn has no significance as a *religious* song: The band's final piece is just an emotional accessory that helps to "get the *Titanic* story right." After all, "Nearer, My God, to Thee" had become so central to the *Titanic* myth that no film aiming at "authenticity" could leave it out. In contrast to the British film *A Night to Remember*, Cameron used the "American" tune "Bethany," which already played a prominent role in Jean Negulesco's 1953 *Titanic* film. Unlike this Hollywood forerunner, however, "Nearer, My God, to Thee" is not a token for religiosity in Cameron's *Titanic*: It is an emotional detail, but does not stand for true faith and resignation into God's will.

In the other instances, religion fares even worse. Again, these scenes primarily serve to add "authenticism": the Sunday service in First Class, which reportedly had higher priority than the lifeboat drill that should have taken place on the morning of April 14, and Catholic priest Father Byles praying with the doomed passengers in the last moments before the sinking. Cameron uses the Sunday service for a moment of dramatic irony: Tellingly, the First Class passengers sing the famous hymn "Eternal Father, Strong to Save," which both in the U.S. and in England is known as "The Navy Hymn," the first stanza ending with the prominent plea "for those in peril on the sea."[31] The ensuing events then will show that the "eternal Father" worshipped by the First Class passengers is not at all "strong to save."

Indifference and irony against Christian religion eventually turn into spitefulness. As the panicking passengers crowd towards the stern, Jack, trapped behind a man reciting Psalm 23, snaps at him:

> PASSENGER: Yea, though I walk through the valley of the shadow of death...
> JACK: You wanna walk a little faster through that valley there?

In this instance, *Titanic* assumes the quality of a teenage flick (just as in the famous scene with giggling Rose giving Lovejoy the finger[32]). The teenage audience no doubt loved Jack Dawson's "witty" quip. More mature spectators, in contrast, must wonder if it really was necessary to debase one of the most traditional texts in Jewish and Christian religion that has been used as a prayer in affliction for several thousand years. Is this supposed to be a tinge of slapstick comedy in the face of disaster? Cameron certainly had a younger, religiously indifferent audience in mind as he inserted this "joke" in his script.

Hubris, the "Old Testament" (and also classical) aspect in the *Titanic* myth, does not play a central role, either. There are, of course, the standard remarks about the *Titanic*'s technological prowess and the ship being "unsinkable." They are not highlighted, though, except for a short scene giving Rose the opportunity to demonstrate her educated sarcasm, as she counters Ismay's eulogy on the ship with a remark quoting Freud. While most *Titanic* films ignore the motif of hubris, Cameron in fact reverts the idea: By focusing so strongly on the wreck, he highlights the tragic contrast between the "ship of dreams" and its tragic doom. It is not hubris that is highlighted (despite the negative image of the arrogant First Class passengers), but the tragedy of the beautiful maiden ship that has become the focus of the film, being inseparably intertwined with the great tragic love story of Rose and Jack.

Religion, elsewhere central to the *Titanic* myth, has thus become a meaningless accessory in the 1997 version. Just as Cameron's interpretation of the other categories in the *Titanic* myth, this phenomenon is intricately linked up with the cultural context of the film, that is, Western society and its values in the 1990s. The issue of gender has been replaced by a virtual, costless feminism, the negotiation of class has been reduced to class-affirmative popular stereotypes, nation serves the clichés of a mainstream American audience, and religion has been substituted for a secular *Zeitgeist*: a general spirit in which romanticized love becomes the token for eternity, nostalgia and postmodernist historicism constitute the dominant form of worship, and consumerism as well as a competitive, survivalist attitude dominate the modes of social behavior.

Postmodernist Features in Cameron's Titanic

Throughout the 20th century, the *Titanic* myth has again and again proved to be an ideal matrix for fiction in novel and film, interacting with their present time. In Cameron's *Titanic*, the various aspects of the myth interact perfectly with the aesthetics of the last decade of the century, which can largely be described as "postmodernist." As Diane Negra states in her analysis of *Titanic* as a "survivalist text," the film "displays a number of up-to-the minute concerns characteristic of a broad range of texts in late–twentieth century popular culture."[33] Cameron's *Titanic*, more successful than any film before, can in many ways be described as a *Zeitgeist* document, presenting postmodernist negotiations of romantic love, the popular use of nostalgia and historicism, current concerns of class and economic survival, the encouragement of a general consumerist attitude, and the reflection of all these concerns in popular culture. These aspects interact with the *Titanic* myth, turning Cameron's version into the ultimate postmodernist *Titanic* tale.

Cameron's *Titanic* preaches the secular religion of inextinguishable romantic love. This central issue is epitomized in Celine Dion's mega-hit "My Heart Will Go On," which sold more than 15 million copies worldwide (thus being one of the best-selling singles in history) and proved to be the ideal preparation for the theatrical release of the film. *Titanic* tied in perfectly with popular culture's longing for love as remedy for everything and all. The religious concept of eternity has been substituted for everlasting love. Rose's dying dream, in which she finally is reunited with the lover of her youth, ends in a white screen: Consciousness has been dissolved in the lovers' ultimate union — and the audience is ready to take this final vision, underlaid by the comforting sounds of Dion's song, home in their minds and hearts.

As scholars of popular culture have shown, this concept of the *Titanic* tale as an epic love story, based on female subjectivity and romantic feelings, is aimed at a primarily female audience, regaining a vital segment of the traditional Hollywood audience after decades of more action-based, male-oriented productions.[34] Cameron set this concept from the very start, noting the basic pitch for his film back in 1995 as "*Romeo and Juliet* on a boat."[35] Within this concept, the heavy accent on technology and technological means was not regarded as a means in itself, but as auxiliary in telling a character-based story and engaging the audience's emotions.[36] It will be shown below under "Recipe for Success" how the story of the ship and the love story of the main characters are inseparably entangled with each other, creating an emotional impact more overwhelming than in any *Titanic* film before.

With his focus on a great love story on an historical canvas, centering on a strong female protagonist who becomes involved both in the upheavals of her times and in the personal upheaval of her romantic love, Cameron takes up the grand tradition of pre–1960s Hollywood.[37] The *Titanic* story, a major disaster in times of social and political upheaval, with the poignant aspect of lovers and families being separated in the face of death, offered the perfect fabric to revive this tradition. Since the disaster also provides ample opportunity for action and technology, Cameron had the chance to offer something for all: action-adventure, aimed primarily at young males, and the large frame of the romantic epic, drawing women into the theaters. Due to the overwhelming dominance of the love story, though, it was the latter, girls and women, who constituted the majority of the audience — and they took their boyfriends, husbands, and families along. Thus, *Titanic* covered an unusually broad segment of the worldwide audience.

Yet it is not the story of romantic love alone that made *Titanic* so attractive to a late 1990s female audience. As discussed under the aspect of gender, the particular frame of the narrative turned the tragic love story into a tale of (alleged) female emancipation, and it transported the historical drama right into the audience's present time. Women of all ages, from teenage girls to grandmothers, were welcome to identify with Rose, her youthfulness, her rebellious spirit, and her eventual wisdom. "A woman's heart is a deep ocean of secrets," is old Rose's (embarrassingly banal) conclusion at the end of the tale. This feels just fine for any female viewer — have we not all known all the way through how special our personal experiences are? Costless liberation, a rich and adventurous life, wisdom and a spellbound audience (that is, the treasure hunters listening breathlessly to Rose's tale), and above all, everlasting love, from youth into old age: Any woman is welcome to identify with this role model. (And, fortunately for the average female viewer, Kate Winslet alias Rose DeWitt Bukater was *not* the super-slim standard Hollywood star: Female viewers did not feel fat in comparison with her.) Wisdom for all, a model for all, and love for all: a message that resonated with the movie's female fans.

Another central aspect that links the *Titanic* myth with postmodernist aesthetics is the strong concern for history and authenticity in Cameron's *Titanic*. Ever since *A Night to Remember*, *Titanic* filmmakers had been bound to the *Titanic* code, to a meticulous awareness for every detail of the historical *Titanic* story. It is obvious from 1958 onwards how scenes defined as "historical truth" in Walter Lord's 1955 novel become indispensable building blocks in *Titanic* narratives, warranting that "the story is right." Cameron with his obsessive sense of detail developed this regard to the extreme. His *Titanic* is the culmination of a specific aspect in the development of the *Titanic* myth — but it is also indicative of the 1990s and their specific relation to history.

Postmodernist aesthetics have a highly ambiguous relation to history. Quite generally (as can be seen in the almost complete abolition of the historical perspective in academic disciplines most affected by postmodern scholarship), postmodernism displays an almost celebratory disregard for history. History is "old-fashioned," it is the present time alone that counts, and after all, everything is subjective. And if "historical fact" is denounced as "construction" (which accordingly must be deconstructed), if everything in fact is relative, why bother with history at all? There is, however, also another attitude to history in postmodern society, most strikingly expressed in the ubiquitous television documentaries on history with their notorious reconstruction and re-enactment of the historical event in question. History can be "experienced" by meticulous reconstruction, up to the most accurate detail. It is this attitude to history that is typical of postmodernist historical film — and that has been developed unto perfection in Cameron's *Titanic*.

Thus, the well-known and well-studied interiors are painstakingly reconstructed, and the exterior is recreated at a scale of 90 percent (that is, with a length of 775 feet), offering the most spectacular prop ever. (The ship was in fact not scaled down at all, but Cameron left out a few stretches of the overall length that were not needed in any of the scenes. The funnels had to be reduced by 10 percent to fit this reduction.) Period clothes were created in excessive detail, and the "true moments" of that night (according to the tradition of *Titanic* lore) are inserted wherever possible. Cultural analysis has identified traces of Antiquarianism in this obsession with detail: an understanding of history informed by an aesthetics of the souvenir. The ship assumes the function of a giant museum or even vitrine: filled with historical objects and historical people, who constitute the "authentic" background to the fictional love story and thus make it "real."[38] It has become a sport among *Titanic* fans to spot as many "authentic" details as possible in the overall setting. Even the color is conceived as "period": Cameron wanted his image of the historical era to blaze with color, using both light and color as a visible token of upper class luxury.[39]

This approach of postmodernism is both monumental and obsessive: According to Gaylyn Studlar, "Cameron's *Titanic* is not indicative of a postmodern disregard of history but instead demonstrates the cinematic strategies of a monumental history essential to the classic Hollywood paradigm in its parallelist conception of events and nations."[40] The monumental stance, which in film culture builds on the strong fundament of the Hollywood tradition of historical epic, is combined with a truly fetishist concern for "getting it right": As Alexandra Keller puts it, "Virtual history, a uniquely postmodern entity, in which a presentation of past events comes to the viewer so loaded with detail that there can be no refuting it, seems to take the place of historical discourse."[41] Regard for history thus turns into virtual history, into a fetishism of detail—and eventually into false historicity.

The fetishist regard for detail in historical epics of the 1990s does in fact correspond to Roland Barthes's "reality effect," which has been drawn upon in the analysis of Academic painting: Accurate details signify the category of the real, their function is to give credibility to the "realness" of the work as a whole.[42] Due to the overload of "authentic" detail, Cameron's *Titanic* convinces us that the story is "true": Cameron's obsessive imperative to use originals, that is, the original plans of construction, the very companies who had produced the equipment of the *Titanic* back in 1911–12, and real material rather than fake, has become an indispensable aspect of the movie's tale of success. Accurate detail became the hallmark of the film production, thus creating a myth of facticity. On this fundament of "authenticity," any message can be sold as "true," as Alexandra Keller illustrates with regard to *Titanic*:

For Cameron to get the facts of the ship correct, down to the last detail, means — to him — that whatever ideological structure falls out will also be right, accurate, and, one assumes, natural, organic to both the ship and the narrative. Cameron's is, then, the quintessential blockbuster approach to history.[43]

There are clearly ideological messages that are transported in *Titanic*, as exemplified by the categories of gender, class, and nation. The obsession with authenticity helps to render them "true" and "correct." In fact, as the 1958 film *A Night to Remember* has shown, the *Titanic* story does not need this accuracy in detail in order to unfold its emotional potential. The British filmmakers did go to great lengths to build on the witness-based details exposed in Walter Lord's novel, but they had no problems in adding fictitious scenes. Their adherence to historical detail was relaxed, not obsessive.[44] In contrast, Cameron's fetishism of accurate detail turns out to be the climax in the development of *Titanic* films since 1958. Yet it equally is a very clear expression of postmodernist aesthetics: History is put to use, it is rewritten and shaped in the discourse, culminating in a "nearly rabid desire to *own* history."[45] Alexandra Keller sees this attitude generally reflected in the late 20th-century phenomenon of the blockbuster, that is, a specific form of postmodernist popular art:

> [Blockbusters] aspire to become history not by doing anything but by appearing, or passing, as history. And in this they are exemplary postmodern simulacra. The claim to be the event comes before the event itself and, thus designated, becomes the event (in attendance, ticket sales, expense, profit, merchandise, consumer ethos). It does not become history, as it pretends; it replaces history. One of the great ironies of *Titanic* and its extraordinary global popularity is that the actual sinking of this ship today would probably be a smaller blip on the historical radar screen than the film about it has been.[46]

Cameron's version of the *Titanic* story clearly is linked to the general historical development of the representation of *Titanic* in film. Yet in its attempt to offer "authentic history," it is also undeniably an "authentic document" of its own time.

History and historicism are closely linked to nostalgia. Again, this has been a central aspect in the *Titanic* myth since Lord's *A Night to Remember*. With Lord's novel and the 1958 film based upon it, nostalgia became the dominant mood in the remembrance of *Titanic*. The ship has become a symbol for a better, more innocent, chivalrous time — a world forever lost. In cinema, the recreation of this world goes hand in hand with a revelry in the lost beauties of the upper class: *Titanic* with its splendid First Class interiors and its splendidly dressed First Class passengers offers the perfect object for the evocation of such a dreamed past. From 1958 onwards, a nostalgic tone dominated *Titanic* movies; both *S.O.S. Titanic* and the 1996 mini-series continued in this vein. Cameron, who underlined the importance of at least *A Night to Remember* as inspiration for his film, duly adhered to this important *Titanic* tradition — and he added the wreck, which since its discovery in 1985 had become an icon for the *Titanic* as a dying queen.

Yet it is by no means only the tradition of *Titanic* representations that spurred the strong note of nostalgia permeating the entire film. As several scholars underline, *Titanic* absorbs and indeed perfects an important phenomenon of the 1990s: a widespread contemporary cultural fusion of nostalgia and consumerism.[47] History, imagined and idealized, is turned into a longing for a better world — and commodified as a utopian vision:

> Because of its particular structure and imagery, *Titanic* has touched contemporary audiences longing for something not readily available or particularly credible in the age of irony at the end of history: namely, "authentic emotion" felt as "historic experience." This longing ultimately confuses the "histrionic" and the "historic" with the "historical." In other words, *Titanic* is a highly effective cultural expression of what Susan Stewart, in *On Longing: Narratives of the Miniature, the Gigantic, the Souvenir, the Collection*, calls ... "the social disease of *nostalgia*."[48]

Titanic is not alone in this "social disease." It is characteristic of the 1990s that several Hollywood blockbusters inculcated the general predilection for nostalgia in form of heritage films, promoting the desirability of bygone lifestyles and landscapes.[49] In fact, there are numerous features that *Titanic* shares with the heritage films of the 1990s[50]:

- conspicuous consumption
- a fetishistic approach to objects
- an overall pervasive sense of loss and nostalgia
- an emphasis on female central characters
- a dominant concern with the lives and lived spaces of the upper class (while the lower class appears in romanticized vignettes)
- a central dilemma of class and gender conflict

Titanic fits excellently into the heritage pattern: like the heritage films, it is obsessed with recreating the past in nostalgic perfection; the space it offers is not a British manor, but a splendid British ship; it dwells on the lavish settings and costumes, and shares the heritage cult of authenticity.[51] Tellingly, it is the details of the "authentic" settings that were duly commodified and thus turned into souvenirs: Rose's dresses are for sale as tailor-made replicas or — less costly — as sewing patterns; you can buy a Rose doll (or rather a Kate Winslet doll?) with varying numbers of "original *Titanic*" dresses, and the Heart of the Ocean diamond necklace is available as a high-priced replica. Equally, traveling shows began to exhibit the objects that were used as props in the movie, drawing large audiences to have an "authentic" look at *Titanic* (the film prop or the historical ship? both melt into each other).[52] Nostalgia, founded on alleged "authenticity," became conveniently merged with consumerism. As shown above, the historical setting is turned into false historicity, an aspect that is underlined by Sean Redmond: "What is recaptured in the heritage-like setting of *Titanic* is not some authentic, accurate, informed sense of the past but the surface level reproduction of a commodity fetish."[53]

Julian Stringer terms this construction of a nostalgic feeling "imagined nostalgia": The film encourages viewers to miss something they never actually had been denied. "As such, *Titanic* represents nostalgia without lived experience or collective historical memory."[54] The creation of an imagined nostalgia, a longing for something one had not even missed, is, in fact, the very principle of consumer advertisements: The beautiful images of nostalgia, released from the fetters of reality, can be marketed anywhere in the world. They present a perfect past, the splendid image of an innocent era in which the little injustices of society still were tolerable and everybody somehow had a chance to participate in the luxury of the rich. It is a dream-like, nostalgic past, represented by the "ship of dreams." The wreck, framing the story of this better world, adds to its poignancy: In the end, the ship is redeemed and sails on in everlasting beauty. It is the spirit of the heritage film, transferred to the most historical of all ships.

Heritage film is not the only genre that has had a major influence on the conception of Cameron's *Titanic* tale. Again, the variety of genres and their mixing is a token of postmodernism: Take all the bricks that you can use to construct something spectacular. Scholars have discussed the mixing of genres in Cameron's *Titanic*, emphasizing the important role of epic romance, action-adventure, rites of passage, heritage, historical epic. If the result succeeds in drawing a large audience, as *Titanic* did, the film becomes a representative of a meta-genre, the blockbuster, which developed its specific characteristics in the final decades of the 20th century.

Titanic is not singular, but most spectacular in this development. It makes sense to link it to the rites of passage film (Susan Sydney-Smith enumerates various historical films of the late 1990s dealing with sea journeys and metaphorical ships[55]), and there is certainly a large amount of heritage in the setting. Most important, though, is the specific combination of action-adventure and the epic romance. This fusion is at the heart of Cameron's concept, merging the story of the *Titanic* disaster with an individual, fictional love story (cf. below). Up to the mid–90s, Cameron had become famous for his technological action films, including a number of science fiction and underwater settings. Now, he combined this gift with a romance in an historical setting, making technology — both within the plot and as means of production — the servant of emotion.

Both his concept and its realization hark back to the Hollywood tradition of epic filmmaking. Peter Krämer points out that *Titanic* exposes several of the traditional thematic concerns of historical epic:

- it offers a transatlantic topic (thus bridging the gap between the tradition of American national epics and that of European and biblical epics)
- it foregrounds the grandeur of the ship, the splendor of First Class, and the nobility of many passengers
- it emphasizes the injustice, oppressiveness and self-destructiveness of the class-based, capitalistic society
- it advocates the necessity for the removal of the class-based European social order that had been transported by Anglo-Saxon pioneers over the ocean (however, the disappearance is also wistfully mourned, just as in Civil War and Western epics)
- it puts a central focus on the conflict between the desires for freedom and the forces of oppression[56]

In these conspicuous correspondences between *Titanic* and the historical epics of Hollywood's Golden Age, the woman's perspective is rather unusual — but again, in *Gone with the Wind*, this perspective has a famous Hollywood forerunner. Yet it is not only the plot and its presentation that recall the grand epics of the great Hollywood era: The external factors — budget, prestige, and box office — which express the mega success in terms of hard cash, equally put *Titanic* in a line with Hollywood's greatest films. *Titanic* is a modern — or postmodernist — smash hit that capitalizes on its strong links to the great Hollywood tradition.

Alexandra Keller connects *Titanic* with a new, postmodernist aesthetics that comes forth in the blockbuster as "meta-genre":

> In many ways *Titanic* is both anomalous and inevitable. It is the apotheosis (so far) of life under blockbuster culture.... Not only is *Titanic* evidently a film for all, it is a *product* for everyone, the ice cream flavor nobody dislikes, and of which everyone wants seconds.[57]

A characteristic feature of the postmodernist blockbuster is its general superficiality. The issues discussed above all are in line with the characteristic features of the blockbuster: While creating the impression (and, with the audience, the tear-driving fact) of great emotion, the seemingly fundamental issues such as gender, class and nation are presented as easily consumable stereotypes. The same applies to history: History is replaced by spectacle and thus commodified.[58] Due to the monumental display of historical backdrop and the overwhelming wealth of accurate detail, viewers are persuaded into thinking they've seen "history as it really was"—a phenomenon that Alexandra Keller terms "the Blockbuster Historical Paradigm."[59] The experience of watching thus does not lead to an autonomous, critical investigation of the past. Rather, it instigates to repeated viewings and thus to repeated consumption of the sterilized, perfect presentation of the past. The various messages about female emancipation, class, and nation are absorbed in the paradigm of commodity. The result is an emotionally charged, pleasant delusion:

> *Titanic*, as the world's most successful blockbuster, so expertly reframes its proposed concerns of romance, class, gender equality, technical prowess, and historical accuracy as sheer commodity that it has become as ubiquitous and as all-encompassing as global capitalism itself. It presents its viewers with extremely pressing and vital issues in an ostensibly rigorous historical context. But by tacitly framing its concerns in terms of consumption, it offers its audience the easy way out, while still leaving them with the impression that they have participated in something of vital importance.[60]

As a blockbuster and thus as a commercial product, Cameron's *Titanic* indeed was a global success. Yet none of the pressing social questions that are an indispensable part of the *Titanic* myth and have let it surface again and again in the course of the 20th century is actually made a subject of reflection and discussion. As shown above, these questions are presented in the form of popular stereotypes, easy to consume, easy to forget. They are enlarged by the monumental disaster—but none of these questions actually is taken up as a socio-political problem. This is, in fact, not really a defect: it is not a blockbuster's job to reflect and solve problems. The blockbuster formula builds on success and popularity. This excludes a serious reflection of sociopolitical problems right from the start.

And this is the very hallmark of postmodernist aesthetics, even of postmodernist strategy in real life: It is surface communication that is the focus—not the contents and not the problems themselves.

Finally there is one aspect of 1990s *Zeitgeist* that distinguishes Cameron's *Titanic* quite clearly from all earlier films. A central part of the *Titanic* myth is the chivalrous behavior of the passengers in the face of death. Up to 1958, *Titanic* films carefully reproduced this aspect: It is the tragedy of the sinking that is the focus, not the survivors' story. Passengers behave in a restrained, dignified way. This idealization begins to change with *A Night to Remember*: The 1958 film was the first to display hysteria in several scenes and to integrate post-disaster scenes. With Second Officer Lightoller, for the first time a *survivor* is made the hero in a *Titanic* tale; accordingly, it is he who has the last word in the post-disaster scene.[61] However, Lightoller's heroism is not displayed on a large scale. On the contrary: He is a paragon of dutifulness, helping the victims even while he himself is struggling in the icy water. Indeed, the fight for survival is not an issue in the traditional *Titanic* story; such a fight was regarded as disgraceful in the 1912 discourse (epitomized in the social disgrace of Bruce Ismay). If *Titanic* films expose the survival motif at all, it is projected on villains, either historical (Ismay) or fictitious (the historical instance of a male passenger who escaped with a woman's shawl over his head, conveniently projected onto whichever unpopular character in *Titanic* films).

Cameron's *Titanic* is quite different in this respect. As Diane Negra shows, the film can indeed be regarded as "a survivalist text" due to its strong focus on two characters who do everything to survive — in extreme cases even disregarding the needs of other people.[62] Jack, the independent globetrotter, openly declares, "I'm a survivor!" Rose, originally a dependent, immobile First Class lady, quickly learns from him: In extreme danger, she even ignores the need of her fellow victim. Resting in relative security on the railing of the sinking stern, she exchanges a glance with a desperate Third Class girl dangling over the abyss (in fact, this is the Norwegian emigrant Helga Dahl, with whom Jack's friend Fabrizio falls in love in the uncut version of the film). Gone is the solidarity with the Third Class passengers that was so exuberantly demonstrated at the Third Class party: Where Rose would increase the danger for her already endangered life, she does not extend a hand, but wordlessly watches the destitute woman fall and die. In the end, after Jack has put her (alone) on the floating door, thus sacrificing his own chances to be saved, Rose again follows the individualist doctrine of survival. Spurred by the promise to survive, which Jack forced from her in his last moments, she pushes her lover's body down into the depths and jumps back into the icy water to get a chance to be saved.

Jack and Rose are entirely self-reliant. They — miraculously — get all the information they need, they do not heed authorities, they find their way through the labyrinth of corridors, they even succeed where the professional in charge failed (namely to unlock the gate that blocks their way under rising water). In her desperate effort to release Jack from his handcuffs, Rose does not receive help from a steward when she, a spoiled First Class passenger, urgently asks for it (quite a new experience for her, no doubt); she serves the steward with a bloody nose and learns to help herself. This underworld scene in the frighteningly deserted corridors, with the light flickering and the ship groaning in its agony, is the actual rite of passage for this fastidious upper class girl: She transforms from a civilized, well-behaved lady to a fierce survivor.

9. James Cameron's Titanic (1997) 205

Survivalism, "a loosely structured yet pervasive belief system and set of practices focusing on disaster preparedness,"[63] played an increasing role in the 1990s, linking up with millennium-oriented fears. Diane Negra identifies the near-miraculous endurance of a small, privileged group of survivors in the face of catastrophic disaster as an emergent narrative paradigm in the 1990s: Building on the initial series of disaster films in the 1970s, categories of disaster and millennial fear merge in the 1990s, giving evidence of "a discursive climate in which themes of disaster and disaster readiness were prevalent on many cultural fronts."[64] In this light, the tremendous success of *Titanic* may, amongst other factors, be attributed to "its status as a seminal example of the new survivalist text."[65]

In contrast to other survival narratives, though, the survivor group is reduced from the prevalent family or one-example-of-each-species structure to the very nucleus of the primeval couple, underlining once more the idiocentrism of their absolute, self-reliant love. Of this primeval couple, one part eventually can die, since the story is told in retrospect, giving evidence (quite tangibly through old Rose's granddaughter Lizzy) that Rose did survive and multiply.

Like contemporary class anxieties (a middle-class on the brink of the social abyss), millennial survival fears are exposed and eventually mitigated in Cameron's *Titanic*. If Rose survives and in the end presents the impressive retrospective on a rich, fulfilled life, why should the same not be valid for every single viewer? Cameron enjoyed adding another, real-life example for successful survival in the media rave about the film: He notoriously encouraged his stylization as a discoverer, adventurer and survivor — after all, he had survived impending financial disaster and prevented the failure of his megaproject, and came out "King of the World." Like fictional character Brock Lovett (who in several ways is a reflection of the Cameron persona), he was gradually transformed by the *Titanic* experience. Or so he said:

> At that point [as Cameron landed the submersible on the Boat Deck of the wreck and spent some time reflecting the historical events right at the place where they had happened], I realized I was approaching it wrong, and that the important thing, maybe even more important than getting the footage, was capturing the emotional significance of the ship and what happened to it, and what happened to the people on it.[66]

Fictional treasure hunter Lovett will express the same experience in a more cinematic phrase, which, of course, was coined by Cameron himself: "I never got it. I never let it in"— confirming that he eventually *has* "got it." The hardcore techies of the 1990s are transformed by human tragedy; *Titanic* opens them up to the fears and anxieties of mankind. These fears are then emotionalized and commodified, resulting in an overwhelming narrative of disaster and survival. The end presents paradise regained, a triumphant new era, the apotheosis of survival, encoded as everlasting love.

Cameron's *Titanic* has transformed the *Titanic* myth. In a very postmodernist fashion, the film exploits the aspects of the myth that are apt for an epic tale, selecting and combining them to constitute spectacle on an unprecedented scale. The *Titanic* disaster has notoriously been regarded as the "largest disaster in maritime history" (regardless of the ship disasters with much greater loss of life). Thus it offered the perfect canvas for this end-of-the-century epic. The historical ship turns into a vehicle for present-day concerns, as summarized by Gaylyn Studlar: "James Cameron's *Titanic* ... uses the White Star's *Titanic*, both pre- and post-sinking, as a milieu, as space, an 'architectural presence' upon which it projects temporary anxieties and fantasies that appeal to a broad, indeed, multi-million member audience."[67] The myth itself had become a commodity, and it sold tremendously well. Cameron's *Titanic* brought the story of the disaster back into collective awareness as no other *Titanic* film has done. The price, however, was a fragmentation and reinterpretation that can be seen as consumerist usurpation of history. The *Titanic* myth had entered its postmodern phase.

The Recipe for Success

Whatever critics and scholars may say about postmodernist shallowness, poor repartees, commodification of emotion and anxieties, superficial spectacle and false historicity, there is no way around the fact that Cameron's *Titanic* is one of the most successful films ever. Susan Sydney-Smith enumerates a number of factors that contributed to the overwhelming success of the film[68]:

- a new, female-centered action-adventure cinema
- democratic escapism (signified by the "ship of dreams" motif)
- the cross-class desire of contemporary America
- material profit versus love
- the emblematic significance of "The Heart of the Ocean"
- romancing disaster: framing story and foregrounding of the fictional star-crossed love story
- a past-present narrative structure as part of the postmodern aesthetic discourse
- the connection to millennial anxieties
- the connection to the British heritage genre and to contemporary rites of passage films

- an innovative narrative address for the feature film, drawing upon timeless, epic traditions

Film critics and scholars alike have acknowledged that Cameron succeeded in tying up various contemporary, emotionally charged concerns in a strong and innovative narrative mode that proved attractive to a tremendously large audience worldwide. Scholars have appraised the role of technology in the production, serving to generate the highest possible degree of "emotional realism."[69]

These factors have to be linked with the *Titanic* myth. *Titanic* films proved to be very successful whenever they were made; Part One of this book has shown why this myth offered the perfect matrix for fictional film from 1912 up to Cameron. In the first part of Chapter 9, I discussed how Cameron used and treated the central categories of the myth, with the second part of Chapter 9 showing the influence of postmodernist aesthetics on the specific treatment of the historical event in the 1997 film. It must now be asked how Cameron created an inseparable bond between the fictional main plot (the love story) and the historical event (the ship, its disaster, and its mythification)—and how he cast this specific combination of fiction and history in a form that displays the handwriting of a master artisan.

Cameron himself jotted the recipe for the film down in 1995: "*Romeo and Juliet* on a boat."[70] That is, a classic story of star-crossed lovers in an unusual setting: good chances for success. But it is not just any boat they are put on, it is the *Titanic*—even better chances for success, not least, since international fascination with the *Titanic* had been revived and boosted by the discovery of the wreck in 1985, followed by ample presentation in film and the media. Cameron took these ingredients and merged them into a compelling romantic tale: a foolproof formula for success.

Thus, *Titanic* presents a large-scale romantic story with two inseparable strands: the romance of the ship and the romance of the central characters.[71] The former is a vital strand in the historical *Titanic* story, which has defined the disaster of the *Titanic* as singular and unforgettable. The romance of the ship builds on the *Titanic*'s extraordinary nature. At least in April 1912, she was the largest ship on the oceans, the most luxurious liner ever built, allegedly the most beautiful ship in the world. This romance of the beautiful maiden ship that died on an icy night before its maiden voyage was consummated is inseparably linked to the topos of human hubris: The tragedy of the beautiful ship lies in the delusion of mankind who believed in being able to master nature with technology. Thus, beauty is paired with technology: The romance of the ship also is a technological story. The ship, beautiful and strong, untouched and innovative, the "last word" in technology, is the star. The technology of the *Titanic* is exuberantly celebrated in the film: Images of engine rooms, giant engines, pistons in motion, and the massive ship propeller impart the impression of a living organism — technology come to life, the healthy, functioning body of the ship. On the other hand, it is the technology of the film production that became part of *Titanic*'s fascination and success. Cameron, master of technology in filmmaking, translated this story accordingly, with an unprecedented investment in life-sized sets, original material, and digital effects.[72] The computer generated visual effects play a vital role in bringing the "main character," the *Titanic*, to life.[73] They enable the audience to see the ship from all angles, to have full views of its impressive size, to be taken onto and into the *Titanic*. Due to advanced film technology, *Titanic* is a feast for *Titanic* lovers — and it convinces the audience that the story is "real," just as the emotions are "real."[74] The romance of the ship has become palpable "reality."

The other strand of his romantic epic is the human story: the romance of the two central characters, a classic story of star-crossed love. It is inseparably linked to the ship. The symbiosis of these two strands is so strong that Cameron relinquished the elsewhere indispensable element of subplots: Except for the treasure hunter story in the frame narrative, there is no subplot in the entire film. Not a single minor character has been so much individualized to be granted a subplot of their own. In fact, Cameron had inserted both a minor love story in Third Class and scenes on the *Californian* in the original script, yet these scenes had to be cut in the final version. The result is a monolithic concentration on the two entangled strands of the main story, uniting the ship with the main characters. Indeed, the famous poster for the film precisely reflects what this film is about: Jack, Rose, and — shown more prominently than either of them — the ship.[75] The story of the *Titanic* and the story of the lovers mutually support each other: Without the *Titanic*, the love story would be insipid, and without the love story, the ship would not come alive.[76]

Aylish Wood has shown how the strands of the ship and of the lovers continually intertwine: At vital points in the film, the ship — feminized both according to maritime tradition and in Cameron's presentation[77] — and the main characters share the same structure of feeling.[78] Jack and Rose, actually the focus characters of the film, become *functional* in the story of the ship. Cameron himself presented this idea as a basic tool in making the audience familiar with the ship and its aura: "I've woven their romance from the stern to the bow and through every interesting place and event in between, allowing us to experience the optimism and grandeur of the ship in a way that most of her passengers never did."[79] But Jack and Rose are not only instrumental in conveying the aura and the setting of the *Titanic*. They serve to make the entire process of the sinking visible, to give an impression of "how it felt." The two fictional main characters define the dramatic space of their tragic fellow:

> The Jack-Rose story is woven through the known events of the sinking of the ship so as to include all the points of action as they happen, as well as other experiences of both classes of the journey; we follow Jack and Rose through a first-class dinner *and* a steerage dance, Rose is present when one of the iceberg warnings arrives, both are on deck when the iceberg hits, and they manage to stay just a little ahead of the water as it rises deck by deck through the ship. Jack and Rose are out on the top deck along with the first-class passengers *and* are locked in below in steerage; Rose both leaves on a lifeboat *and* stays on the ship as it goes underwater; and she is later left behind in the water by the lifeboats *and* is saved by them.[80]

Thus, Cameron's idea of setting a cross-class romance on the doomed ship not only serves emotional purposes, it also gives the audience the chance to really get to know the third — or first! — main character, namely the *Titanic*. Jack and Rose are at the stern and at the bow, they meet several times on the Grand Staircase (defined as the center of the luxurious liner), they involuntarily explore the labyrinth of the Third Class corridors, they whirl through the engine rooms and enter the silent sanctity of the cargo room, turning it into the sanctity of their most private moment. Unrealistic as this carefree omnipresence may be, it gives the audience a chance to "experience" the *Titanic* "as she really was."

The main narrative of *Titanic* falls into two sequences which are separated by the pivotal point in the historical *Titanic* story: the collision. The pre-collision sequence is, as in earlier *Titanic* films, celebratory, a eulogy on the ship and its technology, reflected in the development and erotic climax of the human love story.[81] This sequence establishes the geography and the overwhelming luxury of the ship, offering a sort of animated version of the famous White Star publicity brochure from 1911, peopled with the historical personages from the maiden voyage. *Titanic* is shown from all angles — even the propellers — in blazing colors and with impressive fly-overs, translating Rose's epithet "ship of dreams" into visual reality.

The collision is the very center of the main story (also proportionally in the script). It offers, as Aylish Wood points out, a point of stillness, of perfect balance between forward and backward moving — yet there is nothing hopeful in this poise, since we know the inescapable outcome.[82] The post-collision sequence, counterpart to the celebratory first sequence, then plays out the long-drawn tragedy of the *Titanic*, involving the tragedy of the star-crossed lovers — and, by the way, of some 1,500 men, women and children. Since the audience has come to know the *Titanic* in her splendor and her pride, the sinking is felt as a personal tragedy: The ship is moaning and groaning, slowly dying, with sudden fits as if in feverish agony. From the outside, the *Titanic* offers a pitiable view with her bow sinking deeper and deeper. Again, with the image of the beautifully lit ship lying helplessly underneath a starry sky, Cameron takes up a motif that was known since 1912, presented in a moving description by the otherwise so sober Lawrence Beesley:

> The night was one of the most beautiful I have ever seen: the sky without a single cloud to mar the perfect brilliance of the stars, clustered so thickly together that in places there seemed almost more dazzling points of light set in the black sky than background of sky itself; and each star seemed, in the keen atmosphere, free from any haze, to have increased its brilliance tenfold and to twinkle and glitter with a staccato flash that made the sky seem nothing but a setting made for them in which to display their wonder. They seemed so near, and their light so much more intense than ever before, that fancy suggested they saw this beautiful ship in dire distress below and all their energies had awakened to flash messages across the black dome of the sky to each other; telling and warning of the calamity happening in the world beneath.... And so in these conditions of sky and air and sea, we gazed broadside on the *Titanic* from a short distance. She was absolutely still — indeed from the first it seemed as if the blow from the iceberg had taken all the courage out of her and she had just come quietly to rest and was settling down without an effort to save herself, without a murmur of protest against such a foul blow.[83]

Cameron's visual translation of this image has become an icon in *Titanic* culture: The slowly drowning queen, lying helplessly in the water, in perfect quiescence, unimpaired by the panic of the human masses crawling on her decks. *Titanic*'s slow death is dignified yet it is highly emotional and ends in humanized agony. The encroaching devastation of the ship appears to be a personal one: "In the final moments, where each shriek and cry is accompanied by the shudder and groan of the ship, and a precipitous fall accentuates the extreme angles of the ship in water, the human tragedy and the technological tragedy are inseparable."[84]

In Cameron's film, the death of the *Titanic* is turned into one of the most sustained of all disaster sequences.[85] This is worthy of the *Titanic*'s status as "greatest maritime disaster," yet it is also realistic. One important factor why the disaster became so memorable was the peculiar timing of the sinking: Two hours and forty minutes, too short for help to arrive, too long to die a fast death without becoming aware of the disaster that has struck. Long enough to live through the dramaturgically "perfect" process from innocent curiosity via inquietude, concern, and anxiety to desperation. Long enough for painful separations and dignified resignation. It is this potential of the

9. James Cameron's Titanic (1997)

Titanic (1997): With Cameron's film, the sinking ship lying lit in the water has become another symbol for the slow death of the *Titanic* (Twentieth Century Fox/Paramount Pictures).

historical *Titanic* story that is played out to the fullest in Cameron's film with its extremely extended disaster sequence. And yet, Cameron did not really make use of this historical potential. The exclusive focus on Jack and Rose and their action antics up and down through the ship actually thwart the chances for a slow development along the lines of classical tragedy. In contrast to almost all other passengers, Jack and Rose know right from the start that the *Titanic* will sink, so that there is no gradual awakening. It is fight for survival, from the moment of the collision. Accordingly, the sinking, experienced through their eyes, is a long-drawn action sequence, reeling from one disastrous scene to the next, even including the cheap effect of a gunfight. The audience is indeed tied into the lengthy sinking, yet at the cost of the realistic, painful drama which the two-hour evacuation on April 15, 1912, actually had to offer.

Despite this trip into overdone action cinema, the main character in Cameron's *Titanic*, the famous ship, was brought to life as in no other *Titanic* film before. It was Cameron's love for technology, his obsessive sense for detail, his unlimited curiosity and perfectionism that helped to breathe new life into the *Titanic*—that is, into the ship which is so demonstratively depicted as dead and decrepit in the first twenty minutes of the film.

In order to achieve the effect of miraculous resurrection, digital morph technique is put to the best conceivable use. While Cameron already used this technique of seamless dissolve in his earlier films for special effect, in *Titanic* it assumes a specific significance: It shows that within the contrasting exterior there remains the same unquenchable youthful spirit, the same soul, be it *Titanic* or the narrator Rose (who, through her narrative, brings *Titanic* back to life). The morphing technique creates the strongest link between the narrator's (and the audience's) present time and the historical time of 1912 — it visualizes the simultaneity of both periods in Rose's mind and takes the viewer on a journey through time.[86] It is this technique that makes *Titanic* real and gives the ship a soul.

It was exactly this desired effect of linking the present with the past that prompted Cameron to use the morph technique. According to him, the fading of Jack and Rose in the central moment on the bow, as the ship transforms from the beautiful young *Titanic* into the pathetic wreck, was intended to show them as "youthful spirits, somehow still alive and attached to the ship in the depths."[87] The morph technique creates an eerie effect, making visible the simultaneousness of various time layers within the consciousness of a human being. A consciousness that is then extended to the audience, drawing the viewers into the story, "never letting them go," as Dion sings while the audience is gradually being transported from the reality of the film to the reality of the theater:

> The spiritual, ghostly presence of the characters and events of 1912 in the lives of the film's present-day characters, mirrors the imaginary presence of the film's actors and actions in the cinema auditorium.... Indeed, audiences were unwilling to let go of the film, many returning to see it again and again, and many more trying to relive the experience of the film outside the cinema.[88]

It is indeed ironical that it was technology that redeemed the violated ship on the bottom of the ocean. After all, the belief in the limitless possibilities of technology, coined as human hubris, had been designated as the actual *reason* for the sinking in the *Titanic* discourse of 1912. Cameron continued and perfected what Robert Ballard had begun with the discovery of the wreck in 1985: The technological failure of 1912 was redeemed by the technological prowess of the 1980s, the maiden voyage finally was consummated, the long journey of the *Titanic* had found its poignant, yet somewhat happy end due to the wonders of modern technology. Modern technology brought the famous ship back to the surface; the IMAX *Titanica* film and numerous documentaries enabled a worldwide audience to "go back to *Titanic*." Cameron, who dived down twelve times in the pre-production phase, added the missing link by making the wreck the poignant hero of an emotional narrative, a hero that eventually is brought back to life, revived in the original splendor and eventually transfigured in a vision of eternal youth and beauty.

Advanced film technology endowed both the ship and the love story with life. Cameron, experienced director of action–science fiction spectacles and enthusiast of technology, was the right person to achieve this aim. In

9. James Cameron's Titanic (1997)

Titanic, romance would not have worked without technology. In the end, both female and male viewers appreciated the filmmakers' achievement.

There is one sequence that stands out most distinctly amongst *Titanic* films: the sinking. No other film has gone to such lengths to depict the most disastrous moment in the *Titanic* catastrophe. Cameron's approach to the *Titanic* story is characterized not only by an obsessive accuracy, but also by a relentless curiosity. Cameron offers answers to what everybody with the slightest interest in the *Titanic* story has always wanted to know: what were the last moments on the ship? How did the great drama unfold between 2:15 A.M. and 2:20 A.M. in the night of April 15, 1912? How did the lost souls, the 1,500 people who remained on the ship, cling to their lives, comfort their doomed children, try to save themselves as the stern rose higher and higher into the air? And, spurred by discovery of the wreck in two parts, *how* did the most dramatic moment occur, the breaking of the gigantic hull? What exactly happened as the stern fell back, how did it eventually sink? How did the people act and react on this giant, murderous roller coaster? Cameron has imagined all this to the last detail and given an (allegedly) definite (because immediately visual) answer to these questions.

Survivor Jack Thayer, who jumped into the water as the ship went down and miraculously ended up on Collapsible B, later described the last moments on the ship: "We were a mass of hopeless, dazed humanity, attempting, as the Almighty and Nature made us, to keep our final breath until the last possible moment."[89] Cameron takes up this poignant motif: the mass of people, without hope, yet instinctively fighting for survival up to the last moment. The craze on the stern is counterbalanced by a few romantic images: an elderly couple lying on a bed and affectionately holding hands,[90] a mother in Third Class soothing her children before they will forever fall asleep. The focus of this sequence, however, remains on the action scenes. Cameron offers, as *Titanic* films since 1958 have done, a densely clipped montage of numerous shots that show the final disaster in the various parts of the ship, adding up to a coherent image of the catastrophe. Yet it is the exterior scenes that are unique. We are confronted with the "mass of hopeless, dazed humanity," hastening up and up on the stern, as far away from the water as possible, then, in a perspective from the water, the tortured body of the ship, the rising stern with the massive screws coming out of the water — digitalized, yet awesome, spectacular and terrifying in the "real" dimensions of the 1912 disaster. People lose their footing, topple down along the massive, perpendicular hull, some hit the screws — there is gruesome realism. Just as it really would have been? Cameron satisfies our curiosity and pins down a version of the final minutes that seems to be definite and true due its overwhelming visualization. He takes the most famous icon of the *Titanic* disaster — the stern standing upright against the night, with the gigantic ship going relentlessly down — and imbues it with life through animation. The visual experience of catastrophe is enhanced by the immediate auditory sensation: screams, yells, groans, splintering, and the hammering action music of James Horner, confirming that this is disaster in its most tangible form.

A little later, Cameron in unprecedented realism translates yet another horrifying motif of the historical *Titanic* event into cinematic experience. Numerous survivors told about the screams of the victims dying in the water as the most terrifying experience of that night, haunting them for decades to come.[91] Among the *Titanic* film directors, it is Cameron alone who shows the enormity of this cry in his *Titanic* version, zooming out visually and acoustically from Rose's individual perspective to the masses of the people fighting in the water. This is a disaster on an enormous scale, and Cameron makes it believable through image and sound.

Yet Cameron also offers comfort. It is the epic romance that leaves the final fingerprint in the film, abandoning the realistic reconstruction of death and providing the audience with a feeling of "everything will be all right" — for ever and ever. The end of *Titanic* is a celebration of love, of social integration, of the *Titanic* as nostalgic concept of a better past that somehow can promise us a better future. It leaves the realm of reality and sells the dream as true. History is rewritten: The *Titanic* is restored in its original beauty, the lovers are united, applauded by the resurrected victims of all classes (note that henchman Lovejoy, who was devoured into the hellish abyss of the breaking hull, is *not* among the happy crowd!), and they will probably sail on into eternity, in immortal youth and beauty.[92] Present and past melt into each other, old is made new again, paradise is regained. In line with the two intertwined strands of the film's story, this paradise is the ship *Titanic*, and it is resurrected from death through love:

> Made visually manifest in Rose's dying dream, the ship becomes a classless milieu by virtue of the heroine's inner life. Thus, the ship is reclaimed, not by the treasure-seekers who find the wreck through advanced technology, but through the force of love.[93]

Music helps drive the message home: Dion's song sets in with this finale, constituting a transition from the paradisiac vision of the resurrected *Titanic* to the "real" world of the audience, yet promising that this epic of love will haunt them in their dreams.[94] In the typical function of film music tied in as soundtrack album, the theme song enables the audience to take the emotional experience home with them and re-visit it whenever they listen to the song.[95]

9. James Cameron's Titanic (1997)   215

Together with the visual memory of the final scene, the song has become the most effective "memento" of Cameron's *Titanic*.

This ending — that is, both the dream/dying vision and the song as its acoustic correlate — is highly effective as the crown on a large-scale romantic epic. Yet again, it is tied up with both strands of the film's story: It is not only the crowning vision of the love story, but it also relates closely to the *Titanic* myth. The apotheosis of Rose, Jack, the *Titanic* victims, and the ship itself translate another vital aspect of the *Titanic* myth into a powerful cinematic statement: The tragedy of the *Titanic* has been turned into triumph.

In order to achieve its powerful impact, the final vision had to integrate something that was new and unique in the tradition of *Titanic* films: the wreck. Cameron's film would never have become a global success without the wreck and the frame story linked with it. The integration of the wreck of the *Titanic* added several vital aspects to the film:

- the triumph of present-day technology
- the fascination of the deep-sea space
- the contrast between materialism and romantic idealism, between greed and love
- the dignified poignancy of the decrepit, lonesome maiden ship — and its miraculous resurrection in Rose's imagination
- the seamless transition between past and present, offering the audience a modern experience while transporting the viewers back to 1912

Again, the wreck underlines that the *Titanic* is the main character of the film — and that it is inseparably linked with another human main character, namely Rose, who alone has the power to bring the ship back to life. Since its discovery in 1985, the wreck had been present in collective awareness, being turned into the fascinating, enigmatic subject both of the spectacular IMAX film of 1995 and of numerous documentaries and television programs. Cameron capitalized on this media presence and used it as the starting point to restore the wreck to the "ship of dreams." As described above, the morph technique was the medium of the oscillation between the two temporal frameworks. It made sure that the audience would be able to embark on this voyage in time, held rapt by the double presence of old and new, by the youthful spirit and the breathtaking beauty represented both by the ship and by Rose, despite their poignantly aged exterior in the frame narrative.[96] Having accompanied Rose through space and time in her emotions and imagination ever since 1912, the *Titanic* re-emerges in powerful juvenescence: The physical distance between Rose and the ship, between the female main character and her transforming experience on the *Titanic*, is dissolved. The audience — both the fictional group on the research ship *Keldysh* in the frame narrative, and the real viewers in the movie theater — is irresistibly drawn into this experience.

Without the wreck and the frame story, Cameron's *Titanic* would be a period film blazing in nostalgia, based on an overblown love story. The wreck gives this epic the poignant, nostalgic quality that has characterized the *Titanic* myth since 1955. It breaks down the distance between the present and the past — and thus, it turns a story of kitsch into a transfigured memory of something that really existed. Whatever one thinks about the concept of "*Romeo and Juliet* on a boat," the wreck has added a quality to this *Titanic* tale that renders it unique among *Titanic* films.

Along with the wreck, the present-day frame story is highly relevant for the success of Cameron's *Titanic*. It offers the audience the medium for identification, the ability to submerse themselves in a story whose true dimension only becomes clear in the course of the enthralling narrative. Vivian Sobchack identifies several functions of this frame.[97] It serves as:

1. a "submersible device" to slowly descend and relocate oneself in a "lost" past history both public and private
2. a "spherical device" that encircles and contains both past — present and public — private
3. a "protective device" that allows for mediated but seemingly "authentic" experience, keeping real trauma, but not real emotion, at bay

Being anchored in present time, the frame turns the tale of the *Titanic* into "just a story," maintaining a certain safe distance to the disaster. At least, we know that the main character and narrator, Rose, has survived. Her audience on the *Keldysh* tells us how to react: become enrapt with her narrative, let ourselves get carried away. Or, to say it with Lovett's words: to let it in.

In Chapter 3, under "Framing Devices," the significance of this frame for the entire film has been presented. Both in terms of structure and character development, the frame is vital to interconnect and balance present and past. The decisive link between the temporal spheres are Rose and the ship, who have existed independent of each other for 85 years and have yet remained joined in a symbiosis of common existential experience. The various motivic arches link the beginnings and endings both of frame and main narratives — the result is a coercive stringency in the narrative, creating a feeling of cyclicity (Sobchack's "spherical device").

Proportionally, the frame constitutes a somewhat irregular mounting of the main story: a lengthy sequence of twenty minutes to anchor the film in present time and expose both the foreign underwater world encompassing the wreck and the main character, who then will lead us down and back to *Titanic*, and at the end of the film, a much shorter, much more concentrated closing sequence that only contains two moments of significance, namely Rose dropping the diamond into the Atlantic and her final vision of a rejuvenated *Titanic*. Originally, the proportions were more balanced with a lengthier diamond sequence in the end, letting treasure hunter Brock Lovett see and touch the diamond before Rose throws it into the sea.[98] The cut of this scene made sense, though: Together with Lovett, the audience got the message without the necessity of such a blunt demonstration.

The main story, covering 168 minutes in the final version, then is classically built. The collision occurs right at the center — indeed the "point of no return," in which the first celebratory sequence irrevocably is displaced by the impending tragedy of the *Titanic*. This midway climax is prepared by three scenes of rising eroticism between Rose and Jack in close succession: the bow scene with the first kiss, the drawing scene, and the erotic consummation of their love in the car. The first two scenes are linked to the narrator's present time, with two dissolves to the wreck and to old Rose's intense eyes — a token of the ageless intensity of her feelings, as she (for the first time in her life) revives these events through her narrative. The next climax in the script (the Moment of Truth), three-quarters through the main story, is Rose's jump out of the lifeboat back onto the sinking ship: the emphatic renewal of her contract with Jack. The sinking occurs halfway through the "third act" of the main narrative — spectacular as it is, it is not the end. There is indeed no great, disastrous climax of the main narrative: Due to the frame construction, we are prepared for a retelling of the *Titanic* disaster that opens the way for a continual development into the present time, explaining how and why Rose came to be the wise, self-reliable, extravagant, yet down-to-earth old lady of the frame narrative.

Cameron did not sit down with a calculator to create a classic three-act linear structure as he wrote the treatment for the main story. It is obvious, though, that he placed the climactic points carefully within the script, with a strong awareness for proportion and dramaturgical development. The interconnection of frame and main story, the various arches, and the convincing dramaturgical structure of the main story, involving the audience emotionally with the two leading characters, Rose and the *Titanic*, have contributed decisively to the great success of *Titanic*. After all, a film running longer than it actually took the *Titanic* to sink — that is, over three hours[99] — must have an excellent structure to keep the audience enthralled.

Finally, Cameron's *Titanic* abounds with imagery that is strongly linked to narrative traditions in world literature and film. Indeed, the film is saturated with allusions in word and image to the great narratives and films.[100] This makes the tale strong and convincing, anchoring it firmly in Western narrative tradition. Again, it is hardly conceivable that Cameron would have consciously constructed a mosaic of little building stones. Instead, the density of literary and cinematic allusions in his *Titanic* tale reflects his experience and mastery as a storyteller. The iconic images mostly come as natural, melted together in a strong, emotionally absorbing narrative.

Cameron's obsession for knowledge and detail is clearly reflected in the script and its visual translation. After his dives to the wreck had convinced him of the potential of a large-scale *Titanic* story, he immersed himself in studies of the historical event and its translation into film. Most of the scenes and the entire setting reflect these studies. Cameron's excessive love for detail is by no means merely a postmodernist approach to history as discussed in the preceding chapter — it is just as well a homage to the *Titanic* code as it was laid down with the 1958 film *A Night to Remember* and had been perfected since then. Viewers have commented on "how Cameron pulls subplots, scenes and whole sequences from all the previous *Titanic* movies," enumerating details and entire scenes that were "drawn" from earlier films since 1943.[101] It is problematic, though, to calculate what and how much exactly Cameron has "pulled together" from other films. Although there is no doubt that the collage and processing of earlier film subjects and imagery is a typical technique in Cameron's work as screenwriter and director,[102] *Titanic* is a subject where a strong reliance on and quotation of earlier scenes and images can by no means be avoided. The story is fixed, and ever since *A Night to Remember* there have been stock motifs, stock scenes, and stock personages that simply have to be included to make the story "real"— in short, the *Titanic* code, which no film director aiming at a realistic rendition of the disaster could ignore. There are indeed memorable shots and motifs in Cameron's *Titanic* that seem to be drawn directly from earlier *Titanic* films. Nevertheless, these are standard scenes and standard images that hardly can be left out if one visually imagines the story of the *Titanic* and its passengers — for example, the poignant looks of lovers who are separated as the lifeboat is lowered.[103] One could, of course, draw motif charts and try to prove how much Cameron has "adopted" from earlier films — motifs such as a passenger who is locked in and liberated with a fire axe, or a Third Class passenger jumping out of his bunk right into the water on the floor belong to the more conspicuous instances.[104] Yet such a search for motif precursors would be an idle game: The impact of Cameron's film and the persuasiveness of his narrative will not be undone by pointing out details that have been seen before. In order to present the "authentic" story of the *Titanic*, Cameron was indeed forced to include as many of the well-known details as possible. Their combination into a new, stringent narrative and their complete absorption as background matter do in fact support the story of Rose and the "ship of dreams," since they create a welcome effect of recognition, implying that this is the "authentic" story of the disaster as it had been told by other filmmakers before.

A typical example for the transformation of visual and narrative traditions into something new is the famous bow scene. This scene has become the icon of the film — and since 1997, it has been turned into an icon for "Titanic as such." Political satire has capitalized largely on this scene, using it as symbol for a careless course towards disaster.[105] Cultural analysts have used this scene to point out the tradition of women as figurehead, the feminized body of the *Titanic* as symbolized in Rose, or famous forerunners of such an image in the Golden Age of Hollywood.[106] Yet the famous scene also alludes to other traditions in art — one of which is in fact strongly linked up with the *Titanic* myth.

Rose's position on the bow is almost identical with a classical Greek posture: the arrival of the victorious goddess Nike of Samothrace. Since the statue from the second century BC not only honors the goddess, but also celebrates the victory of the sea battle against Antiochos III of Syria, there are clear references to a female body as figurehead of a ship. Nike of Samothrace, now exhibited in the Louvre museum in Paris, is one of the most celebrated sculptures in the world, with numerous replicas being made in Europe and the U.S. — not only as sculpture, but also in commercial design and popular culture, such as the Rolls-Royce radiator figurine and the first FIFA World Cup trophy.[107] Although the original sculpture has lost its arms, Nike's wings and the stumps of her arms indicate that the female personification of victory stood in a position that was eventually taken up by Cameron — including the drapery flowing in the wind.

Yet there is still a missing link between the famous sculpture and the famous scene in Cameron's film to be found, a distinctly "Titanic" connection: The year 1931 saw the unveiling of the Women's *Titanic* Memorial, a thirteen-foot-tall granite statue honoring the men who perished on the *Titanic*, saving the lives of women and children. Although actually representing a male figure, the drapery and the outstretched arms of this sculpture again seem to prefigure the famous Cameron position: From afar, one might indeed take the memorial in Washington, D.C., as homage to Cameron's film.

The visual similarity between Nike of Samothrace and the Women's *Titanic* Memorial and Rose on the *Titanic*'s bow once more stresses the emphasis on the feminine in Cameron's tale. While the image of the goddess Nike offers a female allegory of victory, the *Titanic* memorial was not only donated by a women's association, but also designed by a woman, namely artist and

220 Part II. Major *Titanic* Films

Titanic (1997): The famous bow scene may have been modeled on The Winged Nike of Samothrace (above) and the Women's *Titanic* Memorial in Washington, D.C. (opposite page).

sculptor Gertrude Vanderbilt Whitney. Eventually, this famous image is translated into the female beauty on the bow of the ship, merging the two main characters, Rose and the *Titanic*, into eternal unity.[108]

Cameron's large-scale movie unites several layers of artistic and cinematic tradition and fuses them inseparably with the *Titanic* myth and the cinematic *Titanic* code. It is an up-to-date, in many ways postmodernist reinterpretation of the myth, yet it also contains numerous timeless elements that endow the combination of love story and historical disaster narrative with its persuasive power. As in the other *Titanic* films, the dominant categories of the *Titanic* myth — gender, class, nation — play an important role. It would be amiss to condemn their negotiation along romantic stereotypes in Cameron's film: After all, Cameron intended to create a Hollywood blockbuster and not a critical investigation of controversial aspects in society. In this respect, *Titanic* is in no way different from the earlier cinematic *Titanic* tales.

New, however, is the inseparable fusion of a romantic love story with the story of the ship: No other *Titanic* film has interwoven the ship's fate so intensely with the story of a loving woman. It was Cameron's intention to translate the incomprehensible scale of the disaster into human terms. According to narrative tradition, it was a love story that had to be the agent for such a translation — yet in turn, it is also the stereotypical image of eternal love that brings the ship back to life. The *Titanic*, appearing as a pathetic, dying wreck in the first part of the film, is revived by being anchored in the memory and experience of a woman. And this revival, leading to an eternal rejuvenation of the "ship of dreams," is not restricted to the "reality" of the film: With Cameron's film, the *Titanic* has forcefully re-entered collective awareness — on a global scale.

10

The *Titanic* Code
Recurrent Motifs in Titanic *Films*

What is a "*Titanic* film"? Basically, it is a film about the historical ship *Titanic*, covering its maiden voyage and its sinking. This basic mould leaves a large margin, a tremendous space for imagination to fill. However, the examination of the major *Titanic* films has shown that they have a lot in common, especially since 1958. The basic pattern has been fleshed out almost alike in these films, increasingly with the same details and scenes over and over again. This is, of course, due to the historical realities of the *Titanic* story and the increasing desire for historical accuracy. As shown in Chapter 6, Walter Lord's *A Night to Remember* and its "translation" into film created a detailed pattern, saturated with "historical" detail, which came to be regarded as obligatory for any retelling of the *Titanic* story: the *Titanic* code.

A comparison of the six major *Titanic* films shows that the majority of the recurring motifs are part of this code, based on the historical facts of the voyage, the ship, its passengers, and its crew. These motifs can be grouped under a limited number of themes, which correspond to the central categories of the *Titanic* myth. As can be seen in the table, the historical themes and motifs actually need very little fictional addition in order to be turned into a functioning feature film.

Historical Motifs	*Themes* (Titanic *Myth*)	*Fictional Motifs*
First Class splendor		
Structure of the ship	Class	Class clichés
"Steerage" (party / gates)		
Women and children first		
Pain of separation		Love stories (all classes)
Men's chivalrous behavior	Gender	Young hero
"Molly" Brown		Young heroine
Man in women's clothes		

Historical Motifs	Themes (Titanic Myth)	Fictional Motifs
Captain Smith		
Officers and crew		
Wireless operators	Nation / Britishness / Race	National / racial stereotypes
Historical passengers		
Panic / pistol shots		
Bruce Ismay		
Ice warnings ignored	Hubris / Speed / Greed	Speed record / Blue Riband
Titanic as "unsinkable"		
Iceberg		
Band's last piece	Religion / Hubris	"Nearer, My God, to Thee"
The Sinking		
Scenes in the lifeboats	Aftermath:	Mourning vs. reunion
Carpathia	Mourning and resignation	
Californian	Irony of fate / Scapegoat	Notion that the *Californian* could have helped

The actual historical story of the *Titanic* is inseparably linked with the *Titanic* myth that emerged as soon as the ship had sunk. Their relation is reciprocal: While the myth developed out of the many historical details narrated in the testimonies and personal accounts, these details are used in film to support and strengthen the ideological messages encapsulated in the categories of the myth. Film, in turn, cemented the myth. The following chapter examines the mutual interplay of history, myth, and fiction, summarizing the findings of the preceding analyses. Special attention is paid to music in the *Titanic* myth, both in its historical guise and as a technique of heightening emotion in *Titanic* films.

Recurrent Motifs: History, Myth, and Fiction

The impressive luxury of First Class and the general complex structure of the ship (divided into different classes and professional spaces), which were so much appraised and admired in 1911–12, are a welcome motif to underline the issue of class in *Titanic* films. Fictitious stereotypes of the various classes — especially First and Third — add to an image of the *Titanic* as microcosm of late Edwardian society, with shots from the engine rooms adding a glimpse of the "underworld" of the lowest working class. The focus clearly lies on First Class (even in Cameron's cross-class love story), which offers the perfect setting for a lavish film. Third Class, in turn, mainly is represented through the parties in the common room that historically took place on April 13 and

14, 1912, offering opportunity for the use of music, dance, and stereotypes of the "poor but happy lot."

In the course of the evacuation then, the image of Third Class being locked in is cited again and again — an historical detail, yet above all functioning as a demonstration of the outrageous injustice of the social system. The historical fact of the large families in Third Class, who all perished, is used in indirect ways (excepting the 1996 mini-series, in which the fictional Jack family with its four children is involved in a subplot): It is Third Class, where the bonds of family play an important role, supporting the image of poor but life-affirming people (whose zeal for life quite naturally results in many children).

With few exceptions, most notably the 1953 Hollywood film, families do not play a role in First Class: Here, it is rich and noble couples who are highlighted, yet rarely ever any children. The three children of the (fictitious) First Class Lucas family in *A Night to Remember* are given another function than the children in the Third Class families. Whereas the latter form an especially pitiful part in the "mass of hopeless, dazed humanity" that has no chance for a place in a lifeboat, the function of the three First Class children is to define the problem of gender roles. The unheard-of "revolt" of Liz Lucas against the will of her husband ("I'm not going, Robert") is stopped dead by his reminding her of her duty to their children. She is forced to think as a mother and therefore is not granted free choice about her own person and her own fate.

Indeed, the principle "women and children first" with the concomitant pain of separation is highly welcome as emotional element in film; it is here, during the evacuation, where gender roles most clearly are defined and negotiated. Screenwriters use this element of heightened emotion for their main plots: *Titanic*, a ship that is doomed to sink, separating lovers, spouses, and families, is the perfect matrix for a strong love story. A favorite detail is the Straus couple, which already in 1912 was elevated to the paragon of matrimonial love and loyalty. However, Isidor and Ida Straus are only used as an historical vignette in *Titanic* films and never turned into characters with a plot of their own. For cinema, a stronger story than the loyal elderly couple that meekly accepts their doom is necessary.

Not surprisingly, it is in the category of gender and gender relations where the essential fictional elements are added in *Titanic* film scripts: love stories that translate the true dimension of separation and loss in the *Titanic* disaster into a cinematic experience. Most popular are the tragic tales: separation forever, the tragic sacrifice of the male partner and the tearful survival of the woman. Minor love plots, in contrast, allow for a happy end: the heroic conduct and miraculous salvation of a young hero, typically effected through his fall into a lifeboat while he is selflessly helping with the evacuation. His fall, must, of course, knock him unconscious, otherwise it would be un-heroic for a young man to remain in a lifeboat.¹ Women, in contrast, are expected to act according to their gender role as valid in Western society at the time of the disaster: passive objects who gratefully — and, in the case of the *Titanic* disaster, tearfully — accept the gentlemanly respect shown to them.

More rarely, the survivalist attitude of a woman is added to the gender spectrum. Usually, the role of the "strong woman" (including comic overtones) is projected on "Molly" Brown, adopting the historical details of her courageous conduct in the night of April 15, 1912. James Cameron is the only screenwriter and director who eventually chose a fictional young woman, intent upon survival, as heroine for the film. Tellingly, love is necessary to imbue her with the necessary survivalist vigor, so that Cameron's "modern" stance is not really feminist, either. All earlier films, in turn, content themselves with the traditional gender roles for the female passengers of the *Titanic*, using "Molly" Brown as a curious little vignette — again confirming her historically anchored image as woman beyond gender norms.

In contrast, there is the behavior of the men, which equally constitutes an important part of the gender complex in the *Titanic* story. The chivalrous conduct especially of the First Class men (the Second Class men, of whom 92 percent were lost, are never mentioned!) is both historical and a cliché (best expressed in Benjamin Guggenheim's oft-quoted phrase "We've dressed up in our best and are prepared to go down like gentlemen"[2]). In order to contrast this "natural" male behavior following the accepted code of honor in Edwardian times, much has been made out of Bruce Ismay and the legend of the First Class passenger who put a woman's shawl over his head: The blemish of cowardice that each male survivor later had to defend himself against turned out to be a wonderful motif in film. In reality, there were two male passengers "escaping in women's clothes"; both were Irishmen travelling in Third Class and in both cases it was a spontaneous reaction to a terrifying situation rather than a deliberate act of cowardice. While twenty-four-year-old Edward Ryan entered Lifeboat 14 with a towel wrapped around his head and was later uncovered by Fifth Officer Lowe, who was in charge of the boat, twenty-one-year-old Daniel Buckley was saved by a woman throwing a shawl over him.[3] *Titanic* films preferably collate their fate, presenting a male passenger who intentionally dresses up as a woman and later is scandalously disclosed. Thus, the 1912 legend of sneaking cowardice is adopted in film in order to demonstrate "wrong" male behavior in the face of disaster. Preferably, it is a First Class passenger who commits this act of cowardice, underlining the abnormity of his behavior in an otherwise "noble" class.

J. Bruce Ismay did not sneak into a lifeboat. He quite openly stepped into Collapsible C, since there were no more women and children in the vicinity and still free places in the boat. Generally, there was nothing reproachable in this act, as it was confirmed at the inquiries — yet Ismay, president of the White Star Line, First Class passenger and survivor, was turned into a "brute" right from the start. False statements were published in the media that he had entered the very first lifeboat to be lowered, that he had collected a crew of his own, that he had privileged other millionaires.[4] In *Titanic* films, the depiction of his conduct varies from open accusation (the 1943 anti–British film) via a more restrained critique (the majority of films) to open compassion for a tortured and eventually broken man. Except for *S.O.S. Titanic*, he does not assume the role of a leading character; he is generally used as a welcome stereotype to criticize the arrogance and lowly character of the very rich and powerful.

Contrasting with this stereotype, Captain Smith, the officers and the crew — especially the wireless operators — are generally used as paragons of dutifulness and reliability, supporting the nation stereotype of "being British." The historical Captain E.J. Smith, who was unofficially regarded as "commodore" of the White Star Line, can more or less be seen as tragic figure. His general popularity and his pride at the outset of the maiden voyage contrast with his doom in the end; the poignancy is enhanced by the oft-quoted statement that the *Titanic*'s voyage was supposed to be his last before retirement.[5] Yet in *Titanic* films, his stature of a tragic hero remains pale. He is (historically correct) not on the bridge as the collision occurs, and his general responsibility for the ship (especially for the high speed despite the awareness of the ice danger) is in most cases toned down — which, in fact, corresponds to the conclusion of the 1912 inquiries that acknowledged his responsibility but did not condemn him. Most films perpetuate the idealized image of Captain Smith as it had been created after he had gone down with the *Titanic*: the good-natured "millionaires' captain," a person of natural authority, professional, reliable, and dutiful unto death. They also render his helplessness in the course of the evacuation, following testimony that his resolution decisively slackened in the final two hours, yet this is not displayed as critique, being of little interest in a setting where the focus lies on the growing desperation of the passengers and the pain of separation.

Except for *A Night to Remember*, where Second Officer Lightoller is turned into the hero of the film, the other officers and crew are primarily used as staffage in *Titanic* films: historical characters who play their historical roles, no more. Only in the 1943 film does a fictional German officer play an important role in order to decry the alleged corruption and unprofessional behavior of the British *Titanic* crew. Ship architect Thomas Andrews, in turn, has been a favorite with *Titanic* filmmakers from 1958 onwards. In line with the testimonies of the survivors, he is used for a positive minor role, an historical vignette representing British reliability, kind-heartedness and composure.[6] In most films he appears as selfless adviser to the afflicted, who in the end poignantly (and according to historical witness) remains in the Smoking Room without even attempting to save himself. His pensive posture before the painting *Plymouth Harbor* and his (fictitious) final act of stopping the clock at the historical moment 2:20 A.M. are invariably used as touching detail in the dramatic mosaic of final disaster.

Among the crew, it is the wireless operators who play a more conspicuous role in cinematic *Titanic* narratives. They are treated somewhat ambiguously: In the first part of *Titanic* films, where the ship and its luxuries are celebrated, they are depicted as adventurous young men, dutiful but overworked; it appears to be the fault of the far too communicative First Class passengers with their silly messages that Jack Phillips inadvertently spikes the *Mesaba* ice warning instead of sending it to the bridge. A fatal, yet somewhat forgivable error: After all, we can see how hard the young wireless operators have to toil. This professional error is entirely offset after the collision: Jack Phillips and his assistant Harold Bride appear as the young heroes, setting duty as their first priority—unto death. This image is enhanced by the historical (yet probably invented) story of the stoker who tries to steal Phillips's lifebelt while the operator still is trying to call for help, though already released from his duty.

Having sunk with the *Titanic*, Captain E. J. Smith was venerated as professional, reliable, and dutiful unto death (public domain).

The eulogy on the

British nation is contrasted with stereotypes of other nations, especially in Third Class. It is inevitably non–British Third Class passengers — again according to the (ideologically biased) testimonies of 1912 — that try to storm the lifeboats. Like the media in 1912, filmmakers love to adopt the dramatic motif of an officer shooting into the air — or even shooting a passenger — as the situation turns to panic. This motif is part of the myth; according to the testimonies of 1912, Fifth Officer Lowe fired a few shots along the ship's side to assuage rising panic, yet no person was shot, and certainly not by First Officer Murdoch.[7] Racial stereotypes, in turn, are rarely played out in *Titanic* films, excepting the Nazi propaganda film of 1943. However, historical as well as fictional passengers are used to display stereotypes of Americanness, which is recommended as a "better way of life" both in the 1953 and the 1997 Hollywood productions.

The motif of speed is rarely used as a dominant factor in the cinematic disaster tale. The White Star Line's (or, more personally, Bruce Ismay's) desire to run the maiden voyage with a good speed are occasionally mentioned, just as the (historical) speculations of the passengers with regard to speed.[8] It is the 1943 propaganda film alone that focuses on this motif as a main factor to disparage the British owners of the *Titanic* (ignoring the fact that the *Titanic* actually was owned by the American Morgan trust International Mercantile Marine). In other films, speed is a detail belonging to historical staffage, as part of the general pride in the technological prowess of the ship. Typically, it is linked with the minor character of Bruce Ismay; in the 1943 film, John Jacob Astor (presented as British) is turned into Ismay's equally ruthless, capitalist counterpart.[9]

The motif of hubris, so strongly used in religious and moral analyses of the *Titanic* disaster in 1912, generally is taken back in *Titanic* films. Even the 1943 film, which tries to highlight this motif in order to accuse "British greed," did not really succeed in this respect: A large-scale disaster with 1,500 people drowning or freezing to death does not support a moralistic stance about hubris and punishment, but involuntarily invokes compassion. It is hard to construct a villain on the *Titanic* who is so loathsome that the audience enjoys his punishment; as the 1996 mini-series with the villain Doonan shows, such a construction verges on parody. If the motif of hubris can be traced in *Titanic* films, it is primarily linked with the sublime power of nature, translated visually into views of ice fields and icebergs that contrast the innocuous life on the luxury liner. (In *S.O.S. Titanic*, this visual and dramatic contrast is a structural element in the script.) Nature, sublime and indifferent, is shown as a *force majeure*, a power beyond mankind's pathetic pride in technological prowess.

The horror of sublime nature unfolds in two obligatory scenes: the collision and the final moments of the sinking. Both are climactic in a story that in fact is a disaster tale. Every film uses the dramatic potential of the circa thirty seconds between the sighting of the iceberg and the collision (a sequence gradually initiated by outlook Frederick Fleet's suddenly freezing stare); James Cameron, in his love for technical detail, has made the most of this dramatic sequence. The frantic action on the ship (triggered acoustically by the three bell strikes and the cry "Iceberg right ahead!") contrasts tellingly with the stillness of the berg lying simply in the water. In its dignified tranquility, it represents the superior force of nature: It is the berg that is the stronger part in "the convergence of the twain." In the 1953 film, the aphoristic exchange "Did we hit it?" "No, sir. It hit us" puts the true relation between man and nature into words. Tellingly, it is a (defrocked) priest who discloses the power of nature: While the historical element of religion is strongly reduced in *Titanic* films, there is still the superior force of nature that remains.

The same relation is found in the sinking — but the superior tranquility of nature is yet disturbed by mankind's desperate scream after the ship has gone down: the "appeal to the whole world" that Lawrence Beesley so impressively described in his report on the sinking.[10] *Titanic* films generally do not endeavor to translate the enormity of this scream into a cinematic experience.[11] Through a visual and acoustic zoom, James Cameron gives an impression of the sheer dimension of hundreds of people fighting for their lives in the water. Yet no film really can translate this horror into image and sound.

The 1953 Hollywood film chose quite another solution for this climactic moment: The horror of forsaken mankind, thrown into the icy abyss of death, is covered by religion. There are no screams in the water; instead, the sound of a hymn covers the ineffable.

It is "Nearer, My God, to Thee" that generally takes the place of religion in *Titanic* films — yet it is nothing more but a clichéd surrogate for this important aspect of the *Titanic* myth. "Nearer, My God, to Thee" is historical in so far as it came to be regarded as the last piece played by the band in the moment of the sinking — despite the fact that the band most likely did *not* play this hymn and certainly not until the water went up to their waists (see below). In the 1912 *Titanic* myth, the hymn came to symbolize resignation into God's will. In the earliest *Titanic* films, it was taken up both as a "historical" element and as a performative means of catharsis, with the hymn being sung by the audience at the end of a silent film screening. Later, the religious dimension of this hymn, felt and embraced by the early audiences, was lost; there remained the pseudo-historical element of this hymn having been the "psalm at the journey's end."[12]

Thus, the hymn has become an icon for religiosity in the *Titanic* tale, yet it is void of any religious meaning or message that would be transported by the film. At the same time, it has been turned into an icon for the modest heroism of the "little people" on the *Titanic*: Just like the stokers and the engineers down in the bowels of the ship, the musicians fulfill their duty, unto the most extreme degree, namely death. Their inner nobility and modest heroism becomes increasingly underlined in *Titanic* films: *A Night to Remember* for the first time depicts them as a group of crew members who, after having been released from duty, voluntarily stays on. "Nearer, My God, to Thee" turns into an expression of their own state of mind, of their personal inclination, contrasting with the light popular music that was their usual fare and that they had played during the evacuation to keep panic at bay.[13] That a religious hymn is the music that really is near to their hearts in this situation is underlined by the cellist spontaneously singing the words of the hymn. His song hovers over the water and turns into a dirge for the dying *Titanic*. Cameron further underlines the inner nobility of the musicians with Wallace Hartley's maybe overdone, yet still moving "Gentlemen, it has been a privilege playing with you tonight." Just as in *A Night to Remember*, the musicians turn away after they have been released from duty, only to return and join in one after the other, as Hartley begins to play the first phrase of "Nearer, My God, to Thee" all for himself. This is, of course, fictional, yet it adds to the historical stylization of the *Titanic* musicians to heroes, reflecting their tremendous fame after the sinking.

With *A Night to Remember*, historical scenes in the lifeboats, as reported by survivors, began to be integrated into *Titanic* films. From now on, *Titanic* films would also show the aftermath of the disaster, characterized by mourning and resignation. The lifeboat scenes add an eerie "nocturne," but also scenes of moral courage with "Molly" Brown in Lifeboat 6 exhorting the women to row (thus keeping them from freezing to death) and quarreling with the notoriously pessimistic Quartermaster Hichens. Both *A Night to Remember* and the 1996 mini-series include scenes on the dramatically endangered Collapsible B, floating upside down with some thirty men balancing on the keel. It is only the 1996 and 1997 films that go to the extreme and show countless bodies floating in the water; in the Cameron film, a dead Third Class woman is holding her dead baby in her arms.[14]

From 1958 onwards, various scenes on the *Carpathia* are added. They follow both the testimonies and the fictional plots of the respective film: The mourning of the survivors is contrasted with unexpected, joyful reunion. Generally, though, the *Carpathia* scenes are quiet and subdued, giving a realistic impression of the trauma that haunted the survivors.[15]

With *A Night to Remember*, the *Californian* was equally brought onto screen. Again, this inclusion of a third ship reflects the historical facts, as depicted by Walter Lord in his documentary novel. Referring to the protocols of the inquiries, Lord adopted the view that his namesake Captain Stanley Lord had been guilty of non-assistance to a ship in distress. For screenwriters, this was a perfect motif: Contrast the heartrending distress of the beautiful *Titanic* with the sleepiness of an insignificant little liner that lies in visible distance yet simply does not help! The historical distress rockets as well as a signaling lamp become part of the *Titanic* code. They intensify the emotional drama unfolding on the sinking ship — arousing again and again the hope (even in the audience, who should know better) that maybe the ship on the horizon will understand. The *Californian* does *not* understand, although her watch officer does wonder, and rightly so; after all, the *Titanic* did not send the correct distress signals. This historical fact is neither shown nor discussed in film, though, so that the sleepy (translate: dumb, foolish, irresponsible, or: simply criminal) Captain Lord is turned into the perfect scapegoat. As *A Night to Remember* was released, the historical Captain Stanley Lord, by then eighty years old, engaged a lawyer, who even after Lord's death continued to fight for exoneration. In vain: First the 1912 inquiries, then — with overwhelming power of persuasion — the film versions of the *Titanic* tale forever anchored the image of his alleged negligence in collective awareness.[16]

In contrast, the effectiveness and altruism of Captain Rostron of the *Carpathia* are highlighted, again corresponding to Walter Lord's depiction; both in his 1955 and his 1986 books, Lord loudly sang the praises of the *Titanic* survivors' "savior."[17] Rostron indeed acted quickly, and rushing to the *Titanic*'s aid with all the power that could be gathered on his little liner, he took little heed of the danger for his own ship, running at highest possible speed through the ice region. (As a responsible captain, he did double the outlooks and held concentrated watch himself, and he did of course slow down as icebergs were sighted — a tacit counter-image to Captain E. J. Smith's negligence.) Thus, Rostron turned out to be one of the dutiful heroes in the *Titanic* tale, an ideal motif for film.

Good guy, bad guy — good ship, bad ship: The *Californian* and the *Carpathia*, both historical, both part of the *Titanic* myth, proved to be perfect accessories in cinematic *Titanic* tales. They add a double irony of fate: On the one hand, the ship that is in palpable distance, yet blind and dumb, on the other, the good Samaritan, too far away to arrive in time. Between these poles of dramatic irony, there is the *Titanic* in dire distress, sinking deeper and deeper — a perfect triangle for cinematic effect.

Quite generally, dramatic irony constitutes a vital technique in *Titanic* films. It relates to an essential part of the *Titanic* myth: the endless series of "ifs."[18] From the very start of the *Titanic* debate it was underlined (partly as a strategy of the White Star Line and its parent company International Mercantile Marine) that the disaster had been a blow of fate, with the many details of the voyage contributing to its fatal outcome like elements in a Greek tragedy. With Walter Lord's *A Night to Remember*, the idle but poignant speculation "what if" became an indispensable part of *Titanic* narratives. It is ideal for a translation into film, since it offers countless opportunities for dramatic irony — often without words, just a close-up shot of the spiked ice warning from the *Mesaba*, or the earphones in the *Californian* wireless office resounding with the desperate "CQD" while the wireless officer is asleep. Or the numerous statements of the *Titanic*'s technological superiority, epitomized in the innocent yet presumptuous line "This ship is unsinkable." Dramatic irony is a favorite device in filmmaking, providing the audience with a feeling of satisfaction: We know what the poor guys in the film do not yet know. In the face of impending disaster (which they do not suspect), their careless, self-confident, arrogant little whims and acts assume a status of poignancy or even tragedy. Thus, the motif of hubris is broken, exposing the pathetic vanity and self-delusion of mankind. Since most of these people are to die, we do not really condemn them — and wish that they, only once, would heed all the little signals that come as a warning.

One fictional shot has turned into a favorite device of dramatic irony in films featuring the *Titanic* story as accessory within a non–*Titanic* main plot. In the 1933 film *Cavalcade*, two innocent lovers stand at the railing and discuss their bright future together. As they turn away, the camera zooms in on a lifebuoy, hanging just where the optimistic lovers have been standing: *Titanic*. The tell-tale life buoy offers the perfect ironic twist in films where *Titanic* is to play an instrumental role in the development of a non–*Titanic* plot: It is here where it is revealed that something will go terribly wrong in the so far innocent course of the story.[19]

Despite dramatic irony and tell-tale life buoys, an important motif in the *Titanic* myth has hardly ever been taken up. The premonitions, abundant in the post-disaster discourse, rarely figure in *Titanic* films.[20] An exception is the 1996 mini-series *Titanic*, in which (historical) maid Alice Cleaver's nightmares about a drowned baby return as a structural device. Another shot in this series shows a decrepit old woman on the Southampton docks foreboding disaster on sea. She is, of course, ignored by the boarding First Class passengers. Yet these shots are melodramatic and in no way convincing. In fact, the *Titanic* story offers so much opportunity for dramatic irony in film that the metaphysical premonitions simply are too much of a good thing and end up appearing as overdone and in bad taste.

As is seen in the table at the beginning of the chapter, the historical story indeed offers more than enough for a dramatically engaging tale about the *Titanic* and the fate of her passengers and crew. Historical detail is so abundant — the circumstances surrounding the construction, the maiden voyage, the disaster, and its aftermath, the individual stories of the 2,200 passengers and crew, the fate of the survivors and the victims' families — and it has been so well researched in the past decades that there would in fact still be many possibilities to devise new *Titanic* films with yet unexploited focuses and plots.

Music to Drown By: Music in the Titanic *Myth*

In several ways, music plays an important role in the *Titanic* myth and its translation into film. The most conspicuous link between music and the *Titanic* is of course the hymn "Nearer, My God, to Thee," which has caused much dissension in *Titanic* scholarship, yet in popular culture invariably is used as the music played as the ship went down. "Titanic" as a tale is unthinkable without this music:

> [T]he rhythm of the shipboard narrative is one of activity subsiding into restfulness, followed by a slow awakening which accelerates into curiosity, alarm, despair and — finally — with an almost symphonic resolution into a quiet, calm and dignified acceptance of fate. When we hear the myth of the *Titanic*, then, it is as though the band provide the incidental music.[20]

In the conservative interpretation of the *Titanic* disaster, namely the disaster as an act of God in answer to human hubris *and* a deplorable tragedy for hundreds of innocent men, women, and children, "Nearer, My God, to Thee" offers the perfect music to accompany the last dramatic moment. Its religious character and musical solemnity are entirely fitting: As Richard Howells points out, the final piece of music creates a "suspended moment of quiet dignity" right at the most dramatic moment, elevating the ship disaster to a universal tragedy of mankind.[21]

At the same time, this music represents the personal fate of the people on the *Titanic*. The legend about the final piece of music is inseparably linked with the glorification of the eight musicians, who have become an indispensable element of the *Titanic* myth, anchored in collective awareness with a large-scale memorial concert on May 24, 1912, a broadside printed by the Musicians' Union in support of their families, and a memorial erected in Southampton.[22]

The musicians' fare was varied: The band, consisting of a quintet and a

10. The Titanic Code

Having allegedly played until the very end, the musicians of the *Titanic* were stylized into heroes. The Musicians' Memorial at Southampton is a typical example of their public veneration.

trio, had a basic repertoire of 342 tunes which the musicians could play in harmonized version from memory. Most of this was light music for entertainment: ragtimes, overtures, arrangements, potpourris, and paraphrases from popular operas and operettas, suites from light classical music, waltzes.[23] Besides this First Class entertainment offered during teatime, in the Reception Room and the Café Parisien, and in after dinner concerts, the musicians were obliged to accompany the hymns in the Sunday services. In addition, bugler Peter W. Fletcher would play the tune "The Roast Beef of Old England" to announce meals in the First Class dining room — a feature used for slightly mocking remarks in several *Titanic* films.

Beside this music reserved for First Class, there is evidence of hymn-singing in Second Class, while Third Class is used for "ethnic" music underlining the vigor and earthiness of the *Titanic*'s poorest passengers. Historically, there was an Irish passenger, Eugene Patrick Daly, who brought his uileann pipes aboard and played on them as the ship left Queenstown (he was one of the few men who went down with the ship but were saved on the upturned Collapsible B). There is no evidence of who played which music at the Third Class party on April 13 — yet there doubtlessly were gifted musicians, some with their own instruments brought along, among the large number of Third Class passengers. *Titanic* films draw largely on these opportunities for inserting realistic music in the setting. Together with the music of the film score, these musical moments increase the emotional impact of the *Titanic* tale, in whichever version it is told.

The Final Song

The identity of the last piece of music played by the band is one of the most-discussed issues in the *Titanic* myth. Which was the piece that the band last played and when exactly did they play it? The myth opts for "Nearer, My God, to Thee"— played right as the ship went down.

According to the testimonies of the survivors, there are in fact three main contenders for the final piece: "Nearer, My God, to Thee," a piece named "Autumn," and a waltz from the *Titanic* band's repertoire, "Songe d'Automne."[24] The latter two possibilities follow the testimony of wireless operator Harold Bride. In an interview with the *New York Times* published on April 19, 1912, Bride stated:

> The water was then coming into our cabin. From aft came the tunes of the ship's band, playing the ragtime tune, "Autumn." Phillips ran aft, and that was the last I ever saw of him alive. I went to the place where I had seen the collapsible boat on the Boat Deck, and to my surprise I saw the boat, and the men still trying to push it off.... I felt I simply had to get away from the ship. She was a beautiful sight then. Smoke and sparks were rushing out of her funnels. There must have been an explosion, but we heard none. We only saw a big stream of sparks. The ship was gradually turning on her nose — just like a duck does that goes down for a dive. I had only one thing on my mind — to get away from the suction. The band was still playing. I guess all the band went down. They were heroes. They were still playing "Autumn." Then I swam with all my might.[25]

Much has been made of Bride's statement. Although he clearly said that "Autumn" was a ragtime, other newspapers took up the name he mentioned and referred to it as a hymn — doubtlessly desiring a more religious musical finale to the disaster. In *A Night to Remember*, Walter Lord took up the notion that the last piece played was the Anglican hymn "Autumn"; he referred to Bride's professional training in accurate listening as evidence for the correctness of his memory, though Bride in fact had stated in the original interview that "Autumn" was a ragtime.[26] Hymnologists then began to discuss the matter and showed that the ascription remained highly problematic, not least because hymns generally are referred to by their first line and not according to the name of their tune.[27]

The "ragtime 'Autumn'" would in fact refer to Archibald Joyce's waltz "Songe d'Automne," which was No. 114 in the repertory of the *Titanic* musicians.[28] Generally known as "Autumn," this waltz was a major hit in London in 1912; any British musician obliged to play light music on his job would have known it.[29] It is quite likely that the band played this waltz among the pieces that were meant to keep the passengers calm in the course of the evacuation; maybe it was even the last piece before they were released from their duty.

However, the waltz had no chance against the overwhelmingly popular notion that "Nearer, My God, to Thee" had been played as last piece. The hymn became the musical icon both for the band's imperturbable sense of duty until the very end and for a general Christian resignation into God's will, shared by the *Titanic* survivors. It was this statement of the "final song" that was desired in the disaster's aftermath, a comfort to the bereaved and a religious morale for the entire public.

Several passengers in fact confirmed that "Nearer, My God, to Thee" had been the last piece of music that the band had played. However, these are women who had been put into lifeboats at an early stage and were far away from the *Titanic* as she sank. Survivor Colonel Archibald Gracie, who had gone down with the ship, emphatically denied that this hymn had been played:

> It was now that the band began to play, and continued while the boats were being lowered. We considered this a wise provision tending to allay excitement. I did not recognize any of the tunes, but I know they were cheerful and were not hymns. If, as has been reported, "Nearer My God to Thee" was one of the selections, I assuredly should have noticed it and regarded it as a tactless warning of immediate death to us all and one likely to create a panic that our special efforts were directed towards avoiding, and which we accomplished to the fullest extent. I know of only two survivors whose names are cited by the newspapers as authority for the statement that this hymn was one of those played. On the other hand, all whom I have questioned or corresponded with, including the best qualified, testified emphatically to the contrary.[30]

Unfortunately, Gracie does not mention when the band actually stopped playing — he, as one of the men who remained on the Boat Deck as the bow went underwater, would have been an important witness on this question. In any case, his statement that a playing of "Nearer, My God, to Thee" at an earlier stage during the evacuation indeed would have been regarded as a "tactless warning of immediate death" and in all likelihood have created the very panic that the music was supposed to prevent, is very interesting. At first sight, it refutes the popular opinion that a religious hymn was appropriate in such a situation. Yet Gracie quite clearly refers to an earlier stage of the evacuation: Would a hymn as the very last word of the musicians, uttered at a time when there no longer was any doubt about the situation, not have been adequate after all? It is this romantic image that is taken up in *Titanic* films.

Nevertheless, the issue remains a problem. "Nearer, My God, to Thee" does in fact have three different tunes, two of which are used in England ("Horbury," composed by John B. Dykes and used by various protestant denominations, and "Proprior Deo," composed by Sir Arthur Sullivan and used in the Methodist church), and one by Protestants in the U.S. ("Bethany," composed by Lowell Mason). Which one would the band have played? And did those English and American passengers who claimed to have heard "Nearer, My God, to Thee" recognize the *same* melody?

It is frequently quoted that "Nearer, My God, to Thee" would have been the personal choice of bandleader Wallace Hartley. According to an article in the British paper *Daily Sketch* published on April 22, 1912, Hartley had once stated to a fellow musician that in the case of ending up on a sinking ship, he would play "O God, Our Help in Ages Past" or "Nearer, My God, to Thee" as his final piece.[31] Hartley was a devout Methodist; on his grave stone the hymn has in fact been engraved with the Methodist tune by Sir Arthur Sullivan. If "Nearer, My God, to Thee" had indeed been Hartley's personal farewell, expressing his acceptance of God's will, he would doubtlessly have chosen the tune of his own denomination. Would any of the passengers have recognized the unusual tune? *Titanic* directors, at any rate, chose either the American "Bethany" tune or the English "Horbury."

The media and popular opinion did not bother with such finicky musical questions. The press and popular culture — issuing souvenirs such as postcards, handkerchiefs, musical compositions on the sinking, and stone memorials — irrevocably confirmed: It was "Nearer, My God, to Thee" that had been played as the ship went down.[32] Accordingly, the hymn was sung at Wallace Hartley's funeral in his home town Colne (the public attention of this funeral varied, according to various sources, between 30,000 and 40,000 people), and the opening phrase of the tune was carved into the foot of his grave monument. In public perception, the complicated question of the tune was as irrelevant as the question how likely it was that the testimonies of the survivors could be correct: "It seemed now that the story of 'Nearer, My God, to Thee' was one of agreement rather than documented fact."[33]

The media documentation of the "Titanic Band Memorial Concert" in London discloses how such general agreement was constructed in public opinion. On May 24, 1912, a major concert was organized by the Orchestral Association to honor the eight musicians of the *Titanic*, involving the seven chief orchestras in London and some of the leading conductors of their time. Altogether 500 musicians were conducted in turn by Sir Edward Elgar, Sir Henry Wood, Landon Ronald, Thomas Beecham, Percy Pitt, and Willem Mengelberg. In the end the large audience sang "Nearer, My God, to Thee." As recorded by the *Daily Sketch* (May 25, 1912), this collective act of remembrance turned into the emotional climax of the concert:

> The supreme moment of the day came when Sir Henry Wood led the orchestra through the first eight bars of Dykes' version of "Nearer, My God, to Thee" and then, turning to the audience, he conducted the singing to the end — quite 10,000 people intense with emotion, sang in unison what is now one of the world's most famous hymns, and the effect was such that women wept and men had difficulty in mastering their feelings."[34]

However, the *Daily Sketch* does not only emphasize the emotional impact of the hymn being sung as an act of religiously imbued remembrance. In the same paragraph it cements the notion that it had indeed been this very hymn that the band had played on the sinking ship:

> To two ladies sitting in a box near the Royal party, the hymn made special appeal, and their emotions were evident. The last time they had heard it was from a small boat loaden to the water's edge and the band playing the hymn on the Boat Deck of the sinking *Titanic*.[35]

It is quite questionable if the two *Titanic* survivors should indeed not have heard the hymn between the night of April 15 and the concert on May 25, 1912: by the end of May 1912, "Nearer, My God, to Thee" had become "common property" in the *Titanic* complex. It had been presented as "final song" countless times in print and in performance, both in churches and in the movie theaters; it would have been quite a feat not to have heard it anywhere in the six weeks between the disaster and the concert. It is obvious from the context of the newspaper report that the "quotation" of the two survivors, whether the statement ever was made or not, serves to reinforce the poignancy of the report about the concert. It can hardly be taken at face value.

Psychology is in fact the decisive factor in discussing the plausibility of "Nearer, My God, to Thee" as final song played on the *Titanic*. Richard Howells convincingly argues that this belief may actually refer back to the disaster of the steamer *Valencia* in 1906, which ran aground only 60 feet off the steep cliffs of Vancouver Island and, after two tormenting days and in full view from the shore, sank with more than 100 people still on board.[36] In this tragedy, the remaining passengers eventually sang, as it was reported in numerous papers, "Nearer, My God, to Thee" (is this the truth — or just an earlier myth?). There is some likelihood that this notable detail of the *Valencia* disaster still was on people's minds and became immediately projected onto the *Titanic*:

> Just as "Be British!" was "what we would have expected and wanted" Captain Smith to have said as his final words, so "Nearer, My God, to Thee" was just what was required as the *Titanic* sank. The fact that it was not true was hardly the point."[37]

The same psychological pattern can be traced in the common belief that the musicians played until the very last moment, even "until they were waist high in water," as it was determined in the nascent legend.[38] Realistically seen, this notion is absurd — just try to play the piano on a strongly slanting plane, or a cello with the water up to the waist. But the *Titanic* myth does not heed realism. Again, it is the romantic notion of the brave musicians attending to duty until the very last moment and then, released from this duty, ending their lives with a dignified musical resignation into God's will.

We do not know what happened to Hartley and his band in the end. Captain Smith probably released them from their duty, as he did with other crew members. It may well be that they nevertheless played on. Where else should they have gone in the midst of rising chaos? It may well be that they chose something else than their usual fare as their final piece, maybe even a hymn. It may have been "Nearer, My God, to Thee" just as well as any other hymn. It may equally have been the popular waltz "Autumn," which Bride stated to have heard as he fled from the wireless office. We do not know, and this does not even matter. Public opinion immediately focused on "Nearer, My God, to Thee," and thus this hymn became an indelible part of the *Titanic* myth.

As such, it was invariably adopted in the cinematic translation of the *Titanic* myth. After all, this "psalm at the journey's end," in combination with the musicians' relentless sense of duty, offered a powerful emotional statement in film. As Jeffrey Richards rightfully observes: "There is no doubt that sequences in which the orchestra on the doomed ship plays 'Nearer My God, to Thee' (whether in the Mason or Dykes versions) have a powerful mythic and spiritual resonance which is wholly absent from the versions in which 'Autumn' is played."[39]

In fact, "Autumn" is hardly ever played in cinematic *Titanic* tales. Nearly all *Titanic* films use "Nearer, My God, to Thee," following the tradition that was established with the first silent films in 1912 (here, the hymn would be inserted as an intertitle or played as film music). The sound film productions of 1929, 1943, 1953, and 1997 all feature the American version ("Bethany") of the hymn. This tune is equally used in the American motion pictures *Cavalcade* (1933) and *History Is Made at Night* (1937) as well as in the NBC production *No Greater Love* (1996), which all include a *Titanic* sequence. The British film *A Night to Remember*, in turn, features the English tune "Horbury," which is eventually turned into the closing orchestral music of the film score.

Very few films deviate from the general consensus that "Nearer, My God, to Thee" was the final song: The 1956 NBC television version of *A Night to Remember* (produced immediately after the publication of Walter Lord's documentary novel) follows Lord's original conclusion that the hymn tune "Autumn" had been played; this was taken up in the 1979 film *S.O.S. Titanic*, which again follows Lord's documentary novel in utmost detail. The 1996 mini-series *Titanic*, in contrast, uses an unusual solution: both "Nearer, My God, to Thee" and Archibald Joyce's waltz "Songe d'Automne" are played, the latter following the original statement of Harold Bride. However, both pieces only reverberate faintly throughout the rising panic. In fact, this effect is highly realistic — nobody in the general chaos would really have listened to the music (if it was played at all until the very end), and certainly no one in the lifeboats would have heard it.[40]

By choosing "Nearer, My God, to Thee" as final hymn in *A Night to Remember*, producer William MacQuitty turned against Lord's conviction expressed in the 1955 book that the final piece had been the Anglican hymn "Autumn." As Jeffrey Richards describes, MacQuitty had in fact consulted fifty of the survivors "and was persuaded by their firm conviction that the hymn had been played."[41] Seen from today's stance of oral history, the complete ignorance of psychological patterns of recollection appears to be almost amusing: Decades after the notion of "Nearer, My God, to Thee" as "final song" had been anchored in collective awareness, the belief that this was correct and that it reflected their own "true experience" had of course been cemented in the survivors' minds. Now, one hundred years after the disaster, this belief has been irreversibly "confirmed" in collective awareness, due to endless reiteration in film, books, articles, and on the Internet: "Nearer, My God, to Thee" will always remain the "final song" played by the band as the *Titanic* sank. It is one of the many *Titanic* legends that never will die.

Music and Class

The social structure of the *Titanic* was reflected in music. Best known is the music for First Class, epitomized in the band under Wallace Hartley. Ironically, these members of the crew were registered as Second Class passengers, since they were not directly under contract with the White Star Line, but hired through the agency C.W. & F.N. Black of Liverpool. (However, they were by no means given Second Class cabins, but were accommodated in the far more modest crew quarters.) The band consisted of two ensembles, a quintet and a trio, featuring the combinations 2 violins — bass viola — cello — piano (quintet) and violin — cello — piano (trio).[42] As mentioned above, it was their duty to play light music in the First Class public rooms, give after-dinner concerts and play hymns in the Sunday service. Accordingly, First Class is musically characterized by cultivated entertainment; in *Titanic* films, the waltz "The Blue Danube" is often quoted as a favorite musical icon, while in the evacuation scenes the band — historically correct — plays ragtimes.[43]

This light music is contrasted by the hymns sung at the service in the morning of Sunday, April 14. In First Class, this service was presided over, as tradition had it, by Captain E.J. Smith. Contrary to the *Titanic* films of 1979 and 1997, there is no evidence of the "navy hymn" "Eternal Father, Strong to Save" (also known as "For Those in Peril on the Sea") having been sung. Instead, Colonel Archibald Gracie recalls "O God, Our Help in Ages Past" as last hymn in this service. Yet even this hymn contains a twist of poignant dramatic irony, as underlined by Gracie:

> What a remarkable coincidence that at the first and last ship's service on board the *Titanic*, the hymn we sang began with these impressive lines:
>> O God our help in ages past,
>> Our hope for years to come,
>> Our shelter from the stormy blast
>> And our eternal home.[44]

It was not a "stormy blast" but an iceberg that, twelve hours later, turned the *Titanic* passengers and crew into "those in peril on the sea." Legend has it that they, under the musical leadership of the *Titanic*'s band playing "Nearer, My God, to Thee," resigned into God's will, many of them returning to their "eternal home" in this ordeal.

Was this noble resignation, accompanied by trained musicians, a privilege to First Class only? Or would the other classes have joined in?

Hymns are in fact the only musical fare that can historically be linked to Second Class. Characteristically, there is almost nothing known about music in Second Class, corresponding to the minimal attention that this "inconspicuous" class has received in the *Titanic* myth and *Titanic* films. The only notable instance is in fact a hymn service organized by Second Class passenger the Rev. Ernest Courtenay Carter from London on the evening of April 14 — a musical prayer meeting ironically taking place a few hours before the collision. The service was held in the Second Class dining room, with around a hundred passengers participating, that is, more than a third of all Second Class passengers.[45] Following the tradition of hymnal and prayer services, the Reverend Carter introduced each hymn with a short introduction about its history, its theological meaning, and its author. Here, "Eternal Father, Strong to Save" eventually was sung; among the other hymns there figure "There Is a Green Hill Far Away," "On the Resurrection Morning," "Lead Kindly Light," and, as final hymn of the evening, "Now the Day Is Over."[46] Tellingly, the hymn-singing was not accompanied by the professional musicians hired by the White Star Line, but by musically gifted passengers: Robert Douglas Norman, an electrical engineer from Glasgow traveling Second Class, played the piano, and Marion Wright from Yeovil, Somerset, who crossed the Atlantic to join her fiancé in Oregon, sang various solo parts in the hymns. (Interestingly, there obviously existed a piano as permanent facility in the Second Class dining room, implying that music-making was regarded as a regular pastime in this class.)

The service lasted until about ten o'clock, followed by coffee and refreshments. The Reverend Carter is said to have thanked the purser for the use of the room, adding that the ship was "unusually steady." His final remark, about ninety minutes before collision, sounds like dramatic irony from a film script: "It is the first time that there have been hymns sung on this boat on a Sunday evening, but we trust and pray it won't be the last."[47]

This scenario fits quite well with the general image of Second Class: unobtrusive, modest, yet committed. A professional class without glamour, yet firm in their standing. Talking about musical clichés, Anglican hymns are quite the right icon for these people in late Edwardian times.[48]

It is Third Class where most ample musical *couleur locale* is added. As with most clichés in the *Titanic* story, there is an historical grain of truth to the stereotype of ethnic, life-affirming music in the "steerage" accommodations: At least one Irish emigrant, farm laborer Eugene Patrick Daly from Athlone, Westmeath, brought his uilleann pipes, a traditional Irish instrument, for which he later claimed a compensation of $50.[49] Before his emigration, Daly had been a member of the Irish National Foresters band at Athlone; his daughter later described him as "not only a piper, but a great Irish step dancer in his young years," who "played all the jigs and reels and hornpipes that were danced to by serious set dancers."[50] In addition, the *Evening World* from April 22, 1912, mentioned that "Eugene P. Daly, the rescued Third Class passenger, was playing the bag pipes in the third cabin to the amusement of his fellow passengers shortly before the iceberg was struck."[51] Thus, the perfect basis for the musical steerage cliché was given: traditional Irish dance music, the stereotype of the poor people's zeal for life.

Yet it is not only lively dance music that is associated with Daly's musical gifts: On the tender *America*, transferring the Irish passengers from Queenstown to the *Titanic*, the experienced amateur musician is said to have played several native Irish airs to the great joy of his fellow Irish travelers.[52] His final farewell to Ireland, as the *Titanic* left Queenstown, then was the traditional piece "Erin's Lament."

Irish dances, native airs, and a wailing lament as farewell to Ireland all have become musical stereotypes in the cinematic depiction of Third Class on the *Titanic*, most notably in the film score of Cameron's *Titanic*. Yet there were numerous other nationalities among the Third Class passengers, taking their cultural and musical heritage along on the voyage. What about their music? It is likely that the musical fare, especially at the party of April 13, was much more varied. Irishness, marketed as "commodity" in the more recent *Titanic* films, has superseded the musical variety that doubtlessly existed in Third Class.

The various classes and their music offered welcome stereotypes to filmmakers. The "social geography" in the *Titanic*'s structure is supplemented with a "musical geography," expressed through the musical icons of cultivated light music, English Protestant hymns, and "ethnic" Irish music. These icons conceal the fact that reality, both social and musical, was much more complex, even within the closed space of the *Titanic*.

The Film Music

In filmmaking, the musical stereotypes on the *Titanic* offer welcome opportunity for inserting diegetic musical moments, that is, "real" music performed as part of plot and setting. This music serves both to define social spaces and to add emotionally charged characterizations of the various protagonists or dramatic situations (such as the performance of solo songs or dances at the Third Class party). "Nearer, My God, to Thee," whether historical or not, does of course figure prominently in almost all films.

However, the principal role of emotional expression in film is given to non-diegetic music, that is, the music of the film score which does not represent a part of the plot, but serves as an expressive means to underline dramatic situations and the emotional reactions of the protagonists — "film music" as applied in the general sense of the term. Diegetic music is part of the overall film score, and it may assist in underlining emotional expression, yet it is non-diegetic music that offers the true space for musico-dramatic expression.

With the exception of the film music to Cameron's *Titanic*, the film scores have hardly received attention in the history of *Titanic* films. Indeed, most of them are not very notable. None of the films up to 1958 goes beyond the conventions of lush orchestral film scores, adding drama and emotion where they predictably belong. In the 1953 film, with a film score by Sol Kaplan, the collision scene is interesting: shrill violins keep on throughout the relatively long-drawn scene, sounding like an alarm — a forerunner of the famous violin stabs in *Psycho*? The post-collision sequence then is devoid of music; instead, there is a constant enervating alarm hooting into the night. Unauthentic, but effective. A similar effect, though with quite a contrary message, is applied in *A Night to Remember*: Here, the notable hooting concert at the *Titanic*'s outset imparts an image of triumphant technology. It is a symphony of technology — and a twist of dramatic irony, since we know how this triumph soon will end.

Both the 1953 *Titanic* film and *A Night to Remember* are unusual in that they almost entirely relinquish film music. In *A Night to Remember*, this is part of the documentary stance. Apart from the obligatory diegetic clichés (for the first time featuring distinctly Irish music in Third Class), the film contains hardly any music at all. Only in the scenes that impart the growing unrest and eventual panic does dramatic orchestral music set in to underline the increasing distress, especially of the Third Class passengers. As the lights go out in the final minutes, this music again adds a dramatic impulse. The rest of the score then is an orchestral version of "Nearer, My God, to Thee," which has been so memorably exposed as diegetic music in the sinking. As a musical soundtrack, the orchestral version accompanies both the prayers of the horrified survivors in the lifeboats and the end credits set over the images of tragic flotsam. Thus, film composer William Alwyn quite tangibly provides the "symphonic finale" of sweet resignation which has been identified as indispensable conclusion of the *Titanic* tale.

In the 1996 mini-series, its low budget is most clearly reflected in the music. The television production features sweeping orchestral music that evinces a scent of cheapness — canned music, no doubt. The only scene in which the film score has something notable to contribute is, as discussed in Chapter 8, the larger-than-life sequence of the sinking. It is music that envelops the moments of the sinking, elevating it to the universal disaster of mankind as which it was regarded in contemporary perception. The music in itself — again broad strings — is not really remarkable, yet the combination of the suddenly dominating music with the multiple disaster scenes in slow motion, the reaction of the horrified survivors in the boats, and the reverberating, increasingly dominant screams turn this sequence into an impressive climax.

The most interesting film scores were created for the 1979 and the 1997 *Titanic* films. Just as the film itself, the score of the 1979 television production *S.O.S. Titanic* has received far too little attention so far. The producers hired one of the more prolific contemporary English composers, Howard Blake.[53] The score is classically conceived, using a large orchestra and building on main themes that fulfill the function of emotional signifiers, returning at telling moments throughout the film.[54] There are four themes that stand out most clearly. The most interesting feature of the score is that they all are developed out of the opening tragic brass theme:

1. "tragic theme": a dramatic, tragic theme dominated by brass instruments: representing fate, the tragedy of the *Titanic* (brass, string accompaniment)
2. "insanity / ice theme": a jagged, disquiet string theme developed from the accompaniment of the tragic theme (strings)
3. "lament": a plaintive theme, representing the helplessness and misery (oboe, flute)
4. Dies irae motif: four-note motif, accompanying the moments of the sinking in manifold reiteration (flute, oboe, later also brass)

The main theme of the film score, labeled "tragic theme" in this analysis, is a musical statement of the tragedy of the *Titanic*. It underlies the opening credits, returns several times throughout the film and prominently features at the end. All other themes are developed out of it. Thus, an overall musical expression of tragedy permeates the score. The amply used diegetic music, in turn, offers a poignant contrast, representing the ingenuous confidence in technology and progress, the passengers' joy of life, and the band's heroic behavior in the face of disaster.

The tragic theme frames the film, accompanying images of the ice field and the menacing bergs that open and close the story. In this audio-visual combination, the music strengthens the theme of sublime nature as superior force, thus disclosing the pathetic delusion of human hubris. The musical means used by Blake are long-cherished stereotypes in romantic music and film composition: a somber, grave minor theme played in low brass instruments (trombones or horns; the instrumentation varies), long-held high violins adding tension to imbue the massive theme with a certain expectancy (of "the convergence of the twain"?), and intermittent, hard brass chords beating down like blows of fate. This theme returns again and again, whenever the large-scale tragic dimension of the *Titanic* and her passengers' fate is underlined in the course of the film. In some instances where urgency is to be imparted (such as the *Carpathia* speeding toward the sinking *Titanic*), dramatically reiterated blows in the strings are added — another effective device in classical film composition to convey dramatic urge.

The strings offer a counter-theme that first appears as accompaniment within the tragic theme, but quickly develops into an independent theme of its own: a disturbed, jagged melodic line, disquieted by vibrant reiterations, a musical signifier for unrest of a mind verging on insanity. It is linked with Ismay and represents his despair that brings him to the brink of madness. Thus, it uncannily sneaks in as Ismay is shown on the *Carpathia*, isolated, unreceptive, close to hallucination. Yet the theme also stands for the general ice danger that will be *Titanic*'s doom: In the opening sequence of the film, the jagged strings are first linked with the ice field, played as a distinct theme as the first lifeboats appear among the bizarre icebergs and flakes. This theme returns as wireless operator Phillips receives the *Mesaba* ice warning, and then, just before the collision, as ice flakes are shown floating in the water and the fatal berg is sighted. After this explicit linking with the ice, the theme returns to Ismay, representing his disturbed state of mind as he — rebuffed by Fifth Officer Lowe — realizes that he is only a passenger and thus has to watch helplessly how the ship sinks.

Besides the first two themes standing for deep tragedy and trauma, there is a plaintive, poignant theme played by the oboe or, alternatively, by the flute — that is, by woodwind instruments traditionally used for laments and "sweeter" emotions. In fact, this theme is a variant of the opening brass theme: The tragedy of universal destiny is turned into a more personal lament. Tellingly, this theme is for the first time fully played as Second Officer Lightoller writes a letter to his wife in the evening after the departure from Southampton. The departure, a sequence of utter triumph and optimism, now is countered by the darker colors of night, by Lightoller describing the near-collision with the liner *New York* as the *Titanic* left Southampton (an historical incident which was regarded as a bad omen by some passengers) — and by the melancholy oboe theme. The theme will return during the evacuation as Ismay wanders around the Boat Deck in silent despair, unable to help, unable to save the ship and its passengers.

The same instrumentation is used for the final theme, which in fact consists of little more than four notes reiterated again and again in varying registers and by varying wind instruments. Melodically, the four-note motif takes up the opening notes of the tragic theme. Setting these notes into equal rhythmic values, Blake has in fact turned this head-motif of his main theme into a quotation from the famous Latin sequence *Dies irae*, whose general significance turned from a liturgical piece into a musical signifier of death and condemnation in the 19th century (see next page).[55] *Dies irae*, in Roman Catholic liturgy the sequence in the Requiem Mass, has been laden with associations since the Requiem became an important asset in church composition. Since the Baroque, the sequence, which depicts in powerful imagery the "day of wrath" (that is, the Judgment Day), has been a climax of Requiem compositions. There is a line of tradition from the Baroque settings via Mozart's famous *Requiem* (1791) to the apocalyptic brass outburst at "Tuba mirum" in Hector Berlioz's *Grande Messe des Morts* of 1837.[56] However, it is another composition by the highly imaginative romantic composer Berlioz that set the standard for the use of the Latin sequence in film composition: In the Fifth Movement of his famous *Symphonie fantastique* (1830), "Dreams of a Witches' Sabbath," Berlioz uses the original chant melody of the sequence to musically depict the entry of Satan. Introduced by uncanny bells (a Satanist perversion of church bells ringing), the famous first line of the chant is presented in unison by heavy brass. Signifying the climax of a witches' Sabbath, the ancient liturgical melody has been perverted into the contrary of its original meaning. From then on, it would in musical composition irrevocably be associated with evil powers, doom and disaster. In this romantically imbued perversion, the first line of the *Dies irae* became part of film music tradition, the most famous instance being the opening of Stanley Kubrick's *The Shining* (1980), where Berlioz's ominous brass setting of the sequence is combined with an electronic score. The melodic line or just the opening notes of the *Dies irae* recur again and again in film scores as signifiers of disaster and death.

Blake's version of the famous motif is somewhat attenuated due to the use of the "pastoral," lamenting instruments oboe and flute. It therefore assumes associations of mourning and regret over the fate of the *Titanic* and its doomed passengers, imbuing the scenes of the sinking with a deep poignancy. However, there are also scenes of panic on the Boat Deck; the motif is played here with heavy brass instruments, clearly recalling Berlioz's use of the *Dies irae*.

The main theme in Howard Blake's film score to *S.O.S. Titanic*, the Dies irae motif developed from the main theme's first four notes, and the medieval sequence *Dies irae*, which stands for death and mourning and is recalled by this motif in the film score.

10. The Titanic Code

In the end, the tragic theme returns, again combined with the view over an indifferent, terribly beautiful ice field. It is this theme that prevails and, due to motivic interrelation with the other themes, permeates the entire film. Yet after its first statement in the grave brass instruments, it is repeated by the oboe: The film ends with a bittersweet, deeply poignant sound.

In addition to Blake's new-composed film score, there is an unequaled variety of diegetic music in *S.O.S. Titanic*. The various pieces of "real" music serve to define the cultural and social spaces on the *Titanic* (and in Southampton and Queenstown insofar as these places are connected with the *Titanic*), supporting the statement that the film makes about the respective situation with the means of setting, dialogue, and overall atmosphere:

Space and Context	*Diegetic Music*	*Statement*
Southampton, White Star pier just before departure	brass band playing "Rule Britannia"	pride in British technological prowess
Queenstown, tender taking Third Class passengers to the *Titanic*	Irish airs (recorder and bagpipe)	Irish culture, simplicity, farewell to Ireland
Titanic, First Class public rooms before departure	light celebrative music	"So much gaiety" (Ismay's recollection): triumph and beauty of the luxurious ship
Titanic, First Class dining room	light classical entertainment	cultivated First Class life
Titanic, Café Parisien	— dance music and varieté song — tango — waltz	— joy of life — comic relief (Molly Brown) — innocence and joy of life (contrasted with the ice field)
Titanic, Turkish Bath	pseudo-oriental music (non-diegetic)	comic relief, exotism, eroticism
Titanic, First Class Protestant Service	hymn "Eternal Father, Strong to Save"	dramatic irony, poignant contrast to the ice field
Titanic, Third Class common room	— Irish dance music — romantic ballad (solo song + piano)	joy of life, simplicity and vigor, romance
Titanic, Second Class Library	dead silence	seriousness and inconspicuousness of Second Class
Titanic, Boot Cleaners' office	humming of a popular English folk song	innocence and simplicity of the dutiful working class
Carpathia, Wireless office (with Cottam preparing to go to bed)	humming of a popular song (humoristic "good night")	dramatic irony and contrast to the incoming distress call

Space and Context	Diegetic Music	Statement
Titanic, First Class Staircase and later Boat Deck during evacuation	*Titanic*'s band: ragtimes and other light music	dramatic irony and poignant contrast to the fatal situation
Titanic, Boat Deck in the sinking	*Titanic*'s band: hymn "Autumn"	poignancy of the final song

Although a "realistic" element in the setting, much of the diegetic music in fact serves for dramatic irony: the pride in technological prowess expressed by the march "Rule Britannia" as the *Titanic* departs (the flagship of the British White Star Line soon will lie on the floor of the ocean), the innocent good-humored folk songs of the dutiful crew (with wireless operator Cottam's humoristic "Good night, ladies" offering a dramatic contrast to the *Titanic*'s call of dire distress beeping simultaneously through the discarded earphones), the First Class passengers' trust in God and fate while they sing "for those in peril on the sea," the light entertainment music in the early stage of the evacuation, inducing the passengers to dance and enjoy themselves as the ship is sinking.

Importantly, the music of First Class is not used as a sign of stiffened, arrogant culture, as it will be rather clumsily in Cameron's film. Instead, it serves as an exuberant expression of the joy of life which the beautiful new *Titanic* represented. Accordingly, brilliant, celebrative music on the ship forcefully sets in as Ismay painfully remembers the optimistic moments before departure, with his agonized words "so much gaiety" leading into the main narrative. In contrast to the musical class stereotypes in other *Titanic* films, the diegetic music in *S.O.S. Titanic* draws an entirely positive image of First Class. The First Class dance music in the Café Parisien and even the overdone tango serve to display the First Class passengers' joy of life, without any deprecation of the more luxurious surroundings these passengers can afford. Like the passengers in Third Class, they simply enjoy the entertainment and the dance in the evening, and just as in Third Class, this innocent enjoyment constitutes a poignant contrast to the fate awaiting them. It is the Astor couple's waltz that most clearly displays this dramatic function of the diegetic dance music: Their dance, illustrating the deep love they feel for each other, is intercut with images of an menacing iceberg at night, and while the gallant waltz continues, the dreary soughing of the wind goes right through the music.

A corresponding effect is used in the Protestant Sunday service, where the innocent trustfulness expressed in the hymn "Eternal Father, Strong to Save" is intercut with the looming ice field. This time, the sound of the hymn (visually "underlaid" by images of the beautifully clad First Class passengers and their well-behaved children) uncannily interferes with a frenzied high vibrato in the violins that fills the clumsy, yet calming sounds of the hymn with a disturbed tension.

While in Third Class, traditional Irish dance music and the solo performance of a folk ballad continue the tradition set by *A Night to Remember*; Second Class starkly contrasts through its silence. The two representatives of this class first meet in the perfect stillness of the Second Class library, which underlines their serious, reflective attitude to life. In contrast, the victualling crew is for the first time granted a few scenes, thus a voice and even some music of its own: cheerfully lilted English songs, a little tongue-in-cheek, a musical stereotype for the good-humored little people doing their little duty in the microcosm of the ship.

A new feature is the folk music on the tender that transfers the Irish passengers to the *Titanic*. Taking up the historical motif of Eugene Daly playing Irish airs, this music underlines the alleged character of the Third Class passengers: innocent, more down-to-earth, yet also vulnerable, just as the recorder's voice. An unexpected addition is the pseudo-oriental music in the Turkish Bath scene. This music is, in fact, not diegetic (there would have been no music in the Turkish Bath), yet it is conceived as "sonic interior" of the exotic facility on the *Titanic*. Its overtly exotic musical stereotypes underline the scene's function as comic relief. Yet this relief again is brutally juxtaposed: Another memento shot of a sublime iceberg in the cold of the night follows the lush sensuality of the Turkish Bath scene.

It is these sudden contrasts that clearly demarcate both the various social spaces on the ship and the difference in character and atmosphere. Ismay's painful memory explodes into brilliant light music, the serious silence in the library is countered by the light-hearted varieté song in the Café Parisien, the exotic strains in the erotic humidity of the Turkish Bath are juxtaposed with the deadly cold of the wind over the ice field. The ample use of diegetic music thus has a clearly expressive function in *S.O.S. Titanic*, enriching the broad kaleidoscope of life on the *Titanic* with a strongly emotional dimension.

Finally, director William Hale also made expressive use of a few sound effects. The proud hooting at departure, mixing with the band's "Rule Britannia," probably imitates the model of *A Night to Remember*, offering a symphony that glorifies the triumph of technology. The pride of the signals later is countered by the squawking alarm in the engine rooms as water breaks in, and by the agonizing noise of the steam being let off— an historical detail that made communication almost impossible during the preparations for evacuation. These sounds of technology are again uncannily juxtaposed with the superior sounds of nature: the icy wind soughing over the ice field, foreboding destruction and death. It is a quiet "music" that accompanies the shots of the ice field, yet it is awe-inspiring, since it gives evidence of a power stronger than any technological accomplishment.

Music thus plays a major role in *S.O.S. Titanic*. Yet in the theatrical version many interesting points of the score are cut, while the original version with the full amount of music only is available in bad quality on YouTube. With its richness and unusual variety of music-scene relations, the score of this film in many ways actually is more interesting than the commercial hit of Cameron's composer James Horner.

In contrast to the music for *S.O.S. Titanic*, Horner's score for Cameron's film has received ample attention — but above all, it has sold better than any soundtrack album ever. Just as in most other aspects, the 1997 film eclipses all other *Titanic* films with regard to the music. Indeed, music plays a major role in the film's success. As Kevin J. Donnelly put it: "*Titanic* was a musical event as well as being a cinematic event."[57] Apart from the overwhelming success of pop star Celine Dion's hit "My Heart Will Go On," two soundtrack CDs were released (the first being the best-selling soundtrack album ever[58]), and at least 24 CD albums came out that in some way tied in to the film. "This makes *Titanic* the film music event of the last century," to quote Donnelly's conclusion.[59]

The music of Cameron's *Titanic* falls into two distinct quantities that have to be examined separately in their relation to the film. The first and best-known is Dion's theme song, the other is the general film score by Horner with its distinctly Irish (or Celtic) flavor. Both represent important factors in the film's overall marketing success.

Generally, the story of *Titanic*'s film music turns out to be a miniature replica of the blockbuster's success story of strong commitment, high risk and eventual mega-success.[60] With a 100-piece orchestra recording in the premiere orchestral room in town, the music budget quickly went over the top. Since Horner had the common package deal, including a flat fee covering the comprehensive costs for the music, he was soon in danger of ending up without any salary at all.[61] Just like Cameron himself, he risked a tremendous personal deficit while investing everything to get his work on *Titanic* done. Yet in the end, he certainly did not become poor because of this movie.

The story of the theme song resembles another Hollywood fairy tale. Cameron originally refused putting a song in his film — ironic as it may sound, he did not want to "go commercial" at the end.[62] Horner, however, followed his intuition, which in the case of *Titanic* told him that a song was needed. He secretly contacted songwriter Will Jennings to write the lyrics to a song he deemed adequate, and invited Dion to sing it. After some persuasion on part of her husband and manager René Angélil, Dion recorded a demo version (according to

10. The Titanic Code

Paula Parisi, she eventually loved the song). Horner then circled Cameron for weeks, waiting for the perfect moment to present the song. Finally, the decisive moment, not only for the song, but for the film as such, had come:

> After a particularly sunny week, "a good long streak of positive vibes," Horner handed the director a DAT tape. "There's something I want you to hear," he said. Cameron played the song several times, saying nothing. He recognized the theme, so he knew clearly that it had been written for his film, but how in the world did he get this recorded? Finally, after what seemed like a long time to Horner, Cameron turned to the composer and said, "This is great."[63]

A beautiful fairy tale for a fairy tale song—which soon turned into hard cash plus an Oscar statuette. In fact, Cameron was realistic rather than romantic: He instinctively realized that this song would become a major commercial success and as such tie in perfectly with the film. More importantly, he realized what the song would do for the film, how it would capture the audience:

> It seemed, on reflection, the correct way to finish the film, giving voice to the ideas and emotions of the film and putting them out there in the world, in the fabric of everyday life.... Cameron knew the song would get the big push. People would get hit by two or three bars of it, relive that emotion and, in a Pavlovian display of empathy, want to see the film again."[64]

It turned out that Cameron was one hundred percent right. "My Heart Will Go On" became one of the most successful singles ever, it was the perfect appetizer for the film and boosted *Titanic*'s success to a truly unique degree.[65]

Yet Cameron was also right with regard to the contents and function of the song: The quite banal text perfectly summarizes the dominant ideas of the epic love story. Love, substituting the aspect of religion in the *Titanic* myth, transcends time and space, offering eternal bliss. "My Heart Will Go On" is the musico-textual essence of *Titanic*.

The same technique of drawing together the most important ideas of the film is found in the musical structure of the song. Jeff Smith has shown that "My Heart Will Go On," constituting the "theme of love" in the overall film score, in fact integrates elements from the score's various major themes, which function as musical signifiers for death, nature, fate, and transcendent love: "Through this system of shared musical associations, 'My Heart Will Go On' not only reminds us of Jack and Rose's undying love but also brings back *Titanic*'s depiction of class struggle, historical spectacle, epic tragedy, and technological folly."[66]

In its function as film music underscoring action, the song strongly increases the emotional impact of key scenes in the love story: the bow scene with the first kiss, Jack drawing Rose, the love scene in the car, Rose being lowered in the lifeboat and coming to the decision to jump back onto the ship. Then it finally emerges in full guise as a musical correlate to the utopian final vision of the film. Thus, it has indeed been turned into a souvenir to be taken home, back into "the fabric of everyday life," as Cameron predicted. The prominent position and emotion-laden film context of "My Heart Will Go On" spurs the desire to hear the song over and over again (after the film premiere, radio stations virtually drowned in requests for having the song played), thus re-experiencing the film through music. Yet it equally spurred the desire, as Cameron sensed, to want to see the film over and over again.

Less than a year after the premiere, a new version of "My Heart Will Go On" accommodated these two desires. By combining Dion's song with dialogue and sounds from the film, the song as part of the album *Back to Titanic* was turned into the album's emotional climax, summarizing the entire epic love story between Rose and Jack in 4:40 minutes. The dialogue marks the four essential stations in the development of the love story: Jack's declaration of love, Rose's first clear sign of amorous devotion, the lovers' first separation, and the last words between the two, which at the same time are Jack's legacy to Rose's further life. The listener re-experiences these four film scenes through the fragments of dialogue[67] and is thus drawn into the emotional narrative of *Titanic* by means of various sound phenomena and their specific combination: the voices of film stars Kate Winslet and Leonardo DiCaprio; the singing voice and the emotional performance of Celine Dion; the structure of music aiming at creating and intensifying emotion through instrumentation, tone color and timbre, articulation, melody, harmony and rhythm; finally, the sound effects that, though low-key, decisively contribute to the atmosphere of the last two representations (especially the tender kiss "sealing" the lasting bond of love between Rose and the dying Jack). These elements interact throughout the entire track, since the dialogue excerpts are also underscored with instrumentals from the song. The combination of the dialogue with the song as the film's "theme of love" together with Dion's specific voice articulation maximizes the emotional impact of the song. Dion's hit as edited on this soundtrack album is no longer a piece of vocal music in itself, but has been transformed into a renewed experience of the most popular scenes in the film, which are evoked in the combination of music, dialogue and sound. Horner and Cameron indeed were right when they envisaged the tremendous importance this song would have for *Titanic*.

Despite the overwhelming popularity of Dion's song, it is the entire score of *Titanic* that became famous. From the very start, Cameron had a clear idea of what he wanted and what he did *not* want. Tellingly, he desired something "contemporary," exactly in line with the general treatment of this "period" theme for a contemporary 1990s audience. For him, the desired "contemporary" sound was the New Age vocalist style of Enya, whose music he put on the temp track.[68] In fact, he had music supervisor Randy Gerston approach Enya in the hope that she would do the score, yet Enya declined. This was probably good luck for the film, since no doubt the experience of an established film composer was needed to meet both Cameron's desire for a special, ethereal sound and the general necessity of creating a large-scale score that would carry through a three-hour motion picture. Although both Horner and Cameron explicitly stated that they had avoided doing a "Hollywood 1940s type big-drama score," the score in fact evinces several traits of exactly the grand Hollywood film music tradition, namely a structure around several themes and leitmotifs, a broad range of orchestral color, and the use of music to enforce character, setting and action, preferably in a grand emotional sweep.[69] The special feature of Horner's score that both enthralled Cameron and a global audience is the distinctly "Irish" (or, more generally, Celtic) color, creating the sound that Cameron originally desired. As shown in Chapter 9, this effect is mainly achieved through instrumentation, which blends a traditional Irish instrument, the uilleann pipes (that were also historically played on the *Titanic*), with synthesizers and vocals.[70] This is combined with a large-scale orchestra, which however is wisely used, rarely drowning the tunes in full orchestral sound. The result offered an attractive sound for everyone, especially in the context of popular culture in the 1990s — an important part of the blockbuster recipe.

For Horner, this instrumentation was in fact not new: As Kevin J. Donnelly underlines, he frequently uses Irish instrumentation and musical style as a "universal" symbol of emotion and sentiment in his film music.[71] In the score of *Titanic*, the "Celtic" sound is used as a symbol for the nostalgic past, as a lament for the *Titanic* and for a better time — thus, the music ties in with the general feeling of nostalgia, which both is a specific element in Cameron's concept and an important feature of the *Titanic* myth. The uilleann pipes' lament is linked with Dion's song, serving as introduction — yet it occurs also independently, as a general expression of mourning for the dead, and, more broadly defined, as a musical signifier for the mysteries of nature, the sea, and the cruelties of fate.[72]

The other themes are clearly distinguished in their expression, representing other states of mind.[73] A broad, heroic tune (involving vocals, full orchestra, and synthesizer bells) forms a sonic equivalent to the moments of celebration and optimism as the *Titanic* sets out and Jack declares himself "King of the World." Rose's theme, in turn, is more lyrical, a chamber setting for flute, piano, and synthesized vocals. In the context of the scenes where it occurs, it emphasizes the themes of lost love, memory, and nostalgia — altogether a sweet, melancholic, yet not Irish sound. Most important is, of course, the love theme of "My Heart Will Go On." As mentioned above, it integrates all other themes of the score. This integration not only created an "overarching sense of musical unity and organicity," it also offered smooth transitions between themes and leitmotifs within the score.[74]

The same sense of unity in sound and expressiveness is imparted in the soundtrack album. The "Celtic" quality, often described as "timeless" in reviews, permeates the film score, creating an "ephemeral, heavenly space that runs parallel with and across the other spaces" that are defined by the diegetic music (light classical music for First Class, lively Irish folk music in Third Class).[75] As Donnelly has shown, this specific quality ties in with the general commodification of "Irishness" in the 1990s, which again is linked to the New Age and World Music market.[76] In *Titanic*, these elements form a persuasive symbiosis that is projected onto the historical disaster. In the 1990s, it seemed to be both politically correct and emotionally attractive to mourn the loss of the *Titanic* with the dreamy sounds of a lost culture. Commercially, the recipe was perfect.

The Sounds of Death

It is not only music that is vital to convey the "feel" of the *Titanic* disaster, sound plays an equally important role. The *Titanic* story features a dying ship and thus uncanny sounds of creaking and moaning. In addition, there was the nightmare of the screams after the ship had gone down, haunting many survivors for the rest of their lives. During the evacuation, the extreme noise of the steam and the detonation of the distress rockets would intensify the drama unfolding on the decks. While sound effects generally play an important dramaturgical role in film,[77] the *Titanic* story indeed has much to offer to enhance the emotional drama of the "night to remember."

In the 1953 film, for the first time a sound effect really becomes conspicuous in a *Titanic* film: of all sounds, it is the fictional alarm that becomes the increasingly enervating sign that something is terribly wrong on the luxurious ship. Such a general alarm did not exist on the *Titanic*; it might have saved lives, since an alarm system would have warned many innocuous passengers of the deadly danger after the collision. The noise of the steam and the detonation of the distress rockets are historically based sound effects that are used in most films, since many survivors mentioned their effect. While they were loud and dramatic, it was the uncanny sounds of the wounded ship that foreboded death. Roy Baker, the director of *A Night to Remember*, was the first to make ample use of this highly expressive effect. He got it served on a silver platter: The set itself made the necessary creaking sounds as it was winched up to create the tilting deck effect, and these sounds were picked up by the microphones.[78] In a way then, Baker used the original sound. Baker also was the first director to use the testimony about the cries in the water. From then on, this important feature of the *Titanic* disaster would be taken up in every production.

James Cameron with his obsessive ambition for utmost authenticity developed the sound effects to perfection. For him, sound editing was vital to make *Titanic* come alive.[79] Every detail was of importance, every sound effect had its carefully styled expressive function: "He was like a conductor of a huge symphony," sound designer Chris Boyes said.[80] The high-tech whirring of the submarines as they visit the wreck, the throb of the engine (that is, triumph of technology), the creaking of the winch as Rose's lifeboat is lowered (sounds etching themselves into the memory of an emotional experience), the horror of the groaning ship in darkened corridors, the deadly gush of water as it breaks through a door — every detail contributes to the triumph and the tragedy of the *Titanic* story. And even in the age of digital sound design, unusual inspiration and its creative processing were urgently asked for:

> The creaks and groans played a huge role in defining the splitting and sinking of the ship. ... The big groans of the sinking and splitting ship were among the earliest effects he fashioned. Cameron actually got to spot the snapping, metallic sounds into his temp. Dozens of individual tones are interwoven for the final effect. Boyes harvested the sounds from a variety of sources. The most dramatic was a ship that was actually docked in San Francisco bay, where it strained against its moorings in rough weather. He then "processed them heavily," ending up with something that sounds "almost like crying."[81]

Indeed, the scene where Rose is lost in the deserted Third Class corridors, with the light going out and deep subwoofer groans of the sinking ship perfecting the horror, is among the scarier ones in *Titanic*. While the music adds "emotion," it is the sounds that etch themselves in as "the real experience." In this respect, Cameron certainly created a masterpiece.

Yet there is one sound that cannot be recreated — not even by Cameron, who at least offers some impression of "how it really was" in his film. Numerous survivors told about the horror of the cries of the people dying in the water.[82] Some underlined that this horror in fact should be met with silence:

> But although the *Titanic* left us no such legacy of a wave as she went to the bottom, she left us something we would willingly forget forever, something which it is well not to let the imagination dwell on — the cries of the many hundreds of our fellow-passengers struggling in the ice-cold water. I would willingly omit any further mention of this part of the disaster from this book, but for two reasons it is not possible — first, that as a matter of history it should be put on record; and secondly, that these cries were not only an appeal for help in the

awful conditions of danger in which the drowning found themselves,—an appeal that could never be answered,—but an appeal to the whole world to make such conditions of danger and hopelessness impossible ever again; a cry that called to the heavens for the very injustice of its own existence; a cry that clamoured for its own destruction.[83]

The traumatizing effect of this experience was confirmed by others. Second Officer Lightoller later indicated that people indeed had fallen ill and eventually died because they continued to dwell on this memory. Other survivors were no longer able to expose themselves to situations that would sonically remind them of the universal cry (such as the roar of the crowds in a football stadium).[84] It would demand the art of an Alfred Hitchcock to translate the psychological horror of this experience into film. Although Cameron effectively illustrated the enormity of these cries by enlarging the visual and acoustic perspective from Rose's personal experience to the hundreds of people fighting for their lives in the icy water, the narrative stance of his film does not leave room to dwell extensively on this most traumatizing of all moments. It is probably best to follow the recommendation of survivors Beesley and Lightoller: Despite the audience's insatiable hunger for the cinematic recreation of awesome disaster, there are moments that should better be met with silence and respect.

Conclusion
Making Titanic *Immortal*

"She's a ship with a ready-made Oscar": Film critic Ernest Bett's evaluation of the *Titanic* does not only pertain to the ship's representation in the 1958 film *A Night to Remember*.[1] Although public interest in 1911–12 concentrated on the *Olympic* as first ship of the spectacular new Olympic class, the *Titanic* with her slightly larger tonnage was a celebrity as she set out for her maiden voyage. Her sinking made her a star, and the special circumstances of this accident — after all, just one among thousands on the North Atlantic — turned her into an immortal archetype of maritime disaster, ideal for translation into film.

The myth about the *Titanic*, which began to emerge in the hours right after the sinking, is constituted of elements that have been identified as dominant issues in Western narrative tradition: gender, class, nation, race, religion, and human hubris. These elements are crystallized in the master narrative of the *Titanic* disaster, advocating a set of conservative values in times of social upheaval on both sides of the Atlantic. The *Titanic* became instrumental in the general political and social discourse. On the foil of the beautiful — and therefore desirable — First Class setting, which the *Titanic* so impressively provided, these conservative values are recommended as true, stable, everlasting. In narrative versions of the *Titanic* tale, in sermons, and in the visual representation of the disaster, the undesired aspects of the story and its context (such as social injustice, defects in navigation, carelessness in safety measures and the priority of profit interests) were blinded out. Thus, a pattern was forged that transformed the *Titanic* story from tragedy to triumph.

Film was the perfect medium to take this pattern up and to strengthen and develop it. In several ways, the *Titanic* story, not only in 1912, but also in later decades, coincided with important stages in film history. Just as the

Titanic sank, film was about to become the key medium both in the news and entertainment sectors.[2] The German and Danish silent films made on the disaster in 1912 and '13 were among the first notable European motion pictures. The 1929 film *Atlantic* then was one of the first films with an integrated soundtrack (in Germany, it was the first sound film ever released). Later *Titanic* productions represent characteristic profiles in international filmmaking; the discovery of the wreck in 1985 largely depended on the development of a new deep-sea film technology—and "techie" director James Cameron scored the *Titanic* home run by combining the *Titanic* film tradition both with the specific aesthetics of the 1990s and with the latest feats of cinematic high tech. *Titanic* is unthinkable without the film medium.

From the very start, the *Titanic* story and myth developed in close symbiosis with film, developing a tradition in the cinematic representation of the *Titanic* disaster which I have chosen to call the "*Titanic* code." This code covers the general narrative presentation of the story, individual scenes and historical personages, combining it with the great human themes of Western narrative tradition as they are crystallized in the *Titanic* myth. It is a code perfect for film drama: In addition to the myth's central themes, which constitute ideal ingredients for any film plot, the historical *Titanic* story displays a narrative rhythm that exactly corresponds to a classic tragedy. The many details, both on the ship and among the passengers and crew, provide the screenwriter and the director with endless opportunities for contrast, conflict, development, and final resolution. The basic structure—the voyage, the collision and the sinking of the *Titanic*—can be fleshed out with human interest stories, both fictional and historical, relying on the probed force of various archetypes in storytelling. Yet in its perfect pacing, the basic outline of the maritime disaster can just as well constitute the story itself: the ship as a star, as it was presented in *A Night to Remember*.

The social microcosm which the ship constituted then provides the screenwriter with an almost endless number of possibilities: a large number of protagonists, some well-known, many only identified by name (and therefore open for fictionalization), the very rich in First Class and the poor emigrants in "steerage," numerous character stereotypes, and the various strata of the crew with their specific responsibilities. The variation of these elements is held together and elevated by the forceful background story and a strong overall structure with consistent, recognizable details. It is the inescapable doom of the *Titanic*, her passengers, and the crew that adds a special note of poignancy to all the little human stories and skirmishes that unfold until the fatal moment. The sinking then becomes the watershed, the touchstone for true character, the catalyst for reconciliation and rediscovery of love and identity.

The setting, too, offers perfect opportunities: the splendor of the late Edwardian era, displayed on the most luxurious and most impressive ship at that time. It is not a coincidence that no *Titanic* feature film ever has placed the main story in Third Class — or in "boring" Second Class or even in the engine rooms. All films, even Cameron's *Titanic* with its alleged "political correctness" regarding class, focused on the luxuries of First Class. This is most attractive to the audience (indeed, even modern-day viewers dream of luxury) — but it also gives the best chance to be "authentic," since it was the magnificent First Class interiors that were most conspicuously advertised in 1911–12 and are best known until today (again, in great part due to their detailed depiction in film and media). Although rarely made a main point in *Titanic* films, the motif of hubris links up with this setting: Without explicit comment, the dramatic destruction of these splendid, virgin locales by the force of nature impressively represents the downfall of hubristic mankind. The *Titanic* marks the end of an era, the end of these beautiful First Class settings and their obsolete, yet timelessly attractive lifestyle.

Most *Titanic* films cover this dramatic end of an era with a thick layer of nostalgia. Nostalgia is vital both in the *Titanic* myth and in film. Since the publication of Walter Lord's *A Night to Remember* and the release of the film version, nostalgia, the longing for the better world represented by the *Titanic*, has permeated narrative representations of the *Titanic* story. Even James Cameron, who turns the "end of an era" feeling into a modern-day lesson for the American Dream, eventually wraps his emancipatory message in nostalgia. It is not the delicate First Class lady but the self-reliant survivor who prevails in his version of the *Titanic* story: a female survivor, entitled to her personal pursuit of happiness as she enters the New World. However, this cliché remains a dream, just like the virtual resurrection of the everlasting *Titanic* at the end of Cameron's film. Thus, nostalgia even permeates this postmodernist *Titanic* tale, epitomized in the wistful message of the title song.

With Lord's novel and its 1958 film version, both nostalgia and authenticity have become the new fundament for the *Titanic* code: Any film aiming at a serious representation of the disaster has to follow the "authentic" pattern stipulated by Lord in his — in fact quite uncritical — conglomeration of survivors' testimonies. The story has to be recreated in utmost detail, with the "authentic" personages, scenes, and motifs, with dialogues and statements that by now have achieved the authority of scriptural verses. This detailed reconstruction then has to be veiled with nostalgia, a mixture of mourning for the victims and mourning for a time in which luxury still was somewhat innocent, people knew where they belonged, men still were chivalrous, and women meek.

The *Titanic* code in film has become relatively fixed: No other disaster has been studied in so much detail, from the ship's construction plans via the individual passengers' and crew members' biographies to the very words spoken at certain vital moments (many of them fictitious, yet turned into "authenticity" in the *Titanic* myth). Indeed, such a detailed and fixed pattern as fundament for a script is unique in the history of film. It is a challenge, but also a chance for a screenwriter. The comparison of the four films following the "code," starting with *A Night to Remember* that set the standard in 1958, shows the advantages and problems of such a starting point for a feature film. The 1958 docudrama and the 1997 epic romance stand at opposite ends of the scale; both offer highly convincing versions of the *Titanic* tale, displaying utmost craftsmanship in their respective genre and ambition. Tellingly, even *A Night to Remember* inserts fictitious little strands which, representing class "types" rather than realistic people, work much better than the strictly "authentic" setting in *S.O.S. Titanic*, where historical personages were provided with quasi-"historical" love interests. The 1997 film then takes this technique to the extreme, entangling the exceedingly well-researched historical story of the ship with the fictional and highly romantic story of two young lovers. Thus, the four *Titanic* films since 1958 show the broad spectrum of possibilities that even a strict adherence to the *Titanic* code still allows for. History does not block the license for fiction.

Indeed, the relationship to history has been the touchstone in the development of *Titanic* film. Cinematic representation of history has always been a tightrope walk with a precarious balance between "authenticity" and the exigencies of film drama. Few historical incidents have offered such a rich field of experimentation as the *Titanic* disaster. It is a field without limits, offering all variants of historical license. Thus, the 1953 Hollywood film, widely condemned for its "historical inaccuracies" by *Titanic* enthusiasts, offers perfect melodrama in the Hollywood style of the 1950s. History is not the point — yet it may just as well become the focus, as in the 1979 television film *S.O.S. Titanic*.

It is amazing, though, how much the *Titanic* code has fettered the filmmakers' imagination: On the background of a well-known disaster story with a perfect pacing, they have a microcosm with some 2,200 passengers and crew at their disposal — how many stories would *Titanic* still yield? And yet, it is always the same pattern, always the same historical people (or their stereotypes, that is, some rich First Class passengers or some poor but happy emigrants), always the same scenes that are depicted. Why has nobody done a story focusing on the fate of the Navratil family? A matrimonial drama in France, ending with Michel Navratil kidnapping his two little sons under a false name in an attempt to start a new life in the United States via a voyage on the *Titanic*. In the face of disaster, the two toddlers then are put on a lifeboat with no one to care for them. The father drowns, the children are saved and become known as "the *Titanic* orphans" in the international media — until their mother in Nice recognizes her boys in a newspaper article and, overjoyed, takes them back to France. What more could one wish for as a perfect film script?

Or what about the Belfast workers — or the stokers from Southampton? Why has nobody asked about their *Titanic* experience? Ennis Watson, a fifteen-year-old apprentice electrician from Harland & Wolff, was overjoyed when he was chosen to join the shipyard's guarantee group on the maiden voyage. His family doubtlessly felt honored: Their son, yet an apprentice, on the maiden voyage of the *Titanic*! Along with his eight colleagues, among them ship architect Thomas Andrews, the boy died in the sinking.[3]

And what about the musicians, who were stylized into heroes in 1912 — but whose families never got even a cent of compensation, neither from the White Star Line, nor from the Liverpool agents, who yet had the nerve to send the parents of violinist Jock Hume a bill for the White Star buttons on their drowned son's uniform? In 1912, the musicians were venerated as paragons of duty and commitment; yet in *Titanic* films they only serve as a touching little vignette. These committed artists could offer quite a story. Erik Fosnes Hansen took the clue with his bestselling novel *Psalm at the Journey's End* (1990). A film version of the European *fin-de-siècle* panorama that Hansen unfolds is overdue.

And the aftermath? Why has nobody until now used the ample material of the 1912 United States and British inquiries for a legal drama? It is clear that quite a lot was covered up in these inquiries, it is clear that there were strong interests of powerful companies and tycoons involved, and it is clear that a considerable number of the witnesses had to fear for their jobs in case they presented the "wrong" version. The fates of many individuals and families were directly connected with the inquiries, depending on their results; it would be easy to construct a strong story around them. Yet some fantasy would indeed be needed to construct a satisfactory happy end for a movie audience: after all, the decisive responsibilities were covered up in 1912, so that the outcome does not quite offer the triumph of law and order desirable for a successful legal drama.

There is so much to be done about *Titanic* yet. James Cameron's version may be seen as the epitome of a postmodernist *Titanic* story — in its monumentality it seemed to be the last word in *Titanic* film. But now that the limits and problems of postmodernist aesthetics have become abundantly visible, *Titanic* does emphatically ask for new retellings and new perspectives.

Has anyone ever thought about a film made from the iceberg's point of view?

There is much to be done. Now as then, the *Titanic* story offers the perfect script. It encapsulates the great themes of storytelling, putting them again and again up for discussion and negotiation. The sinking of the *Titanic* will, due to the enduring myth and due to the special circumstances of the incident and its historical context, always remain the archetype of maritime disaster. As such, *Titanic* holds a lasting fascination as long as there are stories of seafaring, disaster, and love beyond death to tell. The *Titanic* myth will remain unsinkable.

Chapter Notes

Preface

1. Richards 2003, 10.
2. Biel 1996, 132.
3. The body of literature is vast. A few recommended titles presenting important threads of discussion are Rosenthal 1999; Rhodes and Springer 2006; Ebbrecht 2007a and 2007b; in German, Hohenberger and Keilbach 2003 (esp. the contribution by Sylvie Lindeperg) and, with a special focus on visual representation, Steinle 2009.
4. Foster 1997, 13f.
5. Walter Lord, preface to the 1976 illustrated version of *A Night to Remember*, here quoted from Richards 2003, 10. Cf. Lord's extended variation on this list in Lord 1986, 16f.
6. Cf. Heyer 1995; Biel 1996; Foster 1997; Howells 1999a; Köster and Lischeid 1999, and various essays in Bergfelder and Street 2004.
7. The curious phenomenon of various actors who appeared in more than one *Titanic* film is documented in Appendix A of Anderson 2005.
8. Bristow 1995, 7.
9. Howells 1999, 74–78.

Introduction

1. Cf. Eaton and Haas 1986, 216.
2. The term "archetypal vignettes" is taken from David M. Lubin's study on Cameron's blockbuster (Lubin 1999, 87).
3. Anderson 2005, 1.
4. A considerable number of the reported premonitions and omens is listed in Hyslop, Forsyth and Jemima 1997, 105f; extensive discussion of "psychic forewarnings" is offered by Behe 1988.
5. Lord 1955, xi–xii. The novella *Futility or the Wreck of the Titan* describes how the largest ship in the world, named *Titan*, collides with an iceberg on its maiden voyage and sinks. The measurements and technical data of the fictitious ship are surprisingly close to those of the *Titanic*; further correspondences are the ice damage on the starboard side, the approximate position of the disaster, the *Titan*'s port of registration and port of destination. Robertson's novella was reprinted immediately after the sinking of the *Titanic* and became regarded as a prophecy of the *Titanic* disaster. Cf. Spignesi 1998, 268–309 (including a reprint of Robertson's novella). On the considerable number of premonitions of the disaster cf. Behe 1988.

6. The novel *Atlantis* in turn was made into a silent film by the Danish director August Blom. Released in 1913, the film could draw on the massive public attention engendered by the *Titanic* disaster that appeared like a fulfillment of Hauptmann's vision. Cf. Chapter 3, "Early Films and Newsreels 1912/13."

7. Barthes 1972, 67.

8. A considerable number of legends is presented by Hintermeyer 2003; cf. also Goss and Behe 1994. Ghost ships frequently figure in various forms of art and in feature film; the most famous instance is offered in Richard Wagner's romantic opera *The Flying Dutchman* (1843).

9. Anderson 2005, 94–142 (here, only English-language documentaries are included; there do in fact exist countless *Titanic* documentaries in other languages). Apart from film, Anderson's *Titanic* bibliography covers literature (documentary and fictional books, poems, short stories, articles and essays), dramatic renditions (plays, musicals, songs), and software and internet sources. A more extensive, annotated bibliography focusing on literature is offered by Rasor 2001.

10. Cf. Bergfelder and Street 2004, 2, where the alignment of the *Titanic* disaster and 20th-century experience is taken as starting point to present the variety of cultural, literary, and cinematic perceptions and representations of the 1912 incident.

Chapter 1

1. Howells 1999, 1.

2. The summary is based on the following main sources: Eaton and Haas 1986; Bristow 1989; Lynch 1992; Bristow 1995; Eaton and Haas 1996; Störmer 1997; Spignesi 1998; Störmer 2000, and articles and biographies in the Encyclopedia Titanica. An excellent short summary of the historical event with much detailed information is found in Howells 1999a, 13–36.

3. The third ship was to be the *Gigantic*, eventually named *Britannic* by the White Star Line. Construction, which started on 30 November 1911, dragged on beyond the beginning of war. The *Britannic* was thus never used as a passenger ship: she was put into service as hospital ship in 1915, struck a mine off the Greek coast in 1916 and sank in less than an hour.

4. Up to 1929, the command "hard astarboard" would bring a ship to port and vice versa, relating the rudder to the stern. From 1929 onwards, the command has indicated the direction the bow is supposed to take. The correctness of Murdoch's maneuver is extensively discussed in Bristow 1995, 54–67.

5. The occasional argument that Murdoch should have steered the ship right onto the berg, thus avoiding the damage along the side of the ship which eventually led to the sinking, does not take rules of seamanship into account. Cf. Störmer 1997, 182f.

6. Lord 1955, 21.

7. On the sending of the wrong distress signals cf. Bristow 1995, 265–68 (wireless distress call) and 142–57 (distress rockets).

8. An extensive discussion of the *Frankfurt* question is offered ibid., 287–363.

9. Tellingly, she is missing in the 1943 film, which entirely focuses on propaganda against "England's greed" and therefore ignores most of the American passengers (with John Jacob Astor having been turned into an English lord).

Chapter 2

1. The most important theories are discussed in Howells 1999a, 37–59.

2. Ibid., 37.

3. Bergfelder and Street 2004, 1f.

4. Cf. Howells 1999a; Biel 1996; Foster 1997.
5. On the social and racial upheavals in the United States, cf. Biel 1996, 9–21.
6. Cf. ibid., 132.
7. Ibid., 128.
8. On the justification of men's attempts to justify their survival, which automatically involved the suspicion of unchivalrous, even cowardly behavior, cf. Biel 1996, 27f.
9. Ida Straus' famous oath was a paraphrase of Ruth 1:16.
10. At the American inquiry, only three witnesses from Third Class testified. At the British inquiry, not a single Third Class survivor was called. Instead, the Third Class passengers were represented by a barrister (W.D. Harbison), who concluded that "no evidence has been given in the course of this case that would substantiate a charge that any attempt was made to keep back the third class passengers" (Howells 1999a, 96f, quotation on p. 97).
11. Howells 1999a, 18, and endnotes 19 and 20 on p. 165.
12. On the role of the Second Class passengers in the *Titanic* myth, cf. ibid., 90f.
13. http://www.imdb.com/title/tt0051994/trivia (09.08.2011), source not given.
14. As Chapter 7 shows, the tripartite class structure is a constitutive plot element in this *Titanic* film.
15. This incidence was related by Harold Bride in a report he made to the Marconi Company on 27 April 1912 (the report is transcribed on http://www.Titanicinquiry.org/USInq/AmInq14Bride01.php, 08.08.2011).
16. Bristow 1995, 319f.
17. The great exception in this rather unbecoming presentation is Second Officer Lightoller in the 1958 film; cf. Chapter 6.
18. Cf. Howells 1999a, 99–119.
19. The issue is more complex. Captain Smith did certainly act according to custom — but to the custom of the shipping companies, namely regarding the schedule as imperative. At the inquiries, there were contradictory testimonies as to the speed in an ice region; Smith should clearly have reduced speed. As loyal servant to his company, he took the risk, setting highest priority on the schedule. It is not clear if Bruce Ismay encouraged him, yet there is positive evidence that the president of the White Star Line expected the *Titanic* to arrive earlier than scheduled. Cf. Bristow 1995, 220.
20. The German silent film *In Nacht und Eis*, produced right after the disaster, translates this legend into film.
21. It is only *S.O.S. Titanic* that adopts the (historically based) motif that Andrews actually was born and grew up in Belfast and felt homesick for Ireland on the voyage.
22. Walter Lord describes this scene according to an anonymous steward's testimony (Lord 1955, 71). The scene has become a favorite in *Titanic* films; here, the steward is invariably substituted for a fictional encounter between one of the film's main characters and Mr. Andrews.
23. Gracie 1913, 34.
24. Benjamin Guggenheim became famous for his "noble" statement "We've dressed up in our best and are prepared to go down like gentlemen" accompanying his refusal to put on a lifebelt and fight for survival. Guggenheim's words were reported in the New York Times on 20 April 1912; cf. the transcription of the article on http://www.encyclopedia-Titanica.org/guggenheim-dying-sent-wife-message.html (08.08.2011).
25. Young 1912, here quoted from Howells 1999a, 63. Young published his book *Titanic* already in May 1912.
26. A detailed study on the Irish *Titanic* passengers and crew members is offered by Molony 2000.
27. Cf. Chapter 9.
28. Thus the formulation in Fifth Officer Harold Lowe's apology to the Italian Gov-

ernment after he had stated in the U.S. inquiry that he had fired shots to prevent "Italian" immigrants from jumping into the lifeboats (quoted after Spignesi 1998, 85).

29. Cf. Molony 2000, 9–11.
30. Cf. Howells 1999a, 118f.
31. Cf. below, Chapter 10, "The Final Song."
32. In the 1953 production, he is given a fictionalized character of his own, namely that of the defrocked priest George Healey, who after a major explosion goes down into the engine rooms to offer comfort to the stokers trapped there.
33. Biel 1996, 59–84.
34. Cf. Heyer 1995, 157f.
35. Cf. the astute analysis in Howells 1999a, 136–52.
36. Cf. the publicity brochure *White Star Line Royal & United States Mail Steamers "Olympic" & "Titanic,"* Liverpool 1911, and the various brochures and technical journal articles listed in Howells 1999a, 201–203.
37. Quoted after Bristow 1989, 159; a corresponding statement by Franklin is quoted in Howells 1999a, 143 (however, in both cases there are not reliable sources given). Franklin's statement in any case caused media critique, since on Tuesday, 16 April, it was clear that his belief in the *Titanic* being "unsinkable" had crassly failed (Howells 1999a, 143f).
38. On the false messages released about the *Titanic* in the course of 15 April 1912, cf. Bristow 1989, 155–65.
39. In *Titanic* films, this motif of the *Titanic* being "unsinkable" is used for dramatic irony, yet it does not, as in the myth, present human hubris as actual *cause* of the disaster.
40. Biel 1996, 53. Cf. ibid., 57: "The *Titanic* carried meanings that defined and shored up the status quo against disquieting change; in this way the conventional narrative served as a conservative critique of the incipient modern age. When it denounced uppity women, workers, blacks, and immigrants and invoked 'commonsense' rules of social order, the critique defended privilege against threats both real and imagined."
41. Cf. the reproduction of the famous Bamforth postcard series, which epitomize the kitschy religious interpretation of the disaster, in Bottomore 2000, 63f (a few of the postcards are also reproduced on http://www.greatships.net/Titanic_ba.html, 09.08.2011).
42. Biel 1996, 97–132.
43. "*Titanic*: Novel of an Era," published in 1938 as *Titanic: A Novel*, translated by Erna McArthur (London: M. Secker).
44. To my knowledge, this novel was never translated into English. In Germany, however, it became so popular that it was reprinted many times until the 1980s; in 1998 a radio feature *Titanic* was broadcast that still was based on this novel with all its factual mistakes and romanticizations.
45. Cf. Iversen 1999 and the short account in Biel 1996, 168–71.
46. The relative value of historical U.S. dollar amounts varies strongly according to various factors, cf. Samuel H. Williamson, *Seven Ways to Compute the Relative Value of a U.S. Dollar Amount, 1774 to Present*, MeasuringWorth, March 2011, http://www.measuringworth.com/uscompare/index.php (11.06.2011).
47. Cf. Iversen 1999, 33–36.
48. This booklet was reprinted several times and was followed by Bancroft's *The Unsinkable Molly Brown Cookbook* in 1966.
49. In fact, she was one of the first American women to run for a political office — even before women had obtained the right to vote.
50. In the 1996 mini-series *Titanic*, a fictitious scene in Lifeboat 6 is added, with the maiden Aase recognizing the villainous crew member Doonan, who raped her on the *Titanic* just moments before the collision. The scene ends with Aase and Doonan in the water; it is "Molly" Brown who then saves the life of Aase.

51. The 1979 production *S.O.S. Titanic* offers a shot of "Molly" Brown comforting children survivors on the *Carpathia*; in the 1996 mini-series *Titanic* it is actually "Molly" who is nursing the critically ill Aase on the *Carpathia* until Jamie finds her and takes care of his beloved.

52. An excellent analysis of Lord's narrative technique is given by Biel 1996, 151-54.

53. Lord 1955, 89.

54. Cf. Biel 1996, 157: "The *Titanic* resonated in the fifties because it provided a nostalgic alternative to a world in 'rude transition' to the atomic age. Just as the 'return' to the nuclear family and 'traditional' gender roles seemed to offer security amid the constant threat of nuclear war, so did the *Titanic* provide shelter in the 'memory' of a safer time and even in the recollection of a quainter kind of disaster."

55. The belief that more lifeboats would have saved more people is a fixed and dominant aspect of the *Titanic* myth — and it is wrong. As it was, the two and a half hours until the sinking were just enough to lower eighteen of the twenty lifeboats that the *Titanic* had. The last two, Collapsibles A and B, were swept from the deck in the sinking while the officers still tried to cut them loose. Even if there had been more lifeboats, there would have been no time to fill them with people and lower them. Thus, the only and essential scandal connected with the lifeboat question is that far too many boats were lowered half empty and that men who would well have had place were denied entry into a boat. — For an extensive discussion of the lifeboat question, cf. Bristow 1995, 415-35.

56. Eaton and Haas 1996, 20.

57. The script is reprinted in Writers Guild of America 1957, 81-118.

58. Cf. Chapter 3.

59. A subtle analysis of the broader cultural context of the discovery is offered by Biel 1996, 208-25. Cf. the short presentation of the event and its significance in Chapter 3, "The Dying Queen."

60. Cf. Sandler and Studlar 1999 and Chapter 9.

61. Cf. Störmer 2000.

Chapter 3

1. Cf. Howells 1999a, 120.
2. Finlayson and Taylor 2004, 131.
3. Biel 1996, 46.
4. The wireless operators were in fact not members of the White Star Line crew. At the time of the *Titanic*, wireless telegraphy was a new technology, and if it was at all installed on ships, it was run by the telegraphic company which provided the equipment and the staff to the shipping companies. This is an important reason why communication between the wireless operators and the officers was not as coordinated as it should have been. The primary task of the operators was, in the interest of their company, to send commercial telegrams by passengers. Messages from other ships regarding nautical issues were forwarded to the bridge, but did not have utmost priority and were not necessarily understood by the operators. In the case of the *Titanic*, Jack Phillips and Harold Bride could not know that the ice was right on their route when they received the various ice warnings. An extensive introduction to the history of wireless telegraphy and its relation to the transatlantic transport is offered by Bristow 1995, 232-86. In *Titanic* films, however, the wireless office is represented as a category of the same kind as the bridge and the chart room: a professional sphere which — allegedly — was directly involved with the ship's navigation.
5. This is, in fact, highlighted in at least two *Titanic* films: while the 1979 production features Daniel Marvin, son of the American film producer Henry Norton Marvin, filming on the *Titanic*, in the 1996 film it is the fictional main character Jamie who dreams of a career in recently established Hollywood.

6. Most detailed information on this film is offered by Bottomore 2000, 106–15.
7. Mills 1995, 18.
8. Bottomore 2000, 70.
9. Details on these short sequences ibid., 89.
10. On Harbeck as passenger on the *Titanic*, cf. ibid., 27–47.
11. Quoted after ibid., 39.
12. Ample information on Charles Urban and his work is given on http://www.charlesurban.com/. On the *Titanic* episode cf. Bottomore 2000, 7.
13. A short section is shown on YouTube under the search word "SS Olympic (1910)."
14. Cf. Bottomore 2000, 76. Ample information on the various montage newsreels is offered ibid., 69–104. Details on the extant 1912 films featuring the *Titanic* are summarized ibid., 142–48.
15. Description from an article in the 1912 *Motion Picture News*, quoted after Bottomore 2000, 76.
16. Cf. ibid., 80.
17. On this film and its reception in Europe and the United States, cf. ibid., 115–24, Wedel 1997, and Wedel 2004.
18. Lehmann and Wiehring von Wendrin 1997.
19. More information in Mottram 1988, 167–69, and Gunning 2011.
20. Assistant directors were Robert Dinesen — later a successful director in Denmark and Germany — and the 26-year-old Hungarian director Mihály Kertész, who would become famous as Michael Curtis with his Hollywood film *Casablanca*. On the film, cf. Mottram 1988, 156–61.
21. Unlike Morgan Robertson's novella *Futility or the Wreck of the Titan* from 1898, Hauptmann's novel never received international attention as a "prediction" of the *Titanic* disaster. Incidentally, Hauptmann was awarded the Nobel Prize in Literature in 1912, primarily in recognition of his dramatic works. On the relation between the novel and the film version cf. Gunning 2011.
22. *Motion Picture World*, 6 June 1914, 1358f, quoted from Bottomore 2005, 125.
23. Stephen Bottomore mentions British plans to film a mock shipwreck for a scene in a 1914 motion picture and some other productions both in Europe and the United States that included a shipwreck scene. A notable case is the animated toy filmloop featuring a multi-funnel liner approaching and colliding with an iceberg. The ship sinks right beside the berg, with some lifeboats being left on the surface (a few frames are reproduced in Bottomore 2000, 126).
24. For a detailed analysis of this film cf. Peck 2004; cf. also Mills 1995, 21–31.
25. Exterior scenes, which become more frequent toward the end of the film, were filmed at Tilbury Docks in London. It is not definitely known which ship was used; in all likelihood it was the P & O liner *Mooltan*.
26. Mills 1995, 21–26.
27. "Atlantic" still was an unfortunate choice in the eyes of the White Star Line: the suffix -ic had been traditional for White Star ships since the line was founded in 1869, and, indeed, a White Star liner called *Atlantic* was wrecked off Halifax in 1873 (that is, in the same precincts as the *Titanic*).
28. Mills 1995, 26–29. These remarks serve to enhance the dramatic irony of the situation.
29. Although the name "Titanic" was equally avoided in the German version, the German press quite openly spoke about the *Titanic* when discussing the film, and made use of the occasion for propaganda against the British competition. Cf. Mills 1995, 24–26.
30. The scene just before the end, in which dozens of men from Third Class are led into the First Class Smoking Room and offered gratis drinks with the words "Come on,

my lucky lads. We're all one class now. And the drinks are all one price" does in no way mean a leveling of classes: "It is understood that only in this situation, *in extremis*, social distinctions cease to be relevant" (Peck 2004, 118).

31. Robert Peck points out that one important aspect of the myth, hubris, is missing (Peck 2004, 118).

32. Mills 1995, 30.

33. According to Robert Peck, this racist scene was even highlighted in the publicity package as "most realistic" (Peck 2004, 118f). In reality, there was not a single black person among the passengers or crew on the *Titanic*.

34. Cf. Richards 2003, 15, and Peck 2004, 119.

35. A detailed account of this failure in film history is given by Schaefer 1986. Cf. also Mills 1995, 32–40.

36. British Wreck Commissioners' Inquiry, Day 12, question 14197 (Testimony of Officer Charles Herbert Lightoller), http://www.Titanicinquiry.org/BOTInq/BOTInq12 Lightoller03.php (08.08.2011).

37. Memo to Selznick's assistant Daniel T. O'Shea, 16 June 1938, quoted from Schaefer 1986, 62.

38. The anecdotes and references are quoted in Schaefer 1986, 57f.

39. Quoted from ibid., 67.

40. Since the Jack family has four children who all perish with their parents, there might be an allusion to the historical Goodwin family, which perished on the *Titanic* and in later *Titanic* research became best known among the several large Third Class families that went down with the ship. The Goodwin family, however, is not known for having been specifically religious, as the fictional Jack family is, so that the 1996 film family is not necessarily an historical allusion.

41. Cf. the short overview in Mills 1995, 112–25, and the detailed filmographic information ibid., 128–30.

42. As Jeffrey Richards notes, the entire finale is a precise recreation of the *Titanic* disaster with almost all known details (Richards 2003, 16).

43. The individual episodes are summarized on http://en.wikipedia.org/wiki/The_Time_Tunnel (08.08.2011).

44. On the various appearances of the *Titanic* in the 1980s and early 1990s cf. Mills 1995, 118–24.

45. It is regarded by many reviewers as the worst animated film ever made, cf. http://www.imdb.com/title/tt0330994/ (08.08.2011).

46. Including footage from the larger-scale *Titanic* productions is in fact a typical technique in low-budget films and series involving a *Titanic* scene.

47. The best aspect of the film is the score by John Barry, which in some reviews was favorably mentioned.

48. Mills 1995, 111. On the production and its failure cf. ibid., 96–111.

49. One-sixteenth was the limit for a realistic effect, since any smaller model would clearly have shown by the proportion of water drops and waves that a model was used (ibid., 99).

50. Biel 1996, 209.

51. Cf. Ballard 1987, 79–84.

52. Statement at the press conference on 9 September 1985, quoted from Ballard 1987, 101.

53. Ibid., 197–201.

54. The conflicting statements are summarized in Lord 1986, 251–53.

55. On the nature of the damage, cf. Chapter 1.

56. Cf. Ballard 1987, 206.

57. Ibid., 33f.

58. On the desperate efforts to take clear pictures after the discovery of the wreck cf. ibid., 93f; on the problem of the distribution of footage (with some stations picking up pictures via satellite as they were sent to media partners) and the conflicts that derived from this problem, ibid., 96–98.

59. The Columbia Television mini-series *Goliath Awaits* (1981) presents the idea that 337 survivors of a shipwreck managed to exist in a wreck over decades by extracting drinking water and oxygen from the sea. Allegedly, the idea harks back to musings what it would be like to find the *Titanic* wreck and people still alive in the ship (Mills 1995, 121f).

60. Cf. Spignesi 1998, 318–26.
61. Ballard 1987, 213.
62. Cf. Biel 1996, 210f.
63. Cf. Frensham 1996, 42f.
64. Ibid., 99.
65. Spignesi 1998, 332.
66. Frensham 1996, 41.
67. Ibid., 43–45.
68. On the disaster film genre cf. Keane 2001.
69. Cf., for example, Gardiner and van der Vat 1995, presenting the theory that the White Star Line exchanged *Titanic* for the *Olympic* (which had been damaged in a collision in September 1911) and intentionally arranged the sinking as an insurance scam. Although the theory is absurd, it received a considerable amount of attention.
70. On *Titanic Orgy* (1995) and *Titanic 2000* (1999) cf. Anderson 2005, 110f.
71. Frensham 1996, 57.
72. Ibid., 119f.
73. There is only an indirect allusion to them in *S.O.S. Titanic*, which only Titanic experts will be able to fully understand, knowing that the British inquiry was criticized as a "whitewash": "Of course they'll have some — routine little inquiry and give themselves a nice soothing coat of white wash! Nothing will have changed" (fictional American teacher Leigh Goodwin to Lawrence Beesley on the *Carpathia*).
74. Quoted from the 1958 film, cf. the more extended version of this text in Lord 1955, 81f.
75. Quoted from Frensham 1996, 124.
76. On the decisive difference between the original TV version and the abridged theatrical version of *S.O.S. Titanic* cf. Chapter 7 below. The original version with the framing device is found on YouTube.
77. Cf. the analysis of this final scene in Chapter 9.
78. Lord 1955, 134f.
79. As a flashback shows, Rose does realize just before the arrival that she has the incredibly precious diamond in her pocket, but — as she explains to treasure hunter Brock Lovett in the uncut film version — she never made use of it, relying entirely on her own resources. In the final cut, the explanation and the pathetic scene, in which Rose lets Lovett touch the diamond before she throws it into the ocean, is deleted, much to the advantage of this scene's impact.

Chapter 4

1. Cf. Moeller 2000; Quanz 2000; Kleinhans 2003; Giesen and Hobsch 2005.
2. Cf. Richards 2003, 17.
3. On the changes and cuts that can be deduced from the synopsis of the 1943 program, cf. Malone 2004, 127f.
4. For details cf. Peck 2000b. Robert Peck points out that the premiere did not take place in Paris, as usually stated.

5. On the details of the 1943 *Titanic*'s withdrawal from distribution cf. Peck 2000b.

6. Having been reported by screenwriter Zerlett-Olfenius, Selpin had a confrontation with Goebbels, was subsequently arrested and two days later found dead in his cell. Rumors that he had been murdered by the Gestapo per Goebbels spread among the film crew, but were quickly suppressed by the authorities.

7. On the complicated after-war history of the film and its distribution in Germany cf. Peck 2000a.

8. There were very few Germans in First Class on the *Titanic*, and only one of them was actually resident in Germany at the time they embarked on the *Titanic*: passengers Antoinette Flegenheim (resident of New York since 1892), Adolphe Saalfeld (resident of Manchester), and Alfred Nourney (born in the Netherlands but lived in Cologne), as well as the Wideners' maid Amalie Henriette Gieger. Only Nourney could serve as a character of some originality in film — but certainly not as paragon of German virtue. Using the pseudonym "Baron von Drachstedt," 20-year-old Nourney had originally purchased a Second Class ticket and was later transferred to First Class cabin D-38 for a considerable surcharge. He obviously enjoyed being taken for an aristocrat and became known for behaving rather indecently in Lifeboat 7 and on the *Carpathia* (cf. the entry "Alfred Nourney" in the Encyclopedia Titanica). On the young German ship expert Wilhelm Müller, who apparently traveled as First Class passenger on president Ismay's personal invitation without being included in an official passenger list, cf. Bristow 1995, 205–31.

9. In the original version of the novel, the German officer was called Max Dittmar-Pittmann. Dittmar-Pittmann was a real person, a German sailor who in the 1920s (falsely) claimed that he had been Third Officer on the *Titanic*. Felinau integrated him into his novel (promoting him to Second Officer) and included a foreword by Dittmar-Pittmann that confirmed that the events as depicted in the novel were true. In the second version of the novel, which came out in 1943 (that is, in the same year as the production of the *Titanic* film was finished), Dittmar-Pittmann has been substituted by the German officer Petersen. It is not known if the change of the name was prompted by a cooperation with screenwriter Zerlett-Olfenius or if Felinau himself chose the new name. Felinau did in any case distance himself from the film during production: although the central motif, namely the *Titanic* as victim of gambling on the stock exchange, is taken directly from his novel, the novel itself is not anti–British. In the post-war editions of Felinau's novel, Petersen is turned into a Dane and presented as Third Officer. On the fictitious officers on the *Titanic*, especially Max Dittmar-Pittmann and Hans Erik Petersen, cf. the website "The Fictional Officers of the *Titanic*" by Monika Simon, http://www.oocities.org/melissa_mcf/pittmann.html (04.08.2011), where primary and secondary literature is quoted.

10. In the film itself, their anchoring in British aristocracy is not made explicit, yet they are described as "Lord and Lady Astor" in the program for the premiere, thus contributing to the anti–British stance of the film.

11. Hedi and Franz most clearly display a role model coming from the tradition of drama and opera: as manicurist and musician, thus part of the *Titanic* victualling crew, they do — virtually — represent the pair of burlesque servants providing comic relief. The burlesque element lies in the ridiculously short span of their falling in love, which prompts Hedi at once to cancel her long-standing engagement to a German neighbor lad — by the way, the only time in the film a telegram is sent that has nothing to do with the stock market.

12. Paul Malone quotes a 1940 issue of the weekly *Filmwelt* magazine devoted to six types of women portrayed in German cinema, where actress Sybille Schmitz, who plays Sigrid Olinsky in *Titanic*, is counted among the "dangerous women" (Malone 2004, 124; on the various types of women in NS cinema cf. Fox 2000, 12f).

13. This reflects the often-cited admonition of First Class passenger Lucian Philip Smith, who gently ordered his wife to leave him.

14. The 26.5 knots the *Titanic* makes in the Nazi film are fictitious; the *Titanic*'s maximum speed was 23 knots, which she never reached on her maiden voyage. Yet not even the fictitious speed hits the point: the Cunard liner RMS *Mauretania* was capable of traveling at 27 knots, so that the 26.5 knots, to which the *Titanic* is pressed in the film, would just as well have been useless.

15. This is a pun that cannot be translated into English: "Außerdem kann man sie nur dann richtig beurteilen, wenn man sie aus der Fassung bringt. Genauso wie die Frauen!" The word "Fassung" refers both to the mounting of a jewel and to a person's composure, indicating that the true value of a woman can only be judged when she is provoked to lose countenance.

16. Here, there might be a hint at the historical Lady Duff-Gordon, who, sitting with her husband in a scandalously empty lifeboat, discouraged the crew members from going back to help the victims in the water.

17. Cf. Malone 2004, 125.

18. Ibid., 124, with reference to various studies on cinema in the Third Reich in notes 20 and 21.

19. Malone 2004, 125f.

20. Mills 1995, 41.

21. Cf. the analysis in Koldau 2010, 196–214.

22. User review by "tieman64 from United Kingdom," dated 19 October 2010 (http://www.imdb.com/title/tt0036443/usercomments?start=20, 08.08.2011).

23. Peck 2000a, 432f.

24. In fact, there are conjectures that the final court scene may have been added at the instigation of Goebbels, who may not have been content with the film's propaganda line upon first viewing — which would mean that the film might originally have ended with the sinking of the ship. Cf. Peck 2000b, 67, and Moeller 1998, 328 note 57.

Chapter 5

1. User review on the Internet Movie Database (http://www.imdb.com/title/tt0046435/usercomments?start=40; 08.08.2011), signed "8-Foot from Montgomery Village, Maryland," dated 18 September 1999.

2. Among the anachronisms are the students' song *Yard by Yard*, which was published in 1926 only, and, more conspicuously, the dance Navajo Rag, which in the film serves to teach Europeanized Annette some fresh American culture. The Charleston-like Navajo Rag became popular in the Twenties only.

3. Biel 1996, 157.

4. Cf. Finlayson and Taylor 2004, 132.

5. Ibid., 141.

6. Cf. Richards 2003, 23f.

7. *Titanic* experts rightly emphasize that the scene at Cherbourg is historical nonsense, since the *Titanic* was far from being sold out and an additional passenger would easily have been able to purchase a First Class ticket.

8. Byars 1991, 8 (quoted from Finlayson and Taylor 2004, 141).

9. Cf. Mills 1995, 64.

10. Right at the opening, a representative of the White Star Line, leaving the *Titanic* at Cherbourg, sanguinely remarks to Captain Smith: "As to your running time, we know you'll exercise normal prudence. However, the company wouldn't resent a record run on her maiden voyage." Smith retains his authority as the captain, but his answer also shows that he heeds the instructions of his employer: "They're good engines, Sir, we use them. Any other instructions from the company?" Throughout the film, the high speed of the ship is emphasized several times. After the collision, however, nobody ever asks the question of fault and error.

11. This stereotype of ailing European culture on the brink of World War I is epitomized in Richard's speech aiming to arouse Annette's wrath that her mother is about to take her to the American Midwest: "With the time difference they should just be sitting down to luncheon in that extraordinary room overlooking the fountains. The dear arthritic old princess sitting under the finest crystal chandelier in Europe and Mr. Paderewski complaining about the draught" (from the second confrontation between Julia and Richard, which leads to Annette breaking with her mother).

12. Due to his physical condition, tennis player Richard Norris Williams II survived as a swimmer; he was eventually hauled into Collapsible A and recovered from severe frostbite due to daily exercise on the *Carpathia*. The other well-known tennis player on board, Karl Howell Behr, was a student like Giff Richards, but at Yale, whereas Giff makes a point of studying at a Midwestern university and not at Princeton (thus underpinning Julia's plea for Midwestern middle-class virtues). Prompted by Bruce Ismay to enter Lifeboat 5, Karl Howell Behr was rescued. Cf. the biographies in the Encyclopedia Titanica.

13. Cf. Chapter 2.

14. Recollection of Frank Goldsmith, according to the quotation on http://www.encyclopedia-Titanica.org/discus/messages/5667/119966.html?1217894619 (Encyclopedia Titanica, Message Board, Discussion thread "Men who were offered but turned down a lifeboat place," entry by Bob Godfrey on 14 May 2007, 08.08.2011). It has not been possible to detect the original source of Goldsmith's recollection.

15. Mills 1995, 60f.

16. On the function of alarm signals in cinematic sound design, cf. Flückiger 2001, 159–63.

17. Biel 1996, 76 and 82f.

18. Ibid., 83 and 128. Cf. above, Chapter 2.

19. Finlayson and Taylor 2004, 141.

20. Ibid., 133.

21. Ibid.

Chapter 6

1. From an extensive viewer comment on http://www.imdb.com/title/tt0051994/usercomments (signed "gus81 from Sydney Australia," dated 13 January 2005; 09.08.2011). On the Internet Movie Database, there are 121 viewer comments to *A Night to Remember*, many of them written in the same vein. Excellent analyses of the film are offered by Howells 1999b; Richards 2003; Street 2004. Cf. also Mills 1995, 66–82, with additional details on the production.

2. Baker 2000, 95.

3. Street 2004, 143; cf. Richards 2003, 39.

4. Street 2004, 143, quoting a review in the *Hollywood Reporter*, 18 December 1958; on the "unobtrusive," "restrained" style of Roy Baker cf. Richards 2003, 41.

5. Street 2004, 148f.

6. Ibid., 150 (quoted according to *Saturday Review*, 13 December 1958).

7. Beesley 1912, 120; cf. Chapter 10.

8. Lightoller 1935, 250.

9. Street 2004, 147.

10. The French term was originally used in the Soviet Montage school, relating to the use of character stereotype in communicating the essential qualities of an individual human character. Sarah Street transfers the meaning to denote stereotypes of class.

11. Even the Grand Staircase, though present in a few scenes, is never pointed out as a special feature on the *Titanic*.

12. Like the Second Class Clarke couple, Patrick Murphy is fictitious, conflating the historically documented acts of various Third Class passengers.

13. In contrast, twenty-eight-year-old Edgar Joseph Meyer had to argue with his twenty-five-year-old wife Leila to make her enter a lifeboat. She eventually consented to go because of their one-year-old daughter awaiting them in New York.

14. In fact, they fight to survive but are eventually smashed by the funnel breaking down as the ship sinks.

15. Richards 2003, 73.

16. Quoted from ibid., 71.

17. Ibid., 99–102.

18. However, nobody ever thought of questioning Lightoller's peculiar way of interpreting the principle "women and children first": had he not insisted on the entirely unnecessary doctrine "women and children *only*," family fathers and other male passengers would have had a chance to fill the spare places in several boats. In fact, Lightoller's interpretation of "the right of nature" turned out to be cruel, bereaving several families of their fathers, brothers, and sons.

19. Captain Smith decided immediately before departure that Chief Officer Henry Wilde from the *Olympic* was to be transferred to the *Titanic*. Thus, William Murdoch, who should have been Chief Officer on the *Titanic*, and Charles Herbert Lightoller, who was supposed to be First Officer, were graded down to First and Second Officer. The originally intended Second Officer David Blair did not travel with the *Titanic*. The reason for this last-minute reshuffle of the senior officers is not known (nor if Smith took this decision on his own account or upon request of the White Star Line). It may have been grounded upon the fact that the maiden voyage had to take place under unusually difficult conditions (such as the abnormally high amount of ice off the Newfoundland coast, which had been announced in the news since March). Wilde and Murdoch both had the Extra Master Patent, that is, the highest qualification in civil navigation, so that the *Titanic* was in the hand of the best officers of the White Star Line.

20. Richards 2003, 74

21. Quoted from ibid.

22. Ibid.

23. Ibid., 76.

24. Cf. ibid., 80f.

25. This is even true in historical incidents, such as the sinking of the German submarine U-*Hai* in 1966, which cost the lives of nineteen soldiers — only the cook survived.

26. Richards 2003, 80.

27. The historical statement was quoted by Lucian's wife Mary Eloise Smith in her affidavit to the United States Senate Inquiry: "I never expected to ask you to obey, but this is one time you must; it is only a matter of form to have women and children first. The boat is thoroughly equipped, and everyone on her will be saved" (http://www.Titanic inquiry.org/USInq/AmInq18Smith01.php; 19.07.2011). Smith's original statement was slightly changed by screenwriter Eric Ambler in order to adapt to the fictional situation of a First Class couple with three little children. On Mary Eloise Smith's later regret about having left her husband, cf. endnote 5 in Chapter 8.

28. This scene, in turn, is followed by one of the most emotional ones in the film, excellently played by actor John Merivale: the farewell of Robert Lucas to his children and to his little son on his arms. For all its brevity, this scene gives a perfect notion of what the separations in the night of 14 April 1912 meant to the victims of the disaster.

29. As the final rocket is fired without any reaction from the ship on the horizon, Smith gravely utters "God help you!" rather than cursing the seamen who disregard his signals of distress.

30. Cf. the quotation of the text in Chapter 3.

31. On the markedly religious character of *Titanic* "buffdom," cf. Biel 1996, 196–202.

32. Richards 2003, 57.

33. Chief Officer Wilde is generally neglected in *Titanic* narratives, probably because no survivor could figure out what his exact role in the evacuation had been and how he eventually died.

34. Cf. http://www.imdb.com/title/tt0051994/usercomments?start=30 (comment by Brigid O'Sullivan, Toronto, dated 8 September 2002), or http://www.imdb.com/title/tt 0051994/usercomments?start=90 (comment by Tracy Priest, Perth, dated 7 November 2008; retrieved 17.07.2011).

35. Cf. Ballard 1987, 197–201; Leonhardt and Rockwell 1993, 120–23.

36. Cf. Lord 1955, 110–14. In *The Night Goes On*, an entire chapter is dedicated to Rostron (Lord 1986, 155–63).

37. The children's playroom is fictitious, and the age of the four lift attendants ranged between seventeen and thirty-one (in contrast to the teenagers depicted in the film). The message of the card player Jay Yates to his sister is one of the historical *Titanic* hoaxes; Yates never was on the *Titanic* (cf. http://www.encyclopedia-Titanica.org/unlisted-passengers-and-crew.html, 04.08.2011). In *A Night to Remember*, the allegedly authentic gambler is conflated with the anonymous victim who called out a blessing to the men on Collapsible B (according to Gracie 1913, 89). These changes and additions in *A Night to Remember* serve to enhance the poignancy of the drama.

38. Igenlode Wordsmith, user comment on http://www.imdb.com/title/tt0051994/usercomments?start=20 (19.07.2011), dated 1 September 2007.

39. A detailed account of the reception both in Europe and the United States is given in Richards 2003, 85–102.

Chapter 7

1. According to his own testimony, Bruce Ismay did not exchange any words with Captain Smith as the latter handed him the *Baltic* ice warning on Sunday, 14 April. The dialogue in the film conflates several statements of Ismay about his remarks to the crew regarding speed as reported in the inquiries.

2. On the function of this theme in the film, cf. the analysis of the film score in Chapter 10 below.

3. Here, dramatic effect supersedes the ambition to be historically correct: the first boat to be picked up by the *Carpathia* was Lifeboat 2, while Madeleine Astor sat in Lifeboat 4.

4. For a contextualization of this scene cf. Chapter 7.

5. "Close beside me — so near that I cannot avoid hearing scraps of their conversation — are two American ladies, both dressed in white, young, probably friends only: one has been to India and is returning by way of England, the other is a school-teacher in America, a graceful girl with a distinguished air heightened by a pair of *pince-nez*" (Beesley 1912, 42f). The fictional character Leigh Goodwin in fact is a conflation of these two women, since in the film she introduces herself as an American school teacher returning home from a trip to India.

6. Cf. below, "Problems of Plot."

7. The little bugler calling them to dinner is, however, fictitious: it was only in First Class that dinner was announced by a bugler.

8. Beesley 1912, 215f.

9. In reality, it was two Irish Third Class passengers, Daniel Buckley and Edward Ryan, who escaped "in women's clothes."

10. Cf. Molony 2000, 30–36.

11. There is a fictitious aspect to the scene, though: in the film it is one of the Irish girls who hands her friend the shawl in order to hide him, while the historical Daniel Buckley (mistakenly) stated that it was Madeleine Astor who covered him with a shawl.

12. Cf. Chapter 7.

13. There is a fictitious scene added with Irene "René" Harris falling and breaking her arm while descending the Grand Staircase. There was no such spectacular accident on the *Titanic*, though it was reported in the press that she had injured her shoulder the day before the sinking (*New York Times*, 20 April, 1912, http://www.encyclopedia-Titanica. org/mrs-harris-gains-strength.html). Walter Lord states that "Mrs. Harris had just broken her arm" (Lord 1955, 10).

14. The children were known as "*Titanic* orphans" until their mother recognized them in a newspaper article and took them back to France (cf. the entry "Navratil" in the Encyclopedia Titanica and Lynch 1992, 170f.).

15. Cf. the quotations in the Encyclopedia Titanica entries for Mary Sloan and Violet Jessop.

16. Viewer comments signed "Florian Weiss from Abilene, Tex," dated 28 January 1999, and "Yourbigpala183-1 from Long Island New York," dated 1 December 2003 (both found on http://www.imdb.com/title/tt0079836/usercomments?start=20, 09.08.2011).

17. On this aspect cf. Chapter 10, "The Film Music."

18. Beesley 1912, 139f.

19. Both the singing in the Protestant Sunday morning service and John Jacob Astor's dance with Madeleine are intercut with images of an ice field in the glaring morning sun and the shots of an iceberg at night, respectively.

20. The dance locale is conspicuously shown to be the "Café Parisien," which, however, would not have been convenient for dance. The interiors rather resemble the original Verandah Café.

21. Even this comic scene has an historical basis: it was reported that at one point at the informal party in Third Class, "a rat scurried through the room, causing the girls to squeal and several men to give chase" (Lynch 1992, 77).

22. The collision as such is not shown. Director William Hale chose an unusual solution, zooming in on the iceberg, on the approaching ship, the iceberg again, and then on the eyes and finally the lips of lookout Frederick Fleet, who numbly utters the fatal sentence "We hit it."

Chapter 8

1. Cf. the user reviews on the Internet Movie Database for *Titanic* (TV 1996), http://www.imdb.com/title/tt0115392/ (20.07.2011).

2. In contrast to the Cameron plot, though, Isabella Paradine is sure to keep her luxurious living standards in her new life with her lover.

3. The latter is rather improbable, since the greatest part of Cameron's shooting was done by the time the TV series was broadcast in November 1996.

4. In *A Night to Remember*, there is one more extensive scene on Collapsible B in order to highlight Second Officer Lightoller as pensive hero.

5. This is a variant of the written statement that Mary Eloise Smith sent to the U.S. Senate Inquiry: "I had not the least suspicion of the scarcity of lifeboats, or I never should have left my husband" (quoted on http://www.Titanicinquiry.org/USInq/AmInq18Smith 01.php, 20.07.2011).

6. Cf. the entries on the Allison family and Alice Catherine Cleaver in the Encyclopedia Titanica.

7. This is presented as fact in Lynch 1992, 214; cf. the correction of this assumption in the Encyclopedia Titanica under the entry "Alice Catherine Cleaver."

8. Park is shown as one of the people who actually survived the sinking but then died of exposure in the lifeboats.

9. This is fictitious, although there had been rumors in 1912 that Jack Phillips had made it unto Collapsible B and died there.

10. Cf. McCarty and Foecke 2008.

11. Cf. Walter Lord's documentation of passengers' statements (Lord 1986, 251–53)

12. In fact, the object of competition would have been the *Lusitania*'s sister ship RMS *Mauretania*, which had held the record for the fastest Atlantic passage for twenty-two years since its first crossing in 1907.

13. The joke, handed down over decades, may have had its origin in Lawrence Beesley's description of a real joke at a time when the collision was not yet being taken seriously: "One of the [card] players, pointing to his glass of whiskey standing at his elbow, and turning to an onlooker, said: 'Just run along the deck and see if any ice has come aboard: I would like some for this'" (Beesley 1912, 61f).

14. Cf. Chapter 10, "The Final Song."

15. The bronze cherub retrieved is in fact not one of the larger cherub statues that were placed on the main staircase landings; it is believed that this smaller statue stems from a side post newel (http://www.rmsTitanic.net/community/blog/159-bronze-cherub-from-Titanics-grand-staircase.html, 20.07.2011). Viewers, however, will not notice the difference and regard the statue seen in the film as identical with the one retrieved and thus as evidence for authenticity.

16. The Flood Myth is not only biblical, but also found in many other cultures and religions, thus being a universal tale of destruction and rebirth (cf. Dundes 1988).

17. The "great wave" is a common feature in *Titanic* narratives: as the bow went down, the Boat Deck was overrun by a great wave caused by the sudden momentum of the forward part of the ship. This wave swept away many people on the deck; in *Titanic* films it is generally shown as a sudden gush of water breaking in over the deck.

18. Viewer comment by "rsks514 from United States," dated 17 February 2005 (http://www.imdb.com/title/tt0115392/usercomments?start=60, 20.07.2011).

Chapter 9

1. Parisi 1998, 147.

2. Cf. the essays in Sandler and Studlar 1999 and Bergfelder and Street 2004.

3. Lubin 1999.

4. Quoted from Krämer 1999, 116 (original quotation in Don Shay, "Back to *Titanic*," *Cinefex* 72, Dec. 1997).

5. Cf. Krämer 1999, 117.

6. Such as some children waving farewell to their father as the lifeboat (in which also Rose is sitting) is being lowered.

7. In fact, Cameron had originally designed the scene with Rose lacing her mother's corset, but in the shooting both Cameron and the actors decided that it would be more dramatically powerful to change the roles (Marsh 1997, 106).

8. Katha Pollitt, "Women and Children First," *Nation*, 30 March 1998, 9, quoted from Keller 1999, 144.

9. Redmond 2004, 203.

10. This is, as frequently happens in *Titanic* films, a self-reflective instance within the film medium: actress Kate Winslet, who became a film star through the film *Titanic*, plays the role of a female character that became an obviously successful actress after her *Titanic* experience.

11. Redmond 2004, 203.

12. Keller 1999, 143 and 145.

13. Cf. Redmond 2004, 200f; Ouellette 1999, 178.
14. Ibid.
15. Ibid., 169 (italics original).
16. For a detailed discussion of these myths as they are negotiated in *Titanic* cf. Ouellette 1999.
17. Even the frame narrative, set in 1996, displays settings that can only be afforded by affluent or extremely well-sponsored people.
18. Parisi 1998, 191.
19. This emphasis on First Class is again reflected in the making-of book published in 1997: large parts of the book focus on the splendid First Class settings and costumes with ample large-scale photographs, while Third Class is represented by the folksy party scene only. Cf. Marsh 1997.
20. The car was listed on the cargo manifest as a 25-horsepower Renault automobile and belonged to First Class passenger William Ernest Carter, who also brought two dogs with him. Carter survived and claimed the notable sum of $5,000 (approximately $110,000 today) for the car and $100 and $200 for the dogs (cf. the entry "William Ernest Carter" in the Encyclopedia Titanica).
21. In fact, this stereotype was even used for the promotion of the film: 20th Century Fox claimed that the sinking of the ship marked the end of "acceptance of class as a definition of birthright" (cf. Ouellette 1999, 177).
22. Keller 1999, 146. Cf. also Redmond 2004, 203, and Ouellette 1999, 186.
23. Cf. Studlar 2004, 158.
24. Negra 1999, 228.
25. For the full quotation of Cameron's intentions cf. Chapter 9, "The Main Categories of the *Titanic* Myth and Their Treatment."
26. Donnelly 2004.
27. Ibid., 205f.
28. Ibid., 210.
29. Ibid., 207.
30. Ibid., 212.
31. This idea is not new, though: *S.O.S. Titanic* contains a corresponding scene with the Sunday morning service of the First Class passengers, in which this hymn is sung.
32. On the anachronism of this gesture cf. Lubin 1999, 59f.
33. Negra 1999, 235.
34. Cf. Krämer 1999, 125: "The film not only returns women to the cinema, but, in a way, also returns cinema to women...."
35. Parisi 1998, 34.
36. Krämer 1999, 116.
37. Ibid., 125.
38. Sobchack 1999, 199–201, esp. 201.
39. Parisi 1998, 112.
40. Studlar 2004, 161.
41. Keller 1999, 147.
42. Linda Nochlin, "The Imagery Orient," *Art in America* 71 (1983), 123, here quoted from Keller 1999, 147.
43. Keller 1999, 149.
44. Cf. the chapter on the making of the film in Richards 2003, 28–37. A typical example for the relaxed attitude to "authenticity" in the setting is given by director Roy Baker: "During the scene of lunch at the captain's table we served the same menu as on the fatal day. There was no need to do this, but some food had to be eaten and it might as well be correct'" (Baker 2000, 101). Authenticity thus was regarded as affordable extra, but not as indispensable premise for the film production.

45. Keller 1999, 151.
46. Ibid., 151f.
47. Stringer 1999, 205; cf. Sobchack 1999; Sydney-Smith 2004.
48. Sobchack 1999, 192, quoting Stewart 1984, 23.
49. Cf. Stringer 1999, 205.
50. Cf. ibid., 208, partly quoting a 1998 review by Robin Buss of *Titanic* and other heritage films for the *Times Educational Supplement*. Cf. also Redmond 2004, 198f.
51. On heritage films and the cult of authenticity cf. ibid.
52. This in turn corresponds to a boom of new memberships in the various Titanic Societies after the release of Cameron's film: the new, often young members were more interested in the actors of the movie than in the actual historical event and the historical people involved. Cf. Störmer 2000, 90–94.
53. Redmond 2004, 198.
54. Stringer 1999, 213. Stringer in turn refers to Arjun Appadurai, *Modernity at Large: Cultural Dimensions of Globalization* (Minneapolis: University of Minnesota Press, 1996), 75–85.
55. Sydney-Smith 2004.
56. Krämer 2004, 170.
57. Keller 1999, 140.
58. Ibid., 143.
59. Ibid., 146.
60. Ibid., 136.
61. Similar traces might be spotted in the 1943 Nazi film, which highlighted the immaculate behavior of fictitious officer Petersen and added a court scene to disclose the disgrace of British injustice. These traces, however, follow the film's propaganda paradigm and are not based on the historical *Titanic* story.
62. Negra 1999.
63. Philip Lamy, *Millennium Rage: Survivalists, White Supremacists, and the Doomsday Prophecy* (New York: Plenum Press, 1996), 14, here quoted from Negra 1999, 223. Diane Negra adds the following features in her definition of survivalism: mistrust of government and authority; a logic of self-sufficiency and self-reliance; a fervent sense of independence; the expectation of the catastrophe; the desire for preparedness.
64. Ibid., 232.
65. Ibid., 235.
66. Quoted from Parisi 1998, 68.
67. Studlar 2004, 156.
68. Syndey-Smith 2004, 185 and 193.
69. Cf. Wolf 2004; Wood 2004.
70. Parisi 1998, 34.
71. Cf. Wood 2004.
72. Aylish Wood fittingly describes the result as "heri-tech" film (ibid., 228).
73. Cf. Wood 2004 and Wolf 2004.
74. Cf. Krämer 2004, 165, and Wolf 2004.
75. Cf. Wolf 2004, 220.
76. Ibid., 216.
77. Cf. Captain Smith's proud order at departure, declaring the *Titanic* as a distinctly female being: "Take her to sea, Mr. Murdoch. Let's stretch her legs."
78. Wood 2004, 229.
79. From Cameron's foreword to Marsh 1997, vi.
80. Wolf 2004, 216f.
81. On the two sequences and their contrast cf. Wood 2004, 230f.
82. Ibid., 230.

83. Beesley 1912, 99f and 104.
84. Wood 2004, 231.
85. Keane 2001, 118.
86. Cf. Chapter 3, "Framing Devices."
87. Cameron and Frakes 1998, x. A few years later, Cameron would continue this concept in his IMAX documentary on the wreck, *Ghosts of the Abyss* (2003), where he inserts "ghosts" in the documentary images (that is, short flashes of historical characters on the various sites of the wreck). In contrast to *Titanic*, this yields a rather pathetic impression. Cf. Chapter 3, "The Dying Queen."
88. Krämer 2004, 166. Reliving and re-enacting the experience has become a common feature in the *Titanic* legacy — the bow scene with the outstretched arms, symbolizing liberation and independence, is frequently used in advertisements (or by children playing on the beach), and in 1998, there were reported several instances of ferry and ship passengers trying to imitate the "Titanic bow climb stunt" (cf. Lubin 1999, 126, endnote 10).
89. Thayer 1998, 343f (originally published in 1940).
90. This elderly, well-dressed couple is probably meant to be Isidor and Ida Straus, although this romantic depiction contradicts the last testimony about their final whereabouts on the Boat Deck.
91. Cf. Chapter 10, "The Sounds of Death."
92. Cf. Krämer 2004, 163. Cf. the analyses and interpretations of the final scene by Negra 1999, 228 and 235; Ouellette 1999, 185; Krämer 1999, 121f; Krämer 2004, 163f; Studlar 2004, 160; Sydney-Smith 2004, 192; Wolf 2004, 220.
93. Studlar 2004, 160.
94. Cf. Krämer 2004, 164.
95. Ibid., 166, cf. Smith 1999.
96. This aged and dignified exterior in fact has a decisive function in the creation of "historicity." Cf. the discussion of the "patina" of old objects as a system of mediation, establishing relations between the past and the present, the living and the dead, in Stringer 1999, 211.
97. Sobchack 1999, 193.
98. This original ending is contained as special feature in the special DVD edition of *Titanic*.
99. In film advertisements, the length of the film was given as "two hours and seventy-four minutes." While Alexandra Keller proposes that this unusual specification of the running time reflected the studios' consensus that the audience would be scared off if a three-hour film was announced (Keller 1999, 152, note 1), it may also have been a tongue-in-cheek allusion to the sinking time of the *Titanic*, in reality lasting about two hours and forty minutes.
100. Cf. David M. Lubin's scene-for-scene analysis (Lubin 1999).
101. Viewer comment on *A Night to Remember*, dated 19 October 2010, cf. http://www.imdb.com/title/tt0051994/usercomments?start=100 (13.07.2011).
102. Cf. the countless connections between *Avatar* and earlier films featuring science fiction and romantic drama with a native protagonist.
103. A first instance of this visual and emotional motif is found in the 1943 film.
104. The axe motif is found in the 1943 film; there is no historical evidence for such an event having taken place on the *Titanic*. The Third Class passenger jumping from his bunk into the water and reacting with some strong language is found in *A Night to Remember*; it is a motif that can easily be imagined, since it was the single men accommodated on the lower decks in the forward part of the ship who were the first passengers to realize that water was coming in.
105. Cf. the countless cartoon versions of this scene coming up when Google Images is searched with the word "Titanic cartoon."

106. Cf. Gerstner 2004, 181f; Lubin 1999, 50f.
107. Cf. Knell 1995.
108. Cultural analysis again relates this image to the ideological message of the film: "She [Rose] emerges from the wreckage of the Gilded Age as the new liberal middle class unfettered by the decadence of the aristocratic bourgeoisie. [...] The new American figurehead — the ideal American woman secure in the arms of her creators — is ready to break free from the excesses of capitalist production in order to remind those who nostalgically yearn for the dream of *Titanic* that we have fulfilled the dream of the future: American progress, creativity, equality" (Gerstner 2004, 181f).

Chapter 10

1. This justification strategy is an historical feature of the discussion that followed immediately after the disaster. Cf. Chapter 1.
2. Cf. Chapter 2, note 24.
3. Cf. Molony 2000, 30–36 (Daniel Buckley) and 191–95 (Edward Ryan).
4. Cf. the 1912 newspaper articles reprinted on http://www.encyclopedia-Titanica.org/Titanic-biography/j-bruce-ismay.html (15.07.2011).
5. In reality, he was supposed to stay on his job until he had carried through the maiden voyage of the third Olympic class ship.
6. Cf. Chapter 2.
7. After the release of Cameron's *Titanic*, the British press reacted with indignation on the depiction of Murdoch's suicide after having shot a Third Class passenger. William Murdoch's descendants and the people of his home town Dalbeattie (Scotland) sued against this depiction; 20th Century Fox officially apologized and donated $8,000 to the city's high school. Yet the depiction of Murdoch in the film did of course remain unchanged.
8. In his 1912 book Lawrence Beesley describes the passengers' interest in speed and early arrival and their eagerness to have daily reports from the crew about this issue (Beesley 1912, 33f).
9. *S.O.S. Titanic*, in turn, uses the Astor couple to form one of the three love strands, playing upon the weak motif of the difference of age between John Jacob and his young wife Madeleine.
10. Beesley 1912, 120.
11. Cf. below, Chapter 10, "The Sounds of Death."
12. Thus the title of the famous 1990 novel by Erik Fosnes Hansen, focusing on the musicians on the *Titanic*.
13. In fact, the "spontaneous" choice of this hymn on part of bandleader Wallace Hartley is again an historical allusion, since it refers to a personal choice which Hartley allegedly would have made in such a situation of distress. Cf. below, Chapter 10, "The Final Song."
14. Again, this scene is by no means fictitious: Cameron may have followed the report of Beatrice Stenke, passenger on the German liner *Bremen*, who had seen numerous bodies when crossing the region where the *Titanic* had sunk a few days after the disaster. Among the bodies, she described a woman "dressed only in her night dress, and clasping a baby to her breast" (Leonhardt and Rockwell 1993, 84).
15. In Cameron's film the decisive change is reflected visually by the muted colors in the *Carpathia* scenes, contrasting with the blazing clarity of color on the *Titanic*.
16. Captain Lord's descendants probably were glad about the fact that there were no scenes with the *Californian* in Cameron's blockbuster. Indeed, the *Californian* had been an integral part of Cameron's script, and some scenes were also shot, but in the end, this strand had to be cut due to the general overlength of the film.

17. Lord 1955, 108–16; Lord 1986, 155–63.

18. The technique is found again in *No Greater Love* (1996) and, in a slightly different version, in the TV serial *Time Bandits* (1981), with the yet unknowing time travelers chatting at the railing.

19. As often happens with large-scale disasters, reports about premonitions and metaphysical warnings abound after disaster has struck (cf., for example, the Belfast shipyard workers' story about the production number of the *Titanic* reading "NO POPE" in reverse: allegedly a bad omen that, however, was not circulated in 1909, when construction of the *Titanic* began, but only after 15 April 1912). The most interesting and oft-discussed case of "premonition" is Morgan Robertson's 1898 novella *Futility or The Wreck of the Titan*, with numerous details of the fictional ship *Titan* corresponding to the later *Titanic* (cf. Introduction, note 5).

20. Howells 1999a, 120.

21. Ibid., 121.

22. This glorification constitutes a stark contrast to the miserable story how both the Liverpool Black Agency (which was responsible for the contract between the musicians and White Star) and the White Star Line refused to pay a rightful compensation to the musicians' families (cf. Lord 1986, 135–48). In the end, the families received support both from the Titanic Relief Fund and through the British Musicians' Union; they were never paid anything by the White Star Line.

23. A list of the entertainment repertoire is reprinted in Spignesi 1998, 250–53.

24. Cf. Lord 1955, 141; Lord 1986, 138–43; Spignesi 1998, 246–49, Richards 2003, 116–21. A detailed discussion of the possible "candidates" for the final piece is offered by J. Marshall Bevil, including a presentation and analysis of the various tunes in question as well as a minute-to-minute reconstruction of the final moments of the ship (Bevil 2004).

25. New York Times, 19 April 1912, quoted on http://www.encyclopedia-Titanica.org/statement-harold-bride.html (16.07.2011).

26. It must be noted that the original documents, such as the *New York Times* article with the interview, were not easily accessible in 1955. Lord probably did not have the opportunity to consult the original interview. In his 1986 book, he then differentiates between Bride's original statement that "Autumn" was a ragtime and the various newspaper versions describing "Autumn" as a hymn (Lord 1986, 141f).

27. Ibid., 139–41; Richards 2003, 118. Richards comes to the conclusion that "the whole 'Autumn' story is a dangerous red herring" (ibid.).

28. Spignesi 1998, 253.

29. Lord 1986, 141.

30. Gracie 1913, 20 (the book was written in 1912).

31. Cf. Spignesi 1998, 248.

32. Examples of popular remembrance are named by Howells 1999a, 121–24.

33. Ibid., 124.

34. Quoted from Richards 2003, 117.

35. Quoted from ibid.

36. Howells 1999a, 129–32.

37. Ibid., 132. Howells concentrates on the testimony of *Titanic* survivor Vera Dick, who came from the neighboring province of British Columbia, where the *Valencia* had gone down (ibid., 131f). The quotation regarding Captain Smith's legendary exhortation "Be British!" comes from F. S. Stevenson, ed., *"Be British": Captain E. J. Smith Memorial. A Souvenir of July 29th, 1914* (Lichfield, Staffordshire, 1914), 31.

38. Philip Gibbs, "The Deathless Story of the Titanic," *Lloyds Weekly News* 1912, 14, here quoted from Howells 1999a, 125.

39. Richards 2003, 121.

40. Lawrence Beesley, who departed at 1:35 A.M. in Lifeboat 13, in fact wrote that

the survivors in his boat "had heard no sound of any kind" from the *Titanic* since they had left her side (Beesley 1912, 120).

41. Richards 2003, 121.

42. The names of the band members and short biographies are given under http://www.Titanic-Titanic.com/Titanic_band.shtml (17.07.2011) and in the Encyclopedia Titanica.

43. *The Blue Danube* is one of the pieces of classical music that have become an icon in Western culture through their use in film and the media (the most famous instance being Stanley Kubrick's *2001: A Space Odyssey*) as well as through their place in special, exposed cultural rituals (here: *The Blue Danube* as traditional encore piece at the annual Vienna New Year's Concert, which is a major cultural event in Vienna). The famous Johann Strauss waltz represents a graceful, nostalgic European culture, which belongs to the past yet still reappears at certain special moments as a glimpse of classic timelessness.

44. Gracie 1913, 8f.

45. In contrast to several survivors' testimony, theological student Stuart Collett, who had assisted in the service, spoke of only 35 participants (cf. http://www.encyclopedia-Titanica.org/a-canadian-reference.html [17.07.2011], quoting the *East Kent Gazette* from 4 May 1965).

46. Cf. the article "Music Played on the Titanic" in the Encyclopedia Titanica (http://www.encyclopedia-Titanica.org/series/4/, 17.07.2011), with links to the individual hymns, where information on the authors and composers is given.

47. Quoted from the Encyclopedia Titanica (http://www.encyclopedia-Titanica.org/Titanic-victim/ernest-courtenay-carter.html, 17.07.2011); a source is not given.

48. By the way, in the evacuation the Rev. Carter and his wife, a couple without children, constituted another "Straus couple": according to their obituary, Lillian Carter insisted on staying with her husband, using the almost "Strausian" words "Let the mothers get to the boats first; you and I must see this out together." Cf. the obituary *The Rev E.C. & Mrs Carter* in *The Times*, 20 April 1912, reprinted on http://www.encyclopedia-Titanica.org/obituary-rev-ec-mrs-carter.html (17.07.2011).

49. A set of uilleann pipes, possibly Daly's, were decades later recovered from the wreck.

50. Marion K. Joyce, *Eugene Daly — By His Daughter*, published on http://www.encyclopedia-Titanica.org/eugene-daly-his-daughter.html (17.07.2011).

51. The article is quoted on http://www.encyclopedia-Titanica.org/two-survivors-call-mayor-ask-relief.html (17.07.2011).

52. Molony 2001, referring to an article in the *Cork Examiner* from 9 May 1912.

53. Blake's score for *S.O.S. Titanic* is listed as op. 284 in his catalog raisonné. Extensive information on Blake and his work is offered on http://www.howardblake.com/index.php (21.07.2011).

54. The term "leitmotif" is not used in this context: the themes are too loosely defined and refer to various fields of meaning rather than a concrete person or concept. They do therefore not fulfil the function of "leitmotifs" in film music (which, as should be noted, is yet different to the leitmotif technique in Richard Wagner's music dramas).

55. In the music example, the sequence in the Dorian mode has been transposed from the original d to f in order to show the correspondence with the themes from Howard Blake's score.

56. In Berlioz's *Grande Messe des Morts*, to the words "The trumpet, scattering a wondrous sound through the sepulchres of the regions, will summon all before the throne" four brass ensembles placed off-stage enter one by one, joined by an extraordinarily large body of percussion. The choral entry then engages some 400 voices.

57. Donnelly 2004, 209.

58. The album remained No. 1 on the Billboard Hot 200 albums chart for ten con-

secutive weeks and sold over 17 million copies worldwide within seventeen weeks (Parisi 1998, 223).
   59. Donnelly 2004, 209.
   60. Many details are given in Parisi 1998, 164–66 and 193–96. Ample information on the successful soundtrack album is offered on http://en.wikipedia.org/wiki/Titanic:_Music_from_the_Motion_Picture (17.07.2011).
   61. Parisi 1998, 194.
   62. Cf. ibid., 194–96.
   63. Ibid., 194.
   64. Ibid., 196.
   65. Cf. Smith 1999.
   66. Smith 1999, 58–60, quoted text on 60.
   67. This effect of the music plus dialogue combination, first used in a radio version of the song, was also mentioned in contemporary reviews. Cf. Smith 1999, 54.
   68. Parisi 1998, 164.
   69. Smith 1999, 55f.
   70. Cf. the discussion of the score with regard to the promotion of "Irishness" in the film, in Chapter 9, "The Main Categories of the *Titanic* Myth and Their Treatment."
   71. Donnelly 2004, 207.
   72. Smith 1999, 57f.
   73. For a short description of the various themes cf. ibid., 56–59.
   74. Ibid., 59.
   75. Donnelly 2004, 207.
   76. Cf. Chapter 9, "The Main Categories of the *Titanic* Myth and Their Treatment."
   77. Cf. Chion 1994; Chion 1995; Flückiger 2001; Chion 2009; Buhler et al. 2010.
   78. This is reported on the Internet Movie Database, http://www.imdb.com/title/tt0051994/trivia (22.07.2011).
   79. Cf. Parisi 1998, 202–06.
   80. Ibid., 203.
   81. Ibid., 204 and 205.
   82. Cf. various quotations in the survivors' entries in the Encyclopedia Titanica.
   83. Beesley 1912, 119f.
   84. Thus the memory of Frank Goldsmith, cf. the entry on him in the Encyclopedia Titanica.

Conclusion

   1. Bett's 1958 review is quoted in Richards 2003, 85.
   2. As a sort of meta-reflection, *S.O.S. Titanic* actually takes the competition between film and stage entertainment up in one fictional scene, confronting young David Marvin and his film camera with theater manager Henry Harris.
   3. A British docudrama made by William Lyons and Neil McKay in 2005, in fact focuses on the construction of the *Titanic* and the Belfast workers; Ennis Watson's fate is one of the strands in the docudrama presentation of various individual shipyard workers.

Bibliography

Anderson, D. Brian. 2005. *The* Titanic *in Print and on Screen: An Annotated Guide to Books, Films, Television Shows and Other Media*. Jefferson, NC: McFarland.
Baker, Roy Ward. 2000. *The Director's Cut*. London: Reynolds & Hearn.
Ballard, Robert. 1987. *The Discovery of the* Titanic. Toronto: Madison.
Barthes, Roland. 1972. *Mythologies*. Selected and translated from the French by Annette Lavers. New York: Hill and Wang (original French edition 1957).
Beesley, Lawrence. 1912. *The Loss of the SS* Titanic*: Its Story and Lessons*. London: W. Heinemann.
Behe, George. 1988. Titanic*: Psychic Forewarnings of a Tragedy*. Wellingborough: Patrick Stephens.
_____. 1999. Titanic*: Safety, Speed, and Sacrifice*. Polo, IL: Transportation Trails.
Bergfelder, Tim, and Sarah Street. 2004. "Introduction." In Bergfelder and Street 2004, 1–11.
_____, and _____, eds. 2004. Titanic *in Myth and Memory: Representations in Visual and Literary Culture*. London: I.B. Tauris.
Bevil, J. Marshall. 2004. "And the Band Played On: Hypotheses Concerning What Music Was Performed Near the Climax of the *Titanic* Disaster." Paper presented at the October 1999 meeting of the Southwest Regional Chapter of the American Musicological Society, Rice University, Houston. Published as a revised version in 2004 on http://home.earthlink.net/~llywarch/tnc02.html.htm (17.07.2011).
Biel, Steven. 1996. *Down with the Old Canoe: A Cultural History of the* Titanic *Disaster*. New York and London: Norton.
Bottomore, Stephen. 2000. *The* Titanic *and Silent Cinema*. Hastings: The Projection Box.
Bristow, Diane E. 1989. Titanic *R.I.P.: Can Dead Men Tell Tales?*, Detroit: Harlo Press.
_____. 1995. Titanic*: Sinking the Myths*. Fresno: Katco Literary Group.
Buhler, James, David Neumeyer, and Rob Deemer. 2010. *Hearing the Movies: Music and Sound in Film History*, New York: Oxford University Press.
Byars, Jackie. 1991. *All That Hollywood Allows: Re-Reading Gender in 1950s Melodrama*. Chapel Hill: University of North Carolina Press.
Cameron, James, and Randall Frakes. 1998. Titanic*: James Cameron's Illustrated Screenplay*. New York: HarperPerennial.
Chion, Michel. 1994. *Audio-Vision: Sound on Screen*. Translated by Claudia Gorbman. New York: Columbia University Press (original French edition 1991).
_____. 1995. *Le son au cinema*. Paris: Editions de l'Etoile.
_____. 2009. *Film: A Sound Art*. Translated by Claudia Gorbman. New York: Columbia University Press (original French edition 2003).

Donnelly, Kevin J. 2004. "Riverdancing as the Ship Goes Down." In Bergfelder and Street 2004, 205–14.
Dundes, Alan, ed. 1988. *The Flood Myth*. Berkeley: University of California Press.
Eaton, John P., and Charles A. Haas. 1986. *Titanic: Triumph and Tragedy. A Chronicle in Words and Pictures*. Wellingborough: Patrick Stephens.
_____, and _____. 1996. *Titanic: Destination Disaster. The Legends and the Reality*. Rev. and ex. ed. Sparkford: Patrick Stephens.
Ebbrecht, Tobias. 2007a. "Docudramatizing History on TV: German and British Docudrama and Historical Event Television in the Memorial Year 2005." *European Journal of Cultural Studies* 10 (2007): 35–53.
_____. 2007b. "History, Public Memory and Media Event: Codes and Conventions of Historical Event-Television in Germany." *Media History* 13 (2007): 221–34.
Finlayson, Alan, and Richard Taylor. 2004. "Reading *Titanic* Politically — Class, Nation and Gender in Negulesco's *Titanic* (1953)." In Bergfelder and Street 2004, 131–42.
Flückiger, Barbara. 2001. *Sound Design. Die virtuelle Klangwelt des Films*. Marburg: Schüren.
Foster, John Wilson. 1997. *The* Titanic *Complex: A Cultural Manifest*. Belfast: Belcouver Press.
Fox, Jo. 2000. *Filming Women in the Third Reich*. Oxford: Berg.
Frensham, Raymond G. 1996. *Screenwriting*. Chicago: NTC (3d ed. 2008).
Gardiner, Robin, and Dan van der Vat. 1995. *The* Titanic *Conspiracy. Cover-Ups and Mysteries of the World's Most Famous Sea Disaster*. New York: Carol.
Gerstner, David. 2004. "Unsinkable Masculinity: The Artist and the Work of Art in James Cameron's *Titanic*." In Bergfelder and Street 2004, 173–184.
Giesen, Rolf, and Manfred Hobsch. 2005. *Hitlerjunge Quex, Jud Süss und Kolberg. Die Propagandafilme des Dritten Reiches. Dokumente und Materialien zum NS-Film*. Berlin: Schwarzkopf & Schwarzkopf.
Goss, Michael, and George Behe. 1994. *Lost at Sea: Ghost Ships and Other Mysteries*. Amherst, NY: Prometheus.
Gracie, Archibald. 1913. Titanic. *A Survivor's Story*. Reprinted together with John B. Thayer, *The Sinking of the S.S. Titanic*. Chicago: Academy Chicago Publishers, 1998, 1–323.
Gunning, Tom. 2011. "Literary Appropriation and Translation in Early Cinema. Adapting Gerhard Hauptmann's *Atlantis* in 1913." In *True to the Spirit: Film Adaptation and the Question of Fidelity*, edited by Colin MacCabe, Kathleen Murray, and Rick Warner, 40–57. Oxford: Oxford University Press.
Hansen, Erik Fosnes. 1996. *Psalm at Journey's End*. Translated by Joan Tate. New York: Farrar, Straus & Giroux (original Norwegian edition *Salme ved reisens slutt*, 1990).
Heyer, Paul. 1995. *The* Titanic *Legacy. Disaster as Media Event and Myth*. Westport, CT: Praeger.
Hintermeyer, Hellmut. 2003. *Rätselhafte See. Untergänge, Aberglaube, Phänomene, Legenden*. Stuttgart: Pietsch.
Hohenberger, Eva, and Judith Keilbach, eds. 2003. *Die Gegenwart der Vergangenheit: Dokumentarfilm, Fernsehen und Geschichte*. Berlin: Vorwerk.
Howells, Richard. 1999a. *The Myth of the* Titanic. Basingstoke: Macmillan.
_____. 1999b. "Atlantic Crossings: Nation, Class and Identity in *Titanic* (1953) and *A Night to Remember* (1958)." *Historical Journal of Film, Radio and Television* 19 (1999): 421–38.
Hyslop, Donald, Forsyth Alastair, and Sheila Jemima. 1997. Titanic *Voices: Memories from the Fateful Voyage*. Stroud: Sutton.
Iversen, Kristen. 1999. *Molly Brown: Unraveling the Myth*. Boulder, CO: Johnson.

Keane, Stephen. 2001. *Disaster Movies: The Cinema of Catastrophe*. London: Wallflower.
Keller, Alexandra. 1999. "'Size Does Matter': Notes on *Titanic* and James Cameron as Blockbuster Auteur." In Sandler and Studlar 1999, 132–54.
Kleinhans, Bernd, ed. 2003. *Ein Volk, ein Reich, ein Kino. Lichtspiel in der braunen Provinz*. Köln: PapyRossa.
Knell, Heiner. 1995. *Die Nike von Samothrake. Typus, Form, Bedeutung und Wirkungsgeschichte eines rhodischen Sieges-Anathems im Kabirenheiligtum von Samothrake*. Darmstadt: Wissenschaftliche Buchgesellschaft.
Koldau, Linda Maria. 2010. *Mythos U-Boot*. Stuttgart: Steiner.
Köster, Werner, and Thomas Lischeid, eds. 1999. Titanic: *Ein Medienmythos*. Leipzig: Reclam.
Krämer, Peter. 1999. "Women First: *Titanic*, Action-Adventure Films, and Hollywood's Female Audience." In Sandler and Studlar 1999, 108–31.
———. 2004. "'Far Across the Distance': Historical Films, Film History and *Titanic* (1997)." In Bergfelder and Street 2004, 163–72.
Lehmann, Kirsten, and Lydia Wiehring von Wendrin. 1997. "Mime Misu—Der Regisseur des Titanic-Films *In Nacht und Eis*." *Filmblatt* No. 6, Winter 1997, 41–48.
Leonhardt, Axel, and Thomas Rockwell. 1993. Titanic: *Studies in the Perfect Disaster*. Copenhagen: Haase.
Lightoller, Charles Herbert. 1935. Titanic *and Other Ships*. London: Nicholson & Watson.
Lindeperg, Sylvie. 2003. "Spuren, Dokumente, Monumente: Filmische Verwendung von Geschichte. Historische Verwendung des Films." In Hohenberger and Keilbach 2003, 65–81.
Lord, Walter. 1955. *A Night to Remember*. New York: Bantam.
———. 1986. *The Night Lives On*. New York: William Morrow.
Lubin, David M. 1999. *Titanic*. London: British Film Institute (BFI Modern Classics).
Lynch, Donald. 1992. Titanic: *An Illustrated History*. Pictures by Ken Marschall. London: Madison Press.
Malone, Paul. 2004. "Goebbels Runs Aground: The Nazi *Titanic* Film." In Bergfelder and Street 2004, 121–30.
Marine Accident Investigation Branch, Department of Transport, ed. 1992. *RMS "Titanic": Reappraisal of Evidence Relating to SS "Californian."* London: H.M.S.O.
Marsh, Ed W. 1997. *James Cameron's* Titanic. Foreword by James Cameron. New York: HarperPerennial.
McCarty, Jennifer Hooper, and Tim Foecke. 2008. *What Really Sank the* Titanic: *New Forensic Discoveries*. New York: Citadel Press.
Mills, Simon. 1995. *The* Titanic *in Pictures*. Chesham: Wordsmith.
Moeller, Felix. 2000. *The Film Minister: Goebbels and the Cinema in the Third Reich*. Translated by Michael Robinson. Stuttgart: Edition Axel Menges.
Molony, Senan. 2000. *The Irish Aboard* Titanic. Dublin: Wolfhound Press.
———. 2001. "A Tender Named America." Dated 13 February, 2001, http://www.encyclopedia-Titanica.org/Titanic-tender-america.html (17.07.2011).
Mottram, Ron. 1988. *The Danish Cinema Before Dreyer*. Metuchen, NJ: Scarecrow Press.
Negra, Diane. 1999. "*Titanic*, Survivalism, and the Millenial Myth." In Sandler and Studlar 1999, 220–38.
Ouellette, Laurie. 1999. "Ship of Dreams: Cross-Class Romance and the Cultural Fantasy of *Titanic*." In Sandler and Studlar 1999, 169–88.
Parisi, Paula. 1998. Titanic *and the Making of James Cameron: The Inside Story of the Three-Year Adventure That Rewrote Motion Picture History*. London: Orion.
Peck, Robert E. 2000a. "The Banning of *Titanic*: A Study of British Postwar Film Censorship in Germany." *Historical Journal of Film, Radio and Television* 20 (2000): 427–53.

_____. 2000b. "Misinformation, Missing Information, and Conjecture: *Titanic* and the Historiography of Third Reich Cinema." *Media History* 6 (2000): 59–73.
_____. 2004. "*Atlantic*: The First *Titanic* Blockbuster." In Bergfelder and Street 2004, 111–20.
Quanz, Constanze. 2000. *Der Film als Propagandainstrument Joseph Goebbels*. Köln: Teiresias.
Rasor, Eugene L. 2001. *The* Titanic: *Historiography and Annotated Bibliography*. Westport, CT: Greenwood.
Redmond, Sean. 2004. "*Titanic*: Whiteness on the High Seas of Meaning." In Bergfelder and Street 2004, 197–204.
Rhodes, Gary Don, and John Parris Springer, eds. 2006. *Docufictions: Essays on the Intersection of Documentary and Fictional Filmmaking*. Jefferson, NC: McFarland.
Richards, Jeffrey. 2003. A Night to Remember: *The Definitive* Titanic *Film*. London: I.B. Tauris.
Rosenthal, Alan, ed. 1999. *Why Docudrama? Fact-Fiction on Film and TV*. Carbondale: Southern Illinois University Press.
Sandler, Kevin S., and Gaylyn Studlar, eds. 1999. Titanic: *Anatomy of a Blockbuster*. New Brunswick, NJ: Rutgers University Press.
Schaefer, Eric. 1986. "The Sinking of David O. Selznick's *Titanic*." *The Library Chronicle* N.S. 36 (1986): 57–73.
Simon, Monika. 2011. "The Fictional Officers of the *Titanic*." Internet publication, http://www.oocities.org/melissa_mcf/pittmann.html (04.08.2011).
Smith, Jeff. 1999. "Selling My Heart: Music and Cross-Promotion in *Titanic*." In Sandler and Studlar 1999, 46–63.
Sobchack, Vivian. 1999. "Bathos and Bathysphere: On Submersion, Longing, and History in *Titanic*." In Sandler and Studlar 1999, 189–204.
Spignesi, Stephen J. 1998. *The Complete* Titanic: *From the Ship's Earliest Blueprints to the Epic Film*. Secaucus, NJ: Carol.
Steinle, Matthias. 2009. "Geschichte im Film: Zum Umgang mit den Zeichen der Vergangenheit im Dokudrama der Gegenwart." In *History Goes Pop: Zur Repräsentation von Geschichte in populären Medien und Genres*, edited by Barbara Korte and Sylvia Paletschek, 146–65. Bielefeld: Transcript.
Stewart, Susan. 1984. *On Longing: Narratives of the Miniature, the Gigantic, the Souvenir, the Collection*. Baltimore: John Hopkins University Press.
Störmer, Susanne. 1997. Titanic. *Mythos und Wirklichkeit*. Berlin: Henschel.
_____. 2000. Titanic. *Eine Katastrophe zwischen Kitsch, Kult und Legende*. Elmshorn: Verlag S. Störmer.
Street, Sarah. 2004. "Questions of Authenticity and Realism in *A Night to Remember* (1958)." In Bergfelder and Street 2004, 143–52.
Stringer, Julian. 1999. "'The China Had Never Been Used!' On the Patina of Perfect Images in *Titanic*." In Sandler and Studlar 1999, 205–20.
Studlar, Gaylin. 2004. "Titanic/*Titanic*: Thoughts on Cinematic Presence and Monumental History." In Bergfelder and Street 2004, 155–62.
Sydney-Smith, Susan. 2004. "Romancing Disaster: *Titanic* and the Rites of Passage Film." In Bergfelder and Street 2004, 185–95.
Thayer, John Borland. 1998. *The Sinking of the S.S.* Titanic. Privately published 1940, reprinted with Archibald Gracie, Titanic. *A Survivor's Story*. Chicago: Academy Chicago, pp. 325–56.
Wedel, Michael. 1997. "Jüngst wiederaufgetaucht — damals untergegangen. Anmerkungen zur Wiederentdeckung des Titanic-Films *In Nacht und Eis* (Deutschland, 1912)." *Filmblatt* No. 6, Winter 1997, 41–45.
_____. 2004. "Early German Cinema and the Modern Media Event: Mime Misu's *Titanic — In Night and Ice* (1912)." In Bergfelder and Street 2004, 97–110.

Wolf, Mark J. P. 2004. "The Technical Challenge of Emotional Realism and James Cameron's *Titanic*." In Bergfelder and Street 2004, 215–24.

Wood, Aylish. 2004. "Expansion of Narrative Space: *Titanic* and CGI Technology." In Bergfelder and Street 2004, 225–33.

Writers Guild of America. 1957. *The Writers Guild of America Presents the Prize Plays of Television and Radio 1956*. With a foreword by Clifton Fadiman. New York: Random House.

Young, Filson. *Titanic*. London: G. Richard, 1912.

Web Sites

Encyclopedia Titanica: http://www.encyclopedia-titanica.org/
  Extensive online encyclopedia with biographies, passenger and crew lists, a large amount of primary sources in transcription, *Titanic* research articles, reviews and a forum for discussion.

Measuring Worth: http://www.measuringworth.com/index.php
  Translation of historical prices and currencies into their present-day value.

The Ships of the North Atlantic: http://www.paullee.com/titanic/northatlanticships.html
  A detailed discussion of the various ships that were close to the *Titanic* in the night from 14 to 15 April, 1912.

The Titanic Historical Society: http://www.titanichistoricalsociety.org/
  Extensive web site with information on the *Titanic* and other White Star ships, including extracts of the Society's journal *The Titanic Commutator*. Partly commercial.

Titanic in Film & Television: http://www.jimusnr.com/index.html
  An overview and concise information on film and TV productions on the *Titanic*, inspired by the *Titanic* disaster or involving *Titanic* episodes; contains many pictures from the various films.

The Titanic Inquiry Project: http://www.titanicinquiry.org/
  Complete transcription of the protocols of the United States and British *Titanic* Inquiries in 1912, including additional affidavits and sources.

The Titanic Photographs Collection. A Collection of Images Taken by Father Frank Browne: http://www.titanicphotographs.com/
  Online edition of *Titanic* passenger Father Frank Browne's *Titanic* photographs.

Titanic-Titanic.com: http://www.titanic-titanic.com/index.shtml
  Extensive, partly commercial web site, including information about the White Star Line, Harland & Wolff and the *Titanic*'s sister ships *Olympic* and *Britannic*.

Index

Numbers in ***bold italics*** indicate pages with photographs.

Abelseth, Olaus 158
Academy Award (Oscar) 111, 182, 253
Adams, Maude 58
Aherne, Brian 124, 128
Allen, Irwin 67
Allison, Bess 48, 86, 171–72, 278n6
Allison, Hudson 48, 86, 171–72, 278n6
Allison, Loraine 48, 86, 171–72, 278n6
Allison, Trevor 48, 86, 171–72, 278n6
Alwyn, William 245
Ambler, Eric 129–30, 135–36, 137, 276n27
America 243
American Dream/American values 60, 112, 114–15, 120–21, 124, 126, 128, 188, 190, 191, 202, 229
American teacher (anon. Second Class passenger) 62, 154, 157, 161, 163, 272n73, 277n5
American Zoetrope 64, 167, 177
Anderson, D. Brian 15
Andrea Doria 15, ***16***, 67
Andrews, Thomas 10, 24, 28, 33–34, 35, 47, 62–63, 98, 127, 137, 140–144, 152, 157, 159–161, 173, 191, 227–28, 263, 267n21
Angélil, René 252
Anglo-Saxon race 34–35, 38, 56, 118
Astor, John Jacob 10, 27–28, 40, 42, 56, 59, 97–98, 101–103, 108, 114, 118, 123, 124, 143, 149, 152–154, 157, 173–176, 187, 229, 250, 266ch1n9, 273n10, 278n19, 283n9
Astor, Madeleine 10, 28, 40, 56, 97–98, 102–3, 114, 124, 143, 149, 152–154, 157, 163–62, 173–175, 250, 273n10, 277n3, 278n11, 278n19
Athinai 70
Atlantic (1929) 39, 48, 55–56, 58, 78, 83, 240, 260
Atlantic 270n27
Atlantis (Hauptmann, 1912) 12, 53, 266n6, 270n21
Atlantis (1913) 53–55, 66, 260
Aubart, Léontine Pauline 165, 173

authenticity 2, 4–5, 42, 47–48, 50, 52, 61, 114, 125, 143–44, 147, 178, 194, 197–199, 201, 219, 223, 234, 261–262, 280n44

Baker, Roy Ward 32, 60, 129–30, 132, 256–57, 280n44
Ballard, Robert 44, 70–76
Baltic 149, 174, 277n1
Bancroft, Carolyn 40
band *see* musicians
Barnish, Geoffrey H. 158
Barrett, Frederick 158
Barthes, Roland 13, 198
Basehart, Richard 128
Beecham, Thomas 239
Beesley, Lawrence 8, 32, 62, 132, 153–54, 155–157, 161–163, 165, 210, 230, 257–58, 272n73, 277n5, 279n13, 283n8, 285n40
Behr, Karl Howell 121, 125, 275n12
Belfast 50, 263, 267n21
Bell, Joseph 140, 158
The Berg (Raymond, 1929) 39, 55
Bergfelder, Tim 29
Berlioz, Hector 248, 285n56
Bett, Ernest 259
Biel, Steven 2, 38, 47, 71, 126–27
Birkenhead 26
Blair, David 276n19
Blake, Howard 245, 247–249, 285n53
Blaker, Richard 58
blockbuster (film aesthetics) 199, 201–203, 221
Blom, August 53–55, 265n6
Blue Riband 22, 27, 100, 173, 224
Borzage, Frank 66
Bottomore, Stephen 50
Boxhall, Joseph Groves 130, 158
Boyes, Chris 257
Brackett, Charles 111, 117, 128
Bradley, Bridget 158
Breen, Richard L. 111, 117, 128

293

294 Index

Bremen 283n14
Bride, Harold 25, 33, 98, 114, 144, 158, 169, 174, 224, 227–28, 236, 240–41, 266n15, 269n4, 284n26
Bristow, Diane E. 3
Britannic (Gigantic) 266ch1n3
British Board of Trade 39, 58
British International Pictures 55
Brown, John Joseph 40
Brown, Margaret Tobin ("Molly") 10, 28, 39–41, 47, 114, 123, 157, 159, 170, 174, 187
Buckley, Daniel 155–157, 226, 277n9, 278n11
Bucknell, Emma 157, 159
Butt, Archibald 114
Byars, Jackie 116
Byles, Thomas 37, 48, 56, 64, 125, 157, 194, 267n32

Calamai, Piero 15
Californian 12, 26, 43–44, 72, 79, 140, 144–45, 158–59, 170, 174, 208, 224, 231–233, 283n16
Cameron, James 1, 6–7, 9, 15, 36, 39, 45, 53, 62–64, 66–67, 73–77, 81, 84, 88–89, 118, 129, 132, 153, 163, 167–169, 175–76, 181, 182–222, 226, 230–31, 244, 250, 252–255, 257–58, 260–61, 263, 278n2
Cap Arcona 110
Carpathia 3, 26–28, 40–41, 51, 68, 85, 87, 89–90, 142, 144–45, 149–155, 159–60, 163, 165–66, 169–70, 172–73, 181, 174, 177, 181, 185, 187, 191, 224, 231–32, 246–47, 249, 269n51, 273n8
Carter, Ernest Courtenay 242–43, 285n48
Carter, Lillian 285n48
Carter, William Ernest 280n20
catharsis 47, 230
Cavalcade (1933) 66, 233, 240
C.F. Tietgen 54
CGI (computer generated imagery) 177, 208, 213
Charters, David 155, 157
Cherbourg 23, 114, 124, 274n7
class 1, 6–7, 15, 30, 30–33, 38, 47, 56, 60–61, 63, 65, 68, 77, 81, 89, 108, 113–14, 117, 127–28, 131, 134–136, 154, 157, 161, 177, 182, 184–85, 187–191, 195, 199, 202, 206, 221, 223, 224, 241–244, 259, 271n30
Cleaver, Alice Catherine 48, 80, 86–87, 169–171, 173, 177, 179–181, 233, 278n6, 279n7
Cleaver, Alice Mary 171
Cold War 43, 60, 137
Collett, Stuart 285n45
Conan Doyle, Arthur 39
Conrad, Joseph 39
"The Convergence of the Twain" (Hardy, 1915) 11, 86, 165
Costigan, James 152, 154–55, 160–61
Cottam, Harold Thomas 145, 158, 249–50
Coward, Noël 106
CQD 25, 51, 54, 140, 144–45, 233

Cunard Line 22, 58, 130, 181
Curtis, Michael (Mihály Kertész) 270n20
Cussler, Clive 69

Dalton, Audrey 128
Daly, Eugene Patrick 35, 155, 235–36, 243–44, 251, 285n49
Dean, Horace J. 158
diamond ("Heart of the Ocean") 88, 90, 184–85, 187, 200, 206, 217, 272n79
DiCaprio, Leonardo 186, 254
Dick, Vera 284n37
Dies Irae 247–48, **248**
Dinesen, Robert 270n20
Dion, Celine 64, 196, 212, 214, 252, 254–55
The Discovery of the Titanic (Ballard, 1987) 71
distress rockets 25, 29, 44, 98, 174, 232, 256, 276n29
Dittmar-Pittmann, Max 273n9
docudrama 78, 148
Doña Paz 10
Donnelly, Kevin J. 192, 252, 255–56
dramatic irony 47, 79, 140, 142, 144–146, 175, 232–33, 249, 267n39
Duff-Gordon, Sir Cosmo 114, 143, 170
Duff-Gordon, Lady Lucy 114, 143, 170, 274n16
Dupont, Ewald André 55
Dyer-Edwards, Lucy Noël Martha, Countess of Rothes 114, 157, 159
Dykes, John B. 238, 240

Eclair Motion Picture Company 49
Elgar, Sir Edward 239
Eliason, Joyce 168
Encyclopedia Titanica 4, 8
end (in *Titanic* films) 84–85, 91, 215
Enya 255
Et drama paa havet (The Great Ocean Disaster, 1912) 53, 260
"Eternal Father, Strong to Save" 165, 194, 242–43, 249–50
evacuation into lifeboats 26
Evans, Cyril 26, 145

Farrell, James 155, 157
Faust (story archetype) 80
Felinau, Josef Pelz von 39, 97, 273n9
Finlayson, Alan 112, 116
First Class stereotype 41, 47–48, 60, 63–64, 83, 104, 113, 135, 165, 167, 190, 200, 209, 244, 260
Fleet, Frederick 23, 43, 79, 158, 230, 278n22
Flegenheim, Antoinette 273n8
Fletcher, Peter W. 158, 234
Foster, John Wilson 5
Fowler, Gene 40
framing device (film script) 84–91, 148–153, 216–17, 224, 262
Frankfurt 25, 144
Franklin, Phillip A.S. 37–38, 267n37

Frensham, Raymond G. 77
Freud, Sigmund 195
Futility or the Wreck of the Titan (Robertson, 1898) 12, 265*n*5, 270*n*21, 284*n*19

Gallagher, Martin 61, 155–157, 161
gender 1, 6–7, 12, 15, 26, 30–31, 38, 41, 43, 47, 56, 59–60, 63, 65, 68, 77, 81, 112–116, 126–128, 137, 141–42, 177, 182, 184–187, 195, 196, 199, 202, 206, 221, 223, 225–26, 259
genre (film) 5, 16, 79–81, 182, 201–203
Gerston, Randy 255
Ghosts of the Abyss (2003) 72, 75–76, 282*n*86
Gibson, Dorothy 49
Gieger, Amalie Henriette 273*n*8
Gigantic see Britannic
Gilnagh, Kate 155, 157
Glynn, Mary Agatha 158
Goebbels, Joseph 95, 100, 102–3, 106–7, 135, 273*n*6, 274*n*24
Golden Globe Award 147
Goldsmith, Frank 275*n*14
Goliath Awaits (1981) 272*n*59
Gracie, Archibald 34, 138, 144, 237, 242
Grade, Lew 69–70
Grand Hotel (film, 1932) 83, 104, 113
Groves, Charles Victor 145
Guggenheim, Benjamin 27, 34, 98, 114, 143, 157, 165–66, 173
Gurney, Rachel 66
Guy, Edward John 158

Hale, William 62, 148, 251, 278*n*22
Halifax 51
Hankinson, Thomas William 158
Hansen, Erik Fosnes 263, 283*n*12
Harbeck, William 50–51, 270*n*10
Harbison, W.D. 267*n*10
Harbraugh, Carl 57
Hardy, John 158
Hardy, Thomas 11, 86, 165
Harland & Wolff 22, 37, 51, 137, 263
Harper, Henry Sleeper 27
Harris, Henry 155, 157, 286*n*2
Harris, Irene (René) 155, 157, 163, 278*n*12
Hart, John 158
Hartley, Wallace 132, 158, 231, 238, 240–41, 283*n*13
Hauptmann, Gerhard 12, 53, 270*n*21
Hays, Charles Melville 27, 114
Heart of the Ocean *see* diamond
Hemingway, Ernest 12
Hichens, Robert 137, 158, 231
Hill, George Roy 44
historicism (in postmodernism) 182, 195, 197–199, 202–3
History Is Made at Night (1937) 66, 240
Hitchcock, Alfred 39, 57–59, 258
Hitler, Adolf 95
Horner, James 192–93, 214, 252–255

Howells, Richard 234, 239–40
hubris 6–7, 13, 15, 30, 37–39, 43, 47, 77, 97, 108, 126, 142, 163–64, 194–95, 212, 224, 229, 233, 259, 261, 271*n*31
Hughes, Howard 57
Hume, Jock 263

In Nacht und Eis (*Shipwrecked in Icebergs*, 1912) 52–53, 240, 260, 267*n*20
Inquiries *see Titanic* Inquiries
International Mercantile Marine Company 3, 22, 28, 37, 101, 229, 233
Irish beauty (anon. Third Class passenger) 62, 155–56, 158, 161
Irishness/Irish emigrants *see* motifs of the *Titanic* code
Ismay, J. Bruce 10, 22, 25, 27–28, 42, 47, 59, 61, 66, 85, 87, 97–98, 100–103, 108–9, 127, 138, 140, 142–43, 149–152, 157, 162, 173–74, 179–80, 191–92, 195, 204, 224, 226–27, 229, 247, 250–51, 267*n*19, 275*n*12, 277*n*1

Jack Dawson (fictional character) 31–32, 35, 63–64, 68, 88–90, 168–69, 184–85, 188–89, 190, 192, 194, 200, 204–5, 208–9, 211–12, 214, 217, 253–255
Jameson, Jerry 69
Jennings, Will 252
Jessop, Violet 158–59, 278*n*15
Jewell, Archie 158
Joughin, Charles John 137, 140–41, 144, 158–59
Joyce, Archibald 237

Kamuda, Edward 44
Kaplan, Sol 244
Keldysh 88–89, 184–85, 216
Kellard, Thomas 158
Keller, Alexandra 187, 198–99, 202–3
Kennedy, Joseph 58
King, Alfred "Alfie" 158
King, Thomas W. 158
Krämer, Peter 202
Kubrick, Stanley 248, 285*n*43

LaManna, Ross 168
Lee, Reginald 158
Lieberman, Robert 65, 167
lifeboat shortage 26, 56, 98, 143, 269*n*55
Lightoller, Charles Herbert 23, 26, 34, 60, 98, 130, 132, 134–35, 137–139, 141, 144, 158, 174, 203–4, 227, 247, 258, 267*n*17, 276*n*18, 276*n*19, 278*n*4
litany of "ifs" 11, 14, 43–44, 138, 233
Lloyd, Frank 66
London 109, 237
London Inquiry *see Titanic* Inquiries
Long, Milton 157, 159
Lord, Stanley 26, 79, 144–45, 159, 232, 283*n*16
Lord, Walter 2, 8–9, 12, 15, 24, 26, 39, 42–

44, 46, 60, 71, 76, 85, 89, 129–131, 134, 138, 142–145, 163, 174, 197, 199, 223, 232–33, 236, 241, 261, 267n22, 269n52, 278n12, 284n26
The Loss of the SS. Titanic: Its Story and Lessons (Beesley, 1912) 8, 32, 62, 153, 162, 165, 210, 230, 257–58, 277n5, 279n13, 283n8, 285n40
Lowe, Harold 35–36, 158, 174–75, 179, 226, 229, 247, 267n28
Lubin, David M. 183
Lusitania 22, 67, 279n12
Lyons, William 286n3

MacQuitty, William 60, 129, 135–36, 241
Malone, Paul 105
Marconi, Guglielmo 51
Marconi Wireless Telegraph Company 3, 25, 28, 52, 54, 267n15
Marvin, Daniel 155, 159, 269n5, 286n2
Marvin, Henry Norton 269n5
Marvin, Mary 155, 159, 163
Mason, Lowell 238, 240
Mauretania 22, 274n14, 279n12
McCarthy, Neil 57
McCawley, Thomas 158
McGee, Frank E. 151, 158
McKay, Neil 286n3
Melville, Herman 12
Mengelberg, Willem 239
Merivale, John 276n28
Mesaba 23, 144, 174, 228, 233, 247
Meyer, Edgar Joseph 276n12
Meyer, Leila 276n12
Mills, Simon 106
Milo Film 58
Misu, Mime 52
Mizner, Wilson 57
Moody, James Paul 158
More, Kenneth 130
Morgan, John Pierpont 22, 101, 229
morph technique 89–91, 211–12, 215–217
motifs of the *Titanic* code: Andrews's final pose 34, 132, 228; binoculars missing 174; breaking of the hull 72–73, 175, 213; Britishness/"Be British!" 33–34, 56, 60–61, 124, 139–141, 147, 176, 191, 194, 224, 228–29, 240; Captain Smith's death 33, 52, 98; Collapsible B 27, 137, 142, 144, 146, 174, 213, 231, 236, 269n55, 277n37, 278n4, 279n9; collision 23–24, 98, 110, 112, 118, 122, 125–26, 168–69, 173, 175, 209, 217, 230, 244–45; cries of the dying 132, 214, 230, 257–58; dance scene/Third Class party 32, 104, 121, 155, 167–68, 189–90, 204, 223, 236, 244, 278n21; engine rooms 48, 108, 117, 122, 137, 143, 156, 179, 192, 208–9, 261; Father Byles praying 37; First Class splendor 104, *105*, 113, 167–68, 177, 189–90, 199–200, 202, 208, 223–24, 259, 261, 280n19; football with ice chunks 140, 174–75; gash 73, 125, 144, 174; Grand Staircase 71, 89, 151, 177–179, *178*, 185, 189, 209, 249, 275ch6n11, 278n12, 279n15; Guggenheim's farewell 34, 159, 165–66, 226, 267n24; ice warnings 23, 149–50, 174, 224, 228, 269n4, 277n1; Irishness/Irish emigrants 32, 34, 63, 97, 135, 155–56, 156, 162, 192–93, 244–45, 249, 251–52, 255–56; Ismay entering a lifeboat 27, 61, 103, 192, 226; joke about ice 144, 279n13; "Latins" and their unruly behavior 97, 106, 229, 267n28; Lifeboat 14 turning back 35, 167, 175; locked gates 26, 64–65, 108, 136, 155, 175, 189, 223, 225; man escaping in woman's clothes 123, 156, 204, 223, 226; Molly Brown (stereotype) 41, 47, 98, 123, 139, 143, 157, 159, 165, 173–175, 180, 188, 223, 226, 231, 249, 267n50, 269n51; nature's power 87, 150, 164–65, 229–30, 249–251; "Nearer, My God, to Thee" 11, 30, 36, 52, 56, 60, 64–65, 66, 81, 85, 107, 112, 117–18, 124–126, 130, 132, 142, 176, 193–94, 224, 230–31, 234, 236–242, 244–45, 284n24; panic 49, 118, 144, 224, 229, 237; premonitions 171, 176, 233, 265n5, 284n19; shooting 49, 97, 167–68, 176, 224, 229; sinking (final moments) 27, 118, 132–33, 177–181, 210, 213–14, 217, 224, 230, 245, 260; speed 100–101, 118, 124, 142, 150, 175, 224, 229, 267n19, 274n14, 274n10, 283n8; stoker stealing Phillips's life jacket 33, 139–40, 175; Straus couple's oath 27, 31, 68, 112, 136, 159, 165, 175, 186, 225, 267n9; unsinkable ship 14, 37–38, 56, 142–43, 175, 224, 233, 267n37, 267n39; wireless office 47, 52, 137, 269n4; young hero falling into a lifeboat 31, 121, 172, 225–26
Mullen, Katie 155, 157
Müller, Wilhelm 273n8
Munch, Edward 180
Murdoch, Willam McMaster 23–24, 26, 28, 33, 43, 97, 144, 158, 167–169, 175–76, 227, 229, 266ch1n4, 276n19, 283n7
Murphy, Kate 155, 157
Murphy, Mary 155, 158
music (film score) 125, 126, 131, 136, 142, 178–180, 183, 192–93, 214–15, 244–258, 285n53, 285n54
music on the *Titanic* 234–244
musicians 118, 126, 132, 158, 193–94, 224, 230–31, 234–35, 238, 240–242, 249, 250, 263, 284n22, 285n42
Musicians' Memorial (Southampton) 234, **235**
"My Heart Will Go On" 64, 196, 214–15, 252–256, 286n58

narrative rhythm 7
nation 1, 6–7, 15, 30–35, 38, 47, 59, 63, 77, 81, 96–97, 113, 126, 128, 139, 177, 182, 184, 191–193, 195, 199, 202, 221, 224, 228–29, 259

Index

Nautilus 13
Navratil, Edmond Roger ("Momon") 157, 159, 262–63, 278*n*14
Navratil, Marcelle 263, 278*n*14
Navratil, Michel ("Lolo") 157, 159, 262–63, 278*n*14
Navratil, Michel ("Louis M. Hoffman") 157, 159, 262–63
Negra, Diane 195, 204–5
Negulesco, Jean 11, 60, 111, 126, 128, 194
nemesis 47
New York 247
New York 21, 40, 51, 65, 88–89, 102, 150–51, 169–174, 177, 181, 184, 187, 191
New York Inquiry *see Titanic* Inquiries
newsreels 50–52
Night Gallery (1970) 67
No Greater Love (1996) 68, 241, 284*n*18
The Night Goes On (Lord, 1986) 145, 232
A Night to Remember (Lord, 1955) 2, 8–9, 12, 15, 24, 26, 39, 42–44, 46, 60, 71, 76, 89, 129, 142–145, 162, 174, 197, 199, 223, 232–33, 236, 241, 261
A Night to Remember (1956, television drama) 44
A Night to Remember (1958) 2, 7, 16, 31–32, 35, 44, 48, 60, 62, 78, 82, 84–86, 96, 98, 109, 129–147, 149, 153, 155–56, 159–60, 162–63, 166, 174, 177, 186–87, 191, 194, 197, 199–200, 203, 218, 223, 225, 228, 231–32, 241, 245, 251, 256–57, 259–262, 267*n*17, 278*n*4, 282*n*103
Nike of Samothrace 219–20
Norman, Robert Douglas 243
nostalgia 42–43, 71, 76, 138–39, 143, 146, 162–63, 183, 193, 195, 199–201, 214, 216, 255, 261
Nourney, Alfred 273*n*8

"O God, Our Help in Ages Past" 238, 242
Ogden, Mrs. Louis M. 153, 158, 163–64
Olympic 12, 22, 26–27, 50, 51–52, 75, 259, 272*n*69, 276*n*19
Olympic class ships 21–22, 50–51, 100, 259
Orpheus (story archetype) 80
Ouellette, Laurie 188

Parisi, Paula 253
Peck, Robert 96, 109
Petersen, Hans Erik (fictitious *Titanic* officer) 59, 97–100, 102–105, 107, 109, 273*n*9, 281*n*60
Peuchen, Arthur Godfrey 171
Phillips, John George "Jack" 23, 25–29, 33, 98, 107, 114, 139–40, 144, 158, 174, 224, 227–28, 236, 247, 269*n*4, 279*n*9
Pirrie, Willam Lord 22, 34
Pitman, Herbert John 158
Pitt, Percy 239
Pollitt, Katha 186
port-around maneuver 24, 266*ch*1*n*4

portmanteau film 83–84
postmodernism 6, 45, 182–184, 195–207, 218, 221, 261, 263–64
Pratt, Edwin John 39
Prechtl, Robert 39, 97
propaganda 96–97, 105–110

Queenstown (Cobh) 23, 235, 243–44, 249

race 6–7, 15, 30, 33–36, 38, 47, 59, 64, 77, 81, 104, 106, 127, 177, 182, 184, 224, 229, 259, 271*n*33
Raise the Titanic! (Cussler, 1976) 69
Raise the Titanic (1981) 69–70
Rank Organisation 133
Raymond, Ernest 39, 55
realism 130, 139, 146–47, 214
Redmond, Sean 187, 201
Rees, Eric 158
Reisch, Walter 111, 117, 128
religion 6–7, 15, 30, 36–38, 47, 56, 59–60, 64, 65, 71, 76–77, 81, 117–119, 126–27, 137, 141–143, 177, 179, 184, 193–195, 224, 230–31, 259, 271*n*40
Reynolds, Debbie 41
Richards, Jeffrey 139, 141, 240–41
Robertson, Morgan 12, 265*n*5, 270*n*21, 284*n*19
Romeo and Juliet (story archetype) 80, 196, 207, 216
Ronald, Landon 239
Rose DeWitt Bukater (fictional character) 31, 45, 62–64, 67–68, 78, 88–91, 153, 184–197, 200, 208–9, 211–12, 214–217, 219, 221, 253–255, 257–58, 272*n*79
Rostron, Arthur Henry 145, 152, 158, 160, 174, 232
Rush, Alfred 125
Russell, Edith 143, 157
Ryan, Edward 226, 277*n*9
Ryerson, Arthur 27, 141, 143, 174
Ryerson, John 174

Saved from the Titanic (1912) 49–50, 65, 240
Schmitz, Sybille 99, **101**, 273*n*12
script (film) 77–91
Selpin, Herbert 59, 96, 104, 107, 273*n*6
Selznick, David O. 39, 57–59
Selznick International Pictures 57–59
Shark Tale (2004) 67
Shaw, George Bernard 39
Sloan, Mary 35, 158–161, 278*n*15
Smith, Capt. Edward John 11, 23–25, 28, 33–34, 42–43, 47, 51–52, 56, 67, 79, 86, 97–98, 101, 103, 110, 114, 118, 124, 128, 132, 135, 139, 142–144, 149, 158, 173, 176, 191, 224, 227–28, **228**, 232, 240, 242, 267*n*19, 274*n*10, 276*n*19, 277*n*1
Smith, Jeff 253
Smith, Lucian Philip 141, 143, 273*n*13
Smith, Mary Eloise 141, 143, 276*n*27, 278*n*5

"Songe d'Automne" 176, 236–37, 240–41
SOS 25, 54, 144, 174
S.O.S. Titanic (1979) 7, 32, 35, 48, 61–62, 68, 78, 82, 84–87, 148–166, 174, 177, 192, 199, 229, 241–42, 245, 245–252, 262, 267n21, 269n51, 269n4, 272n73, 280n31, 283n9, 285n53, 286n2
sound design 126, 131, 245, 256–57
Southampton 23, 50, 88–89, 171, 192, 233, 247, 249, 263
Spielberg, Steven 85
Spinner, Genevieve 40
S.S. Olympic (1911) 51, 227
Stanwyck, Barbara 111, 128
Stead, William Thomas 48, 56, 143
Stebbings, Sydney Frederick 158
Steel, Danielle 68
Stenke, Beatrice 283n14
Stewart, Susan 200
Straus, Ida 11, 27, 31, 34, 56, 67, 98, 114, 118, 124, 136, 141, 143, 157, 173, 225, 282n89
Straus, Isidor 11, 27, 31, 34, 56, 98, 114, 118, 124, 143, 157, 173, 225, 282n89
Street, Sarah 29, 131, 134
Stringer, Julian 201
Studlar, Gaylyn 198, 206
subplot 82, 119, 160–162, 170–71, 173, 208
Sullivan, Arthur 238
survivalism 203–206, 211, 213, 226, 261, 281n62
Survivors' Committee 40
Sydney-Smith, Susan 201, 206
Symons, George 158

Taylor, Richard 112, 116
technology 43, 45, 48, 76, 131, 142, 156, 202, 207–8, 211–213, 215, 229, 233, 245, 251
Thayer, John 27
Thayer, John Borland "Jack" 157, 159, 213
Third Class stereotype 15, 47–48, 60, 63–64, 104, 108, 113, 124, 131, 135, 155–56, 165, 167, 190, 209, 224, 235, 243, 251, 260, 262
Timberline (Fowler, 1933) 40
Time Bandits (1981) 67, 284n18
The Time Tunnel (1966) 67
Titanensturz (Prechtl, 1937) 39, 97
Titanic (Young, 1912) 14, 34
Titanic (aborted film project, 1930s) 39
The Titanic (Pratt, 1935) 39
Titanic (1943) 7, 33, 59, 65, 78–79, 81–84, 86, 95–110, 117, 126, 168, 218, 227, 229, 240, 266ch1n9, 281n60, 282n103
Titanic (1953) 5, 7, 11, 48, 60, 73, 78, 81, 83–86, 96, 139, 147, 172, 186, 194, 225, 229, 230, 240, 244–45, 245, 256, 262, 267n32
Titanic (1996) 7, 48, 64–66, 78–80, 84–86, 167–181, 199, 229, 231, 233, 245, 267n50, 269n5
Titanic (1997) 1, 6–9, 15–16, 36, 39, 45, 53, 62–64, 66–67, 73–74, 78, 81, 84–91, 118, 129, 161, 163, 167, 169, 175–75, 182–222,
229, 231, 240, 242, 244–45, 250, 252–258, 260, 262
Titanic as metaphor 10
Titanic as microcosm 47, 81, 123, 131, 134–136, 154, 170, 223–24, 244, 262
Titanic code 1, 4, 46, 61, 82–83, 91, 143–147, 148, 168, 174–177, 193, 197, 218, 221, 223–234, 260–262
Titanic Inquiries (1912) 3, 28, 56, 98, 109, 124, 144, 149, 263, 267n10, 272n73
Titanic, mille e una storia (or Titanic: La leggenda continua; Titanic: The Legend Goes On, 2001) 6, 68
Titanic porno films 6, 81
Titanic Relief Fund 28, 187
Titanic II (2010) 69
Titanic—Tragödie eines Ozeanriesen (Felinau, 1939) 39, 97
Titanic Wreck (1912) 9
Titanica (1995) 45, 70, 75, 212, 215
tragedy (classic) 11–12, 38, 43, 46–47, 130, 233, 234, 260
The Truth About the Titanic (Gracie, 1913) 8
Twentieth Century–Fox 77, 128, 280n21

The Unsinkable Molly Brown (musical, 1960) 41
The Unsinkable Molly Brown (1964) 41
The Unsinkable Mrs. Brown (Bancroft, 1936) 40f
Upstairs, Downstairs (1971–75) 66–67
Urban, Charles 50, 270n12

Valencia 239–40, 284n37
Vector 10
Voyagers (1983) 67

Wagner, Robert 128
Waterman, Felicity 177
Watson, Ennis 263
Webb, Clifton 111, 114, 128
Whedon, John 44
White, Richard 75
White Star Line 3, 21–23, 25, 27–28, 31, 37, 40, 50–52, 55–56, 58, 73, 86, 100–1, 103, 109, 149, 206, 209, 226, 229, 233, 241, 243, 250, 263, 266ch1n3, 267n19, 270n27, 272n69, 274n10, 276n19, 284n22
White Swan Hotel (Alnwick) 75
Whitney, Gertrude Vanderbilt 221
Whom the Gods Destroy (1934) 66
Widener, Eleanor 114, 124, 173
Widener, George 27, 114, 124, 173
Wilde, Henry Tingle 28, 144, 158, 276n19, 277n33
Wilhelm Gustloff 10
Williams, Richard Norris 121, 125, 275n12
Winslet, Kate 197, 200, 254, 279ch9n10
wireless telegraphy 9
Women's Titanic Memorial 219–221
Wood, Aylish 208–9

Wood, Sir Henry 239
Woods Hole Oceanographic Institution 71, 73–74
Wordsmith, Igenlode 146
wreck of the *Titanic* 9, 21, 24, 39, 44–45, 62, 64, 69–76, 88, 174–75, 184–85, 193, 200–1, 207, 212, 215–16, 218, 221, 260, 272n59
Wright, Marion 243

Yates, Jay 277n37
Young, Filson *14*, 34, 267n25

Zerlett-Olfenius, Walter 96–98, 100–1, 103, 106–7, 273n6
Zola, Émile 103

www.ingramcontent.com/pod-product-compliance
Lightning Source LLC
Chambersburg PA
CBHW051210300426
44116CB00006B/505